Career Theory
and Practice

2
edition

To our families for their love and support
Bill, Merit, and Robert (JS)
Bob, Nick, Erin, Andrew and Patrick (NF)

Career Theory
and Practice
Learning Through Case Studies

2
edition

Jane L. Swanson
Southern Illinois University Carbondale

Nadya A. Fouad
University of Wisconsin–Milwaukee

Los Angeles • London • New Delhi • Singapore • Washington DC

For information:

SAGE Publications, Inc.
2455 Teller Road
Thousand Oaks, California 91320
E-mail: order@sagepub.com

SAGE Publications Ltd.
1 Oliver's Yard
55 City Road
London EC1Y 1SP
United Kingdom

SAGE Publications India Pvt. Ltd.
B 1/I 1 Mohan Cooperative Industrial Area
Mathura Road, New Delhi 110 044
India

SAGE Publications Asia-Pacific Pte. Ltd.
33 Pekin Street #02-01
Far East Square
Singapore 048763

Printed in the United States of America

Library of Congress Cataloging-in-Publication Data

Swanson, Jane Laurel.
Career theory and practice: learning through case studies/Jane L. Swanson, Nadya A. Fouad.—2nd ed.
 p. cm.
Includes bibliographical references and index.
ISBN 978-1-4129-3751-1 (pbk. : alk. paper)
 1. Career development—Case studies. 2. Vocational guidance—Case studies. I. Fouad, Nadya A. II. Title.

HF5381.S937 2009
158.6—dc22   2008041301

This book is printed on acid-free paper.

09 10 11 12 13   10 9 8 7 6 5 4 3 2 1

Acquisitions Editor:	Kassie Graves
Editorial Assistant:	Veronica Novak
Production Editor:	Carla Freeman
Copy Editor:	Paula L. Fleming
Typesetter:	C&M Digitals (P) Ltd.
Proofreader:	Victoria Reed-Castro
Cover Designer:	Arup Giri
Marketing Manager:	Carmel Schrire

Contents

List of Tables and Figures   xi

List of Additional Cases   xiii

Acknowledgments   xv

1. **Career Counseling: An Overview**   1
   Purpose of the Book   2
   Definition and Types of Theories   4
   Clarifying Distinctions Between Theories
       and Theoretical Orientations   7
   Counselor Roles and Settings   8
   Developing Hypotheses and a "Working Model" of the Client   10
   Conducting Career Counseling   13
   Integrating "Career" and "Personal" Aspects of Counseling   16
   Summary   17

2. **The Use of Assessment in Career Counseling**   21
   Selection of Assessment   22
   Types of Assessment   23
       Interests   23
       Needs and Values   24
       Abilities and Skills   24
       Personality   24
       Assessment of Other Constructs   25
       Other Types of Assessment   25
   Ethical Principles and Responsible Use of Assessment   26

3. **The Case of Leslie**   33
   Presenting Issue   33
   Career and Work History   34
   Family Information   36
   Marital Information   37
   Leslie's Expectations for Career Counseling   38

Initial Impressions of Leslie   39
Assessment Information   39
    Strong Interest Inventory (SII)   40
    Skills Confidence Inventory (SCI)   42
    Minnesota Importance Questionnaire (MIQ)   43
    Adult Career Concerns Inventory (ACCI)   44
    Summary of Leslie's Assessment Information   45
Working With Leslie's Case and Assessment Information   46
    Observation 1   46
    Observation 2   47
    Observation 3   48
    Observation 4   49
Conceptualizing Leslie From Various Theoretical Approaches   50

4. Gender-Aware and Feminist Approaches   51
Introductory Review   51
Gender-Aware Counseling   53
Feminist Counseling   54
Gender and Assessment   55
Gender and Theories of Career Development   57
Applying Gender-Aware and Feminist Approaches   59
    Conceptualizing Leslie's Career History   59
    Conceptualizing Leslie's Present Situation   60
    The Case of Diana and Bill   62
Directions and Implications for Career Counseling   64
    Goals of Counseling   64
    Interventions   65
Additional Cases   69
    Case 1: Ellen   69
    Case 2: Brenda   71
    Case 3: Tony   71

5. Culturally Appropriate Career Counseling   75
Introductory Review   75
Career Intervention Models   79
Multicultural Career Counseling Tenets   84
Applying a Multicultural Perspective to the Case of Leslie   85
    Conceptualizing Leslie's Career History   86
    Conceptualizing Leslie's Present Situation   88
    The Case of Norman   90
Directions and Implications for Career Counseling   92
    Goals of Counseling   92
    Culturally Appropriate Career Counseling Model 93

Additional Cases 96
    Case 1: Justino 96
    Case 2: Lian 98
    Case 3: Monica 99

6. Holland's Theory of Vocational Personalities
   and Work Environments 105
   Introductory Review 105
   Applying Holland's Theory 110
    Conceptualizing Leslie's Career History 110
    Conceptualizing Leslie's Present Situation 112
    The Case of Judy 114
   Directions and Implications for Career Counseling 115
    Goals of Counseling 115
    Interventions 116
   Additional Cases 119
    Case 1: Johnny 119
    Case 2: Susan 120
    Case 3: Cynthia 121

7. The Theory of Work Adjustment 125
   Introductory Review 125
   Applying the Theory of Work Adjustment 131
    Conceptualizing Leslie's Career History 131
    Conceptualizing Leslie's Present Situation 132
    The Case of Charles 133
   Directions and Implications for Career Counseling 134
    Goals of Counseling 135
    Interventions 135
   Additional Cases 138
    Case 1: Phil 138
    Case 2: Melissa 140
    Case 3: Linda 141

8. Super's Developmental Theory 145
   Introductory Review 145
   Applying Developmental Theory 149
    Conceptualizing Leslie's Career History 150
    Conceptualizing Leslie's Present Situation 152
    The Case of Karen 154
   Directions and Implications for Career Counseling 155
    Goals of Counseling 155
    Interventions 157

Additional Cases   162
    Case 1: Walter   162
    Case 2: Maria Josefina   163
    Case 3: Deborah and Trish   164

9. Gottfredson's Theory of Circumscription
   and Compromise   169
   Introductory Review   169
       Cognitive Growth   170
       Self-Creation   170
       Circumscription   171
       Compromise   172
   Applying Gottfredson's Theory   174
       Conceptualizing Leslie's Career History   174
       Conceptualizing Leslie's Present Situation   176
       The Case of Gary   177
   Directions and Implications for Career Counseling   178
       Goals of Counseling   178
       Interventions   179
   Additional Cases   181
       Case 1: Dorece   181
       Case 2: Steve   182
       Case 3: Lori   183

10. Social Cognitive Career Theory   187
    Introductory Review   187
    Applying Social Cognitive Career Theory   192
        Conceptualizing Leslie's Career History   192
        Conceptualizing Leslie's Present Situation   195
        The Case of Ron   197
    Directions and Implications for Career Counseling   199
        Goals of Counseling   200
        Identify Foreclosed Options   200
        Reevaluate and Modify Efficacy Beliefs   204
        Identify Barriers and Supports   205
    Additional Cases   206
        Case 1: Jerry   206
        Case 2: Kamisha   208
        Case 3: Jim   210

11. Summary and Integration   215
    Summary and Comparison of the Theories   216
        Applying Theories to Your Own Career Development   220

Integrating Theoretical Perspectives   220
    Contributions of Different Theories
        to Understanding Leslie   221
The Case of George   223
    Working With George   224
    Considering George From Various
        Theoretical Perspectives   225
The Case of Tom   231
    Working With Tom   232
Evaluation of the Major Theories   233
Revisiting Counselor Cognitions   235
Parting Words   236

Appendix A: Leslie's Profiles   239

Appendix B: National Career Development Association
Code of Ethics   253

Index   305

About the Authors   311

List of Tables
and Figures

Tables

Table 6.1   Characteristics of Holland's Personality and
             Environmental Types   106
Table 11.1   Comparison of Theories   218

Figures

Figure 1.1   Gysbers, Heppner, and Johnston's Model of
             Career Counseling   14

Figure 5.1   Culturally Appropriate Career Counseling Model   81

Figure 5.2   Spheres of Influence of Cultural Variables   82

Figure 6.1   Holland's Hexagonal Structure   109

Figure 7.1   Prediction of Work Adjustment   126

Figure 7.2   Relationships Between Adjustment-Style Dimensions   129

Figure 8.1   Super's Life-Career Rainbow   147

Figure 9.1   Gottfredson's Model of Circumscription and
             Compromise   171

Figure 10.1 Predicting Interest Development in Social Cognitive
             Career Theory   189

Figure 10.2 Predicting Vocational Choice in Social Cognitive
             Career Theory   190

Figure 10.3 Predicting Task Performance in Social Cognitive
             Career Theory   191

Appendix A   **Figure1:**
                  Leslie's Strong Interest Inventory Profile   240

                  Figure 2:
                  Leslie's Skills Confidence Inventory Profile   248

                  Figure 3:
                  Leslie's Minnesota Importance Questionnaire Profile   249

                  Figure 4:
                  Leslie's Adult Career Concerns Inventory Profile   252

Appendix B   National Career Development Association
                  Code of Ethics   254

List of Additional Cases

Theory or Approach	Client Name (Age)	Race/Ethnicity	Page
Gender-Aware and Feminist	**Diana and Bill (mid-40s)**	Caucasian	62
	Ellen (50)	Caucasian	69
	Brenda (47)	Hispanic	71
	Tony (19)	African American	71
Culturally Appropriate	**Norman (17)**	African American	90
	Justino (37)	Puerto Rican	96
	Lian (23)	Asian international	98
	Monica (27)	Multiracial: Native American and African American	99
Holland, Vocational Personalities and Work Environments	**Judy (38)**	Caucasian	114
	Johnny (38)	Hmong American	119
	Susan (17)	Caucasian	120
	Cynthia (42)	Caucasian	121
Theory of Work Adjustment	**Charles (early 40s)**	Caucasian	133
	Phil (48)	Caucasian	138
	Melissa (32)	Caucasian	140
	Linda (18)	Korean American	141
Developmental	**Karen (52)**	Caucasian	154
	Walter (65)	Caucasian	162
	Maria Josefina (16)	Puerto Rican	163
	Deborah (33) and Trish (38)	Caucasian	164

(Continued)

(Continued)

Theory or Approach	Client Name (Age)	Race/Ethnicity	Page
Gottfredson, Circumscription and Compromise	**Gary (16)**	Caucasian	177
	Dorece (21)	African American	181
	Steve (39)	Caucasian	182
	Lori (45)	Caucasian	183
Social Cognitive	**Ron (57)**	Caucasian	197
	Jerry (32)	Caucasian	206
	Kamisha (21)	African American	208
	Jim (27)	Caucasian	210
Summary and Integration	**George (54)**	Caucasian	223
	Tom (21)	Caucasian	231

Acknowledgments

We express deep gratitude to the many individuals who have helped us with the first and second editions of this book. First, our thanks to the career development scholars who provided feedback on drafts of the first edition: Nancy Betz, Helen Farmer, Lenore Harmon, and Mary Heppner. We also appreciate the feedback offered by experts in specific theoretical perspectives: Linda Forrest and Stephen Wester (Chapter 4), Rosie Bingham (Chapter 5), Gary Gottfredson and John Holland (Chapter 6), James Rounds and Howard (Tony) Tinsley (Chapter 7), David Blustein and Mark Savickas (Chapter 8), and Steve Brown and Bob Lent (Chapter 10). We thank Jeff Prince, John Westefeld, Mark Leitheiser, Azara Santiago-Rivera, and Chris Finn for feedback on case materials, and we thank the following organizations for providing the materials and scoring of assessment instruments: Consulting Psychologists Press, Career Development & Resource Clinic in the Department of Psychology at Southern Illinois University, and Vocational Psychology Research at the University of Minnesota.

We also thank the students in Nadya Fouad's summer 2008 Foundations of Career Development course at the University of Wisconsin–Milwaukee: Rosin Bergdoll, Melissa Brah, Lisa Engel, Donna Grady, Stacy Ludwig, Greg Mathias, Ginny Patton, Chad Peterson, Haley Pollen, Elizabeth Ojeda, Margaret Rhody, Shana Schloemer, Melissa Sell, and Elizabeth Wall. They provided wonderful feedback on early drafts of the second edition, helped us identify needed changes in the format and structure, and gave their perspectives on the breadth and depth of the cases. Similarly, Sarah Miller at Southern Illinois University provided her expertise and "fresh eyes" to a thorough review of the second edition. We appreciate their help.

Finally, we thank "Leslie" for inspiration.

We are deeply appreciative of the following individuals for their reviews of the second edition: Darlene M. Hannigan, LaSalle University; Margo A. Jackson, Fordham University; Mickey C. Melendez, The State University of New Jersey; and Donna E. Schultheiss, Cleveland State University.

Career Counseling: An Overview   1

Ruth has been out of the paid workforce for 8 years. Her youngest son recently started public school, and she would like to find a job. Ruth has a degree in medical technology and worked in a hospital lab for 5 years before her first child was born. In her geographic area, the job market for medical technologists is poor, so she'd like to consider some other job possibilities. She doesn't know what other options are available.

Harry has worked in the human resources department of a large company for over 20 years. He had been satisfied with his job and had received good performance evaluations. However, he was recently assigned new job responsibilities that he doesn't feel adequately trained to do. Last week, he received a negative report from his supervisor, and he's worried that he might lose his job. Harry has been depressed and angry, and his wife is concerned that he's drinking too much.

Joel is a high school junior who doesn't have any idea what he will do after graduating. His parents want him to go to college, believing that a college education will provide him with opportunities they did not have. However, Joel's grades have been mediocre, and he really doesn't want to go to college anyway. His guidance counselor tells him that he needs to make a decision soon.

❖

Each of these situations represents a struggle with some work- or career-related concern. Because work plays a central role in most people's lives, successful pursuit of work activities is crucial to psychological well-being. Furthermore, vocational issues and mental health issues affect one another in individuals' lives, and work is an important component of overall well-being (Betz & Corning, 1993; Blustein, 2008; Blustein & Spengler, 1995; Spokane, 1989; Spokane & Fretz, 1993). It is important for counselors to understand the crucial impact of vocational issues and to assist individuals in the choice and implementation of their career-related goals so that people's lives are enriched.

Purpose of the Book

The purpose of this book is to provide the reader with hands-on, practical examples of how to apply career development theories to career counseling clients. We view the book as a bridge between career theory and career practice. We wrote the first edition to be used in conjunction with other materials that describe career development theories in depth. In this second edition, we continue to assume that the reader will either use the book as a supplement or read other sources for further information about the theory in question, so the theoretical material in each chapter is presented as a review rather than a comprehensive treatment. This edition includes a new chapter (Chapter 2) highlighting the importance of various types of assessment in career counseling and addressing the role of ethics and professional issues. We also added material to highlight the role of the economy and the changing nature of the workforce that influence the career and work decisions individuals make, first in the present chapter and then throughout the book.

The book is organized to facilitate the integration of theory and practice. Chapter 3 introduces "Leslie," the primary case example used throughout the remainder of the book. We will consider Leslie from a new theoretical perspective in each subsequent chapter to demonstrate how theories can inform the way in which counselors view and work with their clients. In addition to Leslie, a secondary case with an extended analysis will be presented in each chapter. Three additional brief cases will offer the reader more opportunities to practice the application of theory to individual clients. We have added three new pedagogical tools in each chapter: a set of questions inviting readers to engage in personal reflection, a summary of the key theoretical constructs, and a summary of the counselor's cognitions from that theoretical perspective. We also provide additional references at the end of each chapter that provide greater depth for the interested reader.

We brought our own experiences as practitioners, researchers, and teachers to bear on our approach to writing this book. As practitioners, we believe that the theoretical orientation one adopts has a significant impact on how client issues are conceptualized and treated. As researchers, we know that the ethical delivery of career counseling must be based on sound empirical findings. Finally, as instructors, we are committed to helping students make connections between theory, research, and practice in ways that are ultimately in the service of clients. We have attempted to incorporate all of our experiences into the structure of this book by choosing theories that have received empirical support, by highlighting how the theoretical propositions influence views of clients, and by providing considerable case information for analysis and discussion. We have also learned that some students learn best by applying the material to their own lives, and thus we have incorporated personal reflections in each chapter. The personal reflections at the end of this chapter are relatively general; subsequent chapters have personal reflection geared to the content of the chapter.

We also wanted to incorporate our commitment to integrating contextual issues in conceptualizations of clients' concerns. We both have spent our careers conducting research and teaching students about the need to consider a client's gender, ethnicity, socioeconomic status, sexual orientation, and disability status when helping that client to make career decisions. An individual's choices and decisions, or lack of choices, are shaped by his or her gender, family, disability, sexual orientation, and culture, which in turn influence his or her schooling, access to resources, and interaction with the larger environment. Consider, for example, a Latina high school student from a traditional Hispanic family growing up in an affluent suburb of Los Angeles. Her career choices will be shaped by her gender, her family's cultural values, and their expectations of her post–high school decisions. Their expectations may be influenced by their affluence, their beliefs about gender and work, and the influences of the schools in their community. Her expectations will be shaped by her acceptance of her family's expectations and her ability to navigate expectations from her peers, parents, and teachers at her school. Her parents may feel that her post–high school choices are limited to options of which they approve, while she has been encouraged to "dream big" by her counselor. All of these factors will influence her decisions.

Change the example above to an African American heterosexual male student in rural Georgia, or a European American gay male in rural South Dakota, or a European American heterosexual female in an inner-city high school in Boston. While all of these individuals may choose to go to college after high school, the contexts for those decisions are shaped by their gender, family, race/ethnicity, disability, sexual orientation, schooling, and interactions with the mainstream culture in the United States. We think it is critical within ethical practice to consider clients' contextual factors, particularly gender and race/ethnicity. Readers will note the emphasis on the importance of context in several ways. Considerations of gender and culture are integrated into each chapter, a chapter is devoted to each (Chapters 4 and 5), and cases are included to represent the diversity of clients who seek counseling.

We wrote the book with two types of readers in mind. The first type is a student in a graduate-level course, such as theories of vocational psychology or practicum in career counseling, who is learning about theories of career development and how to apply these theories to clients. The second type of reader is an established counseling practitioner who wants additional resources to strengthen his or her delivery of career services or who is expanding the focus of his or her work to include career issues.

In this chapter, we focus on the role of theory in career counseling, beginning with a definition of *theory* and a description of types of career development theories. We then describe the theories selected for this casebook and discuss how to use theories, particularly as a means to develop hypotheses about clients. We will discuss the settings and roles in which career and work-related counseling may occur. Finally, we present some models of conducting career counseling, including a discussion of how career and personal issues might interact in individuals' lives.

Theories of career development tend to be primarily psychological in nature; that is, they focus on characteristics of individuals that help explain the careers they enter, the ways that they adjust to work environments, or the processes by which they make career choices or changes. However, these theories do not exist in a vacuum: The larger economic and social systems in which an individual resides play crucial roles in the type of decision that is made or even whether a decision can or needs to be made at all. For example, when the national (or global) economy is booming, an individual may see many opportunities available and may feel little risk in deciding to leave a current job for one in another organization or field or to pursue further education. On the other hand, when the economy is in a downturn, the same individual may see few opportunities and may not be able or willing to risk any work-related changes. When a labor market is relatively open (more jobs than workers), employers have to offer better salaries and other benefits to attract well-qualified workers; when a labor market is relatively tight (more workers than jobs), employers do not have to compete for workers and may decrease what they offer. These economic factors obviously influence an individual's career development, at particular choice points and in the progression of one's career over a life span, and we will continue to discuss these factors as we consider specific theories of career development.

Definition and Types of Theories

A theory is a series of connected hypothetical statements designed to explain a particular behavior or set of behaviors. We have, for example, theories to explain how people solve problems (e.g., Heppner, Reeder, & Larsen, 1983), to predict causes of stress in the workplace (e.g., Long, Kahn, & Schutz, 1992), or to describe how humans develop socially and psychologically (e.g., Erikson, 1968). Theories serve a very important purpose in psychology and in counseling; they help psychologists and counselors to conceptualize human behavior. In essence, theories guide us in making sense of very complex sets of information about how humans behave to help us understand them and to predict their behavior in the future.

One useful way to envision the role of a theory is to view it as a road map (Krumboltz, 1994). Both maps and theories are representations of reality designed for a particular purpose to help guide the user's understanding of a terrain. Motorists use road maps to facilitate traveling from point A to point B; counselors use career theories to help them explain a client's vocational behavior. Krumboltz notes that maps and theories can be useful for one purpose and not for another. Vocational theories, for example, are useful to help understand career choices but might be less useful in other situations.

Krumboltz (1994) also notes that theories designed to explain and predict complex human behavior must, of necessity, omit some aspects of behavior, distort other aspects to highlight them, and depict some unobservable conditions as reality. Thus, a vocational theory may include some variables that help explain career choices but may omit behavior related to interpersonal relationships. The theory may label some behavior to bring attention to it. The theory of work adjustment (Dawis, 2005; Dawis & Lofquist, 1984), for example, has a number of unique identifiers for work-related behavior, such as satisfactoriness, to highlight those aspects of behavior the theory is designed to explain. Other theories in this book have developed labels to highlight behavior leading to a career choice rather than to highlight behavior in a work setting. None of the theories explains all work-related behaviors, and in this way, theories distort the reality of the very complicated behavior related to making career decisions prior to and following the entry into the world of work. And all theories make some assumptions about internal conditions that are not observable. Super's theory (Super, Savickas, & Super, 1996) includes an assumption that vocational choice is the implementation of the self-concept; this is not directly observable, yet it is a central tenet of his theory.

The theories discussed in this book are attempts to explain some career-related behavior. Each theory overlaps with the others in some ways, but each has distinct constructs. In some ways, however, each theory may be viewed as attempting to explain different aspects of the proverbial elephant; depending on the theorist's vantage point, different aspects of behavior will be emphasized.

Although there is considerable overlap among the major vocational theories discussed in this book, they each explain some unique work-related behaviors and thus are useful guides for counselors. Without a theoretical framework to guide us, we would find it very difficult to make sense of the information clients might bring to us about their work-related problems. To return to the map analogy, we consult a road map before we leave on a trip to know the best way to get to our destination; without a map, we may wander aimlessly. So a good theory helps us to represent reality, understand behavior, and assist clients in understanding their behavior.

We chose seven different theoretical approaches for inclusion in this book. Three of the theories have long histories of scholarship and recognition (Hackett, Lent, & Greenhaus, 1991): Holland's typological theory of persons and environments, Dawis and Lofquist's theory of work adjustment, and Super's life-span, life-space approach. The fourth theory, Lent, Brown, and Hackett's social cognitive career theory, had previously been called an "emerging theory" (Hackett et al., 1991; Swanson & Fouad, 1999) yet has achieved considerable stature in the past decade. A fifth theory, Gottfredson's theory of circumscription and compromise, was included despite having less empirical support due to its appeal to practitioners and its explicit attention to early socialization. Further, we chose to include two additional approaches—feminist and gender-aware perspectives and culturally appropriate career counseling—because they reflect the steadily growing recognition of the critical impact of context on career behavior.

Our decision to include the two chapters related to gender and race and ethnicity does not imply, however, that we consider them "separate" topics. These chapters are placed before the more well-established career theories to highlight their importance and to emphasize the critical role of contextual issues in mainstream career development theories. Moreover, gender and multicultural issues, as well as other contextual issues, are integrated throughout the book in an effort to bring them to the center of discussions about vocational behavior. We encourage readers to contemplate contextual factors, such as gender and race, each time they evaluate a different theoretical perspective or conceptualize a new client.

A danger in presenting each theory separately is that this organization might foster a polarization of the theories, as well as the implication that one must choose a specific theory and not deviate from that choice. Nothing could be further from the truth. What we hope will become evident throughout the book is that each theory has some unique and useful perspectives to offer a consideration of Leslie, the primary case described in Chapter 3. Moreover, each theory may be particularly useful for a specific type of client, as evidenced by the additional cases provided in each chapter. Despite the organizational structure, we encourage the reader to think integratively across the theoretical perspectives, and we will provide some assistance in doing so in the final summary chapter (Chapter 11). There, we will model how we as counselors might approach a case from an integrated theoretical approach, and we will summarize how each theoretical perspective added to our understanding of Leslie.

Clarifying Distinctions Between Theories and Theoretical Orientations

We have introduced several slightly different terms, which may cause some confusion: *theoretical orientation, career development theories,* and *career counseling theories.* The term *theoretical orientation* is most frequently used to describe one's general philosophical stance about the nature of personality and of therapeutic change, such as humanistic, cognitive-behavioral, or family systems. One's theoretical orientation interacts with one's view of career development and of career counseling, although this interaction is rarely discussed because of the manner in which we often compartmentalize career counseling and personal counseling, or career issues and personal issues within counseling. We will revisit the issue of "career versus personal" in a later section.

Our discussion about career-related theories has, thus far, focused on theories of career *development* rather than on theories of career *counseling;* yet they are not identical. Theories of career *development* were devised to explain vocational behavior, such as initial career choice, work adjustment, or life span career progress. The goal of theories of career *counseling,* on the other hand, is to provide counselors with direction for how to work with clients; these theories are more akin to theoretical orientation as defined earlier.

The distinction between theories of career development and career counseling is an important one. In fact, Osipow (1996) contends that no career counseling theory exists. There have been, however, several models for conducting career counseling, and we will discuss one model later in this chapter. Moreover, there have been some efforts to apply psychotherapy theoretical orientations to career counseling, such as psychodynamic career counseling (Watkins & Savickas, 1990) and person-centered career counseling (Bozarth & Fisher, 1990), as well as efforts to more explicitly link career development theories to career counseling (Savickas & Walsh, 1996).

So a counselor might describe her general therapeutic theoretical orientation as cognitive-behavioral, her view of career development as guided by Holland's (1997) typological theory, and her work with clients as following Gysbers, Heppner, and Johnston's (2003) model of career counseling, with additional attention to the client's cultural context. These descriptors do not contradict one another, because they all influence how this particular counselor views her clients and affect her in-session behavior and interventions with clients. Counselors develop their theoretical affinities through exposure to different perspectives and through their own clinical experience.

We advocate that career development theories be used in career counseling to help practitioners determine the most appropriate and effective tools to help clients. This is an ideal situation, however, and one met with some skepticism by practitioners and researchers alike. Lucas (1996) for example, points out that "counselors insist on relevance, [and the theory-driven research published in] journals [does] not provide it" (p. 82).

The biggest concern voiced by practitioners is that career development theories explain pieces of vocational behavior, but no client ever walks into an office with just the exact piece explained by the theory. Practitioners contend that some theories do not adequately explain the career behavior of women, racial and ethnic minority clients, or lesbian and gay clients. They find that other theories do not discuss the interface between work and family or that they do not adequately address the myriad problems a client brings to counseling that include both career and personal concerns. This book does not specifically address the split between practitioners and academicians; there still remains the need for practice to inform science in a substantive way (Osipow, 1996). But we are suggesting that a counselor's solid theoretical grounding helps to shape the way the counselor approaches the client and the questions he or she will ask. The counselor's preferred theory will also help to determine the types of assessment tools used in counseling, as well as the interventions and techniques employed.

Counselor Roles and Settings

Who uses career counseling? Our premise in this book is that all counselors need to understand how work and career decisions are conceptualized. Individuals may seek counseling for a variety of concerns, and an understanding of how those concerns may be affected by work or career is critical to a holistic understanding of the client. Having said this, though, in some settings, career or work counseling is the primary focus of the counselor. Some career counselors have private practices in which all of their clients are seeking help with voluntary career transitions, such as leaving a job to retire or seek another position, or involuntary transitions, such as a layoff or having to return to the workforce following a divorce.

Amundson, Harris-Bowlsbey, and Niles (2009) note that career counseling has evolved from helping an adolescent choose a college and major to counseling individuals at all stages of development with work-related choices and decisions. They highlight seven myths about career counseling that are important for students, professionals, and clients to recognize as myths:

1. Career counselors can give clients tests that tell them what to do.
2. Work decisions are made separately from other life decisions.
3. Career counseling does not address personal concerns.
4. Career counselors do not need training or expertise.
5. Career counseling is the same for everyone, regardless of cultural context.
6. Career counseling is needed only when a decision must be made.
7. Career counseling ends when a decision is made.

We address many of these myths in this chapter and throughout the book. Career counselors at all levels need to be aware that some or all of these myths may shape the expectations that clients or students have when they seek career counseling. It is thus important to help clients understand the ways that career counseling may help them, that a single assessment tool cannot predict the success of a future career choice, and that the scope of career counseling is, in fact, often life and work counseling. It is also critical that individuals seek career counseling from trained professionals. Figler (2007) notes that hundreds of millions of individuals "would say they need help with their careers. Yet only a tiny fraction seek and pay for the services of a career counselor" (p. 98). Figler advocates an annual career checkup, in which individuals seek the help of a career counselor in much the same way individuals make an appointment with a health care provider as a preventative measure. He suggests an annual checkup could consist of one or more of several activities, including a review of skills, career exploration, identification of new competencies needed, career redirection, and job search activities.

Currently, career exploration is most often done by school counselors, who often focus on career development activities as part of their work with students, particularly at the high school level. High school counselors help adolescents manage the anxiety of an uncertain future after high school, navigate the process of choosing a major and college or postsecondary work setting, and understand the relationship between high school activities and grades and future opportunities. The American School Counselor Association (ASCA, 2004) *National Standards for Students* for school counseling programs include three major career development standards:

1. Students will acquire the skills to investigate the world of work in relation to knowledge of self and to make informed career decisions.

2. Students will employ strategies to achieve future career goals with success and satisfaction.

3. Students will understand the relationship between personal qualities, education, training, and the world of work.

College career counselors help students entering college as "undecided" about their major and assist students in exploring various options and building decision-making skills. College career counselors also help students transition to the settings after college, such as work, internships, or further schooling. Finally, many organizations have counselors to help individuals make career decisions within the organization. Large companies may help individuals choose various options, such as ways to advance within the company or how to be involved in other areas of the company (e.g., choosing to work in another country or on another product line).

Individuals may thus provide career counseling as part of their work in a high school or college, in private practice, or as part of a large organization. Each setting has unique professional and ethical challenges for counselors, and we will introduce readers to those challenges through ethical vignettes at the end of Chapter 2.

Developing Hypotheses and a "Working Model" of the Client

Each client who comes for career counseling brings a unique set of personal characteristics and life experiences. Yet a number of common dimensions can guide a counselor's work with clients. The specific dimensions of interest to a particular counselor will be determined by his or her theoretical orientation and the theories of career development and career counseling to which he or she subscribes.

One way in which career development theories influence career counseling is that they suggest hypotheses for further consideration and exploration. Walborn (1996) describes a hypothesis as "an educated hunch that is grounded in theory" (p. 224) or that may emerge from the interaction between the client and counselor. Developing and sharing hypotheses with the client are critical components in any type of counseling or therapy, particularly in career counseling. Regardless of theoretical orientation, counselors have hunches about clients' presenting problems and what might be done to assist them. Moreover, counselors "must be aware of where they are taking the client and, to do so, they must be aware of their hypotheses" (p. 225).

The language we use throughout this book reflects our focus on generating and testing hypotheses, and we strongly encourage the reader to adopt the inquisitive frame of mind that underlies hypothesis generation and hypothesis testing. The structure of the book offers many natural places for the reader to pause and reflect on (a) what is known about a particular client; (b) whether the reader's hypotheses have been confirmed, have been disconfirmed, or need further elaboration; and (c) additional hypotheses or speculations that the reader might make about a client. For example, in Chapter 3, Leslie's case history is first presented and summarized; then, assessment information is discussed and illustrated. The reader will form some impressions about Leslie based on her career history, so the reader should articulate those impressions before reading the section with Leslie's assessment results. Then the reader may review the assessment with his or her impressions and hypotheses in mind and search for confirming and disconfirming evidence.

Development of hypotheses begins with the very first exposure to the client, whether in person or through written intake case information, and is an ongoing process throughout counseling. Hypothesis development may need to be an explicitly conscious exercise for new counselors, but it becomes an automatic process as counselors gain experience. It is important for counselors to be aware of and be able to articulate the hypotheses that they form, whether consciously or unconsciously.

Refinement of hypotheses continues throughout counseling. Walborn (1996) suggests a number of benefits of continual development of hypotheses, including helping the counselor remain an active rather than passive listener, keeping counseling sessions focused, providing alternative interpretations of the client's problem, and fostering a collaborative relationship between counselor and client.

Counselors use all sources of available information to generate hypotheses. Moreover, counselors look for consistent themes across several sources of information as well as for inconsistencies between sources. For example, John's highest interest inventory scores are in the artistic area, and he reports that the course he enjoyed most last semester was art history. However, he is performing poorly in a photography course this semester. These bits of information provide both consistency and inconsistency, resulting in a hypothesis that merits further investigation: John enjoys artistic, flexible, creative environments as a spectator; he doesn't have artistic skills or abilities, nor does he enjoy producing art. How does the counselor then test this hypothesis? The most direct way is to simply offer the hypothesis to John to see how he reacts and to invite him to gather evidence related to the hypothesis. For example, John's counselor might comment, "You seem to have a strong interest in artistic activities, but perhaps more as an observer or appreciator of art rather than as a 'doer' of art. How does that fit?" The goal is to help John discover something new about himself or to clarify something he already knows and help him to integrate it within his view of himself.

Sometimes, clients already know what the counselor offers as a hypothesis; for example, it may be quite clear to John that he doesn't have strong artistic skills but that he still enjoys learning about art. At other times, clients may not have thought about their interests and activities in quite the same way that the counselor has presented the hypothesis, and further discussion helps them to clarify information about themselves. It therefore becomes very important that the counselor makes it clear that the hypotheses are just that—hunches about the client that await further evidence and verification.

Counselors communicate the hypothetical nature of their statements via several methods. First, counselors use tentative language when offering hypotheses to clients so that they are not perceived as statements of fact. For example, a counselor might say, "I'm wondering if you might prefer selling ideas rather than selling products," or, "It seems that you're most comfortable in situations where you clearly know what's expected of you." Second, counselors engage clients in a collaborative effort to develop and examine hypotheses, primarily by paying attention to the development of the counselor-client relationship. If the client feels that he or she is in a comfortable, collaborative relationship, then the client will be more likely to disagree with the counselor if the hypothesis is not accurate. The counselor might ask, "What do *you* think? How does that fit with what you know about yourself?" Finally, counselors need to remind themselves (and their clients) that they are offering hypotheses that are in need of further evidence and to search thoroughly for such evidence: "What other experiences have you had that support your pursuing an artistic career? How else might you 'test out' your interests and skills?"

Walborn (1996) argues that verbal disclosure of a counselor's hypotheses about the client is a necessary, but not sufficient, condition for effective therapy. The way in which hypotheses are shared with the client depends on the stage of counseling; the client himself or herself; the strength of the client-counselor relationship; and, perhaps, the theoretical orientation of the counselor. Within the realm of personal-emotional counseling, Walborn suggests that the presentation of hypotheses differs by schools of therapy. Humanistic approaches use reflection as the major technique because it directs the client's attention to something that the counselor deems important. Explicit disclosure of hypotheses is a fundamental basis of cognitive approaches, and hypotheses are most often related to a client's faulty cognitions. Finally, a variety of methods are used to disclose hypotheses in psychodynamic approaches, such as interpretation and catharsis. These stylistic differences in how hypotheses are offered and explored also may be seen in career counseling. For example, counselors using Holland's theory of vocational personalities might use a didactic style, and feminist counselors would be likely to develop a collaborative approach to developing hypotheses with the client.

A final point is that counselors need to judge whether their hypotheses are accurate. First, the counselor must consider whether the hypothesis is culture bound. In other words, is the hypothesis appropriate for the client's culture and gender, or is it based on the counselor's own cultural background? Accuracy may be determined by the client's reaction to the hypothesis and by gathering further evidence to test its veridicality. Furthermore, Walborn (1996) suggests that the *process* of developing and sharing a hypothesis actually may be more important than the *content* of the hypothesis. In other words, one outcome of hypothesis testing is that the client learns self-exploration skills, which is important in and of itself.

A caveat about formulating hypotheses about clients: Hypotheses and "working models" should never be used to label prematurely, infer conclusions, or make judgments about clients. While it might be tempting for a counselor to think he or she has the client "all figured out," the counselor should always remain open to new evidence and be prepared to alter his or her view of the client in response to new information. Research examining how counselors form and test hypotheses suggests that counselors tend to pay more attention to new information that confirms their hypotheses at the expense of information that disconfirms their hypotheses. This research serves as a reminder that counselors need to consider as much information as possible (Garb, 1998; Pfeiffer, Whelan, & Martin, 2000; Spengler et al., in press).

Conducting Career Counseling

Individual career counseling is an "ongoing, face-to-face interaction between counselor and client" (Swanson, 1995, p. 245) in which the focus is on work- or career-related concerns. Career counseling is also defined as "the process of assisting individuals in the development of a life-career with focus on the definition of the worker role and how that role interacts with other life roles" (National Career Development Association, 1997, p. 1), highlighting the importance of placing career issues within the broader context of individuals' lives. Career services may also be delivered to groups, such as in classes or workshops, and career interventions often include activities that do not require a counselor's presence, such as computer-assisted guidance packages. Although these modes of service delivery are useful, in this book, we will focus on individually delivered career counseling in which there is a relationship between counselor and client. Individual career counseling has been shown to be effective across a large number of studies (Brown & Ryan Krane, 2000; Whiston, Brecheisen, & Stephens, 2003). Brown and Ryan Krane also found that career counseling optimally consists of written exercises, interpretation of assessment tools (e.g., interest inventories), occupational information, role modeling, and helping clients build social support.

Several authors have developed models of career counseling. To return to our earlier discussion of terminology, these are truly theories of career counseling rather than theories of career development, because their purpose is to outline how counseling might proceed. We cannot provide an exhaustive review of each model but will present one model here as an introduction or review. In general, career counseling models are structured around a phase of introduction and relationship building, a phase devoted to exploration of the client's work-related problem, and a phase devoted to helping the client move toward resolution of the problem.

Gysbers et al. (2003) outline a model of career counseling that has two major phases: (1) goal or problem identification, clarification, and specification and (2) client goal or problem resolution. As noted in Figure 1.1, at the core of Gysbers et al.'s model is the *working alliance* between counselor and client, which consists of agreement on the goals and tasks of counseling and formation of a bond between counselor and client (Bordin, 1979). The working alliance is an important component of career counseling in that it creates the atmosphere in which the work of counseling takes place and facilitates the client's trust in the counselor to help the client reach goals. Whiston and Rahardja (2008) recommend that counselors need to help clients develop insight and facilitate exploration of options and potential barriers to achievement of goals.

During the opening subphase of goal or problem identification, the counselor first establishes a relationship with the client and helps the client to identify and explore his or her initial problems. The counselor listens for the client's goals and the concerns that the client brings to counseling. During this phase, the counselor helps to clarify the client's expectations

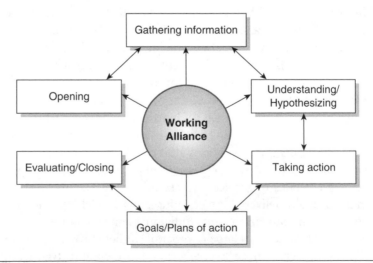

Figure 1.1   Gysbers, Heppner, and Johnston's Model of Career Counseling

SOURCE: Gysbers, Heppner, and Johnston (2003).

for counseling and sets the stage for the counseling relationship to develop. Spokane (1991) notes that one of the critical outcomes of the opening phase of career counseling is the activation of hope that the dilemma or concern will be resolved.

The next subphase is gathering client information, accomplished through the use of standard formal assessment, as well as through qualitative data gathered from the interview about the client's dreams, hopes, and aspirations. This phase is to help both the client and counselor understand the client's self-awareness and worldview, understanding of career history and decision making, and actual or ideal role of work in life. The counselor also listens for the social and personal resources on which the client might build or the external and internal constraints or barriers the client might have.

The last subphase of goal identification is understanding and hypothesizing client behavior, in which the counselor forms some hypotheses about the client that will help to guide counseling interventions. The counselor's hypotheses are based on theories of career development, knowledge and awareness of gender and culture in influencing career and work decisions, and attention to possible client resistance to moving toward goals. Gysbers et al. (2003) note that there may be many reasons for a client's resistance, including fear of change, fear of counseling, fear of responsibility, irrational beliefs, indecisiveness, and faulty processing. Amundson et al. (2009) label this as *client reluctance*. Reasons for reluctance include fear of the unfamiliar, refusal to take responsibility for the problem, job loss or search burnout, previous bad experiences with counseling, and secondary gains for not moving toward a goal. The latter may occur when counseling is a threat to financial benefits as, for example, when deciding on work also means no longer receiving unemployment compensation. Finally, Amundson et al. discuss the occasions when clients are mandated to receive career counseling. For this situation, Amundson et al. recommend that counselors adopt four guiding principles: nondefensive listening and discussion of the situation, empathy with the client's emotions and situation, clarifying the role of the counselor, and supporting the client in his or her progress. Both Amundson et al. and Gysbers et al. highlight the role of the working alliance in successfully negotiating with difficult or resistant clients.

The working alliance is strengthened and fulfilled during these later two subphases of the opening phase. The second major phase, goal or problem resolution, is also characterized by three subphases. In the first subphase, taking action, the counselor uses theory-based counseling interventions to assist the client. The second subphase consists of developing career goals and plans of action so that the client can achieve his or her goals and resolve potential barriers. The last subphase, evaluating results and closing the relationship, is accomplished when the client's goals are achieved.

This model provides a useful paradigm to help counselors work with clients who have career concerns. Embedded in this model is the implicit acknowledgment that individuals bring to counseling a continuum of career-related issues. Clients seek help for career-related problems that are intricately intertwined with their personal lives. A client might, for example, want help getting more information about a career in nursing, then might want help sorting out how training to be a nurse would fit with the responsibilities he or she has for three children at home. The client might decide to seek help responding assertively to demands made by his or her family, then perhaps might return to a more information-oriented need of obtaining financial aid. Gysbers et al. (2003) point out that to work effectively with clients, we need to combine skills in career counseling with skills in personal-emotional counseling. They echo Blustein and Spengler's (1995) call for domain-sensitive counseling, which "refers to a way of intervening with clients such that the full array of human experiences is encompassed" (p. 316). In other words, effective career counselors are able to take the client's concerns as the beginning point of therapy and develop interventions in both career and noncareer domains as is appropriate for the client. In this way, a client's experiences, behaviors, and life roles can be addressed across a variety of contexts.

Integrating "Career" and "Personal" Aspects of Counseling

Because career counseling and personal-emotional counseling developed from different historical traditions and within different specialties of psychology, they are often viewed as independent activities. Haverkamp and Moore (1993) discuss the perceptual dichotomy existing in the profession in which career counseling and personal counseling appear to function as distinct cognitive schemas. They argue that the implicit definition of personal counseling is too broad, consisting of anything not directly related to career; the implicit definition of career counseling, on the other hand, is too narrow, consisting primarily of initial career choices of young adults and neglecting adult work adjustment.

Research suggests, however, that it is unwise to view clients with career issues as substantially different from those with personal issues and that they may experience similar levels of psychological distress (Gold & Scanlon, 1993; Lucas, 1992). Moreover, clients might be less well served or less satisfied with career counseling when evident personal issues are not addressed (Juntunen, 2006; Phillips, Friedlander, Kost, Specterman, & Robbins, 1988). As Hackett (1993) notes, "We are undoubtedly doing our clients a disservice by any attempt to neatly compartmentalize their lives" (p. 110).

A related area of literature highlights the connections between career counseling and mental health outcomes. There is increasing recognition that work and mental health are interwoven and that adult vocational needs are complex (Blustein, 2008; Fouad, 2007; Hackett, 1993; Haverkamp & Moore, 1993; Herr, Cramer, & Niles, 2004). Brown and Brooks (1985) argue that career counseling with adults may be a viable alternative to stress management and even to personal counseling. Furthermore, they argue that psychologists have overlooked the potential of career counseling, and they encourage practitioners to recognize that the source of psychological symptoms may be in the work situation rather than in intrapsychic factors. They also propose that although all practitioners cannot be skilled career counselors, all should become skilled in recognizing situations in which career counseling is an appropriate intervention.

So how shall we conceptualize the connection between career counseling and personal counseling or between career issues and personal issues? Clearly, career counseling can be very similar to personal counseling, but it can also be very different. Career counseling requires the counselor to use many of the same skills that personal counseling requires; therefore, the process, at least at times, can be quite similar. Perhaps most importantly, counselors need to be aware of how career and personal factors are intertwined in their clients' lives and to address clearly the spectrum of issues that clients experience.

Summary

We have presented the preceding issues in some detail, because each is crucial to considering how to apply theories of career development to real client issues. We now turn to a discussion of assessment in Chapter 2. Then we present the primary case of the book, Leslie, in Chapter 3, followed by chapters focusing on gender (Chapter 4) and multicultural (Chapter 5) considerations. Finally, after considering each of the five theories in Chapters 6 through 10, we will return in Chapter 11 to some of the ideas presented here in Chapter 1.

Return to the three vignettes at the beginning of this chapter—brief stories of Ruth, Harry, and Joel. Imagine that any one of these people has come to you for counseling. What impressions do you have of each one? What do you think about his or her work or career concerns? What additional information would you like to know? How might you begin to address the concerns these people have expressed?

Now think back to a time when you had career or work-related concerns, such as an unsatisfying job, an inability to find work, or uncertainty about which career direction to choose. How did these concerns affect other aspects of your life? How did you resolve the concerns? Use the questions in Box 1.1 to guide your personal reflection.

Box 1.1

Personal Reflection

What have been some of the key transition points in my own career and work history? How did I make decisions along those points? Who influenced my decisions?

What assumptions does society make about work? Do I agree with those assumptions?

How has my context (gender, family, race/ethnicity, religion, disability status) helped to shape my career decisions?

References

American School Counselor Association (ASCA). (2004). *ASCA national standards for students.* Alexandria, VA: Author.

Amundson, N., Harris-Bowlsbey, J. G., & Niles, S. G. (2009). *Essential elements of career counseling: Processes and techniques* (2nd ed.). Upper Saddle River, NJ: Pearson Prentice Hall.

Betz, N. E., & Corning, A. F. (1993). The inseparability of career and personal counseling. *Career Development Quarterly, 42,* 137–142.

Blustein, D. L. (2008). The role of work in psychological health and well-being: A conceptual, historical, and public policy perspective. *American Psychologist, 63,* 228–240.

Blustein, D. L., & Spengler, P. M. (1995). Personal adjustment: Career counseling and psychotherapy. In W. B. Walsh & S. H. Osipow (Eds.), *Handbook of vocational psychology* (2nd ed., pp. 295–320). Hillsdale, NJ: Lawrence Erlbaum.

Bordin, E. S. (1979). The generalizability of the psychoanalytic concept of working alliance. *Psychotherapy: Theory, Research, and Practice, 16,* 252–260.

Bozarth, J. D., & Fisher, R. (1990). Person-centered career counseling. In W. B. Walsh & S. H. Osipow (Eds.), *Career counseling* (pp. 45–78). Mahwah, NJ: Lawrence Erlbaum.

Brown, D., & Brooks, L. (1985). Career counseling as a mental health intervention. *Professional Psychology: Research and Practice, 16,* 860–867.

Brown, S. D., & Ryan Krane, N. E. (2000). Four (or five) sessions and a cloud of dust: Old assumptions and new observations about career counseling. In S. D. Brown & R. W. Lent (Eds.), *Handbook of counseling psychology* (3rd ed., pp. 740–766). New York: Wiley.

Dawis, R. V. (2005). The Minnesota theory of work adjustment. In S. D. Brown & R. W. Lent (Eds.), *Career development and counseling: Putting theory and research to work* (pp. 3–23). New York: Wiley.

Dawis, R. V., & Lofquist, L. H. (1984). *A psychological theory of work adjustment.* Minneapolis: University of Minnesota Press.

Erikson, E. H. (1968). *Identity: Youth and crisis.* New York: Norton.

Figler, H. (2007). The annual career checkup. In H. Figler & R. N. Bolles (Eds.), *The career counselor's handbook* (2nd ed.). Berkeley, CA: Ten Speed Press.

Fouad, N. A. (2007). Work and vocational psychology: Theory, research, and applications. *Annual Review of Psychology, 58,* 543–564.

Garb, H. N. (1998). *Studying the clinician: Judgment research and psychological assessment.* Washington, DC: American Psychological Association.

Gold, J. M., & Scanlon, C. R. (1993). Psychological distress and counseling duration of career and noncareer clients. *Career Development Quarterly, 42,* 186–191.

Gysbers, N. C., Heppner, M. J., & Johnston, J. A. (2003). *Career counseling: Process, issues, and techniques* (2nd ed.). Boston: Allyn & Bacon.

Hackett, G. (1993). Career counseling and psychotherapy: False dichotomies and recommended remedies. *Journal of Career Assessment, 1,* 105–117.

Hackett, G., Lent, R. W., & Greenhaus, J. H. (1991). Advances in vocational theory and research: A 20-year retrospective. *Journal of Vocational Behavior, 38,* 3–38.

Haverkamp, B. E., & Moore, D. (1993). The career-personal dichotomy: Perceptual reality, practical illusion, and workplace integration. *Career Development Quarterly, 42,* 154–160.

Heppner, P. P., Reeder, B. L., & Larsen, L. M. (1983). Cognitive variables associated with personal problem-solving appraisal: Implications for counseling. *Journal of Counseling Psychology, 30,* 537–545.

Herr, E. L., Cramer, S. H., & Niles, S. G. (2004). *Career guidance and counseling through the lifespan: Systematic approaches* (6th ed.). Boston: Pearson/Allyn & Bacon.

Holland, J. L. (1997). *Making vocational choices: A theory of vocational personalities and work environments* (3rd ed.). Odessa, FL: Psychological Assessment Resources.

Juntunen, C. L. (2006). The psychology of working: The clinical context. *Professional Psychology: Research and Practice, 37,* 342–350.

Krumboltz, J. D. (1994). Improving career development theory from a social learning perspective. In M. L. Savickas & R. W. Lent (Eds.), *Convergence in career development theories* (pp. 9–31). Palo Alto, CA: Consulting Psychologists Press.

Long, B. S., Kahn, S. E., & Schutz, R. W. (1992). A causal model of stress and coping: Women in management. *Journal of Counseling Psychology, 39,* 337–239.

Lucas, M. S. (1992). Problems expressed by career and non-career help seekers: A comparison. *Journal of Counseling and Development, 70,* 417–420.

Lucas, M. S. (1996). Building cohesiveness between practitioners and researchers: A practitioner-scientist model. In M. L. Savickas & W. B. Walsh (Eds.), *Handbook of career counseling theory and practice* (pp. 81–88). Palo Alto, CA: Davies-Black.

National Career Development Association (NCDA). (1997). *Career counseling competencies.* Columbus, OH: Author.

Osipow, S. H. (1996). Does career theory guide practice or does career practice guide theory? In M. L. Savickas & W. B. Walsh (Eds.), *Handbook of career counseling theory and practice* (pp. 403–409). Palo Alto, CA: Davies-Black.

Pfeiffer, A. M., Whelan, J. P., & Martin, J. M. (2000). Decision-making bias in psychotherapy: Effects of hypothesis source and accountability. *Journal of Counseling Psychology, 74,* 429–436.

Phillips, S. D., Friedlander, M. L., Kost, P. P., Specterman, R. V., & Robbins, E. S. (1988). Personal versus vocational focus in career counseling: A retrospective outcome study. *Journal of Counseling and Development, 67,* 169–173.

Savickas, M. L., & Walsh, W. B. (Eds.). (1996). *Handbook of career counseling theory and practice.* Palo Alto, CA: Davies-Black.

Spengler, P. M., et al. (in press). The Meta-Analysis of Clinical Judgment Project: Effects of experience on judgment accuracy. *The Counseling Psychologist*.

Spokane, A. R. (1989). Are there psychological and mental health consequences of difficult career decisions? *Journal of Career Development, 16*(1), 19–23.

Spokane, A. R. (1991). *Career intervention*. Englewood Cliffs, NJ: Prentice Hall.

Spokane, A. R., & Fretz, B. R. (1993). Forty cases: A framework for studying the effects of career counseling on career and personal adjustment. *Journal of Career Assessment, 1*, 118–129.

Super, D. E., Savickas, M. L., & Super, C. M. (1996). The life-span, life-space approach to careers. In D. Brown, L. Brooks, & Associates (Eds.), *Career choice and development* (3rd ed., pp. 121–178). San Francisco: Jossey-Bass.

Swanson, J. L. (1995). The process and outcome of career counseling. In W. B. Walsh & S. H. Osipow (Eds.), *Handbook of vocational psychology* (2nd ed., pp. 217–259). Hillsdale, NJ: Lawrence Erlbaum.

Swanson, J. L., & Fouad, N. A. (1999). *Career theory and practice: Learning through case studies*. Thousand Oaks, CA: Sage.

Walborn, F. S. (1996). *Process variables: Four common elements of counseling and psychotherapy*. Pacific Grove, CA: Brooks/Cole.

Watkins, C. E., Jr., & Savickas, M. L. (1990). Psychodynamic career counseling. In W. B. Walsh & S. H. Osipow (Eds.), *Career counseling* (pp. 79–116). Mahwah, NJ: Lawrence Erlbaum.

Whiston, S. C., Brecheisen, B. K., & Stephens, J. (2003). Does treatment modality affect career counseling effectiveness? *Journal of Vocational Behavior, 62*, 390–410.

Whiston, S. C., & Rahardja, D. (2008). Vocational counseling process and outcome. In S. D. Brown & R. W. Lent (Eds.), *Handbook of counseling psychology* (4th ed., pp. 444–461). New York: Wiley.

The Use of Assessment in Career Counseling 2

Historically, assessment has been an integral part of career counseling. Use of assessment takes a somewhat broader role in career counseling than in counseling for other issues. In personal-emotional counseling, a test is primarily used by the *counselor* to make diagnostic decisions and recommendations. In career counseling, assessment is used primarily for the *client's* benefit, for self-exploration and self-understanding (Duckworth, 1990; Watkins & Campbell, 1990). Because of this expanded role of assessment, it is particularly important that counselors be knowledgeable, because they need to explain assessment results to clients accurately, clearly, and in the proper context.

We expect that the reader will have prior exposure and training regarding the use of career assessment or will obtain this information elsewhere. It is beyond the scope of this book to provide the detailed information necessary to use each of these tests in a competent manner. We have chosen to include four instruments in the primary case (Leslie) to illustrate how a career counselor might use different types of assessment in counseling.

Seligman (1994) discusses the benefits and limitations of testing and assessment in career counseling. She suggests that tests are useful for summarizing a person's responses to a set of items or questions, then comparing the responses with those made by other people, thus presenting an objective and standardized picture of a person's behavior. Tests can be used to answer *what* questions (What are the client's primary interests? What difficulties is she having in making a career choice?) and *how* questions (How do the client's interests compare with other women in scientific fields? How do her interests fit with her values?). Tests are less relevant to answering *why* questions (Why is the client having difficulty making a career decision? Why don't the client's current interests match past experiences?). The *why* questions may be sources of further hypotheses about the client to explore in counseling.

The ethical use of psychological assessment requires that counselors be well versed in a variety of topics, including how a test is constructed, norm groups, fairness for female and racial and ethnic minority clients, and strategies for interpretation. Results of career assessment should be considered in the context of all other available information about the client. It is critical that counselors choose reliable and valid tests and know the limitations of the instruments that they choose. We recommend that readers consult sources designed to assist counselors in evaluating assessment instruments, such as the checklists offered by Kapes, Mastie, and Whitfield (1994).

Selection of Assessment

Counselors using assessment tools have a number of decisions to make when selecting tools. Test developers should provide information to help counselors decide which tools will help their clients (Joint Committee on Testing Practices [JCTP], 2004). While test developers need to provide this information, test users are ethically obligated to use that information in selecting appropriate tests for their clients (Association for Assessment in Counseling [AAC], 2003a; JCTP, 2004). The first decision is to determine the purpose of the assessment. Career assessment may focus on helping clients make career decisions, including generating and exploring new options or confirming interest in a potential career area. Career instruments may also be used to help individuals clarify needs and interests and predict satisfying occupational choices. Finally, career instruments may be used to help understand and clarify concerns related to the career decision-making process. These different types of assessment tools are described more fully in the next section.

The second major set of questions in selecting career assessment tools concerns the technical aspects of the instrument, including validity and reliability. It is the responsibility of test developers to provide such information in test manuals, and it is the responsibility of test users (counselors) to evaluate this information (JCTP, 2004). Evidence of validity indicates how well the test measures what it is intended to measure. Evidence of validity for an interest inventory, for example, indicates how well the inventory assesses the domains of interests. Clearly, a counselor would not want to measure interests with a tool that may not measure interests. Validity of an instrument is critical to ascertain when choosing an assessment tool to ensure that the assessment results are an accurate representation of behavior or attitudes. Reliability indicates how stable the results are over time, as well as how free the assessment tool is from error. Examining an instrument for a high level of reliability enables counselors to have confidence that the instrument will assess behavior or attitudes in a similar way over time.

The third major set of questions relates to social issues: Is the instrument gender- and culture-fair? Is there evidence that the test developer has taken care to ensure that any differences among men and women or individuals from different cultures are due to differences in the skills or attitudes being assessed, rather than to irrelevant factors (AAC, 2003b)? Test manuals should indicate information about the performance of men and women as well as various cultural groups on the instrument. Counselors also need to assess how similar their clients are to the norm group for the instrument. For example, counselors may not want to use an assessment tool normed on adolescents for adult clients, and vice versa, unless research indicates that the scores may be appropriate for both groups. Again, this information should be available in the manual for use with the instrument.

Types of Assessment

In the realm of career counseling, assessment typically is divided into two broad categories (Betz, 1992; Whiston, 2005). The first category contains instruments that measure some aspect of individual differences relevant to career choice, such as interests, values, needs, skills, abilities, and personality. These instruments have been an important part of career counseling since its beginning. In fact, the development of vocational guidance was intertwined historically with the development of psychometric assessment, and some of these instruments date back nearly 100 years. The second category contains assessment of career-development process, such as decision making, self-efficacy, and career maturity (Swanson & D'Achiardi, 2005).

Both types of instruments may be used as part of screening or intake so that the counselor can assess where the client stands on a number of constructs related to choosing a career. We now present a brief description of each of these constructs and how they are assessed.

INTERESTS

Vocational interests are, without a doubt, the most frequently assessed construct in career counseling (Hansen, 2005), and clients may enter counseling asking for "the test that will tell me what I should be." Interests also play an important role in several of the theories discussed in later chapters, and the majority of measures incorporate Holland's typology (see Chapter 6) or a similar set of constructs. Several measures of interests are currently available and widely used, such as the *Strong Interest Inventory*, the *Self-Directed Search*, the *Campbell Interest and Skills Survey*, the *Kuder Career Search*, and ACT's *UNIACT*. Interest inventories also have been developed for specific purposes; examples include those on career-planning Web sites.

NEEDS AND VALUES

The assessment of work values may be used to clarify a client's reasons or motivations for working, or what he or she expects to gain from a specific job or occupation (Rounds & Armstrong, 2005). Values and needs are central in the theory of work adjustment (Chapter 7), and also are important to other approaches to career counseling. Measures of work values include the *Minnesota Importance Questionnaire*, the *Work Values Inventory*, and measures available on O∗NET.

ABILITIES AND SKILLS

Identification of a client's abilities and skills is an important aspect of career counseling, yet these constructs are less likely to be assessed via formal means than are other constructs, such as interests and values. Objective assessment of abilities is available through measures such as the *ASVAB* and the O*NET *Ability Profiler* (Ryan Krane & Tirre, 2005). However, in the context of career counseling, self-estimates of abilities, such as the *Kuder Skills Assessment* and ACT's *Inventory of Work-Relevant Abilities*, are more likely to be used than objective measures.

PERSONALITY

The assessment of personality could fit into either of the two broad categories; it is an important individual difference related to the choice of a career and is included in theories of career development, yet it also influences how a career decision is made or how career counseling might progress (Swanson & D'Achiardi, 2005). While personality certainly is important to both the process and outcome of career counseling, it is less frequently assessed than other constructs. This may be due to the fact that most objective measures of personality focus on psychopathology or deviance, whereas fewer measures focus on "normal" personality so as to be of value in career counseling. The latter measures include the *Myers-Briggs Type Indicator* and the *NEO Personality Inventory*.

ASSESSMENT OF OTHER CONSTRUCTS

As noted earlier, the second broad category of career assessment focuses on where the client is in the career choice process and includes constructs such as decision making, self-efficacy, and career maturity. These constructs often have emerged from specific theories of career development and, thus, will be discussed in greater depth in later chapters. In contrast to measures of interests, values, abilities, and personality, measures of career development process tend to be more informal; that is, not published commercially. Rather, they have been developed initially as research instruments and later have become available for use with clients. For example, the *Career Decision-Making Self-Efficacy Scale* emerged from social cognitive career theory (see Chapter 10) and was developed to examine the effects of an intervention on self-efficacy. Similarly, measures of career maturity or adaptability emerged from Super's life-span, life-space theory (see Chapter 8) and attempted to quantify an important construct in the theory. Because the category of measures is more informal, the measures tend to have fewer norms or groups available for comparison, and fewer interpretive materials are available to guide the counselor and client.

OTHER TYPES OF ASSESSMENT

Several other methods of assessment are available for the counselor to use in career counseling. The first type, card sorts, may be used to assess any of the previously discussed constructs; for example, card sorts have been developed for interests, skills, and values. Card sorts are used in session with the client (compared to objective or standardized assessment, which is likely to be done outside of session) and are considered a type of qualitative assessment, since the goal is not to arrive at scores or to compare the client's scores to a norm group; rather, the process of completing a card sort reveals information to both the client and the counselor that helps to clarify the client's interests, values, or skills.

Another method of qualitative assessment is through a genogram. Genograms are visual representations of some set of connections in a client's life. Genograms were originally developed within the context of family systems (Bowen, 1978) to chart a client's family history and current relations, but they have been adapted to other settings. As with other types of qualitative assessment, the process of completing a genogram may be at least as useful as the product or outcome of the genogram. That is, the discussion that ensues between client and counselor as they work on the genogram may be very fruitful. As Gysbers, Heppner, and Johnston (2003) note, a genogram has "substantial face validity for clients because it provides them with an opportunity to tell their story within the career counseling context" (p. 202). Moreover, it encourages trust and helps to build the working alliance between counselor and client and may be adapted creatively to fit a variety of needs (Miller, Dillon, & Swanson, 2007; Okiishi, 1987).

Ethical Principles and Responsible Use of Assessment

The National Career Development Association (NCDA, 2007; see also Appendix B), the American Counseling Association (ACA, 2005), and the American Psychological Association (APA, 2002) all include a section in their ethics codes that focuses on ethical mandates for appropriate assessment. These organizations also collaborated with educational professional associations to form the JCTP. This group developed the *Code of Fair Testing Practices in Education* (JCTP, 2004), which outlines the obligations for test users: Test users should administer and score tests correctly and fairly; should report and interpret test results accurately and clearly; and should provide clients with information about the instrument, the use of scores, and where to find more information about the instrument and results.

Counseling and psychological ethical codes address the appropriate use of assessment, in large part because unethical assessment practices may lead to significant client harm. Consider, for example, a client who makes a career decision to be a teacher based, in part, on the results of an assessment of her interests and needs. Imagine that she quits her current job to go back to school for a degree in education. If, however, the test results are invalid or unreliable or were poorly chosen or interpreted, she may suffer a significant loss in terms of time, money, and emotional investment in an unwise decision.

Professional ethical codes emphasize that client welfare is paramount in the assessment process and that counselors need to be competent in the tools that they use. For example, the NCDA *Code of Ethics* (2007; see Appendix B) notes,

> Career professionals do not misuse assessment results and interpretations, and they take reasonable steps to prevent others from misusing the information these tools provide. They respect the client's right to know the results, the interpretations made, and the bases for professionals' conclusions and recommendations. (§ E.1.b)

All ethical codes encourage counselors to inform their clients appropriately of the use of tests and receive their clients' consent to be assessed. All codes emphasize the need to interpret accurately the results of assessment tools and to note the context within which assessment takes place. Finally, all ethical codes address the special issues that arise when career counselors are asked to release assessment results to other professionals. Clients must provide explicit permission to release the assessment results, and information should only be released to qualified professionals.

However, career counselors often are challenged by competing ethical mandates, leading them to engage in ethical decision making. Ethical decision making occurs when a counselor is faced with an ethical dilemma, defined as a situation in which there may be conflicting ethical mandates (i.e., professional codes differ), conflicting moral values, or standards may not easily be applied (Cottone & Tarvydas, 2007). Career counselors face ethical dilemmas inherent to all mental health professionals. For example, counselors are responsible for safeguarding clients' welfare and for ensuring that information shared by the client is kept confidential. But sometimes guarding the welfare of the client means that someone else may be harmed. In that situation, the counselor faces an ethical dilemma and must decide how to act to resolve the dilemma.

There are many ethical decision-making models, but we will highlight Welfel's (2006) 10-step model. Step 1 is recognizing the ethical dilemma in a situation. In the situation above, the dilemma is a potential harm to another individual versus the harm to the client by a breach of confidentiality. Step 2 is examining relevant external facts. The counselor would want to know if the other individual is clearly identified, how feasible and imminent the threat of harm is, and how specific the threat of harm is. Did the client make a vague, nonspecific threat ("I could just shoot her!"), or is there a clear plan in place with means and intent to harm the other individual? Step 3 is consulting professional standards and ethical codes, such as the NCDA *Code of Ethics* in Appendix B. Section B of the *Code* focuses on confidentiality, privileged communication, and privacy, noting that career professionals respect clients rights and "do not share confidential information without client consent or without sound legal or ethical justification" (§ B.1.c.). However, section B.2 concerns exceptions: B.2.a., Danger and Legal Requirements, indicates that confidentiality "does not apply when disclosure is required to protect clients or identified others from serious and foreseeable harm." Welfel's (2006) next steps (Steps 4 and 5) include examining relevant literature (e.g., Cottone & Tarvydas, 2007; Welfel, 2006) and laws. In this example, the counselor needs to be aware of state laws governing confidentiality and duty to warn others of potential harm.

Step 6 involves considering which of the five principles of moral behavior are involved. Counselors' decisions on how to resolve ethical dilemmas revolve around their professional and moral judgment of ethical behavior and their balance of ethical principles. The ACA, the NCDA, and the APA focus on five major ethical principles. The first is respect for autonomy and individuals' freedom to make their own decisions regarding their welfare. The second is nonmaleficence; that is, not to take any actions that would harm clients. The third is to do beneficence, meaning to do good by helping clients or the greater society. The fourth principle is justice and fairness. And the fifth is fidelity and honesty, or to keep promises made. The counselor in the dilemma above faces a conflict between fidelity to the client by keeping the promise of confidentiality and not doing harm to the client versus doing good for the individual potentially harmed. In Step 7, counselors consult with colleagues and supervisors, and in Step 8 they decide what actions to take. In Step 9, counselors inform others, including the client, and in Step 10, counselors reflect on the experience.

As is clear from this example, ethical decision making is most difficult when ethical mandates compete or counselors need to decide on an action when major principles may conflict. Consider the vignettes in Box 2.1, which demonstrate the ethical challenges that may occur for career counselors in various settings. Readers are encouraged to consult the NCDA *Code of Ethics* in Appendix B as they consider each vignette.

Ethical Vignette #1, in a high school setting, may be a conflict between the welfare of many students versus two specific students. It may also be considered a conflict involving the informed consent for two students, the consideration of the validity of the instrument for two students, or multicultural issues in assessment. Counselors may feel that justice conflicts with doing no harm in this situation.

Ethical Vignette #2 takes place in a college setting. The ethical dilemma also involves cultural sensitivity to the client's relationship with her father, but this vignette involves an adult who has the right to refuse to release the information, including to her father. This vignette also highlights the importance of client welfare and the appropriate use of assessment tools. Counselors may feel a conflict between a client's right to autonomy and helping the client (doing good).

Ethical Vignette #3 occurs in an organizational setting, calling into question the appropriate use of assessment and the right of the client to release the results. This case also highlights ethical concerns with confidentiality, informed consent, and the multiple relationships between the counselor and colleagues, as well as between the supervisor and employee. Counselors may feel a conflict between a promise made to the supervisor, doing good for the company, and doing no harm to society (via the patients' tissue analyses).

Finally, the fourth vignette takes place in a private practice. Ethical conflicts in this vignette also include the appropriate use of assessment and release of information, but in this case, assessment may be very helpful to provide some information to the client. However, the counselor appears to have urged the client to take an assessment tool, calling into question whose needs are met by the assessment: Is it the client's need for information or the counselor's need for guidance on how to move the client forward? The counselor may be dealing with the conflicts between principles of doing good and fidelity to promises made to the referring therapist.

In summary, while it is critical to consider the purposes of testing, the characteristics of tests, and the settings and conditions of testing, as well as to be competent to administer and interpret tests (AAC, 2003a), it is even more critical to consider the responsible use of tests in career counseling.

Box 2.1

Ethical Vignettes

Vignette #1

You are a career counselor in a large public high school. You are asked to conduct a week-long unit on career decision making for students in the AP English classes. Your plan is to have two classes on self-exploration, giving students an interest inventory and an ability checklist. Two classes will focus on world-of-work information and college exploration, and the final class will be on decision making. Two African American students refuse to take the interest inventory because they will base their future choices on how to be a credit to their race, not on their interests.

- What would you do in this situation?

- On which ethical codes and professional standards would you base your decision?

- Are you obligated to ensure that all students receive the same curriculum in the class, or can you release the two students from taking the interest inventory?

- What is a multiculturally appropriate response to the two African American students? What is a multiculturally appropriate response to the rest of the class?

Vignette #2

You are a career counselor in a community college. A 35-year-old Hispanic woman comes to you for counseling because she is considering returning to school. She had been taking care of her mother for several years, but her mother passed away three months ago. Her father is encouraging her to become a nurse. Her father is very supportive of her seeking counseling and brings her to each session. He is encouraging you to "give her the test that tells her what to do." He sits outside the door of the counseling session, waiting for her. He says he is there to protect her. He would like to see the results of the assessment tools to ensure she is making the right decision.

- What would you do in this situation?

- On which ethical codes and professional standards would you base your decision?

(Continued)

(Continued)

- Would interacting with the father violate your client's confidentiality?

- Would you consider inviting the father into the career counseling with his daughter? What steps would you need to take if you were to do that?

- Your client feels a very strong obligation to family. Do you have an obligation to include her father in career counseling?

Vignette #3

You are a career counselor in a large company. You are asked by a supervisor at a pathology laboratory to see an employee who works in the lab. Helen, the supervisor, is concerned that the employee has very good skills and is able to provide some guidance to the pathologists. However, she has been very frustrated that he does not follow her rules about the chain of command and continues to believe he can provide diagnoses on his own. She notes that he does not have a medical degree; he is a bachelor's-trained biological technician. She is not only frustrated but deeply worried that his independent work will lead to an erroneous diagnosis, with concomitant legal and ethical issues. She wants you to do some testing to help support her perceptions.

- What would you do in this situation?

- On which ethical codes and professional standards would you base your decision?

- Who is your client—the supervisor or the employee?

- You have information that the employee is less than satisfactory. Would you inform him of this?

- Do you have any ethical obligations to the patients whose tissues are being analyzed by the technician?

Vignette #4

You are a career counselor in private practice. A 25-year-old client is referred by her therapist because she is very indecisive about her career, and her indecision is impeding the other aspects of her therapy. She tells you she is just waiting for God to tell her what to do. She is resistant to taking any assessment tools but finally agrees to take an interest inventory if she can pray beforehand to discern what her interests are.

- What would you do in this situation?

- On which ethical codes and professional standards would you base your decision?

- Would you help the client discern what she is called to do?

- At what point would you decide that her indecision is dysfunctional?

- What are your ethical obligations to the referring therapist?

References

American Counseling Association. (2005). *ACA code of ethics*. Retrieved June 16, 2008, from http://www.counseling.org/Resources/CodeOfEthics/TP/Home/CT2.aspx

American Psychological Association. (2002). *Ethical principles of psychologists and code of conduct*. Retrieved June 16, 2008 from http://www.apa.org/ethics/code2002.pdf

Association for Assessment in Counseling. (2003a). *Responsibilities of users of standardized tests (RUST)* (3rd ed.). Retrieved June 16, 2008, from the Association for Assessment in Counseling and Education Web site: http://www.theaaceonline.com/rust.pdf

Association for Assessment in Counseling. (2003b). *Standards for multicultural assessment*. Retrieved June 16, 2008, from the Association for Assessment in Counseling and Education Web site: http://www.theaaceonline.com/multicultural.pdf

Betz, N. E. (1992). Career assessment: A review of critical issues. In S. D. Brown & R. W. Lent (Eds.), *Handbook of counseling* psychology (2nd ed., pp. 453–484). New York: Wiley.

Bowen, M. (1978). *Family therapy in clinical practice*. New York: Jason Aronson.

Cottone, R. R., & Tarvydas, V. M. (2007). *Counseling ethics and decision making* (3rd ed.). Upper Saddle River, NJ: Pearson.

Duckworth, J. (1990). The counseling approach to the use of testing. *The Counseling Psychologist, 18*, 198–204.

Gysbers, N. C., Heppner, M. J., & Johnston, J. A. (2003). *Career counseling: Process, issues, and techniques* (2nd ed.). Boston: Allyn & Bacon.

Hansen, J. C. (2005). Assessment of interests. In S. D. Brown & R. W. Lent (Eds.), *Career development and counseling: Putting theory and research to work* (pp. 281–304). New York: Wiley.

Joint Committee on Testing Practices. (2004). *Code on fair testing practices in education*. Washington, DC: Author. Retrieved September 17, 2008, from http://www.apa.org/science/FinalCode.pdf

Kapes, J. T., Mastie, M. M., & Whitfield, E. A. (1994). *A counselor's guide to career assessment instruments*. Alexandria, VA: National Career Development Association.

Miller, S. A., Dillon, A., & Swanson, J. L. (2007, May). *Genograms as sources of support, inspiration, and meaningful adolescent self-exploration*. Paper presented at the eighth biennial conference of the Society for Vocational Psychology, Akron, Ohio.

National Career Development Association. (2007). *Code of ethics*. Retrieved June 16, 2008, from http://www.ncda.org/pdf/code_of_ethicsmay-2007.pdf

Okiishi, R. W. (1987). The genogram as a tool in career counseling. *Journal of Counseling and Development, 66*, 139–143.

Rounds, J. B., & Armstrong, P. I. (2005). Assessment of needs and values. In S. D. Brown & R. W. Lent (Eds.), *Career development and counseling: Putting theory and research to work* (pp. 305–329). New York: Wiley.

Ryan Krane, N. E., & Tirre, W. C. (2005). Ability assessment in career counseling. In S. D. Brown & R. W. Lent (Eds.), *Career development and counseling: Putting theory and research to work* (pp. 330–352). New York: Wiley.

Seligman, L. (1994). *Developmental career counseling and assessment* (2nd ed.). Thousand Oaks, CA: Sage.

Swanson, J. L., & D'Achiardi, C. (2005). Beyond interests, needs/values, and abilities: Assessing other important career constructs over the life span. In S. D. Brown & R. W. Lent (Eds.), *Career development and counseling: Putting theory and research to work* (pp. 353–380). New York: Wiley.

Watkins, C. E., Jr., & Campbell, V. L. (1990). Testing and assessment in counseling psychology: Contemporary developments and issues. *The Counseling Psychologist, 18,* 189–197.

Welfel, E. R. (2006). *Ethics in counseling and psychotherapy: Standards, research, and emerging issues* (3rd ed.). Belmont, CA: Wadsworth.

Whiston, S. C. (2005). *Principles and applications of assessment in counseling* (2nd ed.). Belmont, CA: Brooks/Cole.

The Case of Leslie 3

Leslie is a 35-year-old Caucasian woman with a bachelor's degree in secondary education. She is seeking career counseling because she is considering quitting her current job as a math teacher in a large suburban high school. Leslie lives in a midsize metropolitan area in the Midwest; she is married, with a 10-year-old stepson.

Leslie reports a considerable amount of dissatisfaction with her current job, particularly related to the stress of many responsibilities and long working hours, as well as the impersonal nature of the school. Leslie reports that her dissatisfaction has been accumulating for several years but that recent events have brought it to the forefront. First, a newly hired principal has instituted administrative tasks that Leslie finds insulting to experienced teachers, such as requiring teachers to keep a weekly log of their activities, submit lesson plans for review, and file quarterly reports on teaching goals. She reports that these activities are "oppressive" and feels quite angry toward the principal. Second, Leslie has had several interactions with parents this year that discouraged her greatly; the parents showed little involvement in their children's school activities yet expected her to go "above and beyond" her responsibilities as a teacher. This is particularly frustrating because Leslie sees students dealing with increasingly difficult problems at home. She also is frustrated by the lack of intellectual challenge in her job.

On the positive side, Leslie reports that she did have an opportunity last year to teach an elective advanced math course, in which her students were more motivated and capable, and that she continues to enjoy the one-on-one aspects of teaching. She feels she is a good teacher, and she values the relationships that she develops with students. She displays considerable enthusiasm when discussing what she likes about teaching.

Leslie is unclear at this point whether or not she will quit her current job and, if so, whether she will look for another teaching position or a

33

new career. She wants to explore options to remain in education, whether in a traditional classroom or in some other venue. She also wants to explore new career options outside of teaching. She has thought about a wide range of possible career shifts, such as financial planning, social work, technical writing, and engineering. She is willing to consider pursuing further education if necessary for the career direction that she chooses.

Career and Work History

Leslie grew up in a predominantly White suburban area, where she attended public schools. Leslie excelled in a number of subjects in middle school and high school, including math, science, and social studies. She was a member of the French club, was a math tutor for middle school children, and won first place in the high school science fair during her senior year. She did not actively seek out any positions of leadership within the school but was often viewed as a leader by others, in part because she assumed many organizational responsibilities.

Although her family expected her to go to college, she received little direction from them or her high school guidance counselor in choosing a college or selecting a field of study. She delayed making a decision about attending college until the summer after high school graduation and then decided to enroll at a local community college. She chose the community college because many of her friends were going there, it was close to home, and she was unsure about her motivation to pursue a college education and whether she would be successful.

During her first semester at the community college, she enrolled in general English, math, chemistry, and psychology courses. During this time, she ended a relationship with her high school boyfriend and began dating a college student who was home for Christmas vacation. The relationship flourished during her second semester, and he encouraged her to join him at the state university 90 miles from home. She finished her first year at the community college and decided to transfer to the state university, in part to join her boyfriend but also because she was disappointed by the lack of challenge in the math and science classes at her community college.

She entered her sophomore year at the university with a number of possible majors in mind but declared herself as "undecided." She enjoyed taking a variety of classes while in college, and she contemplated a number of diverse options—mathematics, engineering, creative writing, psychology, and premedicine—prior to choosing her major. She enjoyed the challenge of her math classes but did not do well in mechanical drawing. She did not enjoy being the only woman in her advanced math classes, particularly because she had some negative experiences with professors who singled out her mistakes. A number of factors detracted from her serious consideration of a degree in mathematics, including lack of encouragement from professors and not wanting to commit to pursuing a graduate degree. Her lack of motivation to pursue postbaccalaureate training also precluded her from declaring a major in psychology or premedicine, and she decided not to major in engineering because two professors told her she would have a difficult time combining that career with a family. Leslie finally decided to major in secondary education, with an emphasis in mathematics education, because she could easily combine teaching with raising a family, she could still use her math skills, and teaching would not require schooling beyond a bachelor's degree. In addition, she remembered enjoying her experiences as a math tutor in high school in which she had feelings of accomplishment when her students understood difficult concepts for the first time.

Leslie had a satisfying student teaching experience in a medium-sized high school in her hometown, and she received positive feedback and excellent evaluations from her supervising teacher. This experience led her to feel excited and confident about her decision to become a teacher.

After graduating from college, Leslie took a teaching position in a small town about 2 hours from the city in which her family lived. Her first year in the position was very stressful, but she also loved being a teacher. As the only math teacher in the school, she taught a diverse range of classes and students, and she enjoyed the challenge of taking sole responsibility for her classes. She also enjoyed being a part of the community. However, she worked every night and weekend to keep up with lesson preparation and grading. She was the youngest teacher in the school and found it difficult to meet people with whom she could socialize outside of work. She also missed being close to her family, and her workload made it difficult for her to see them on weekends. Her relationship with her boyfriend suffered, and they ended the relationship during her second year of teaching.

After 3 years, Leslie found a teaching position in a large school district in the city in which her family lived and looked forward to being closer to them. She soon discovered that her new teaching position, although slightly less stressful, offered fewer rewards than her previous position. Because she was teaching in a larger school system, she was assigned five sections of freshman algebra, the least desirable teaching assignment. She found her students to be disinterested in the subject, and because they came from a wide geographic area, she no longer felt part of a community. She was also frustrated by the large bureaucratic structure of the school system. She was, however, able to find a greater degree of social support outside of work, including her family and high school friends. She has been in this position for 10 years.

Leslie has a number of interests outside her job, although she does not have much time to pursue any of these interests during the school year due to the time demands of her job. She enjoys several hobbies during the summer, including gardening and other outdoor activities, and teaches swimming lessons at the local YMCA. She also volunteers at the science center, where she maintains the membership records, and she teaches Sunday school at her church.

Family Information

Leslie is the second of three children, with an older brother (age 38) and a younger sister (age 30). Her brother has a bachelor's degree in electrical engineering and works for a company that designs computer equipment. He was recently promoted to vice president of one of the company's product divisions in which he coordinates all aspects of a particular product line, from research and development to marketing and sales. He is married to a woman who is a personnel manager for a retail chain; they have two children. Leslie's sister has a bachelor's degree in nursing and has worked at a number of hospitals and home health agencies. She is currently out of the workforce while she cares for two young children; her husband is the district sales manager for a pharmaceutical company.

Leslie's parents are in their early 60s. Her father is a corporate attorney for a midsize manufacturing firm, specializing in product liability and patents. His bachelor's degree was in chemistry, and he worked as a research and development chemist for 10 years before pursuing a law degree. Her mother attended several years of college but left school when she married Leslie's father. She has been involved in community arts organizations by, for example, volunteering as a docent at the art museum and serving on the board of the symphony orchestra. She did not work outside the home until Leslie's younger sister was in high school. At that time, she found a position with a small business specializing in office interior design, where she continues to work part-time as an administrative assistant.

During college, Leslie's parents stated their support for whatever she chose as a major and provided the financial resources for her college education. Her father strongly encouraged her to major in business, but Leslie found that these classes were her least favorite. Her mother felt that the specific major was not critical as long as Leslie received a good education; she expected that Leslie would not remain in the workforce after marrying and having children. Leslie's family expressed some impatience when it was difficult for her to choose a major; Leslie's brother teased her for "changing her mind so often."

Leslie and her siblings all live within the same metropolitan area as her parents, and they see one another frequently. Leslie has discussed her job dissatisfaction with her family, and they have given her conflicting advice: Her father has renewed his encouragement of Leslie's pursuing a business career, her mother and sister have suggested that now would be a good time for Leslie to have children, and her brother has advised her to quit complaining about such inconsequential aspects of her job.

Marital Information

Leslie has been married to Joe (age 39) for 5 years. Joe has an associate's degree from a local community college and is currently a finish carpenter for a residential contractor. He enjoys his work and takes a great deal of pride in his reputation as a highly skilled craftsman; however, he has been thinking about finding a different line of work due to the job's physical demands and the seasonal fluctuations in available work.

Joe is the older of two sons from a middle-class Hispanic family; both his father and mother are of Mexican descent. Joe's father is a midlevel manager in a hardware store chain. Joe's mother worked as a housekeeper while Joe and his brother were young, but she quit working outside of the home when Joe's father was promoted into management. She has strong connections with the Hispanic community through her involvement in church and neighborhood activities. Joe's brother works as a youth services coordinator, organizing programs at a city-funded community center.

Joe grew up trying to be "American" like the other kids in school. He did not want to acknowledge his Mexican heritage. He refused to speak Spanish at home, he and his parents had great conflicts during his adolescence when he refused to go to church, and he did not include the other adolescents from his Hispanic neighborhood in his circle of friends. His parents were particularly upset when he did not show respect for his grandmother, who came to live with them when he was 15.

Joe graduated from high school with a C average. He did not consider going to college, because he did not enjoy high school and wanted to be working and earning money rather than going to school. The only class he liked in high school was his woodworking class, and he became an apprentice carpenter after graduation. He worked his way up to finish carpenter over 10 years. He has worked for the same contractor for the past 7 years.

After the conflicts with his family during and right after high school, Joe increasingly began to appreciate his Mexican heritage. He began to attend community and neighborhood events, although he chose not to live in the same community as his parents. He identifies himself as a Mexican American but has some resistance to the label "Hispanic." He endorses many traditional Hispanic values: a strong emphasis on family, a preference for smooth interpersonal relationships, and respect owed to elders. He is more ambivalent about appropriate roles for men and women in the family. On the one hand, his mother's highest goal was to stay home to care for her family; on the other hand, he realizes that some women want to work and to be more independent.

Joe's first marriage was to a young Hispanic woman who grew up in the same neighborhood. They married at age 22, and his family was very happy that he would stay within their community. His wife, Maria Pilar, worked as a clerk in a small business. The conflicts in their marriage stemmed from her pressuring him to find ways to earn more money. Like his mother, her goal was to have a family and to be a homemaker. Maria was deeply involved in the Hispanic community and the church, and another source of conflict was his resistance to this level of involvement. Their marriage ended 2 years after their son was born. His first wife has since remarried and moved to another Hispanic community.

Leslie and Joe met through a common friend and dated for 6 months before marrying. Leslie's family was not wholly supportive of her decision to marry Joe, although they did not express their feelings directly to Leslie. Joe's family also had concerns about Joe and Leslie's marriage; his mother was concerned that Leslie was too American. Their marriage has been relatively stable: Leslie describes herself as being happy in her marriage. She does, however, express some dissatisfaction with their relationship, primarily due to what she characterizes as their "lack of communication about important issues." Leslie reports that Joe is supportive of her considering a career change, but she feels that he does not understand why she is unhappy with her job and that he seems hesitant about her returning to school.

Joe's 10-year-old son from his first marriage now lives 300 miles from Leslie and Joe and spends school vacations with them, as well as an occasional long weekend. Leslie wants to have a child, and although Joe has expressed some ambivalence since before they were married, he has been supportive of Leslie's desire. He expects that Leslie would postpone any career decisions if they were to have a child so that she could stay at home full-time until the child was in school. This expectation is consistent with the division of labor that they have assumed, although Leslie is increasingly frustrated that Joe does not contribute more to household responsibilities. Leslie and Joe have had some difficulty related to pregnancy; Leslie had two miscarriages last year. The miscarriages were followed by marital tension and depression, for which Leslie sought individual therapy with a psychologist. Leslie reported that her previous experience with therapy was quite beneficial, although she now wishes that Joe had joined her in therapy.

Leslie's Expectations for Career Counseling

Leslie was referred to career counseling by a coworker who had heard about the availability of career services. She is enthusiastic about career counseling, she is hopeful that the career counselor will help her define her career direction, and she expects to receive information and perhaps advice from the counselor about her "best" career option. She is eager to take the tests that the counselor recommends, stating that she is waiting to hear what the tests will tell her to do.

Leslie feels that she is at a crossroads in her life and is ready to explore her options for her next step. She is evaluating many aspects of her career, family relationships, and marriage. She is looking forward to beginning counseling.

Initial Impressions of Leslie

Before reading the subsequent section with Leslie's assessment results, use the following questions to formulate your impressions of her:

1. What have you learned about Leslie from the information presented thus far?

2. What general impressions do you have of Leslie? What impressions do you have of her as an employee? As a spouse? As a member of her family of origin?

3. What role do you think Leslie's gender has played in her life and career decisions? What role do you think her culture and socioeconomic status have played? What role do you think her husband's culture and socioeconomic status have played?

4. What more would you like to know about Leslie?

5. What observations or hypotheses do you have about Leslie that the assessment data might clarify? What specifically will you look for in the assessment results?

6. How would you describe her primary career issue(s)? How might you prioritize the direction of counseling? Where would you like to begin in working with Leslie?

Assessment Information

Leslie completed four inventories at the beginning of counseling: the Strong Interest Inventory (SII), the Skills Confidence Inventory (SCI), the Minnesota Importance Questionnaire (MIQ), and the Adult Career Concerns Inventory (ACCI). These four inventories were chosen to assess a diversity of components typically considered in career counseling—namely, factors related to career choice *content* (interests, values, and personality) and factors related to career choice *process* (self-efficacy, beliefs, and life span career issues). Typically, clients would take one or two inventories; in Leslie's case, all four were included to illustrate the types of information that might be assessed as part of career counseling.

STRONG INTEREST INVENTORY (SII)

The SII (Harmon, Hansen, Borgen, & Hammer, 2005) is a measure of an individual's vocational and avocational interests. Individuals respond whether they like, dislike, or are indifferent to occupational titles, activities, school subjects, and working with various types of people and whether or not various characteristics are descriptive of them. It is important to note that the SII is not a measure of abilities but, rather, an assessment of an individual's interests.

The SII profile consists of four sets of scales: General Occupational Themes, Basic Interest Scales, Occupational Scales, and Personal Style Scales; each set of scales addresses a different set of questions about the individual. The General Occupational Themes assess an individual's interests in six broad work areas that correspond to Holland's (1997) six vocational personality types, reported in comparison with an individual's same-sex group. The General Occupational Themes are the most global scales and answer questions about work personality (e.g., What am I like? How do I like to work? What types of work environments do I prefer?).

Leslie's SII profile is shown in sections in Appendix A, Figure 1. The profile that she received consists of nine pages: General Occupational Themes in Section 1 (p. 2), Basic Interest Scales in Section 2 (p. 3), Occupational Scales in Section 3 (pp. 4–7), Personal Style Scales in Section 4 (p. 8), and a Profile Summary and administrative indexes in Sections 5 and 6 (p. 9). Compared with other women, Leslie's SII indicates that she has very high interest in the investigative theme (science and analysis), with high interest in the social theme (helping others), and moderate interest in the conventional theme (organization and structure). She has little interest in the realistic area (working with things) and very little interest in the enterprising theme (business oriented, selling) and artistic theme (creative self-expression). Leslie's primary General Occupational Theme code, then, would be investigative-social-conventional, or ISC.

The second set of scales on the SII profile assesses an individual's interests in 30 broad clusters, which may represent vocational or avocational interests, answering the question "What do I like?" The 30 scales are organized in relation to their association with the General Occupational Themes and also indicate the client's level of interest compared with the same-sex group. Six of Leslie's Basic Interest Scales are in the "very high" range: research, mathematics, and science in the investigative theme; teaching/education and religion/spirituality in the social theme; and taxes/accounting in the conventional theme. She also has a high level of interest in computer hardware/electronics (realistic theme). Her lowest Basic Interest Scales are military (realistic theme), and performing arts, visual arts/design, writing/mass communication, and culinary arts (all artistic theme). All of these scores indicate very little interest. The codes for her highest Basic Interest Scales are all investigative, social, or conventional, and the codes for her lowest Basic Interest Scales are artistic, enterprising, or realistic, consistent with the pattern of General Occupational Themes.

The third set of SII scales includes the Occupational Scales, which indicate the similarity of the client's pattern of likes and dislikes to men and women in 122 occupations, arranged on the profile according to their relation to the six General Occupational Themes. These scales answer the question "Who am I like?" based on the assumption that similarity to one's coworkers increases job satisfaction. Scores of 40 and above suggest that the client has interests similar to those of individuals in the particular occupation. Leslie's interests are most similar to those of women who are actuaries, mathematicians, software developers, financial analysts, mathematics teachers, university professors, medical technologists, biologists, bookkeepers, and financial managers; these occupational scales are the top 10 in terms of scores, and all are scores of 59 or higher. Her interests are also similar (scores of 50 or higher) to those of physicists, geologists, chemists, computer scientists, optometrists, science teachers, accountants, credit managers, production managers, technical support specialists, foresters, network administrators, and engineers. There are an additional 12 occupational scales on which Leslie scored between 40 and 50 (see the SII profile for more information). Leslie's interests are least similar (scores of 0 or below) to those of women who are public relations directors, graphic designers, medical illustrators, art teachers, advertising account managers, reporters, English teachers, interior designers, and chefs.

The codes associated with Leslie's highest Occupational Scales are primarily investigative or conventional, and the codes associated with her lowest Occupational Scales are primarily artistic and enterprising. Again, the codes for these scales are consistent with the General Occupational Themes and Basic Interest Scales, with the exception of the social theme. Leslie's interests are moderately similar to only one occupation primarily coded in the social area: special education teachers.

The fourth set of scales is the Personal Style Scales, which assess various aspects of work personality, more specifically addressing the question "What am I like?" First is the Work Style Scale, which indicates the client's preferred level of involvement in working with people. Leslie's score is 54, indicating that she has no marked preference for either working with people or working alone. Leslie scored 56 on the Learning Environment Scale, which assesses preference for learning by doing versus learning through books and traditional lectures. Leslie's score indicates a slight preference for a traditional academic environment over practical learning. The Leadership Style Scale measures an individual's interest in taking charge of others as a leader. Leslie scored 45 on this scale, showing some interest in working alone rather than assuming a high profile as a leader. The fourth personal style scale is the Risk Taking Scale, which measures the individual's level of interest in taking risks and in thrill-seeking activities. Leslie's score is 34 on this scale, indicating that she does not like risk-taking activities and prefers to be careful and play it safe. The final personal style scale is the Team Orientation Scale, which measures working on a task independently versus through teamwork. Leslie's score of 60 suggests that she may enjoy collaborating with others in a team.

The profile summary page of the SII results also contains a set of administrative response summary indexes, which indicate the way in which the individual has responded to the items. The response total indicates the number of items that the client answered out of a possible 291 items. The remaining seven rows of numbers indicate the proportion of preferences that the individual chose for various portions of the SII items, divided among the *strongly like, like, indifferent, dislike,* and *strongly dislike* options. These percentages may be examined to determine the client's response style in completing the SII across the entire profile as well as within specific sections of items.

Leslie omitted one of the SII items (TR index of 317), and she did not respond in an unusual way. She indicated more dislikes than likes, particularly for items regarding occupations, leisure activities, and types of people. She seemed to be fairly sure about her likes and dislikes, as indicated by very few "indifferent" responses.

SKILLS CONFIDENCE INVENTORY (SCI)

In addition to the SII, Leslie also completed the SCI (Betz, Borgen, & Harmon, 1996), shown in Appendix A, Figure 2. The 60-item SCI assesses the level of confidence an individual has in completing tasks associated with the six General Occupational Themes. The overall objective of the instrument is to identify areas for a client to explore. Each scale consists of 10 items, averaged to produce a score between 1 and 5, with 5 indicating very high level of confidence in that area. Leslie has the most confidence in the investigative area, followed by social and conventional (see Appendix A, Figure 2). She has very little confidence in her artistic and realistic skills.

The SCI profile is designed to coordinate with the SII, so the levels of confidence and interest are plotted for each General Occupational Theme. Three scenarios are of particular interest in counseling: Confidence and interest are both high, confidence is higher than interest, or interest is higher than confidence. High confidence and interest in a theme are good areas for further exploration. These conditions apply for Leslie in the investigative, social, and conventional areas. Leslie has two themes (investigative and social) in which both her interests and confidence are equally high and one theme (conventional) in which her interests are lower than her confidence. All three areas are avenues of potential career exploration with Leslie, inquiring whether her interests and confidence could be further developed in these areas. A fourth scenario is represented by Leslie's enterprising, artistic, and realistic areas in which both her interests and skills confidence are low, suggesting that these areas are "low priority" for further exploration.

MINNESOTA IMPORTANCE QUESTIONNAIRE (MIQ)

The MIQ (Rounds, Henley, Dawis, Lofquist, & Weiss, 1981) measures 21 work-related needs, which are grouped into six value categories. An individual's results on the MIQ are presented in two sections. On the first page, intraindividual scores on the 21 needs and six values are plotted relative to one another. The second page consists of comparisons between an individual's need and value profile and reinforcer patterns for various occupations. These two pages provide quite different information: On the first page, an individual is compared only with himself or herself, whereas on the second page, an individual's scores are compared with scores derived from normative occupational groups. An additional type of information is the logically consistent triads (LCT) score, which indicates the degree to which the individual responded in a consistent manner across the inventory.

Several points are important in interpreting Leslie's MIQ profile (see Appendix A, Figure 3). First, scores on the plotted profile (page 1) are "ipsative," or compared with one's own scores. Leslie's scores represent the relative importance that she gave to the responses. Her "high" scores thus reflect the needs that are most important to her, relative to the other needs measured by the MIQ, and her "low" scores represent the needs that are the least important to her. Second, the least important needs may be those about which she is simply indifferent, or they may represent situations that she wants to avoid. Third, it is important to recall the actual statements to which the client has responded and that underlie the need labels. Referring to these statements (presented on the profile) will help clarify the meaning of the scale labels. For example, a client's score on the scale measuring variety is based on his or her endorsement of the statement "I could do something different every day." Fourth, it is useful to examine both the 21 individual needs, as well as the six higher-level categories, to determine the degree of consistency or discrepancy between these two levels of scores.

The LCT score for Leslie's MIQ profile is 92%, suggesting that her responses were highly consistent across the items. Leslie's highest needs on the MIQ are moral values ("I could do the work without feeling that it is morally wrong"), ability utilization ("I could do something that makes use of my abilities"), achievement ("The job could give me a feeling of accomplishment"), and social service ("I could do things for other people"). Her lowest needs are authority ("I could tell people what to do"), independence ("I could work alone on the job"), and company policies ("The company would administer its policies fairly"). Her highest value categories are achievement and altruism, and her lowest value is status.

The second page of Leslie's MIQ profile consists of 90 occupations arranged alphabetically within six clusters, each containing 15 occupations. Each cluster represents a different pattern of important needs and values, and Leslie's MIQ responses are compared with the patterns of each cluster as well as with individual occupations. Two types of information are presented: a C index, which indicates the degree of correspondence between Leslie's scores and a cluster or occupation, and a predicted level of satisfaction (satisfied, likely satisfied, or not satisfied), based on the strength of the C index. Occupations in the satisfied range are italicized.

Examining the clusters first, four of the six clusters have C index values in the satisfied range (Clusters A, B, C, and F). Leslie's highest C index is for Cluster A (0.68), which is characterized by the values of achievement and autonomy and the need of altruism. Cluster C (0.60), with the next highest C index, is characterized by the value of achievement and the needs of autonomy and compensation. Cluster A has a large number of occupations that correspond to Leslie's pattern of values and needs: 13 of the 15 occupations have C index values in the satisfied range.

The occupations in Cluster A include counseling psychologist, occupational therapist, speech pathologist, secondary and elementary school teacher, interior designer, architect, and recreation leader. Additional occupations found in Cluster C include real estate sales agent, beauty operator, and caseworker. Occupations with high C indexes are also found in other clusters, including librarian and medical technologist in Cluster F. The lowest C index is for Cluster E, characterized by the value comfort; none of the 15 occupations has a C index value in the satisfied range. The lowest indexes are for occupations such as production assembler, meat cutter, and solderer.

ADULT CAREER CONCERNS INVENTORY (ACCI)

The ACCI was developed by Super and his colleagues (Super, Thompson, & Lindeman, 1988) to assess issues related to developmental career tasks and stages. The ACCI provides scores on Super's four adult career stages (exploration, establishment, maintenance, and disengagement; see Chapter 8 for more detail), as well as scores for three substages within each stage. A client's scores can be interpreted relative to one another (intraindividually) or by using norms as a point of reference. Scores reflect the amount of concern that a client expresses about various tasks within the stages and substages. The ACCI can be useful in identifying minicycles within maxicycles of Super's theory, which is of particular interest with a client such as Leslie.

Leslie's ACCI profile (see Appendix A, Figure 4) reveals that her highest stage score is in exploration and that her scores decrease with each subsequent developmental stage (that is, establishment is the second highest score, maintenance is the third highest, and disengagement is her lowest stage score). Thus, her primary career concerns are tasks that are typical of the exploration stage of career development.

Moreover, the substage scales within exploration suggest that she is most concerned about the tasks related to specification, closely followed by crystallization, with lesser concern for implementation. Crystallization includes identifying and developing potential career directions, whereas specification emphasizes choosing a specific occupational direction; these two types of concerns are typical for individuals undergoing career transitions (Super, Savickas, & Super, 1996).

An interesting feature of Leslie's ACCI profile is that, although her maintenance score is relatively low, one substage score is markedly higher than the other two within the stage. The maintenance stage is focused on continuation or further development within one's chosen occupation and position. Leslie expressed concerns related to the innovation substage, which indicates a desire to "do something different or at least to do it differently" within one's established occupation (Super et al., 1996). The innovation substage could be viewed as an "exploration and establishment" minicycle within the maintenance stage.

SUMMARY OF LESLIE'S ASSESSMENT INFORMATION

Leslie has clear interests in the social area, such as teaching, social services, and religious activities, and it is important for her to do things for others and to feel good about what she does. She also has considerable confidence in her ability to do these types of activities, although her interest exceeds her confidence. She enjoys working with people but also values working independently. She is comfortable working alone and frequently prefers doing so to being with other people. Her favorite part of teaching is the one-on-one interactions with students versus lecturing in front of the entire class. Her interest in working with people does not include leadership activities, such as managing, persuading, or directing others. She has neither interest nor confidence in enterprising activities.

Leslie appears very comfortable with structure and organization and demonstrates much attention to detail. She is less comfortable when situations are vague or ambiguous and may work to impose structure when none is forthcoming from the situation at hand. She likes developing systems to make her job more efficient.

Leslie also has strong interests in investigative-type activities. She is unfailingly curious and enjoys learning new things. It is important for her to feel that she is accomplishing something, and she enjoys being intellectually challenged. She is confident of her skills as a learner and problem solver. Although she does not have any interest or confidence in artistic activities, she enjoys the creativity involved in solving new problems or figuring out a new way to do a task.

Leslie would appear to be a good candidate for career counseling with many issues that could be profitably addressed in counseling. She is inquisitive and motivated to address her career concerns at this point. Presently, she seems particularly concerned with defining a new direction for herself or creating new opportunities within her original chosen career field. She has some external constraints to her career choices, most notably, difficulty undertaking a geographic relocation due to family obligations. She also has some internal constraints that the counselor might address, such as the power or influence that she gives to others regarding her career and the way in which she undervalues her own ability and performance. In addition, there might be conflicts due to culture that could benefit from exploration with a counselor.

Working With Leslie's Case and Assessment Information

In Chapters 1 and 2, we discussed ways in which counselors might use background information and assessment results to develop hypotheses and form a "working model" of the client. Each hypothesis then may be tested by searching for evidence that either confirms or disconfirms the hypothesis, and the working model can be changed to reflect this new evidence. New hypotheses then emerge from the altered model, and the counselor's view of the client is continually refined.

The information presented in this chapter now may be used to develop hypotheses about Leslie. We will present some broad observations about her, followed by specific hypotheses for further investigation.

OBSERVATION 1

There seem to be some discrepancies about social-type activities, values, and personality style. For example, her social General Occupational Theme score is high, as are several social Basic Interest Scales, yet no social

Occupational Scales are in the "similar" range. She also appears to be somewhat introverted, indicating that she has equal preferences for working alone or working with people but also a slight preference for working in teams.

Hypotheses

- Leslie is likely to enjoy social-type activities, particularly those in which she is helping people, but may also find them tiring and stressful. She may need to withdraw from people to rejuvenate and regain her energy.

- Her interests are dissimilar to those of other women in social-type occupations (e.g., minister, physical education teacher, parks and recreation coordinator). Members of these occupations are likely to be fairly extroverted, and Leslie's lower scores may reflect her relatively introverted nature.

- Leslie's interest in social activities could reflect gender stereotyping; she may feel that she "should" like these activities because of gender-role socialization. The General Occupational Theme and Basic Interest Scales, in particular, may be more readily affected by these influences than are the Occupational Scales because of the transparency of the items.

- Leslie is probably most comfortable when she is in a defined or prescribed role in dealing with others, as is true when she interacts with students as a teacher. She may be less comfortable in less structured interactions.

- Her interest in social-type activities and in working with people might be limited to specific types of people; she indicated "strongly dislike" to over 60% of the items on the Types of People section of the SII.

- Leslie's interest in the social-type activity of teaching also seems to be fairly circumscribed to mathematics. Mathematics teacher is her highest Occupational Scale directly related to teaching and indicates that she has interests very similar to those of other math teachers. In contrast, she has low scores on the elementary teacher, foreign language teacher, and social science teacher Occupational Scales.

OBSERVATION 2

Leslie's low artistic interests are matched by her lack of confidence in these areas, and she has not directly pursued any artistic activities. On the other hand, she does like the creativity that comes with solving problems and designing new methods.

Hypotheses

- Leslie may enjoy artistic activities such as going to concerts or attending museums, but her lack of confidence in her ability to perform artistic activities may have influenced her responses to items on the SII. Alternatively, she may be truly averse to artistic activities.

- Leslie may feel uncomfortable in artistic environments—those characterized by flexibility, creativity, and self-expression—because they are not as structured as she prefers.

- Her mother's involvement in artistic organizations and activities is quite different from Leslie's. Leslie may compare herself with her mother and feel that she is not as capable in artistic endeavors.

- Leslie seems to enjoy creativity as a means to an end—to solve problems or create new ways of doing things—rather than as an end itself.

OBSERVATION 3

Leslie also has low interest and confidence in enterprising activities. Moreover, she ranked as low the MIQ authority item ("telling others what to do"), and her score on the Leadership Style Scale of the SII suggests that she is not comfortable with taking charge or directing others in activities. She has been viewed by others as a leader but has not herself sought out leadership positions. Leslie seems to avoid (as opposed to merely being indifferent to) activities related to leadership or assumption of power or influence. Yet she has taken on administrative duties in her job and volunteer work.

Hypotheses

- Leslie seems to dislike and avoid enterprising-type activities or those that involve active pursuit of leadership roles. Her introverted nature may be antithetical to enterprising activities.

- Her father, with his interests in law and business, may be an enterprising type. Leslie may be disinterested in these activities to set herself apart from her father or because she feels that she cannot match his accomplishments in this area.

- Leslie has been successful in the administrative responsibilities that she has undertaken. These responsibilities may reflect her conventional interests in structuring and organizing details. Moreover, her administrative duties, like her enjoyment of creativity, may be a means to an end.

- Leslie's dissatisfaction with the new principal in her school may be due to her aversion to, or even distrust of, enterprising types. She may feel that he discounts her because she is not like him nor does she value the same things. Leslie may also interpret the new procedures that he has instituted as a sign that he does not respect her ability and experience as a teacher.

OBSERVATION 4

Leslie dislikes taking risks and prefers to "play it safe." Yet she has entered career counseling because she is thinking about changing her career direction, and she seems willing to try new activities and work hard toward goals that are important to her.

Hypotheses

- Leslie's dislike of taking risks may be related to her concern about receiving the approval of others. She may be uncomfortable with trying something if there is a possibility that she will fail or will be judged as deficient by someone else.

- Her willingness to consider a radical career change, in light of her preference to avoid risk, seems to reflect the amount of dissatisfaction she is currently feeling. She may be more willing to take risks than is apparent from her inventory results.

- Leslie seems to have a clear sense of what she likes. Equally important, she seems to know what she dislikes. This fact may reduce the perceived risk of exploring a career change.

Questions for Discussion

Review all of the material related to Leslie that has been presented in this chapter, remembering that there are multiple sources of information, including the background and career history, family information, and the results of the four inventories. The questions listed below will guide your review.

1. What other observations do you make from a review of Leslie's background information? From the results of her assessments?

2. What consistent patterns occur within each separate source of information? Across all of the information?

3. What discrepancies do you observe within each source of information? Across all of the information?

(Continued)

(Continued)

4. List specific hypotheses that you have about Leslie.

5. How would you test these hypotheses? How will evidence that you gather confirm or change your working model of Leslie?

6. How is your working model of Leslie shaped by your sex, culture, and socioeconomic background? How is it shaped by her sex, culture, and socioeconomic background?

Conceptualizing Leslie From Various Theoretical Approaches

The material in this chapter provides sufficiently rich information to begin forming hypotheses about Leslie's career concerns. We now turn to specific theoretical perspectives on working with Leslie. In each chapter, we will add supplementary information about Leslie as appropriate to the specific theory or approach. This additional information is particularly relevant to the "working model" of Leslie that a counselor using a particular theory would be likely to develop.

References

Betz, N. E., Borgen, F. H., & Harmon, L. W. (1996). *Skills Confidence Inventory.* Palo Alto, CA: Consulting Psychologists Press.

Harmon, L. W., Hansen, J. C., Borgen, F. H., & Hammer, A. C. (2005). *Strong Interest Inventory: Applications and technical guide.* Palo Alto, CA: Consulting Psychologists Press.

Holland, J. L. (1997). *Making vocational choices: A theory of vocational personalities and work environments* (3rd ed.). Odessa, FL: Psychological Assessment Resources.

Rounds, J. B., Henley, G. A., Dawis, R. V., Lofquist, L. H., & Weiss, D. J. (1981). *Manual for the Minnesota Importance Questionnaire.* Minneapolis: University of Minnesota.

Super, D. E., Savickas, M. L., & Super, C. M. (1996). The life-span, life-space approach to careers. In D. Brown, L. Brooks, & Associates (Eds.), *Career choice and development* (3rd ed., pp. 121–178). San Francisco: Jossey-Bass.

Super, D. E., Thompson, A. S., & Lindeman, R. H. (1988). *Adult Career Concerns Inventory: Manual for research and exploratory use in counseling.* Palo Alto, CA: Consulting Psychologists Press.

Gender-Aware and Feminist Approaches 4

In contrast to the theories discussed in subsequent chapters, gender-aware and feminist approaches are not theories of career *development*; rather, they are approaches to career *counseling*. (This distinction was discussed in Chapter 1.) Attention is usually given to women's career psychology in discussions of theories of career development; however, feminist career counseling rarely is included. Moreover, the virtual explosion of empirical literature regarding women's career development has not been matched by theoretical development.

Discussions of gender frequently focus solely on women. Indeed, many authors have argued that traditional theories of career development are really theories about and for White, middle-class males, so it is natural to shift our attention to how career theory and practice may better serve women. But clearly, men also are influenced by gender socialization and the gendered context in which they make career choices. The enormous societal changes that have occurred for women brought about changes for men as well—in their conceptions of the role of work in their lives, in the expectations that are placed upon them by society, and in the structure of the family and interpersonal relationships. Gender socialization occurs for both males and females in this society, beginning from birth onward, through childhood, adolescence, and into adulthood.

Much of the literature cited in this chapter is based on earlier writings about feminist therapy in general. In addition, several authors have recently translated these feminist therapy concepts to career counseling, and we draw heavily on these writings to describe feminist career counseling and its applications to Leslie and other clients. Our goal, then, is to synthesize previous literature regarding gender context in career development and in therapy so that readers may view how gender-aware and feminist principles can be applied in career counseling.

Gysbers, Heppner, and Johnston (2003) describe three counseling orientations that take gender into account. First, *nonsexist counseling* (Marecek & Kravetz, 1977) is based on the idea that there should be equity in the treatment of men and women within counseling and clients should be treated as individuals, not as "women" or "men." Second, *gender-aware counseling* (Good, Gilbert, & Scher, 1990) recognizes that gender is integral to counseling and that client concerns are best viewed within a larger societal context. Counselors are encouraged to address gender injustices actively and to work together with the client in a collaborative relationship. Finally, *feminist counseling* (Brooks & Forrest, 1994; Sturdivant, 1980) represents an adaptation of feminist tenets to the practice of counseling.

Gender-aware and feminist counseling approaches share many similar philosophical assumptions, primarily their common emphasis on the centrality of gender in working with clients. Nonsexist counseling, on the other hand, differs in that it advocates a "gender-blind" perspective on clients, which presents some disadvantages in comparison with the two other approaches.

Hare-Mustin and Marecek (1988) discuss two perspectives on studying the social construction of gender, one that emphasizes the differences between men and women and one that minimizes those differences. They characterize the former perspective as prone to "alpha bias," or the tendency to exaggerate differences, whereas the latter perspective is prone to "beta bias," or the tendency to ignore differences. Alpha bias is the predominant view in American society and underpins most psychological theories about gender (see Gilligan, 1982). These theories propose fundamental gender differences as constellations of opposing traits or characteristics (such as feminine vs. masculine, instrumental vs. expressive). Beta bias, on the other hand, has received less attention but also exists in many theories of psychological development. Beta bias is evident in theories and practices that attempt to treat men and women equally yet may inadvertently perpetuate the inequality they hope to redress.

One consequence of alpha bias is that observed sex differences may be overinterpreted as essential "male" or "female" qualities, when they may be due to differences in the social hierarchy. For example, demonstrated sex differences in vocational interests, such as women's interest in social activities, may not be due to women's inherent relational nature but because social-type careers include lower-prestige occupations that are more accessible to women. Moreover, by emphasizing between-group variability, alpha bias leads to minimization of within-group variability. Thus, theories concerning gender tend to overlook differences among women that may be related to race and ethnicity, age, disability status, social class, marital status, parental status, sexual orientation, and so on.

Consequences of beta bias are more subtle in nature and, on the surface, may seem trivial. After all, what's wrong with arguing for little difference between men and women and therefore treating them similarly? However, ignoring special needs of women may also underestimate differential allocation of resources and power and ultimately disadvantage women: "In a society in which one group holds most of the power, seemingly neutral actions usually benefit members of that group" (Hare-Mustin & Marecek, 1988, p. 460). In the realm of career and educational attainment, Betz (1989, 2006) discusses the "null environment" in which individuals are neither encouraged or discouraged but simply ignored. The null environment, according to the originator of the concept (Freeman, 1979), has a greater effect on women because of the cumulative effect of negative messages about their pursuit of career goals.

Gender-Aware Counseling

Gender-aware therapy (GAT) (Good et al., 1990) was developed by integrating feminist therapy with emerging knowledge about gender. The impetus for developing GAT was (a) the perception that feminist therapy was not applicable to male clients and (b) the growing evidence that gender-role socialization also has deleterious effects on men's development and mental health. It is important to distinguish among terms used in this body of literature. *Sex* refers to one's biological status as male or female, whereas *gender* refers to the way in which one perceives and expresses being male or female. *Gender roles* and *gender-role socialization* thus refer to the behaviors and roles that society expects of individuals, based on their biological sex.

Gender-aware approaches highlight the pervasive influence of early gender-role socialization on expectations about work and careers, for both men and women. For men, gender-role socialization in childhood and adolescence encourages boys to restrict their emotional expressiveness and to strive for achievement and competition. Men's expectations of the work world often include assuming a provider role, upward career progression, and acquisition of material possessions that reflect their success. Gender-role socialization for women includes messages that place limits on career aspirations and achievements, as will be discussed in more detail later in this chapter.

Gender-aware counseling acknowledges that male and female role expectations also enter into the counseling process. For example, counseling itself may be "antithetical to the male role" (Mintz & O'Neil, 1990, p. 382), which may influence how the client interacts with the counselor, such as engaging in competitive behavior. Women clients may assume a passive role in the counseling process and may rely on the expertness offered by test results and interpretations. Another focus of gender-aware counseling is the gender-role socialization of the counselor and how it interacts with the gender-role socialization of the client (Mintz & O'Neil, 1990).

Feminist Counseling

The basic underlying belief of feminism is the social, political, and economic equality between women and men. Chronister, McWhirter, and Forrest (2006) describe four tenets of feminist therapy, which they then apply to career counseling. First, *sociocultural conditions* are viewed as the primary source of women's problems, and the presenting issues that they bring to counseling are conceptualized as "originating from socially defined and oppressive sex roles" (Chronister et al., p. 168). An implication of this tenet is that the symptoms women exhibit actually represent adaptive solutions to societal expectations rather than psychopathology or intrapsychic problems. For example, a "dependent" style of career decision making might be viewed as the natural consequence of the role that young women were expected to fulfill in their families and in society at large.

Second, the *personal is political:* Because all women in American society are oppressed, political understanding and solutions are necessary to address the problems that individual women experience. An individual's concerns, then, are best understood within the larger social and societal context. A goal of feminist therapy is to assist the client in differentiating what has been imposed on her by society and what is truly internal, or "to differentiate between external, relatively uncontrollable sociocultural conditions (such as prejudice in the job market) and internal feelings and reactions to these conditions (which are changeable)" (Sturdivant, 1980, p. 79).

A classic example of this tenet is the politics of housework. The manner in which home responsibilities are divided is viewed as not just a personal decision between a woman and her male partner but also as a larger political issue because of the gendered nature in which work and home worlds are constructed. The arena of work is traditionally the domain of men; the arena of home is traditionally the domain of women. Women may be expected to do more housework because their time in the work world is viewed as less valuable to the family (in terms of their level of compensation) and as less important to their self-concept. In a reciprocal fashion, they may have less time to invest in the work world because of their home and child care responsibilities. Thus, an interplay exists between the personal realm and the political realm and, in this case, between the personal realm and the career realm. Personal decisions in the home about the division of labor have political ramifications; political and organizational decisions in the work world have personal ramifications.

The third tenet of feminist therapies is that the relationship between counselor and client is *egalitarian.* The feminist counselor acknowledges her expertise but works to develop a relationship that is based on equal worth and is collaborative rather than hierarchical. Power is inherent in the client-counselor relationship, and the feminist counselor needs to be aware of the sources of her power and the ways in which power may be abused. Moreover, the counselor needs to work to diminish any power differentials that are harmful or exploitative and that reinforce client passivity and dependence (Gannon, 1982). Power-sharing techniques are recommended to reduce the power differential, such as self-disclosure by the therapist and encouraging clients to consider themselves the experts on their own experiences.

Finally, the fourth tenet is related to the *goals of feminist therapy,* which may be viewed as diametrically opposed to the goals of traditional therapy. Namely, feminist therapies reject social conformity and adjustment to unhealthy social conditions in favor of personal self-definition and self-determination. One fundamental belief is that women must achieve both psychological and economic independence.

As noted earlier, both GAT and feminist therapy may be applied to career counseling; in fact, they are particularly relevant given the "gendered context" of career choice and development (see Cook, 1993; Gysbers et al., 2003). This terminology reflects the fact that gender-role socialization permeates all aspects of individuals' development and is therefore crucial in understanding how they perceive their available opportunities as well as their limits. Moreover, recognizing the gendered context of a client's career development entails making those influences an explicit part of the discussion within career counseling so that the client can be empowered to make choices based on a more informed consideration of the intersection of his or her gender-role socialization and the gendered nature of the work environment.

How do these three approaches—nonsexist counseling, GAT, and feminist therapy—relate to career counseling? What are the advantages and disadvantages of a counselor attending to gender issues? Counselors are likely to struggle with the role of gender in career counseling. When should we pay attention to gender differences, and when should we downplay or ignore them? An obvious example is how clients choose to integrate parenting with their careers. Clearly, pregnancy and childbearing are unique to women and have implications for career planning and workplace accommodations. Parenting, however, is increasingly shared by mothers and fathers, also with clear yet overlooked implications for the workplace and career planning. Counselors may routinely ask female clients about their plans for children yet neglect to ask the same questions of male clients. We will return to these questions later in the chapter and as we discuss cases throughout the remainder of the book.

Gender and Assessment

Gender also is relevant to the use of assessment in counseling. Worrell and Remer (1992) discuss four major sources of sex bias in testing: (a) sex-biased items, (b) inappropriate norm groups, (c) sex-biased interpretation, and (d) sex-biased constructs. Because of the focused attention given to gender issues in career development research, most of these sources have decreased substantially in the last several decades. However, counselors should continue to be concerned about the ways in which sex bias may enter into standardized assessment, particularly related to how the counselor interprets the results. And, as Lonborg and Hackett (2006) explain, the debates about sex bias in assessment are "only the tip of the iceberg" when addressing the issue of gender in the context of assessment. They recommend that counselors be particularly alert to how assessment might reinforce the status quo. The profession of counseling clearly provides ethical guidelines related to the use of assessment with women, regardless of the presenting concern (American Counseling Association, 2005; American Psychological Association, 2002; Whiston & Bouwkamp, 2003).

It is imperative that counselors understand the way in which a specific inventory is developed and normed so that they can interpret the results accurately for female and male clients. For example, sex differences in vocational interests have been well documented. However, consensus has not been reached about how to treat these differences, so inventories vary in their approaches.

Brown (1990) offers a set of guidelines for explicitly incorporating gender into assessment, which were adapted for career counseling by Brooks and her colleagues (Brooks & Forrest, 1994; Brown & Brooks, 1991; Forrest & Brooks, 1993). Two guidelines are pertinent prior to assessment. First, counselors need to be familiar with theory and research regarding the role of gender in career development and the differential factors or processes influencing men's and women's career choices. Many resources exist for acquiring this type of information (see Betz, 2008; Betz & Fitzgerald, 1987; Fitzgerald & Weitzman, 1992; Walsh & Osipow, 1994). Second, counselors need to examine their own biases, conscious and unconscious, about women and career development. These biases have the potential to affect counselors' work with their clients.

The remaining guidelines pertain to inclusion of gender in the assessment process (Brown, 1990). First, counselors gather information about clients' views of themselves in various roles over their life spans, including messages from their families of origin and the current or future expectations they perceive for work and family roles. What types of roles do clients anticipate, and how do gender-role expectations relate to these roles? Second, counselors elicit information about the meaning that clients attach to gender relative to their careers. For example, how does a client think about her decision to be an engineer in the context of its being a nontraditional choice for women? Third, counselors explicitly assess the degree to which clients comply with gender-role prescriptions and the positive and negative consequences of their degree of compliance or noncompliance. Brooks and Forrest (1994) suggest three patterns of how gender roles may influence female clients' perceived career options: (a) Overly stereotyped clients may respond passively to career problems and may express interest only in traditionally female occupations, (b) those attempting to conform more to stereotypes may struggle with the ways in which they do not "fit" with expectations, and (c) those attempting to conform less to stereotypes may exhibit more nontraditional behaviors and explore gender-nontraditional occupational choices.

The fourth guideline (Brooks & Forrest, 1994; Brown, 1990) is that counselors need to monitor their reactions during counseling, particularly to clients' noncompliance with gender-role expectations. Fifth, counselors can develop specific hypotheses about the influence of gender-role expectations within the counseling process. Finally, counselors need to evaluate diagnoses and conceptualizations of clients for gender-stereotypic assumptions. These guidelines all serve a single purpose: to integrate a consideration of gender into all that a counselor does with a client, both covertly in the counselor's own reactions and internal processes and overtly in discussions in counseling sessions.

Gender and Theories of Career Development

Theorists generally agree that women's careers may not be adequately explained by traditional theories of career development, at least in their original versions. However, there continues to be some disagreement about whether it is better to modify existing theories, create new theories specifically to address women's career issues, or create theories that explain both men's and women's careers more adequately. Some of this debate parallels the earlier discussion of alpha and beta bias (Hare-Mustin & Marecek, 1988). More specifically, the primary debate is whether separate theories are necessary or desirable. To some, separate theories overemphasize our differences (alpha bias), whereas to others, separate theories are necessary to understand special needs. For example, women continue to perform a larger proportion of child-rearing responsibilities, and, therefore, this needs to be addressed in theories of career development. Harmon (1997) discusses "neglected theoretical categories" that occur when theories are geared toward women. As Harmon (1997) notes, counselors "fail to operate from the broadest possible stance in opening topics for discussion with their clients" (p. 465), such as neglecting to assess a man's self-efficacy for combining multiple roles.

Betz (2005) encourages counselors to attempt overtly to restore options that have been taken away from women through societal sexism and stereotyped socialization. She offers eight recommendations for counseling women who are making career choices:

1. Encourage high-quality and extensive education and training.

2. Encourage as much math coursework as possible, given its role as a "critical filter" in entry to many career fields.

3. Stress decisions that keep as many options open as possible.

4. Define the counselor's role as "catalyst" for creation of new learning experiences for the client.

5. Explore the client's outcome expectations about goals (see Chapter 10 for a discussion of social cognitive career theory), as well as barriers and supports.

6. Remember the crucial role that one supportive person can play in a client's life.

7. Assess the role of culture and ethnicity in the client's decisions.

8. Integrate career theories as appropriate (pp. 268–269).

All of these guidelines are based on research regarding women's career development.

The American Psychological Association (2007) has recently developed *Guidelines for Psychological Practice With Girls and Women*, which outlines important goals for practitioners in working with female clients. Psychologists (and, by extension, other human service providers) are encouraged to do the following:

- Be aware of the effects of socialization and stereotyping.
- Recognize and use information about oppression, privilege, and identity development.
- Understand the impact of bias and discrimination on physical and mental health.
- Use gender and culturally sensitive practices.
- Recognize how their socialization, attitudes, and knowledge about gender may affect their practice.
- Use interventions and approaches that have been found to be effective.
- Foster therapeutic relationships and practices that promote initiative, empowerment, and expanded choices.
- Provide appropriate, unbiased assessments and diagnoses.
- Consider problems in their sociopolitical context.
- Use relevant mental health, education, and community resources.
- Understand and work to change institutional and systemic bias.

These guidelines share common elements of gender-aware and feminist approaches that we discussed earlier.

Box 4.1

Personal Reflection

How have gender role expectations influenced the career decisions that I have made?

How does thinking about gender alter the way I think about work?

What is the "gendered context" of my current career situation?

Applying Gender-Aware and Feminist Approaches

CONCEPTUALIZING LESLIE'S CAREER HISTORY

Leslie's career history contains evidence of early gender-role socialization and corresponding limits placed on her options due to gender expectations. Moreover, she seems to have been struggling throughout her life with balancing nontraditional interests with traditional gender-role expectations. She received mixed messages about careers considered appropriate for women. She did receive support and encouragement for her nontraditional interests, and she was not actively discouraged from pursuing those interests. However, the support was not offered universally by the important people in her life, and often, she felt that other people, particularly her family, were "humoring" her aspirations and choices. For example, her mother indicated that the specific major or career direction that Leslie chose was not crucial, because she probably would marry and have a family rather than be active in the workforce.

Leslie experienced some negative events during college related to her gender, such as being put on the spot by professors as the only woman in her advanced math classes and being discouraged from pursuing engineering because it was said to be difficult to combine with her interest in having a family. Although none of these individual events was overly traumatic, they had the cumulative effect of diverting her from pursuing a math degree.

Moreover, there seem to be times when Leslie was aware of or struggled with the constraints she felt as a woman, although the degree to which these were conscious struggles is unclear. For example, her decision to pursue math education represented a compromise between traditional and nontraditional career paths, yet at the time she could not articulate what she might be giving up in such a compromise.

Leslie did benefit from the influence of role models early in her life, most notably a female math teacher in seventh grade. This teacher served as Leslie's most important role model and source of support. Leslie generally found school to be a supportive environment, beginning in grade school and through high school. However, her success in school and recognition for academic achievement was consistently tempered by clear gender-role expectations about the relatively lesser role of work in her life as compared with marital and family roles.

Gysbers et al. (2003) suggest two factors within the gendered context of adolescence that have particular relevance in understanding Leslie's history. First, boys and girls often receive differential treatment in the classroom, which may occur more often according to gender-role expectations. For example, girls are less assertive about contributing to classroom discussions or offering answers to questions posed by teachers. These differential behaviors may be even more apparent in classes such as math and science. Leslie experienced some teasing by her classmates during middle school and high school and at times chose not to speak in class to avoid being teased.

Second, the college years may be characterized by the "culture of romance" (Holland & Eisenhart, 1990), in which women's career aspirations decrease as they spend more energy in relationship-enhancing activities and make career decisions to accommodate their partners' plans. This pattern was true for Leslie, who transferred from a community college to the university that her boyfriend attended. Luckily for her, it turned out to be a good decision, because the university provided her with more challenging classes and greater educational opportunities.

CONCEPTUALIZING LESLIE'S PRESENT SITUATION

Several aspects of Leslie's current situation may be illuminated by a consideration of their gendered contexts, most notably (a) the circumstances in her specific work environment and (b) her perceptions about her current and future work and family roles.

Leslie's work environment provides opportunities for both growth and development, as well as constricting her behavior in certain ways, based on her role as a female employee. Although Leslie has not experienced any blatant examples of sex discrimination, she has occasionally wondered if her male colleagues have received better teaching assignments. The principal has championed the importance of male role models for the adolescent boys in their school, particularly for those who are having problems at home, and Leslie has overheard other female teachers complaining about feeling undervalued by the principal. She has not yet joined in those discussions but has begun to think more seriously about the validity of their concerns. Moreover, some female teachers have voiced their suspicions that male teachers may be receiving higher merit raises because of the principal's statements about their relatively greater value.

Another factor related to gender at work is that Leslie is the only woman in the math department at her school. Her immediate work environment, then, tends to consist of more traditional "masculine" than "feminine" attributes, even in minor details such as what the math teachers discuss about their weekend activities. Leslie also has less experience than most of her colleagues, which interacts with her being the only woman in how she is perceived by others and how she perceives her treatment by others.

Acknowledging the gendered context of Leslie's current situation allows several perspectives to emerge. For example, part of her frustration with her principal may be due to gender-role expectations that enter into their professional and interpersonal interactions. During her intake, Leslie described the principal's style as "oppressive." One hypothesis is that he treats his teaching staff, most of whom are female, in a sexist manner.

Teachers within Leslie's school volunteer for or are assigned duties that follow gender-typical expectations. For example, female teachers are expected to chaperone dances, and male teachers are expected to supervise athletic events. Furthermore, there are clear messages about female teachers who have or are planning to have children, whereas male teachers' decisions about children are discussed only in the context of salary needs. Leslie has not discussed her desire to have children, and she has kept her difficulties with pregnancy to herself. Yet during a discussion of teaching assignments and an upcoming retirement in her department, the principal asked Leslie about whether she was planning to ask for maternity leave in the next few years. Leslie was uncomfortable discussing her plans and personal life with her principal.

Taking a gendered-context perspective also has implications for a second issue in Leslie's life: taking on the role of parent. Choosing to have children brings many changes in one's life, including major questions about life roles as well as the "minor" decisions that need to be made on a daily basis. All of these changes are influenced by gender-role expectations and vice versa. Here, too, Leslie seems to have received many mixed messages about societal and familial expectations. Her mother and sister believe that her current career crisis is a good reason to quit her job and have children. Her husband expects that Leslie would stay at home until their children are in school and also expects that she will not move ahead with any career decisions at this time because of her desire to have children.

Leslie struggles with articulating her expectations about combining work and family, particularly because her beliefs and hopes are somewhat at odds with her husband's and with her mother's and sister's beliefs. She very much wants to have a child, and she also wants to maintain her involvement in the work role. She continues to view teaching as an ideal occupation to combine with family roles, an attractive feature when she made her initial choice of teaching as a career. Moreover, she has had numerous coworkers as role models, women who have had children and returned to their teaching positions.

When Leslie's mother and sister express their opinions that she quit her job, Leslie finds it easiest just to ignore them. She has tried to explain how she would like to combine work and family roles, but she doesn't feel that they understand why she would want to continue working. Joe's expectations, on the other hand, are more important for Leslie to address, and they have had some arguments about the roles that each of them would assume as parents and as workers. Leslie hopes that Joe will cooperate fully in child rearing once they have a child, although she also expects that she will take primary responsibility for a child. She is more concerned, however, about his expectation that she stay at home until the child enters school, because she has no intention of doing so. She worries that she would "go stir crazy" if she were not working outside of the home.

Questions for Discussion

1. What specific hypotheses would you develop about Leslie from gender-aware or feminist approaches or both? How does using these approaches help you understand Leslie? How might it help Leslie understand herself?

2. In what other ways has gender influenced Leslie's career development throughout her life—as a child, an adolescent, and an adult?

3. How might you work with Leslie from a nonsexist perspective? From a gender-aware perspective? From a feminist perspective?

4. What types of gender-role expectations did Leslie learn from her family of origin? From the educational system? From her work experience? From her husband and his family?

5. How might Leslie's assessment results be influenced by gender? How might the counselor address these influences?

6. Conceptualize Leslie's relationship with her husband from a gendered perspective. In what ways might each of their roles be constrained due to gender-role expectations?

7. How has "the personal is political" been manifested in Leslie's life?

THE CASE OF DIANA AND BILL

Diana and Bill, both Caucasian, are a dual-career couple in their mid-40s. Diana is a systems analyst within the communications industry; Bill is an actuary, most recently with an insurance company. They moved to a new state 18 months ago so that Diana could accept a major promotion within her company. They have been married 20 years and have two daughters in high school.

Bill sought counseling because he is having difficulty finding a new job since their move. For the first few months, he looked for a position similar to the one he'd just left, but he expanded his search when he was unable to find such a job. Before moving, Bill had been successful at his job but was beginning to experience some burnout. The vice president in his division was grooming him to take over a supervisory position, yet Bill had been feeling ambivalent about the promotion. He felt pressured by Diana to take the position, because it was accompanied by a hefty raise and more status within the organization. He felt some relief when Diana's company offered her the promotion and transfer to another state, because it took the pressure off of his decision; he also felt that the move might provide him with a new beginning.

Diana and Bill met as sophomores in college and married soon after graduation. They both wanted a family and thought they'd have a "traditional" marriage, where Bill would provide financially for the family and Diana would stay at home to raise the children. She initially worked as a computer programmer for a small company but quit her job after their first child was born.

Diana reentered the workforce 5 years ago after a 10-year hiatus for child rearing, and she has been very successful at her job. The position for which they recently moved represented a major move up the corporate ladder for Diana. Bill has been supportive of Diana's career and felt relieved that he was no longer the primary breadwinner. On the other hand, he is somewhat uncomfortable with her success because of their shifting roles: He was becoming less committed to his job and career as Diana was becoming more committed to hers. He became angry when his former coworkers made comments that Bill was quitting his job so he could be supported by his wife, and the vice president who wanted to promote him wrote him a weak letter of reference, questioning his drive and ability to achieve.

Neither Bill nor Diana were concerned when Bill did not find a job immediately after their move; he had decided not to spend much time looking until they actually moved and were settled into their new home, and he'd heard that it could take up to a year to find a suitable job given his years of experience. However, now that it's been 18 months, both Bill and Diana are becoming concerned about Bill's continued unemployment. Diana has found herself wondering why Bill hasn't found anything yet and is beginning to doubt that he is investing sufficient time and energy into the job search. She experiences occasional resentment about being the sole wage earner and the increasing financial pressure as their daughters get closer to pursuing college education. Bill vacillates between feeling confident that a satisfactory position will come along and feeling worried that his skills and experience are not good enough. The longer he has gone without a job, the more he has taken over household responsibilities, at Diana's urging.

Questions for Discussion

1. In what way have gender-role expectations influenced Bill? How are they affecting Bill and Diana?

2. How might you help Bill deal with the changes that have occurred because of his inability to find a job?

3. What does the occupational role mean to Bill? How does it fit with his image of himself as a man?

4. How might you help Diana deal with the changes that have occurred because of Bill's unemployment?

5. What does the occupational role mean to Diana? How does it fit with her image of herself as a woman?

BOX 4.2

Counselor Cognitions

How have gender-role expectations influenced the client's career choices?

How do gender roles affect the client's current choices?

How will I foster an egalitarian relationship with the client?

How will I incorporate gender awareness into counseling with the client? Nonsexist principles? Feminist principles?

How might my gender influence my interaction with the client?

Directions and Implications for Career Counseling

GOALS OF COUNSELING

Feminist therapy has been described as more of a philosophical stance than a school of therapy. As such, the tenets of feminist therapy clearly have important implications for the goals of counseling. Perhaps most important, the issue of gender becomes an explicit focus of career counseling and may even permeate every aspect of counseling, including definition of the presenting problem, building a working alliance, choosing and interpreting assessments, designing and implementing interventions, and terminating the counseling relationship.

The four tenets of feminist therapy, described earlier, have been applied to the practice of career counseling (Chronister et al., 2006) and, more specifically, to career assessment (Forrest & Brooks, 1993). In addition, several authors have suggested specific techniques for addressing gender within counseling, which will be applied to Leslie and to Diana and Bill. In the latter case, although Bill is the person who sought career counseling, it is useful to conceptualize the career-related issues of both Diana and Bill, and it may also be helpful for Diana to join Bill in career counseling.

INTERVENTIONS

Sociocultural Conditions as a Primary Source of Women's Problems

This first tenet addresses how problems are conceptualized by the counselor and the client. Feminist counselors emphasize sociocultural explanations and deemphasize intrapsychic explanations in considering a client's problems. Common career problems that women experience, such as work-family conflict, underuse of abilities, limited opportunities, and work adjustment problems, are viewed as resulting from the patriarchal society in which they live (Forrest & Brooks, 1993).

The feminist counselor would begin working with Leslie with an eye toward assessing how societal expectations have shaped her career experiences thus far. One way to do so is to interpret traditional types of assessment (interests, values, skills, personality, work history). A second method is to search specifically for ways in which gender-role issues have affected the client (Forrest & Brooks, 1993; Swanson & Woitke, 1997).

Leslie's Strong Interest Inventory (SII) profile contains scores reflecting same-sex norms, opposite-sex norms, and combined-sex norms—sometimes for the same scales—and the counselor needs to know how properly to interpret these scores. Leslie is likely to ask the counselor why there are two scores for each Occupational Scale and why some of her male-normed scales are higher than the corresponding female-normed scales.

Another perspective on Leslie's SII profile is that her interests are somewhat atypical for women—namely, the primary code of investigative in Holland's (1997) theory. On the other hand, her secondary (social) and tertiary (conventional) codes are more common for women. The counselor is likely to explore the gender-role origins of Leslie's interests and discuss societal expectations for women. Throughout her life, Leslie clearly has been aware that her interest in math was atypical for her sex. She has not, however, really thought about the "gendered context" of her career decisions. One focus of counseling might be analyzing how Leslie has experienced her decisions regarding her nontraditional interests. What benefits has she received from "being different"? What negative experiences has she had because of being different?

A feminist or gender-aware counselor working with Bill also would explore the ways in which gender-role expectations have influenced him. He has been working in an occupation that is traditionally filled more often by men but now finds himself in a new role. Diana's occupational role, on the other hand, has been a bit more nontraditional, and her reentry into the workforce while her husband is unemployed also puts her into a new role. How might they be reacting to these new roles? What does the occupational role mean to Bill? How does it fit with his image of himself as a man? What does the occupational role mean to Diana? How does it fit with her image of herself as a woman?

Gysbers, Heppner, and Johnston (1998) suggest a set of questions to guide an assessment of the gendered context of a client's environment. These questions provide examples of how a counselor might explicitly integrate gender into an assessment of a client's career-related history:

- What messages did you receive as a child about the career options you might pursue?

- In school, did you feel support, discouragement, or a neutral reaction to the development of your interests? Who supported the development of your interests and skills? Who discouraged you about a potential interest area?

- Were you actively encouraged to pursue interests because they were appropriate to your role as a woman (man)? Were you encouraged to pursue interests that were nontraditional for you as a woman (man)?

- What occupational dreams did you discard at some point in your life? Why did you discard them?

Gysbers et al. (1998) also suggest questions to assess the gendered context of a work environment. These questions would be particularly useful for a client dealing with issues related to work adjustment:

- In general, how does your work environment feel to you? What words would you use to describe your work atmosphere?

- What messages have you received about your career opportunities within your work environment? Do they seem limited because you are a woman (man)?

- Are your skills and interests being actively promoted and developed within the organization?

- Have you experienced either subtle or blatant instances of harassment or discouragement in your work environment?

- Have there been times when you felt treated differently because of your sex?

The counselor also may use a gender-role analysis (D. Brown & Brooks, 1991; L. S. Brown, 1986, 1990). As described by Forrest and Brooks (1993), gender-role analysis begins with the counselor's assuming a sociological perspective to gather information about the client's family of origin and his/her beliefs about societal gender-role expectations. The counselor then takes phenomenological perspective to examine the ways in which the client ha created meaning for him- or herself within that background. What did it mean for Leslie to be female in her family while she was growing up? What does it mean for her now with her husband and within her family of origin? What lessons did she learn about gender-role expectations? From Leslie's experience, what happens when women deviate from gender-role expectations? What does gender mean to her when she thinks about her career thus far? When she thinks about her future career and family roles? These same questions are appropriate to consider in Bill's (and Diana's) case as well.

The counselor needs to be aware of external barriers to career development that Leslie has encountered in her academic or work environments (Swanson, Daniels, & Tokar, 1996; Swanson & Woitke, 1997; Worrell & Remer, 1992). Moreover, the counselor needs to be attentive to ways in which these barriers have been internalized into low self-efficacy or self-esteem. Identifying internal barriers as originally emanating from external sources is a unique perspective of feminist therapy.

Another technique that the counselor could use to assess Leslie's, Bill's, and Diana's gender role prescriptions is to use a sentence completion exercise, either in session or as homework. Forrest and Brooks (1993) suggest the following:

Since I am a woman,

  I am required to be _____

  I am allowed to be _____

  I am forbidden to be _____

If I were a man, I would be

  required to be _____

  allowed to be _____

  forbidden to be _____

The Personal Is Political

Application of this tenet in career counseling suggests that a client must be aware of the political and economic realities of society to fully understand her own personal problems. Furthermore, this tenet implies that individual action alone will not resolve the problems that a woman brings to career counseling (Forrest & Brooks, 1993).

Career counseling with Leslie thus would incorporate the "personal is political" tenet by analyzing her concerns within the context of the larger group of women in general and focusing on the sociopolitical commonalities between Leslie's situation and that of other women.

Furthermore, this tenet may be applied by focusing on the power dynamics in her work environment and relationships. The counselor could use a power analysis (Forrest & Brooks, 1993; Worrell & Remer, 1992) to help Leslie identify the types of power that she can and does use in various situations. The goals of a power analysis would be to increase Leslie's understanding about the nature of power, particularly in how power is connected to gender and how she might expand her use of power.

Egalitarian Counseling Relationship

This tenet encourages development of a collaborative, nonhierarchical relationship between counselor and client in which both participants have equal worth regardless of whatever differential expertise or power they bring to their interactions. The counselor can use a number of power-sharing techniques with Leslie. First, the counselor assumes, and encourages Leslie to acknowledge, that she is the expert on herself. This is particularly important to emphasize in the context of using and interpreting standardized assessment results, during which computer-generated profiles are often inappropriately reified. Second, the counselor and Leslie work together in developing hypotheses about her career issues and avoid using jargon in doing so. The egalitarian approach also applies to decisions about assessment, and Leslie would have been involved in choosing specific instruments.

In the context of developing a good working alliance, Leslie and the counselor will begin to discuss their beliefs about gender-role issues. It is important to assess Leslie's level of awareness or acceptance of feminist ideas, because this will affect how she views the gendered context of her career issues and whether she may be in a different place than the counselor in terms of her readiness to discuss gender-role expectations and experiences.

Bill's experience in career counseling may be influenced by whether the counselor is female or male, and gender dynamics may be particularly salient if Diana and Bill decide to pursue conjoint counseling. It would be important for the counselor, whether male or female, to be attuned to these issues.

Essentials for Women's Mental Health: Self-Definition and Self-Determination

This tenet is the one most closely related to counseling goals in that it redefines appropriate goals for women. One explicit goal of feminist therapy that is particularly relevant in career counseling is for individuals to be financially independent; as Fitzgerald (1986) notes, "It is not in anyone's best interest to be totally economically dependent on the good will and good health of another person" (p. 129). Pursuit of this goal with Leslie would entail discussion of how gender-role expectations have limited her choices and how the low wages associated with traditionally female occupations, such as teaching, keep women from achieving independence. Moreover, the counselor could help Leslie view the gendered aspects of her work environment and discuss how she might overcome external and internal barriers (Forrest & Brooks, 1993).

In addition, feminist therapists are enjoined to not overlook critical issues affecting women's lives. With Leslie, the counselor would discuss a wide range of issues, beginning with possible instances of discrimination or sexual harassment in her work environment. A second set of issues concerns the degree to which Leslie's career decisions are governed by economic or financial dependence and how she and Joe will negotiate their respective career or job changes. Moreover, Leslie expressed dissatisfaction with how she and Joe divide household responsibilities and concerns about how they might approach child-rearing responsibilities.

Leslie's capacity for self-definition and self-determination can be assessed by listening carefully to how she talks about her career decisions to date and by her thinking about future career decisions (Forrest & Brooks, 1993). Does she frame her career history in terms of how it has conformed to the desires or influences of other people? Are her interests and goals clearly defined separately from those of people such as her family and husband?

A nonsexist card sort (Brown & Brooks, 1991; Dewey, 1974) also may be used to determine Leslie's perceptions of gender-appropriate options. The cards consist of equal numbers of traditionally male and traditionally female occupations, and Leslie would sort them into three piles: those she would consider, those she would not consider, and those about which she is unsure. The counselor then separates the first two piles of cards into the traditionally female and male occupations and asks Leslie to describe advantages and disadvantages of each group of occupations.

The gender-socialized limits that Leslie perceives may also be assessed via the "discarded dreams" technique (Sargent as cited in Forrest & Brooks, 1993). Leslie would list her career dreams that have been encouraged or discouraged by important people in her life. As she discussed these dreams, the counselor would listen for negative messages that continue to influence her decisions.

Additional Cases

CASE 1: ELLEN

Ellen is a 50-year-old Caucasian woman who entered counseling at a women's center in her community. Her husband, Tim, recently filed for divorce after 27 years of marriage, and Ellen is feeling bewildered. They have three children—two sons aged 21 and 19, who are both in college, and a daughter aged 16.

Ellen and Tim met and married while in college—Ellen as a sophomore and Tim as a senior. Ellen quit school to take a secretarial job to support them while Tim went to graduate school in anthropology. He finished his PhD in 5 years and obtained a faculty position at a prestigious state university. Their oldest child was born during the first year of Tim's new job, and Ellen did not look for work outside of the home. When the youngest child went to elementary school, Ellen contemplated getting a job, but Tim's career was so demanding that she felt it was more important for her to focus her attention on the children and household responsibilities.

Ellen knew that Tim had seemed dissatisfied for the last few years, but his decision to ask for a divorce came as a shock to her. He told her that he wanted to leave the marriage because he was disappointed in how "traditional" their relationship was and that he wished she could be more like the professional women he dealt with daily at the university. Ellen reports feeling "betrayed," because he never expressed these concerns at any time earlier in their 27 years together. She feels that they had an unspoken arrangement in which she would take most of the responsibility for raising their children, entertaining his colleagues, and generally doing whatever was necessary to support Tim's career advancement. Yet now she feels that he is changing the rules and criticizing her for what she felt he wanted her to do.

In addition to her emotional distress about Tim's announcement, Ellen is also thinking about many practical details resulting from the divorce. Tim seems amenable to a fair financial settlement and is committed to providing for a college education for all three children. However, he has told Ellen that he doesn't intend to provide her with any financial support after their youngest daughter leaves home, and Ellen is feeling quite concerned about her future. Ellen will no longer be able to anticipate financial security at retirement, so, at age 50, she would like to plan how she will use the next 15 years to prepare for her own retirement. Because she hasn't been in the workforce for 20 years, however, Ellen feels very unsure of what she could do to support herself. Ellen is thus entering counseling with a variety of pressing issues.

Questions for Discussion

1. How would you conceptualize Ellen's current situation from a gender-aware or feminist perspective?

2. How might it help Ellen to view her situation from a gender-aware or feminist perspective? How would examining gender-role expectations assist her?

3. How might you work with Ellen regarding career planning? How could she identify work-related skills?

4. In what ways would you foster an egalitarian therapeutic relationship with Ellen?

5. What specific interventions or techniques would you like to use with Ellen?

CASE 2: BRENDA

Brenda is a 47-year-old Hispanic woman who is a police officer in New York City. She entered the police academy in her early 20s because her uncle was a cop and she thought it would be "cool" to be a uniformed officer; her uncle encouraged her by telling her she was "tough" and could handle the work. Brenda recently retired from the force after 25 years on the job but now needs to return because her benefits are being reduced. She has taken some community college courses over the years but hasn't pursued a degree. Without a college degree, she feels that she cannot do much other than work for the police department, although she's has grown a little weary of the physical aspect of the work as she's gotten older. At her age, she still has many working years ahead of her, yet she's not sure what direction to take.

Questions for Discussion

1. In what way have gender-role expectations influenced Brenda?

2. How might you help Brenda deal with the changes that have occurred through retirement and now her return to work?

3. What does the occupational role mean to Brenda? How does it fit with her image of herself as a woman?

4. How have Brenda's experiences in a gender-nontraditional occupation affected her? How do these experiences influence her future work?

5. How might Brenda's career be conceptualized from a gender-aware or feminist perspective?

CASE 3: TONY

Tony is a 19-year-old African American sophomore who came to the university counseling center because he is undecided about a major. He has considered physical education or restaurant management, although he does not know much about either of these majors or occupational fields. He states that he wants to make a lot of money and also wants a job where he is his own boss. What he'd really like to do is own and manage a nightclub, and he has thought about many of the details, such as the name and format of the club, the kind of manager he would be, and so on.

Tony is a first-generation college student, and he feels pressure from his parents to complete his bachelor's degree. College was not entirely what he expected, however, and he wishes he could quit and find a job in a nightclub. He wonders if getting a degree will help him anyway. Tony is engaged to a woman who is a junior majoring in marketing, and she is encouraging him to stay in school. They plan to get married after she graduates next year.

During counseling, you ask him about how he envisions his job or career fitting with the rest of his roles in life and use a guided imagery exercise to help Tony think about his lifestyle and his daily activities. When you ask him how working in a nightclub will fit with other aspects of his life, he talks about how it won't affect other aspects of his life because his friends will probably "hang out" with him at the nightclub. You then specifically ask about whether he wants to have children; Tony responds by saying that "Why does that matter? It will be my wife's job to take care of any kids."

Questions for Discussion

1. How would you deal with your feelings and reactions to Tony's statements?

2. How would you encourage an egalitarian relationship with him?

3. What techniques might you use to help Tony explore the various roles in his life? How might you convince Tony of the value of doing so?

4. What gender-role expectations might Tony be experiencing from his parents, particularly as an African American man?

5. What factors might be occurring between Tony and his fiancée? How might their careers and their relationship be conceptualized from a gender-aware or feminist perspective?

BOX 4.3

Summary of Key Constructs

Construct	Definition
Gender-aware counseling	An approach that recognizes gender as integral to counseling in which client concerns are viewed within larger societal context
Nonsexist counseling	An approach that emphasizes equity between men and women and treats people as individuals
Feminist counseling	An approach that explicitly adapts feminist tenets to counseling
Alpha bias	Tendency to exaggerate differences between men and women
Beta bias	Tendency to minimize or ignore differences between men and women

References

American Counseling Association. (2005). *ACA code of ethics*. Washington, DC: Author.

American Psychological Association. (2002). *Ethical principles of psychologists and code of conduct*. Washington, DC: Author.

American Psychological Association. (2007). *Guidelines for psychological practice with girls and women*. Washington, DC: Author. Retrieved September 17, 2008, from http://www.apa.org/about/division/girlsandwomen.pdf

Betz, N. E. (1989). The null environment and women's career development. *The Counseling Psychologist, 17*, 136–144.

Betz, N. E. (2005). Women's career development. In S. D. Brown & R. W. Lent (Eds.), *Career development and counseling: Putting theory and research to work* (pp. 253–277). New York: Wiley.

Betz, N. E. (2006). Basic issues and concepts in the career development and counseling of women. In W. B. Walsh & M. J. Heppner (Eds.), *Handbook of career counseling for women* (2nd ed., pp. 45–74). Mahwah, NJ: Erlbaum.

Betz, N. E. (2008). Women's career development. In F. L. Denmark & M. A. Paludi (Eds.), *Psychology of women: A handbook of issues and theories* (2nd ed., pp. 717–752). Westport, CT: Greenwood.

Betz, N. E., & Fitzgerald, L. F. (1987). *The career psychology of women*. Orlando, FL: Academic Press.

Brooks, L., & Forrest, L. (1994). Feminism and career counseling. In W. B. Walsh & S. H. Osipow (Eds.), *Career counseling for women* (pp. 87–143). Hillsdale, NJ: Lawrence Erlbaum.

Brown, D., & Brooks, L. (1991). *Career counseling techniques*. Needham Heights, MA: Allyn & Bacon.

Brown, L. S. (1986). Gender role analysis: A neglected component of psychological assessment. *Psychotherapy: Theory, Research, Practice, Training, 23*, 243–248.

Brown, L. S. (1990). Taking account of gender in the clinical assessment interview. *Professional Psychology: Research and Practice, 21*, 12–17.

Chronister, K. M., McWhirter, E. H., & Forrest, L. (2006). A critical feminist approach to career counseling with women. In W. B. Walsh & M. J. Heppner (Eds.), *Handbook of career counseling for women* (2nd ed., pp. 167–192). Mahwah, NJ: Lawrence Erlbaum.

Cook, E. P. (1993). The gendered context of life: Implications for women's and men's career-life plans. *Career Development Quarterly, 41*, 227–237.

Dewey, C. R. (1974). Exploring interests: A nonsexist method. *Personnel and Guidance Journal, 52*, 311–315.

Fitzgerald, L. F. (1986). Career counseling with women: Principles, procedures and problems. In Z. Leibowitz & D. Lea (Eds.), *Adult career development: Concepts, issues and practices* (pp. 116–131). Alexandria, VA: American Association of Counseling and Development.

Fitzgerald, L. F., & Weitzman, L. M. (1992). Women's career development: Theory and practice from a feminist perspective. In H. D. Lea & Z. B. Leibowitz (Eds.), *Adult career development: Concepts, issues and practices* (2nd ed., pp. 124–160). Alexandria, VA: National Career Development Association.

Forrest, L., & Brooks, L. (1993). Feminism and career assessment. *Journal of Career Assessment, 1,* 233–245.

Freeman, J. (1979). How to discriminate against women without even trying. In J. Freeman (Ed.), *Women: A feminist perspective* (2nd ed., pp. 217–232). Palo Alto, CA: Mayfield.

Gannon, L. (1982). The role of power in psychotherapy. *Women and Therapy, 1*(2), 3–11.

Gilligan, C. (1982). *In a different voice: Psychological theory and women's development.* Cambridge, MA: Harvard University Press.

Good, G. E., Gilbert, L. A., & Scher, M. (1990). Gender aware therapy: A synthesis of feminist therapy and knowledge about gender. *Journal of Counseling and Development, 68,* 376–380.

Gysbers, N. C., Heppner, M. J., & Johnston, J. A. (1998). *Career counseling: Process, issues, and techniques.* Boston: Allyn & Bacon.

Gysbers, N. C., Heppner, M. J., & Johnston, J. A. (2003). *Career counseling: Process, issues, and techniques* (2nd ed.). Boston: Allyn & Bacon.

Hare-Mustin, R. T., & Marecek, J. (1988). The meaning of difference: Gender theory, postmodernism, and psychology. *American Psychologist, 43,* 455–464.

Harmon, L. W. (1997). Do gender differences necessitate separate career development theories and measures? *Journal of Career Assessment, 5,* 463–470.

Holland, D. C., & Eisenhart, M. A. (1990). *Educated in romance: Women, achievement, and college culture.* Chicago: University of Chicago Press.

Holland, J. L. (1997). *Making vocational choices: A theory of vocational personalities and work environments* (3rd ed.). Odessa, FL: Psychological Assessment Resources.

Lonborg, S. D., & Hackett, G. (2006). Career assessment and counseling for women. In W. B. Walsh & M. J. Heppner (Eds.), *Handbook of career counseling for women* (2nd ed., pp. 103–166). Mahwah, NJ: Erlbaum.

Marecek, J., & Kravetz, D. (1977). Women and mental health: A review of feminist change efforts. *Psychiatry, 40,* 323–329.

Mintz, L. B., & O'Neil, J. M. (1990). Gender roles, sex, and the process of psychotherapy: Many questions and few answers. *Journal of Counseling and Development, 68,* 381–387.

Sturdivant, S. (1980). *Therapy with women: A feminist philosophy of treatment.* New York: Springer.

Swanson, J. L., Daniels, K. K., & Tokar, D. M. (1996). Assessing perceptions of career-related barriers: The Career Barriers Inventory. *Journal of Career Assessment, 4,* 219–244.

Swanson, J. L., & Woitke, M. B. (1997). Theory into practice in career assessment: Assessing women's career barriers. *Journal of Career Assessment, 5,* 443–462.

Walsh, W. B., & Osipow, S. H. (Eds.). (1994). *Career counseling for women.* Hillsdale, NJ: Lawrence Erlbaum.

Whiston, S. C., & Bouwkamp, J. C. (2003). Ethical implications of career assessment with women. *Journal of Career Assessment, 11,* 59–73.

Worrell, J., & Remer, P. (1992). *Feminist perspectives in therapy: An empowerment model for women.* New York: Wiley.

Culturally Appropriate Career Counseling 5

The United States has a long history of grappling with and attempting to come to terms with the changing demographic makeup of its population. The first decade of the 21st century is no exception. In the most recent censuses, a third of the U.S. population identifies as a member of a racial/ethnic minority group (U.S. Census Bureau, 2006), up from 20% of the population in 1990 (Hobbs, Stoops, & U.S. Census Bureau, 2002). The increase is in part due to a change with the 2000 census that allowed individuals to identify as more than one racial/ethnic group. Nonetheless, the U.S. population is increasingly racially and ethnically diverse, and clients will increasingly come from racially/ethnically diverse cultures.

The increasing diversity has had an influence on educational systems, where college enrollment of students of color has increased 62% in the past two decades (National Center for Education Statistics, 2006). However, college completion rates have differed, with only 10% of Hispanic/ Latinos and 18% of African Americans graduating from college by age 29, compared to 30% of Whites and 54% of Asian Americans (National Center for Education Statistics, 2006). There are also racial/ethnic differences in occupational choices, with African Americans and Hispanics underrepresented in professional occupational groupings (e.g., less than 5% of engineers) and overrepresented in lower-paying occupations (e.g., African Americans are 30% of guards and Hispanics are 40% of cleaners; Bureau of Labor Statistics, 2006).

Thus, neither the educational nor occupational landscape is similar across racial/ethnic groups. However, recent studies have shown that these differences are not due to differences in career aspirations or in decision making attitudes but rather to differences in expectations and in perceptions of barriers and opportunities (Fouad & Byars-Winston, 2005). Career counselors who help racial/ethnic minority group members realize their career dreams and challenge foreclosed options may be uniquely positioned to help create a more equitable educational and occupational landscape.

The changing racial and ethnic makeup of educational systems and workplaces has been perceived as both a problem and as a tremendous opportunity for the United States. As a problem, the changing demography is forcing employers, educators, and members of the helping professions to rethink their practices and policies. As an opportunity, the changes are bringing a new energy and vitality to many environments, as multiple perspectives and diverse viewpoints help to create more powerful and effective solutions to complex issues.

These changes are affecting the counseling profession as well. Counselors are faced with an ethical imperative to develop competencies to be both culturally sensitive and culturally responsive (National Career Development Association [NCDA], 2007; see also Appendix B). Counselors are questioning whether current policies and practices are effective for diverse populations, and old notions of uniformity are being eliminated in favor of designing programs to meet the distinctive needs of various cultural groups. Leaders within the profession are demanding that counselors provide culturally appropriate services (American Psychological Association, 2003; Blustein, 2006; Byars-Winston & Fouad, 2006; Sue & Sue, 2007; Worthington, Flores, & Navarro, 2005), and clients from diverse racial/ethnic groups are demanding that they receive those services (NCDA, 2000). NCDA's Gallup poll found that racial/ethnic clients report a need specifically for career services, yet Carter, Scales, Juby, Collins, and Wan (2003) found that racial/ethnic minority students were less likely to remain in career counseling. The surgeon general's report on mental health (U.S. Department of Health & Human Services, 2000/2001) concluded that racial/ethnic minority clients are not seeking or staying in counseling services, possibly because traditional services are not effective. This challenges career counselors to frame their work within a cultural context, helping clients set goals appropriate from their worldview (rather than the counselor's worldview) and using culturally appropriate techniques to best serve all clients. For their part, career counselors are willing to provide appropriate services but are often at a loss to learn how to be more culturally responsive to their clients.

Unlike the theories we will discuss in Chapters 6 through 10, no one theoretical framework has been developed to explain the career behavior of racial/ethnic minorities. Rather, several individuals have called for culturally appropriate career counseling, and some also have described models for appropriate intervention. In this chapter, we will give a brief overview of the issues salient to culturally appropriate career counseling and provide a review of three models. One model, the culturally appropriate career counseling model (Fouad & Bingham, 1995), will be discussed in greater depth and then will be applied to the cases of Leslie and Norman.

All clients operate within a cultural context. Clients are shaped in part by such factors as their gender, racial identity and background, sexual orientation, socioeconomic status (SES), or disability, which help to form their environments and their responses to the environment. A central tenet of all approaches to cross-cultural career counseling is that the most effective career counseling explicitly incorporates those contextual factors. Effective career counselors do not treat all clients the same, assuming their cultural experiences are uniform, but will approach each client as belonging to one or more cultures. For example, a client may be an Asian American married to a White woman, working in a company headed by an African American and living in an ethnically diverse, middle-class neighborhood. He may feel that he belongs to several cultures; some may be more salient to him than others. His counselor needs to be aware of his multiple cultures and how they interact. His goals will reflect his cultural contexts, indicating which are most salient to him.

Culturally responsive career counseling is good for *all* clients. All clients come to counseling with unique biological, social, and developmental experiences that are products of the cultures to which they belong. It is also critical to note that belonging to a culture does not automatically mean that a client will display one characteristic or another. Rather, there is great heterogeneity within groups. Counselors need to be flexible enough to incorporate the cultural variables salient to the client. This requires that the counselor has developed multicultural competencies and is prepared for culturally appropriate counseling (Sue & Sue, 2007).

Culturally appropriate counseling requires that the counselor have knowledge and skills to work with specific cultural groups. For example, a counselor working with Hmong clients in the Midwest needs to know the history of the Hmong immigration to the United States, the development of their written language, and their cultural norms and values. But while counselors need to know certain culturally specific issues, counselors also need to be aware of several overlying variables that may affect many minority group clients. These include the influences of racism, social class, discrimination, acculturation, and immigration status on career behavior, as well as the involvement of family in career decision making.

Racial discrimination and social class have had a strong influence on the career behavior of racial/ethnic minorities in the United States. Such external issues as discrimination and poverty have a disproportionate effect on racial/ethnic groups, limiting the options that individuals may consider and restricting their access to a wide variety of opportunities (Fitzgerald & Betz, 1994). As noted earlier, there is large occupational segregation by race/ethnicity, as well as gender, with an overrepresentation of racial/ethnic group individuals in the lower SES levels and overrepresentation of White men in higher SES levels. The strong relationships between SES and educational attainment and occupational level have led to a continuous cycle of poor and poorly educated minority individuals (Arbona, 1996; Worthington et al.,

2005). Discrimination has also played a role in keeping individuals trapped in this cycle.

To be most effective, career counselors need to understand the role that discrimination has played in the choices of their clients and help their clients realize how discrimination may have limited their perceptions of opportunities, as well as barring them from opportunities. Counselors need to understand the relationship between social class and educational level and how those together may affect the real choices available to clients. Poverty, poor academic training, and the psychological factors related to feeling powerless and unable to plan for the future are realities for many clients. As Fitzgerald and Betz (1994) and Blustein (2006) have noted, the very notion of finding an optimal occupational area is unrealistic for many poor clients. For them, a job that pays for rent and food for their families is of much greater importance than self-realization.

Acculturation and immigration status also are important variables to assess in cross-cultural career counseling. Acculturation refers to the ongoing process by which individuals come into contact with a new culture and how they change and adapt to that culture in behavior, emotion, and thought. It is not a simple linear process, nor is it a process through which individuals automatically lose their original culture. Some individuals may be able to operate quite well in two cultures, in essence becoming bicultural. It is important to ascertain clients' level of acculturation, since this may affect their consideration of various career choices. It also may affect the process they find most useful in career counseling. For example, counseling may be most effective for an Asian American client with strong traditional values if it includes her family.

This previous example illustrates the fourth overarching variable: that for many racial/ethnic groups the weight placed on individual values is less important than the weight placed on collectivistic values. Traditionally, career counseling has focused on the individual with an emphasis on independent decision making, but this emphasis may not be as appropriate for some individuals from traditional ethnic cultures. Rather, they may feel strongly that family approval is the most important variable in choosing a career. Family approval may, in fact, be much more important than individuals' own interests and needs. While effective career counseling has always considered such variables as family obligations, it has been done within the context of also examining interests, abilities, values, and personality. We are suggesting that culturally responsive career counseling acknowledges that cultures vary in the weight placed on all those variables and that, in many cultures, the standard individualistic approach to career decision making may be less effective. For example, a recent qualitative study of Asian Americans showed that family expectations were a strong and all-encompassing influence in their career choice (Fouad et al., 2008).

Cultures differ on a number of variables that influence individuals' career choices. Individuals receive messages from their parents and the cultural milieus in which they were raised that affect their career and work decisions. For example, the U.S. mainstream culture values individual achievement and a large role of work in one's life. In other cultures, collective or group achievement is emphasized, and work is merely one of many roles in one's life. Work may play a role in survival, in helping form relationships, or in helping achieve an identity (Blustein, 2006). Culturally competent career counselors help clients approach career decision making from within the clients' own cultural contexts.

Box 5.1

Personal Reflection

What role does my cultural context play in my career decision?

How have I been affected by the mainstream U.S. cultural expectations about work?

Career Intervention Models

Three models have recently been developed to help counselors conceptualize ways to incorporate culture into career counseling. These models complement one another, each expanding areas that the others do not cover. The most comprehensive model is Leong and Hartung's (1997) integrative-sequential conceptual framework for career counseling. Another model, by Leung (1995), focuses exclusively on career interventions, explicating the outcomes of those interventions. Finally, Fouad and Bingham's (1995) model delineates the career counseling process, identifying specific areas in which culture may play a role. Each model addresses a specific aspect of cross-cultural career counseling.

Leong and Hartung's (1997) model consists of five stages:

Stage 1: Recognition by the client of vocational problems. In this stage, Leong and Hartung suggest that the client's cultural background affects the process by which a client recognizes a problem. For example, two individuals may work in an environment that does not make full use of their abilities, but only one views it as a problem while the other is grateful to have work that pays a salary. Their cultural backgrounds help shape when they view situations as problems.

Stage 2: Help seeking and using career services. Leong and Hartung note that clients' attitudes toward mental health services influence whether they seek help for problems. Leong and Hartung suggest that it is important in this stage to assess barriers to seeking career counseling.

They identify lack of bilingual staff, lack of culturally appropriate services, and cultural mistrust as possible factors that have led to underutilization of career services by culturally diverse clients.

Stage 3: Evaluation of career problems. Leong and Hartung extend other models examined in this chapter by delineating that career problems can be evaluated only if a problem is recognized and if the client seeks professional help for career problems. Once a client comes for counseling, the counselor may use a five-dimension cultural formulation model as a guideline, which incorporates the cultural identity of the individual, a cultural explanation of the problem, an examination of cultural factors in the environment, influence of cultural variables that may affect the relationship between the client and counselor, and an overall cultural assessment and plan.

Stage 4: Implementing career interventions. Leong and Hartung include assessment as a primary career intervention, advocating that after the client's career problems have been evaluated, the counselor and client collaborate to "help the client derive meaning from the assessment results" (p. 198).

Stage 5: Outcome of the intervention. The client returns to the community.

While Leong and Hartung's (1997) model is a comprehensive model of career services for minority clients, Leung (1995) focuses on one aspect, that of career interventions. His model has three levels—systemic, group, and one-to-one—and focuses on educational as well as career outcomes. Leung advocates that the model should incorporate educational outcomes, since education is critical to the career development of racial/ethnic minorities to counteract the cyclical effect of poverty and discrimination. Systemic interventions for career outcomes may include helping school counselors develop special career-related programs that target racial/ethnic minorities; systemic educational outcomes may include developing multiculturally affirming schools. Group educational and career interventions include group career counseling. This is strongly advocated by Bowman (1993) as well. Leung, however, suggests that group career counseling may be more effective if it is structured and if the groups consist of one racial/ethnic group, so that similarity of values and beliefs may be explored. In one-to-one career and educational counseling, Leung advocates that "career issues of minority clients must be understood in terms of the cultural background and beliefs of the client" (p. 562).

Fouad and Bingham (1995) propose the culturally appropriate career counseling model (CACCM), which specifically assesses the impact of cultural variables in each step of career counseling (Figure 5.1). Note that this model is less comprehensive than the Leong and Hartung (1997) model, since it does not explicate the process by which clients arrive at the recognition that they need to seek counseling for help with career problems. The CACCM is an extension of models originally proposed by Ward and Bingham (1993; Bingham & Ward, 1994).

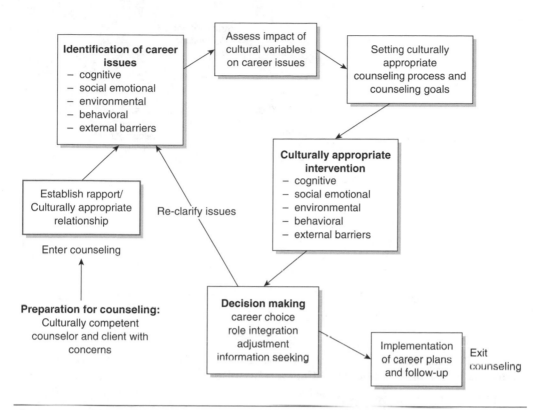

Figure 5.1   Culturally Appropriate Career Counseling Model

SOURCE: Fouad and Bingham (1995).

As shown in Figure 5.1, the CACCM has seven steps:

Step 1: The counselor and client establish a culturally appropriate relationship. In this critical first step, the counselor must work to establish a trusting relationship with the client to develop a working consensus. Culturally appropriate relationships will, of necessity, differ from clients' cultural norms and expectations of counseling and of the counseling relationship. It is important for the counselor to be knowledgeable of general cultural expectations but also to be flexible and to suspend judgment.

Step 2: The counselor identifies career issues that the client brings to counseling. This step is conceptualized as a broad examination of the client's concerns that may be related to vocational issues; these are examined within the client's cultural context. Fouad and Bingham (1995) identify five categories of career issues: cognitive, social/emotional, behavioral, environmental, and external. Clients may, of course, bring more than one of these issues to career counseling. Cognitive issues may include faulty information processing or irrational beliefs about working or career decision making. Emotional issues may include anxiety at work, or a client may be managing anger related to racism that prevents him or her from taking advantage

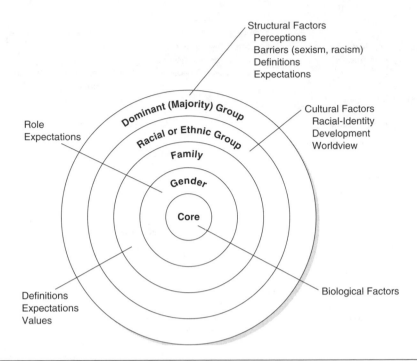

Structural Factors
Perceptions
Barriers (sexism, racism)
Definitions
Expectations

Role
Expectations

Dominant (Majority) Group

Racial or Ethnic Group

Family

Gender

Core

Cultural Factors
Racial-Identity
Development
Worldview

Definitions
Expectations
Values

Biological Factors

Figure 5.2   Spheres of Influence of Cultural Variables

SOURCE: Fouad and Bingham (1995).

of a work-related opportunity. Behavioral concerns may include being referred to career counseling because of a poor interpersonal style or work habits. Environmental issues are those related to the work environment; these include working conditions, coworkers, and supervisors. Fouad and Bingham distinguish environmental concerns from external barriers, which include racial discrimination, oppression, and sexual harassment. External barriers are explicitly defined, because racism and oppression influence career choices for many racial/ethnic group clients. These may operate implicitly, as part of restricting options that clients may consider, or explicitly, as clients are eliminated from positions due to race or gender.

Step 3: The counselor works with the client to assess the impact of cultural variables on the client's career issues. Fouad and Bingham (1995) conceptualize a series of five concentric circles forming a sphere to help identify the way that culture influences vocational behavior (see Figure 5.2):

1. The first, innermost circle represents the core, which comprises the unique aspects of the individual.

2. The next circle, influencing the self most directly, is gender. Gender influences the types of careers that individuals will consider and the way that they implement their career choices. The interaction of gender and culture also affects career choices, as some cultures have more clearly defined expectations of men and women, particularly in relation to gender-appropriate occupations.

Gottfredson

3. The next circle influencing vocational behavior represents individuals' families. Familial expectations, as well as familial norms and values, play an important role in forming individuals' views of work and their work-related decisions. As noted earlier, for some individuals, the family will be a strong influence; for others, the influence of the family will not be as strong.

4. The fourth layer from the center is the individual's racial/ethnic group, including cultural factors such as cultural values, racial identity, and acculturation level.

5. Finally, Fouad and Bingham (1995) conceptualize the dominant culture as the outermost layer of influence on individuals' career decision making.

These spheres are intended to be dynamic rather than static. Thus, at a particular point in one individual's life, the family sphere may be predominant, with strong influence also from the dominant culture. Then, as individuals gain a greater sense of identification with a racial/ethnic culture, the fourth sphere may increase in influence while the dominant culture sphere reduces in influence on their vocational choices.

Step 4: Once the counselor and client have determined the career issues and the influence of culture on those career issues, they set culturally appropriate processes and goals. The counseling process must be culturally appropriate, and the goals of counseling must fit within the client's cultural framework. An example of an inappropriate process is the use of insight-oriented counseling for clients whose culture places little emphasis on individual introspection (e.g., traditional Asian cultures) or an insistence on addressing solely the individual rather than his or her family. Inappropriate goals for the client may include encouraging career choices based on dominant culture values, such as choosing occupations based on prestigious occupations or nontraditional careers for women.

Step 5: Once the goals and processes have been determined, the counselor and client determine and implement a culturally appropriate intervention. Bowman (1993) recommends that group interventions might be particularly effective with racial/ethnic clients. She also recommends including the family in career counseling and encouraging clients to seek same-gender/ethnic group role models. Career interventions often include assessment, which has unique issues when applied across cultures. Subich (2005) and Flores and Heppner (2002) recommend that counselors be aware of the way that culture may influence traditional vocational assessment; they suggest that counselors seek additional ways to help clients clarify and identify the variables important in their career decision making.

[handwritten marginal note: degree of influence of each may vary over time]

Step 6: The counselor helps the client make a culturally appropriate decision. For clients who feel they straddle several cultural contexts, counselors may help clients understand the cultural consequences of each choice. For example, a traditional Latina may be expected by her family to live close to home, and she may have a conflict between embracing the value placed on family and wanting to pursue a college education far away. A counselor may help her understand the consequences of each decision and help her choose the right decision for her.

Step 7: This step involves implementing the client's plans and following up.

Although no studies have examined the effectiveness of the CACCM, per se, Ihle et al. (2005) reviewed empirical studies related to each of the steps. They concluded that racial/ethnic match between counselor and client was important to clients of color and that the client's perception of the counselor's cultural competence was almost as important. They also concluded that much more research is needed to understand if, and how, a culture-centered approach is effective. Heppner and Heppner (2003) also note the importance of investigating the role of culture in career counseling. More information is needed to understand how the culture of the client and the counselor interact and how that influences the career counseling process.

Multicultural Career Counseling Tenets

Gysbers, Heppner, and Johnston (2003), working with Helen Neville, outline five central tenets that are hallmarks of traditional career counseling against which counselors must guard as they work from a multicultural perspective. The first is the tenet of individualism and autonomy. As noted earlier, most traditional career counselors focus on the individual as the primary decision maker. In fact, the family unit is the decision maker for many clients, particularly those from cultural minority groups.

The second tenet is an assumption of a certain level of affluence. In other words, most career theories assume that clients can afford to spend time exploring their interests, values, and abilities and then to seek additional training prior to implementing a career choice. However, as discussed earlier, many individuals do not have the economic luxury to do anything other than find a job that pays for necessities, and in fact, for many working poor, their salaries do not even cover basic needs. This is particularly the case for racial/ethnic minorities, who are disproportionately overrepresented in lower socioeconomic levels.

A third tenet of traditional career counseling is that opportunities are available to all individuals who work hard. In reality, the American dream of success based on hard work is the American nightmare for individuals who are restricted in their career choices due to racial and sexual discrimination, as well as discrimination based on sexual orientation or social class.

A fourth tenet is that work is central in people's lives. But work may not be central for some individuals because of their experiences of institutional racism or because their cultures place higher value on other aspects of life.

The final tenet is that of linearity in the career counseling process. Traditional career counseling, consisting of knowledge of self, knowledge of the world of work, and finding a match between the two, is the epitome of the White cultural focus on linear, rational, and objective thinking. But for some racial/ethnic group clients, a more intuitive approach may be more beneficial than a linear one.

Applying a Multicultural Perspective to the Case of Leslie

Counselors applying a multicultural perspective would consider the questions in Box 5.2. Counselors actively bring their cultural frameworks, values, and worldviews into their thinking. These factors shape the way that they develop hypotheses about a client and inform specific steps or strategies of career interventions. Counselors examine their own cultural competence with their clients, how the cultural context is influencing their clients and the counseling sessions, and how they are being effective with their clients.

Box 5.2

Counselor Cognitions

What is my plan for working with this client?

What are my gaps in knowledge about the client's context?

How is my cultural context framing the way I view the client?

How am I interpreting the client's information?

What are my strengths and areas of challenge in working with this client?

How is the client's cultural context shaping his or her perception of work?

How have the client's multiple contexts influenced his or her work decisions?

What are the client's external and internal challenges?

CONCEPTUALIZING LESLIE'S CAREER HISTORY

Leslie grew up as the middle child of a relatively affluent White, middle-class family in a large metropolitan area in the Midwestern United States. Her ethnicity is not specified, other than to note that she is Caucasian. She is, however, a product of one or more cultures that transmitted values and messages about being a Caucasian woman in the United States. Giordano and McGoldrick (1996) note that "all people are ethnic. . . . It is a fact of our identities, one over which we have no choice" (p. 428). European Americans often conceptualize themselves as not having a culture, as being "regular" Americans. However, their cultural backgrounds, whether their ancestors came from the Mediterranean, Eastern Europe, or Western Europe, have shaped the way they view the world, their relationship with nature, the way they define family, the way they define work, and their view of time. To understand fully Leslie's career history, it is critical to understand the cultural messages she received growing up as a White woman.

Katz (1985) discusses several aspects of the White culture. She notes that "Whites share similar cultural dimensions that constitute a separate, unique culture" (p. 616). She explicitly identifies several components of White cultural values and beliefs. These include a focus on individualism, with its emphasis on autonomy and independence; a focus on competition; and a value placed on winning. There is a strong pragmatic orientation, with an emphasis on doing something about a situation or problem. Future planning is stressed, and progress and growth are valued. The scientific method is the favored mode, with preference given to rational and linear thinking and to decision making based on objective as opposed to subjective information. Status and power are based on position and title, and value is placed on economic possessions. The world is viewed as a place to master, rather than as a place to tolerate or in which to coexist with nature. Family is primarily viewed as the nuclear family rather than as an extended family including many generations. The Protestant work ethic predominates: hard work is good, and working hard brings success. Time is viewed as a saleable entity that is apportioned out according to set schedules; deviations from time schedules are not tolerated.

Leslie received messages from her family consistent with White cultural expectations. She was taught to work hard, as evidenced by her excellent academic work in high school. Her family expected her to plan for the future in anticipating that she would go to college. However, they also clearly conveyed a value on individualism and autonomy in not giving her much direction or guidance in choosing a career or a major. Her father communicated a value placed on pragmatic gain in recommending that she enter a business field, although this did not coincide with her interests. Her family also may have transmitted several values in showing their impatience with her decision-making process. They may have indicated that she ought to be more rational and linear in her decision making, taking the information she had and simply making a decision with it. This also is consistent with a preference for doing something about a situation perceived as problematic rather than living with it. Leslie's family also appears to have conveyed messages about appropriate careers for their children that allowed them to gain positions of power and status.

Leslie also received messages of appropriate behavior as a White woman; some of these messages are in direct conflict with appropriate behavior as a White individual. White women are expected to be nurturing and to put others' needs before their own. They are expected to be caring and to be kind and helpful to others, particularly other White people. They also are perceived as being emotional, weak, illogical, and needing security from others. Thus, the culture tells White women to be independent *and* dependent, logical *and* emotional. White women are expected to be passive *and* to take control of a situation. They are to be nurturing *and* autonomous. Leslie seems to have received these mixed messages. She was to be autonomous in making a career decision, but her mother communicated that she should not pursue that career at the same time she was taking care of a family. Her parents may have communicated that the occupation of teacher is a more appropriate occupation for a woman than going into a math or science career, since she would be taking care of others as a teacher. She may also have received messages that it is more appropriate to rely on others to help make decisions rather than being emotionally independent. She may have received messages to avoid positions of leadership and power.

It is not clear what Leslie's perceptions of other races were while she was growing up. She grew up in a suburb of a large midwestern city; she may have grown up in a racially segregated environment. If so, then she had little contact with individuals of other races while she was growing up, thus having little opportunity to develop a consciousness of herself as a member of a racial/ethnic group or to develop a knowledge or understanding of other groups. On the other hand, Leslie may have grown up in a racially integrated neighborhood and may have had significant interpersonal relationships with children from many cultural groups. She may have developed a strong sense of herself as a member of a racial group and an appreciation of and understanding for other cultures. She may, in fact, have spent a great deal of time exploring her own cultural heritage(s) and may have gained an appreciation of the role of White privilege in the United States. Whichever the case, her early upbringing and the messages her family, neighborhood, and school gave her about her own race and about other races helped to form her later racial perceptions and attitudes.

Leslie moved to her first job in a small town in the Midwest, which was most probably homogeneously White. Her frustrations with the job appeared to have little to do with the culture of the town, but rather with the workload in her job and with the lack of a social support network.

She had ended her relationship with her boyfriend, whose ethnicity is not given. She met her husband, Joe, when she was nearly 30. He is second-generation Mexican American. Joe appears to have had some ambivalence about identifying with his Mexican American heritage. He wanted to conform to the dominant culture's behavioral expectations when he was an adolescent, refusing to speak Spanish or to attend church with his family, but his first marriage was to a Hispanic woman from his neighborhood. He appears to have become more involved in his community and to have developed a greater appreciation for the traditions and values of his heritage. After his marriage dissolved, he appears to have retained his sense of identity as a Mexican American. Although he eventually married a White woman, Leslie, and no longer lives in his family's neighborhood, he still self-identifies as a Mexican American and has embraced many traditional values.

Joe and Leslie's marriage appears to be problematic for both sets of in-laws. Leslie's marriage to a member of another ethnic group may have been an issue for her parents. There are indications that they accepted him as a member of the family, since Leslie and Joe spend a fair amount of time with her family. Leslie's family's initial concerns for her marriage to Joe may have been due less to his ethnicity than to her marriage to a divorced father of one son; they also may have reacted due to their own prejudices and lack of racial awareness. Social class may be another factor that influenced Leslie's family's reaction to Joe, since Joe's educational and occupational level are quite different from those of the rest of her family. Joe's mother has said she thinks Leslie is too American. This may have caused conflicts for Leslie with her mother-in-law; it may also cause conflict between Joe and Leslie if Joe feels torn between his family and his wife.

CONCEPTUALIZING LESLIE'S PRESENT SITUATION

Conceptualizing Leslie's current situation from a multicultural perspective includes examining Leslie's behaviors and values from the multiple cultural contexts in which she lives. She is a close member of her White family and continues to be influenced by their expectations and values. She is married to a Mexican American man, who has expectations for her behavior that may stem from his own cultural background and values. She works in a high school setting that may have a racially diverse faculty and students.

Leslie's family has conveyed to her that she should be pursuing a career that will give her position and economic benefits and have also suggested that she should start a family; the latter connotes that she cannot both work and raise a family. They again show some impatience with what they perceive as her slow decision making. Her father is still advocating a business career, her mother and sister still suggesting that she stop working to have children. Her brother communicates that she is perhaps making an emotional decision in examining her career choices; he has labeled her dissatisfaction as complaints about inconsequential aspects of her job.

Leslie's husband, Joe, also expects that she would stay home if they have children. She feels that though he is supportive of her changing careers, he is less supportive of her returning to school. The role of women in the traditional Hispanic family is one of being subservient to their husbands and of caring and nurturing children, a role to which his mother conformed. A woman is expected to be passive and dependent on her husband. Caretaker of the family is her predominant purpose in life. On the other hand, Joe indicates that he knows that women should be able to be independent. Leslie may be violating some of his expectations in her interest in pursuing a career change. Though she and Joe want to have a family together, she may be reluctant to assume the role that he wants her to play in that family. It is not clear whether Joe expects her to play a particular role with his son. Leslie and Joe's lack of communication may be due to differences in cultural values; she may be focusing on discussing all her concerns with him, thereby creating conflict, while he may be motivated by the Hispanic value of smoothing over conflicts and having harmonious relationships.

Finally, Leslie works in a high school that may or may not be racially diverse in the students she is serving and the faculty with whom she works. Whichever the case, race may be playing a role in Leslie's decisions. Her perceptions that parents are uninvolved in their children's education may actually be due to a cultural difference in attitudes and behaviors. What she is interpreting as lack of involvement may be a cultural respect for authority and viewing the teacher as the expert. Similarly, her perceptions that students are having more difficulties at home may be due to her own racial assumptions about problems. In other words, Leslie may be interpreting her students' behavior from a cultural deficit model, thus concluding that they are dealing with many problems at home.

Questions for Discussion

1. What specific hypotheses would you develop about Leslie from culturally appropriate counseling approaches? How does using these approaches help you understand Leslie? How might it help Leslie understand herself?

2. What role may Leslie's worldview have played in her career development and choices?

3. How could you balance increasing awareness of race and ethnicity as possible influences in Leslie's decision making with an appreciation of her racial consciousness? Where might this be problematic?

4. How could you empower Leslie to make different types of decisions?

(Continued)

(Continued)

5. How may culture have interacted with Leslie's family of origin and her familial obligations to shape her behavior?

6. What role may sexism and racism have played in Leslie's decisions and in the outcomes of those decisions?

7. How might cultural issues influence the relationship between Leslie and Joe?

THE CASE OF NORMAN

Norman is a 17-year-old African American male who is referred to a counselor to help him "adjust his attitude." He is a junior in high school and needs to find a job. Norman is the youngest son of three children. His father is a cook for a large catering company, and his mother is a nurse; they have been divorced for 10 years. His oldest brother is in college, majoring in business, and his older sister is currently working as a receptionist and hopes to return to school to become a paralegal assistant. Norman has lived primarily with his mother, though she has asked him to live with his father twice during his high school years, when she felt she was not able to "manage" him.

Norman currently has a C average and has taken elective courses in manufacturing and in computers. Norman entered high school with a B average. However, he did not do well in his eighth-grade math and science classes, and his eighth-grade counselor encouraged him to take classes that would prepare him for a vocational technical school, such as applied math courses and business writing. His mother initially expressed some concern about this plan of study, hoping that Norman would enter a college-preparatory curriculum, but Norman did not want to go back and ask his counselor to change his schedule. In addition, his friends were signing up for the same courses, and he thought he'd be able to change once he was in high school. Unfortunately, the curriculum has been less flexible than he thought, and he has been unable to shift to a college-preparatory track.

The course that Norman enjoyed the most during his first year in high school was manufacturing. He enjoyed the material, he enjoyed working on the class projects, and he enjoyed the practical nature of the course. He was less enthusiastic about his other classes; he thought they were either irrelevant or boring. His mother became concerned during his sophomore year that he was not doing well in school. They began to have conflicts at home about his grades and about his friendships with several boys at school. This was the first instance in which he lived with his father, who helped him refocus on school, and his grades improved. He returned to live with his mother during the summer after his sophomore year, since her schedule permitted her to be home more than his father. He lived with his father once more during his junior year for 2 months, returning to his mother's home when he and his father disagreed about the time spent with his friends.

Norman's freshman year manufacturing teacher encouraged him to continue in this track and to apply for an apprenticeship with a manufacturing company. While he did not secure a formal apprenticeship, he did join a cooperative program during his junior year that enabled him to work part-time during the afternoon and take classes in the morning. He enjoyed the work, although he also felt bored at times with the relatively mundane tasks he felt he had to do. He was learning about cell manufacturing and quality improvement techniques in his manufacturing classes at school but was not seeing those policies implemented in the manufacturing company. He began to question his supervisor about the discrepancy between what he was doing and what he had learned in class. The supervisor complained to the teacher, and the teacher referred Norman to the school counselor. The teacher was primarily concerned that Norman learn to adjust his attitude, since questioning supervisors may lead Norman into problematic situations on the job.

Norman was angry that he was referred to his school counselor. He did not think he had a "problem" or that his attitude needed to change. He was resistant at first and did not trust what the counselor would eventually tell his teacher. His counselor, a White woman, reassured him that their sessions would remain confidential and that they would talk together about what she would say to his teacher. She encouraged him to think about how they could work together. They talked a great deal about Norman's feelings and thoughts about working in a factory, and Norman acknowledged his boredom and how uncertain he was about another career choice. They also talked about whether Norman should have conveyed his opinions about his internship to the supervisor, and if so, how he could do that. Norman decided he would like to explore his interests and the possibility of going to college instead of entering an apprenticeship.

The counselor found that Norman's vocational interests were primarily in the Realistic and Investigative areas. Norman also scored high on the Mechanics & Construction, Mathematics, and Science Basic Interest Scales, as well as Management, Law, and Politics & Public Speaking Basic Interest Scales. Norman was most similar to men who are engineers, farmers or ranchers, research and development managers, computer systems analysts, and auto mechanics.

Questions for Discussion

1. What cultural values did his family transmit to Norman?

2. What role may racism have played in Norman's school and career history?

3. What role may Norman's parents and siblings have played in Norman's decisions?

(Continued)

(Continued)

4. What cultural variables would you want to incorporate in career counseling?

5. What are some possible career interventions you could use?

6. What cultural strengths could you emphasize in working with Norman?

7. How should you work to "adjust Norman's attitude"? Is that an appropriate request on the part of the instructor?

Directions and Implications for Career Counseling

GOALS OF COUNSELING

The goal of counseling from a multicultural perspective is for counselors to deliver culturally appropriate interventions for clients, recognizing that clients come from unique sets of environments and contexts. Before this can happen, however, counselors must have knowledge of their own culture and the way their values, biases, and behaviors reflect that culture. They must have knowledge of and understanding of other groups' worldviews and how individuals' worldviews affect their values and behaviors. In other words, counselors must be multiculturally competent. The goal of multiculturally competent career counseling is to help clients make the most culturally appropriate career decisions that fit within the context of their lives. Readers are referred to Sue et al. (1998) for further delineation and explanation of multicultural counseling competencies.

Some of the tenets discussed earlier may be important for their counselors to keep in mind when examining Leslie's and Norman's career histories. Leslie has consulted with her family and her husband; her husband, in particular, appears to play an influential role in Leslie's career decisions. The counselor should be aware that Leslie may choose to incorporate her husband in her decision making. Leslie also may have perceived that opportunities were not available to her because she is a woman. The counselor could help her explore some of those assumptions.

Norman's counselor needs to be aware of her own biases and assumptions about African Americans and be open to Norman's perceptions of his experiences. She will need to be aware of the role that racism and discrimination may have played in Norman's schooling and work opportunities. She will also want to be open to the role that racial differences may play in the relationship between herself and Norman and work to feel comfortable in discussing this openly with him. Finally, she should be aware of ways that she can advocate for him within the school system to enable him to have more options.

CULTURALLY APPROPRIATE
CAREER COUNSELING MODEL

Step 1: Establishing a Culturally Appropriate Relationship

In the first step, the counselor sets the context for a working consensus (Bingham & Ward, 1994). This includes exhibiting empathy, warmth, and positive regard. The counselor and Leslie would discuss Leslie's expectations for counseling, which are shaped by her cultural background. The counselor might ask Leslie, "What do you expect of counseling and of me as your counselor?" Leslie most likely expects that the relationship would be a fairly egalitarian one and that the counselor has some information to share with her. She may also expect that the assessment tools will help her clarify her interests and needs and point her in a particular direction.

Norman's counselor in the case above sets the context for a working consensus by addressing Norman's anger at the referral for counseling and reassuring him that she was working to help him, rather than his teacher. Norman felt that he was being "sent to be fixed," and the counselor discussed her role as a school counselor, telling him that what he said would be kept confidential. She also encouraged him to set goals for his time with her and explored with him what had made him unhappy and bored at the factory.

Step 2: Identification of Career Issues

The counselor then helps the client identify his or her career issues. Counselors also help clients explore additional environmental issues, such as the role that race and ethnicity may be playing in their current environment, external barriers such as possible sexism or racism operating in the work environment, and how gender-role expectations may have influenced their prior decisions. Leslie's career concerns may include her dissatisfaction with her job, her desire to explore other career possibilities, and her desire to make a career decision of which her husband can be supportive as initial issues for counseling. Norman's career issues include uncertainty about how to make a career decision, how to change the educational track he is on, how to handle his supervisor and teacher, and what other options he could choose.

Step 3: Assessing the Impact
of Cultural Variables on Career Issues

In the third step, the counselor helps explore how behavior has been a product of the client's culture and whether these are behaviors the client wants to continue or to change. For example, the counselor may state,

"Leslie, you have been dissatisfied with not being able to teach advanced classes but have not said anything when those were assigned to others. You indicated that your mother taught you to play along and that women don't make a fuss. You could choose to be more assertive, which may change the assignments you get. Is this something you would like to change?" The counselor may also explore how Joe's Hispanic background and values have contributed to the role he expects his wife to play. The counselor could help Leslie examine how her culture and her husband's culture have interacted to help create the conflicts she has experienced in her marriage.

Using the spheres diagram (Figure 5.2), the counselor could help Leslie examine how her gender has influenced her own and others' expectations of her and the roles that she has been taught she should play. The counselor may then help her examine how her family and the values that they have conveyed have influenced her career decisions. The counselor could ask Leslie to identify her cultural heritage and help her understand how her culture has influenced her behavior. The counselor may say, "Leslie, you indicated that you are White. Tell me what ethnic group your family identifies most with. Let's look at how that culture may have influenced you." Finally, the counselor may help Leslie examine how the majority culture has affected her, both in giving her privileges as a White woman and in restricting her options due to sexism.

Norman's counselor might also use Figure 5.2 to help Norman think about the role that racism may have played in his options to this point. She might ask him to consider the messages his family has given him about being an African American man in the United States and how racial differences may have influenced the interactions with his teacher and supervisor. She would also explore the messages he received from his family about working and about how he feels about working in a predominantly White environment.

Step 4: Setting Culturally Appropriate Processes and Goals

The counselor works with the client to establish the goals that the client wants to achieve in counseling. Leslie may choose to decide whether to leave teaching or not. In addition, she may want to gain further clarity on how she has accepted messages from her family about being indecisive and overly emotional and how cultural values have influenced her marriage. Norman might decide to switch to a college track in high school or continue to seek an apprenticeship. His goal may also include how to negotiate differences with his supervisor and teacher.

Step 5: Implementing Culturally Appropriate Interventions

In Step 5, the counselor incorporates the assessments that clients have taken, as well as implementing additional interventions that appear appropriate for the goals that clients have set for counseling. For example, Leslie's first goal is to make a decision about whether to stay in the teaching profession or choose another career. Norman's is whether to stay on a vocational track or change his high school classes to prepare to go to college.

The counselor first incorporates the results of the Strong Interest Inventory in counseling. In Norman's case, the counselor wants him to consider a wide variety of occupations, including those that may require more education. She wants to ensure he does not prematurely foreclose options due to racism. Norman's counselor also may advocate within the school system to help him switch to a more college-preparatory program and help him build the skills to do well in these classes.

Clients often restrict their options to gender-stereotypic occupations; Leslie's counselor may help her examine her interest areas other than the female-traditional ones. For example, Leslie's counselor could help her explore interests in the Investigative and Conventional areas, examining the General Occupational Themes and Basic Interest Scales. Thus, the counselor asks her to discuss her interests in Math and Science, as well as in data management and processing. The counselor could also ask Leslie to discuss the occupations in the Investigative and Conventional areas. Leslie may, however, prefer to accommodate her husband's wish that she not seek further schooling; this will limit her options to those careers that she could enter with a bachelor's degree in secondary math education. Interestingly, her Skills Confidence Inventory indicates that she is quite confident about her skills in the nontraditional Investigative areas; her counselor may want to explore this further with her.

Leslie's Minnesota Importance Questionnaire indicates that her highest values are consistent with her cultural expectations: Achievement, Ability Utilization, Moral Values, and Social Service are her highest needs. The counselor could help Leslie examine which of those values are important for her to feel rewarded in an occupation and how she interprets those needs. For example, the counselor may say, "Your highest need is Achievement. Tell me what that means for you, when you feel that you have accomplished something."

Hartung et al. (1998) suggested that many of the assessment tools that Leslie completed may be used within a cultural framework, advocating the use of a qualitative approach. For example, the counselor may examine the items or scales in the Adult Career Concerns Inventory from a cultural perspective within the interview. Thus, the counselor may ask Leslie to discuss her concerns on implementing a career within the context of the cultural differences in her marriage.

Additional interventions that the counselor may employ include the 42-item Career Checklist (Ward & Bingham, 1993). Leslie identifies the issues that influence her career decision making, such as familial obligations; understanding of her abilities, interests, and needs; confidence; knowledge of the world of work; personal or sociopolitical obstacles; decision-making confidence; view of the relationship between education and work; ability to dream; and belief that personal parameters affect career choice. The Career Checklist may help Leslie clarify barriers and obstacles to achieving her goals.

If Leslie's counseling goals include examining the role that culture plays in her decision making and in her marriage, the counselor may invite Joe to be part of career counseling. The counselor may use fantasy exercises to help Leslie identify how she would like to shape her career. The counselor could ask Leslie to find role models who are women in nontraditional occupations to help her explore how such an option would fit in her life. Additional strategies include the use of genograms to help Leslie examine how her family has defined appropriate careers for men and women. Finally, the counselor may ask Leslie to examine the role that culture may play in her decision to leave teaching: "How comfortable are you with teaching a racially diverse student group? Could your decision be related to the different races of your students or of other faculty? Could your decision to leave be due to sexist policies or behavior on the part of your principal?" If so, these issues may be a result of a lack of racial understanding or lack of knowledge of various racial/ethnic groups' cultural values and behavior, and they could be addressed in counseling.

Step 6: Decision Making and Step 7: Implementation

Following the interventions, the counselor helps clients make a decision relative to their goals and then helps them formulate a plan to implement it. For example, Leslie may decide to confront Joe and her family about their expectations that she behave in sex-appropriate ways. Leslie's counselor could help her formulate specific steps to implement her decision; the counselor might help Leslie to work on assertiveness skills, role-playing a confrontation. Her counselor would help her to identify some specific goals she wants as a result of the confrontation, such as more equitable sharing of household tasks or support for a decision to go to graduate school. Norman's counselor may help him make a decision to talk to the teacher and decide to pursue a different educational track.

Additional Cases

CASE 1: JUSTINO

Justino is a 37-year-old single man from Puerto Rico. He has lived in Atlanta, Georgia, for the past 6 years, while he was a pilot for a major commercial airline. He is seeking career counseling because he has just learned his job was eliminated when his company merged with another airline. Justino graduated from a college in Puerto Rico with a bachelor's degree in airway sciences and received his commercial pilot's license after graduation. He worked for a small commuter airline in Florida for several years after college and then felt very fortunate to get a position with a major airline. His primary routes were in the United States, though he occasionally was able to fly to Europe and Puerto Rico. He loved his work, loved the prestige of being a pilot, and enjoyed the considerable salary he earned. He states several times that his family is very proud of him because of the prestige associated with being a pilot.

Justino is the oldest son of four children. His father worked as an engineer for the government in Puerto Rico. His mother stayed home until her youngest child went to school and then became a real estate agent. His family lives in San Juan, near many of Justino's aunts and uncles and cousins and grandparents. Several of Justino's cousins work in the United States, as does one brother and sister. The family accept that there are more opportunities for their children in the United States, but they expect weekly communication and frequent visits. Justino has gone home often, since his airline flew to San Juan. He was expected to be at his parents for every major holiday and family event, and he enjoyed his ability to travel and his position in the family as the eldest son.

The news that he would be laid off is devastating to him. He knew that the merger of the two airlines would result in some job losses, but thought he had enough seniority to remain employed. The job outlook for pilots in commercial airlines is not very good, and he does not want to take the pay cut to go back to work for a commuter airline. He has wanted to be a pilot since he was a small child and has never thought of doing something else. He is ashamed of losing his job, worried that his family will see him as a failure and that he will bring disgrace to them.

Questions for Discussion

1. What is the first thing you would focus on as the counselor?

2. What role may Justino's ethnic identity play in his decisions?

3. What cultural values may his family have transmitted to Justino?

4. What cultural variables would you want to incorporate in career counseling?

5. What are some possible career interventions you could use?

6. What cultural strengths could you emphasize in working with Justino?

CASE 2: LIAN

Lian is a 27-year-old woman from Taiwan. She has come to the United States for graduate school in psychology in the southern part of the United States. She graduated from National Taiwan University, one of the most prestigious, and most competitive, universities in Taiwan. She did very well in her undergraduate work and was strongly encouraged by her mentors to come to the United States for graduate work. She is nearing completion of her PhD in psychology and is seeking career counseling because she does not know if she should return to Taiwan or seek a university position in the United States.

Lian is the middle of three children. Her father is an accountant, and her mother helps take care of Lian's grandmother. Lian's older brother, Tai, is also studying in the United States and is nearing completion of a medical degree. He has at least 3 more years of medical training before he finishes. Her younger brother, Wei, will start an engineering graduate program in California in the fall. Lian's parents are very proud of their children, but they feel that it is time for their daughter to come home. Her mother needs help taking care of Lian's grandmother; her father has been recently diagnosed with diabetes and also needs more care.

Lian has done very well in her graduate work in experimental social psychology. She has been part of a very productive research team and has published several articles with her major professor. This past year, she helped him write a federal grant, and it included a postdoctoral fellowship. He has just offered it to her, providing her an opportunity to stay in the United States at least another year. The fellowship would also provide her the opportunity to conduct a systematic search for a university position. Lian is struggling with whether to take the fellowship or return home. She knows her mother needs her help, and it is her obligation as a daughter to go back to Taiwan. However, she enjoys her work very much, believes she is on the track to pursue an academic career in the United States, and knows she would not have the same opportunities in Taiwan. She also does not want to disappoint her adviser, who has helped her a lot. She has not talked to him about her dilemma, feeling guilty for not accepting the fellowship immediately.

Questions for Discussion

1. What is the first thing you would focus on as the counselor?

2. What role may Lian's ethnic identity play in her decisions?

3. What cultural values may her family have transmitted to Lian?

4. What cultural variables would you want to incorporate in career counseling?

5. What are some possible career interventions you could use?

6. What cultural strengths could you emphasize in working with Lian?

CASE 3: MONICA

Monica is a 27-year-old woman who is of Native American and African American descent. She is seeking career counseling because she has lost her government subsidy and must enter the workforce. Monica is the mother of three children, ages 10, 8, and 6. The oldest child is the daughter of a White man; the younger two are children of a relationship Monica had with an African American man who also accepted her first child as his own. The latter relationship has ended. Though the children continue to see their father, his contribution to the household income must be supplemented to support Monica and her three children.

Monica's parents are both biracial. Her mother is half Cherokee and half African American and identifies primarily with her Cherokee heritage. She volunteers at a local museum devoted to Native American history and culture. Her father is half Sioux and half African American; his primary identification is with the African American community, where he is a community police officer. Monica grew up in a middle-class, racially mixed neighborhood, the younger of two children. Her sister, who is 5 years older, is employed as a day care worker, which enables her also to care for her own children. Monica's sister is married to an African American man, who owns his own plumbing company.

Monica did not finish high school, since she dropped out when she was pregnant with her first child. Although her high school had day care available and her counselor encouraged her to complete her high school degree, Monica wanted to concentrate on her baby and on her boyfriend. However, shortly after the child was born, the baby's father left town, and Monica has not seen him since. She went on public aid after he left. She was too depressed to find a job and then began her relationship with Rick. Her government subsidy continued. Rick helped support her and her daughter, and the two additional children that they had together, until their relationship ended. Monica's primary support system consists of her family and friends in her apartment building, most of whom are African American, though feels no particular identification with either the Native American or African American community.

Monica learned last fall that her government subsidy was going to be eliminated this month. She did not know what to do, since she had no skills, no degree, and no job history. Her family encouraged her to seek career counseling some time ago, but she was embarrassed at her lack of skills and did nothing until she learned her last check would come next week.

Questions For Discussion

1. What is the first thing you would focus on as the counselor?

2. What role may Monica's biracial status and her ethnic identity play in her decisions?

(Continued)

(Continued)

3. What cultural values may her family have transmitted to Monica?

4. What cultural variables would you want to incorporate in career counseling?

5. What are some possible career interventions you could use?

6. What cultural strengths could you emphasize in working with Monica?

Box 5.3

Summary of Key Constructs

Construct	Definition
Traditional versus culturally centered career counseling	Traditional career counseling tends to focus on the individual, be linear, assume independent decision making, assume equal opportunity, and assume that work is central in people's lives. Culturally centered career counseling tends to acknowledge the role of the family in decision making, barriers due to discrimination, and that work may play a smaller role relative to other roles in clients' lives.
Leong and Hartung's (1997) integrative sequential model	This five-stage model of career interventions begins with recognition of a problem and ends with the outcome of the client returning to the community.
Leung's (1995) career interventions	Career interventions may be classified as individual, group, or systemic. They focus on outcomes, including educational outcomes.
Culturally appropriate career counseling model (Fouad & Bingham, 1995)	This five-step model of career counseling explicitly incorporates culture in every step.

References

American Psychological Association. (2003). Guidelines on multicultural education, training, research, practice, and organizational change for psychologists. *American Psychologist, 58,* 377–402.

Arbona, C. (1996). Career theory and practice in a multicultural context. In M. L. Savickas & W. B. Walsh (Eds.), *Handbook of career counseling theory and practice* (pp. 45–54). Palo Alto, CA: Davies-Black.

Bingham, R. P., & Ward, C. M. (1994). Career counseling with ethnic minority women. In W. B. Walsh & S. Osipow (Eds.), *Career counseling with women* (pp. 165–195). Hillsdale, NJ: Lawrence Erlbaum.

Blustein, D. L. (2006). *Psychology of working: A new perspective on career development, counseling, and public policy.* Mahwah, NJ: Lawrence Erlbaum.

Bowman, S. L. (1993). Career intervention strategies for ethnic minorities. *Career Development Quarterly, 41,* 14–25.

Bureau of Labor Statistics. (2006). *Labor force statistics from the Current Population Survey.* Table 11: Employed persons by detailed occupation, sex, race, and Hispanic or Latino ethnicity. Retrieved April 21, 2008, from http://www.bls.gov/cps/home.htm#data

Byars-Winston, A., & Fouad, N. A. (2006). Metacognitions and multicultural competence: Expanding the culturally appropriate career counseling model. *Career Development Quarterly,* pp. 187–201.

Carter, R. T., Scales, J. E., Juby, H. L., Collins, N. M., & Wan, C. M. (2003). Seeking career services on campus: Racial differences in referral, process, and outcome. *Journal of Career Assessment, 11,* 393–404.

Fitzgerald, L. F., & Betz, N. E. (1994). Career development in cultural context: The role of gender, race, class, and sexual orientation. In M. L. Savickas & R. W. Lent (Eds.), *Convergence in career development theories: Implications for science and practice* (pp. 103–117). Palo Alto, CA: Consulting Psychologists Press.

Flores, L. Y., & Heppner, M. J. (2002). Multicultural career counseling: Ten essentials for training. *Journal of Career Development, 28*(3), 181–202.

Fouad, N. A., & Bingham, R. (1995). Career counseling with racial/ethnic minorities. In W. B. Walsh & S. H. Osipow (Eds.), *Handbook of vocational psychology* (2nd ed., pp. 331–366). Hillsdale, NJ: Lawrence Erlbaum.

Fouad, N. A., & Byars-Winston, A. M. (2005). Cultural context of career choice: Meta-analysis of race/ethnicity differences. *Career Development Quarterly, 53,* 223–233.

Fouad, N. A., Kantamneni, N., Smothers, M. K., Chen, Y. L., Fitzpatrick, M. E., Guillen, A., et al. (2008). Asian American career development: A qualitative analysis. *Journal of Vocational Behavior, 72,* 43–59.

Giordano, J., & McGoldrick, M. (1996). European families: An overview. In M. McGoldrick, J. Giordano, & J. K. Pearce (Eds.), *Ethnicity and family therapy* (pp. 427–441). New York: Guilford.

Gysbers, N. C., Heppner, M. J., & Johnston, J. A. (2003). *Career counseling: Process, issues, and techniques* (2nd ed.). Needham Heights, MA: Allyn & Bacon.

Hartung, P. J., Vandiver, B. J., Leong, F. T. L., Pope, M., Niles, S. G., & Farrow, B. (1998). Appraising cultural identity in career development assessment and counseling. *Career Development Quarterly, 46,* 276–293.

Heppner, M. J., & Heppner, P. P. (2003). Identifying process variables in career counseling: A research agenda. *Journal of Vocational Behavior, 62,* 429–452.

Hobbs, F., Stoops, N., & U.S. Census Bureau. (2002). *Census 2000 special reports: Demographic trends in the 20th century* (CENSR-4). Washington, DC: U.S. Government Printing Office. Retrieved April 21, 2008, from http://www.census.gov/prod/2002pubs/censr-4.pdf

Ihle, K. H., Fouad, N. A., Gibson, P., Henry, C., Harris-Hodge, E., Jandrisevits, M., et al. (2005). The impact of cultural variables on vocational psychology:

Examination of the Fouad and Bingham (1995) culturally appropriate career counseling model. In R. T. Carter (Eds.), *Handbook of racial/cultural psychology* (pp. 262–285). New York: Wiley.

Katz, J. H. (1985). The sociopolitical nature of counseling. *The Counseling Psychologist, 13,* 615–624.

Leong, F. T. L., & Hartung, P. J. (1997). Career assessment with culturally different clients: Proposing an integrative-sequential conceptual framework for cross-cultural career counseling research and practice. *Journal of Career Assessment, 5,* 183–201.

Leung, S. A. (1995). Career development and counseling: A multicultural perspective. In J. G. Ponterotto, J. M. Casas, L. A. Suzuki, & C. M. Alexander (Eds.), *Handbook of multicultural counseling* (pp. 549–566). Thousand Oaks, CA: Sage.

National Career Development Association (NCDA). (2000). *Career connecting in a changing context: A summary of the key findings of the 1999 National Survey of Working America.* Retrieved April 20, 2008, from http://www.ncda.org/pdf/gallupwhitepaper.pdf

National Career Development Association (NCDA). (2007). *Code of ethics.* Retrieved April 21, 2008, from http://www.ncda.org/pdf/code_of_ethicsmay-2007.pdf

National Center for Education Statistics. (2006). *Enrollment by sex, race and ethnicity.* Table 192. Retrieved April 21, 2008, from http://nces.ed.gov/quicktables/result.asp?SrchKeyword=enrollment+by+race&topic=Postsecondary&Year=2006

Subich, L. M. (2005). Career assessment with culturally diverse individuals. In W. B. Walsh & M. L. Savickas (Eds.), *Handbook of vocational psychology: Theory, research, and practice* (3rd ed., pp. 397–421). Mahwah, NJ: Lawrence Erlbaum.

Sue, D. W., Carter, R. T., Casas, J. M., Fouad, N. A., Ivey, A. E., Jensen, M., et al. (1998). *Multicultural counseling competencies: Individual, professional and organizational development.* Thousand Oaks, CA: Sage.

Sue, D. W., & Sue, D. (2007). *Counseling the culturally diverse: Theory and practice* (5th ed.). New York: Wiley.

U.S. Census Bureau. (2006). *American community survey.* Table B02001. Retrieved April 21, 2008, from http://factfinder.census.gov/servlet/DTSubjectShowTablesServlet?_lang=en&_ts=239807025436

U.S. Department of Health and Human Services. (2000/2001). *Mental health: Culture, race and ethnicity (A supplement to mental health: A report of the surgeon general).* Rockville, MD: U.S. Department of Health and Human Services, Public Health Office, Office of the Surgeon General. Retrieved September 17, 2008, from http://www.surgeongeneral.gov/library/mentalhealth/cre/

Ward, C. M., & Bingham, R. P. (1993). Career assessment of ethnic minority women. *Journal of Career Assessment, 1,* 246–257.

Worthington, R. L., Flores, L. Y., & Navarro, R. L. (2005). Career development in context: Research with people of color. In S. D. Brown & R. W. Lent (Eds.), *Career development and counseling: Putting theory and research to work* (pp. 225–252). New York: Wiley.

Additional Readings

Adams, E. M., Cahill, B. J., & Ackerlind, S. J. (2005). A qualitative study of Latino lesbian and gay youths' experiences with discrimination and the career development process. *Journal of Vocational Behavior, 66,* 199–218.

Chung, Y. B., & Harmon, L. W. (1999). Assessment of perceived occupational opportunity for Black Americans. *Journal of Career Assessment, 7,* 45–62.

Cook, E. P., Heppner, M. J., & O'Brien, K. M. (2002). Career development of women of color and White women: Assumptions, conceptualization, and interventions from an ecological perspective. *Career Development Quarterly, 50,* 291–305.

Gomez, M. J., Fassinger, R. E., Prosser, J., Cooke, K., Mejia, B., & Luna, J. (2001). *Voces abriendo caminos* [Voices forging paths]: A qualitative study of the career development of notable Latinas. *Journal of Counseling Psychology, 48,* 286–300.

Juntunen, C. L., Barraclough, D. J., Broneck, C. L., Seibel, G. A., Winrow, S. A., & Morin, P. M. (2001). American Indian perspectives on the career journey. *Journal of Counseling Psychology, 48,* 274–285.

Richie, B. S., Fassinger, R. E., Linn, S. G., Johnson, J., Prosser, J., & Robinson, S. (1997). Persistence, connection, and passion: A qualitative study of the career development of highly achieving African American Black and White women. *Journal of Counseling Psychology, 44,* 133–148.

Walsh, W. B., & Heppner, M. J. (Eds.). (2006). *Handbook of career counseling for women* (2nd ed.). Mahwah, NJ: Lawrence Erlbaum.

Holland's Theory of Vocational Personalities and Work Environments

6

Theories of person-environment fit, such as Holland's theory (Holland, 1997) and the theory of work adjustment (Dawis, 2005; Dawis & Lofquist, 1984), are considered evolutionary extensions of earlier trait-and-factor counseling (Chartrand, 1991; Rounds & Tracey, 1990), which, in turn, had its roots in a social reform movement at the turn of the 20th century (Parsons, 1909/1989). Person-environment psychology is grounded in the basic assumption that a reciprocal relationship exists between people and their environments; that is, people influence their environments, and environments influence people (Walsh, Price, & Craik, 1992). Perhaps nowhere has this fundamental idea been more thoroughly implemented than in the realm of vocational psychology; in fact, the history of vocational psychology as a scholarly field is intimately intertwined with the evolution of person-environment models applied to career behavior (Swanson & Chu, 2000).

Holland's theory of person-environment fit has been an influential force in vocational psychology since its introduction over four decades ago. Part of the theory's appeal is due to the simple and intuitively meaningful premises on which it is based. Holland (1997) described his theory as answering three fundamental questions. First, what characteristics of persons and environments lead to positive vocational outcomes (such as satisfying career decisions), and what characteristics of persons and environments lead to negative vocational outcomes (such as indecision or dissatisfying decisions)? Second, what characteristics of persons and environments lead to career stability or change over the life span? Third, what are the most effective ways of providing assistance to people with career concerns?

Holland's theory is based on the underlying premise that career choice is an expression of one's personality and, thus, that members of an occupation have similar personalities and similar histories. He described four working assumptions of his theory. First, most individuals can be described in terms of their resemblance to six personality types—realistic, investigative, artistic, social, enterprising, or conventional. These types are perhaps best considered as model or theoretical types that describe an individual or with which an individual may be compared. Each personality type has a characteristic set of attitudes and skills to use in response to problems encountered in the environment, and each encompasses preferences for vocational and leisure activities, life goals and values, beliefs about oneself, and problem-solving style (see Table 6.1). An individual is rarely a single "pure" type; rather, individuals are more likely to be a combination of several types, with one type that is dominant and other types that are secondary.

Table 6.1   Characteristics of Holland's Personality and Environmental Types

Type	Self-Concept and Values	Potential Competencies	Typical Work Activities and Environments
Realistic	Emotionally stable, reliable Practical, thrifty, persistent Shy, modest Uncomfortable talking about self Traditional values	Mechanical ability and ingenuity Problem solving with tools, machines Psychomotor skills Physical strength	Job with tangible results Operating heavy equipment Using tools Physical demands Fixing, building, repairing
Investigative	Independent, self-motivated Reserved, introspective Analytical, curious Task oriented Original, creative, nonconforming	Scientific ability Analytical skills Mathematical skills Writing skills Perseverance	Ambiguous or abstract tasks Solving problems through thinking Working independently Scientific or laboratory settings Collecting and organizing data

Type	Self-Concept and Values	Potential Competencies	Typical Work Activities and Environments
Artistic	Independent, nonconforming Self-expressive Intuitive, sensitive, emotional Impulsive Drawn to aesthetic qualities	Creativity, imagination Verbal-linguistic skills Musical ability Artistic ability	Creating artwork or performing Working independently Unstructured, flexible environments that allow self-expression
Social	Humanistic, idealistic, ethical Concerned for welfare of others Tactful, cooperative, generous Kind, friendly, cheerful Understanding, insightful	Social and interpersonal skills Verbal ability Teaching skills Ability to empathize with and understand others	Teaching, explaining, guiding Solving problems, leading discussions Educational, social service, and mental health organizations
Enterprising	Status conscious Ambitious, competitive Sociable, talkative Optimistic, energetic, popular Aggressive, adventuresome	Verbal skills related to speaking, persuading, selling Leadership skills Resilience, high energy, optimism Social and interpersonal skills	Selling, purchasing, leading Managing people and projects Giving speeches and presentations Financial, government, and political organizations
Conventional	Conscientious, persevering Practical, conservative Orderly, systematic, precise, accurate Careful, controlled	Efficiency, organization Management of systems and data Mathematical skills Attention to detail, perfectionism Operation of office machines	Organizing office procedures Keeping records and filing systems Writing reports, making charts Structured organizations with well-ordered chains of command

SOURCE: Adapted from Harmon, Hansen, Borgen, and Hammer (2005); Holland (1997); Sharf (1997).

Types develop as a "product of a characteristic interaction among a variety of cultural and personal forces including peers, biological heredity, parents, social class, culture, and the physical environment" (Holland, 1997, p. 2). These experiences lead to an individual's preference for some activities over others; the preferences then develop into strong interests, which lead to related competencies. An individual's interests in conjunction with his or her competencies form a specific "disposition" that allows the individual to "think, perceive, and act in special ways" (p. 2).

The second assumption in Holland's theory is that environments can be categorized as one of six model types—again realistic, investigative, artistic, social, enterprising, or conventional. The environment's type is determined by the dominant type of the individuals who compose that environment. Because different types of people have varying constellations of skills, abilities, and so on, they prefer to surround themselves with other people who are similar to them: "Where people congregate, they create an environment that reflects the types they most resemble" (Holland, 1997, p. 3). Each environment has a characteristic set of problems and opportunities, as well as requiring differing activities and competencies and offering different rewards (see Table 6.1).

The third assumption of Holland's theory is the heart of the person-environment fit theories—namely, that "people search for environments that will let them exercise their skills and abilities, express their attitudes and values, and take on agreeable problems and roles" (Holland, 1997, p. 4). In a reciprocal manner, environments also search for people, through activities such as social interactions and recruitment and selection practices.

Fourth, personality and environment interact to produce behavior. Knowing an individual's personality type and the type of his or her environment allows us to make predictions about a range of possible outcomes, such as vocational choice, job tenure and turnover, achievement, and satisfaction. Theories of person-environment fit require some mechanism to describe the degree of fit. The mechanism in Holland's theory is the six types, which can be used to describe either persons or environments, thus allowing a description of how individuals match with their environments.

In addition to the four working assumptions, Holland proposed secondary assumptions that outline specific and predictable ways in which the types are interrelated. The first is usually referred to as *calculus:* The six types are arranged in a hexagonal structure, with the distance between types inversely proportional to their theoretical interrelations (see Figure 6.1). That is, types adjacent to one another share more in common than the types that are opposing in the hexagon; for example, realistic types are more like investigative types than they are like social types.

Furthermore, Holland postulated four constructs to describe the relationships between types within people or environments and between

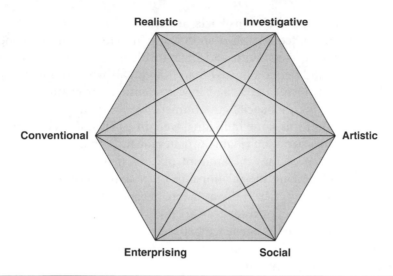

Figure 6.1 Holland's Hexagonal Structure

SOURCE: Holland (1997). Reproduced by special permission of the publisher, Psychological Assessment Resources, Inc., from *Making Vocational Choices*, 3rd ed., © 1973, 1985, 1992, 1997, by Psychological Assessment Resources, Inc. All rights reserved.

people and environments: congruence, differentiation, consistency, and identity. The concept of *congruence* occupies a central role in Holland's theory. Congruence refers to the match between a person and his or her environment in terms of the six types specified by the theory. An enterprising individual working in an enterprising environment is considered highly congruent as compared with the same individual working within an investigative environment. Congruence is hypothesized to be related to important outcomes, such as job satisfaction and job tenure. As Holland (1997) described it, "Persons in congruent environments are encouraged to express their favorite behavior repertoires in familiar and congenial settings. In contrast, persons in incongruent environments find that they have behavior repertoires that are out of place and unappreciated" (p. 56).

Differentiation pertains to the degree of definition of an individual's interests; interests are considered well differentiated when there is a clear distinction between what an individual likes and dislikes. *Consistency* is a reflection of the "internal coherence" (Spokane, 1996) of an individual's interests in terms of the hexagonal arrangement; an individual with artistic and investigative interests would be considered to be more consistent than an individual with artistic and conventional interests. *Identity* provides "an estimate of the clarity and stability" (Holland, 1997, p. 5) of a person's identity or goals, interests, and talents. Like other constructs in Holland's theory, differentiation, consistency, and identity are used to describe both individuals and environments. Thus, environments as well as people may be characterized by their level of differentiation, consistency, and identity.

These four additional constructs are useful for making predictions about vocational outcomes. More specifically, individuals who are congruent, differentiated, consistent, and high in identity are predicted to be more satisfied and better adjusted than individuals who are incongruent, undifferentiated, inconsistent, and low in identity. For example, a social individual working in a social environment would be happier and more productive than if this same individual were in a realistic environment.

The hexagonal structure (Figure 6.1) in Holland's theory thus has three functions. First, it defines the amount of consistency in an individual's interests by referencing the relationship of primary, secondary, and tertiary types to one another in the hexagon. Second, in a parallel fashion, it defines the amount of consistency in an environment. Finally, the hexagon defines the amount of congruence between an individual and his or her environment by providing comparisons of the distance between an individual's type and the environment's type.

John Holland was awarded the APA Distinguished Professional Contributions Award in 1996, and his address (Holland, 1996a) focused on the strengths of his theory, as well as areas that still needed further research. One area he identified as needing further investigation was the lack of explanatory power of the construct of congruence. As noted earlier, the greater the fit between work personality and environment, the greater the job satisfaction. However, research has shown the relationship to be relatively small (Spokane & Cruza-Guet, 2005). Gottfredson (1999) points out the strengths of Holland's career and theory, including the practical utility of the theory for counselors. Betz (2008) notes that Holland's theory was among the most widely researched and supported in vocational psychology and has been incorporated in many career assessment instruments, programs, and interventions, including the major governmental occupational information system (O*Net).

Box 6.1

Personal Reflection

What were my aspirations at ages 12, 15, 18, and 23? Are there consistent patterns of interests across these daydreams?

Applying Holland's Theory

CONCEPTUALIZING LESLIE'S CAREER HISTORY

Leslie's history suggests a stable personality type of investigative and social; she pursued activities in these domains even in childhood. For example, as a child she "played school" with her sister, and in high school she enjoyed her math and science courses and became a math tutor. She has enjoyed working with others through these early activities, as well as through her current hobbies of teaching swimming and teaching Sunday school. Her conventional tertiary code is reflected in her enjoyment of tasks that require attention to detail and developing systems for managing information. For example, she particularly enjoys organizing her lesson plans and keeping track of her students' progress in her current teaching job, and she chose to be membership coordinator in her volunteer work at the local science center.

It is useful to consider whether Leslie's lack of interest in realistic, enterprising, and artistic activities is because she avoided these areas or because she did not have the opportunities to develop interests in these areas. Holland (1997) suggests that "to some degree, types produce types" (p. 17), primarily because parents engage in activities related to their own types, creating circumstances through which children may develop interests. Leslie's father is a corporate attorney, suggesting that he is an enterprising type, which may have led to his encouraging Leslie to pursue a business career. Her father also may have some interest in investigative activities, as evidenced by his bachelor's degree in chemistry and his work in patents and product liability. Leslie's father, then, ostensibly served as a role model of both enterprising and investigative interests, yet she developed interest in the latter but not the former.

Leslie's mother is an administrative assistant at a small business, which would typically be considered a conventional- or enterprising-type occupation. However, this occupation may not be an accurate reflection of her type, because it may have been a choice of convenience rather than an expression of her personality. Moreover, since her job is at an interior design firm, the environment actually may have strong artistic elements, which would be consistent with her involvement in artistic volunteer activities, such as being an art museum docent and being active on the symphony board. As with her father, Leslie's mother may have served as a role model for artistic and conventional interests, and Leslie developed interests in one area (conventional) yet not the other (artistic). It would seem, then, that Leslie grew up in an environment in which she was exposed to artistic, enterprising, investigative, and conventional activities. Her brother also developed investigative interests, expressed in his choice of engineering as an occupation, and her sister pursued social and investigative interests in becoming a nurse.

Leslie entered college undecided about her major. She knew that she enjoyed taking advanced math classes and that she had been frustrated by the lack of challenge in those investigative areas in the community college she first attended. Her strategy when she first went to college seemed to be to explore many areas, although most of the options she explored were in the investigative area: engineering, medicine, psychology, and mathematics. There is little information about her social interests in college, either in the coursework she enjoyed or in any outside activities in which she engaged during those years. These two sets of interests—social and investigative—are not wholly consistent in that they are not adjacent to one another on Holland's hexagon. As is true of many individuals with inconsistent interests, Leslie's difficulty with career decision making may have been due to the apparent incompatibility of her investigative and social interests. Leslie's solution was to choose math education, which reflected both types of interests.

The other focal point of Leslie's history from Holland's perspective is evaluation of the environments in which she has been. While she was growing up, her primary environments were her family and various educational settings. Her family represented a heterogeneous environment, with artistic and enterprising elements, as well as investigative and conventional characteristics. Her educational environments were most likely characterized as investigative, particularly in her choice of the more specialized environment that a college math major represented.

CONCEPTUALIZING LESLIE'S PRESENT SITUATION

Using Holland's theory to understand Leslie's current career dilemma focuses attention on both her characteristics and the features of her environment. First, Leslie's personality type of investigative-social-conventional (ISC) can be further examined in terms of the constructs of Holland's theory. Her Strong Interest Inventory (SII) profile is well differentiated, with the investigative interests representing a high peak in her profile and the artistic interests representing a clear low point. Leslie's three highest scores (I, S, and C) are also differentiated from each other, with I clearly higher than S or C. In terms of Holland's hexagonal arrangement of types, Leslie's investigative, social, and conventional interests represent an inconsistent pattern—that is, interests that are not adjacent to one another on the hexagon. Finally, Leslie's vocational identity is fairly clear and stable: She knows where her interests lie, even though they may feel contradictory, and she has maintained these fundamental interests since high school.

An analysis of Leslie's current work environment reveals some important information. In general, high school teachers are likely to be predominantly social types; however, math teachers (conventional-investigative-realistic) and science teachers (investigative-realistic-social) are the colleagues with whom Leslie spends most of her workday. Moreover, her principal is likely to be characterized by social and enterprising interests. From the perspective of person-environment fit, math and science teachers may generally perceive some incongruence in their work environment within a typical high school setting. The particular school in which Leslie works may be characterized as fairly heterogeneous and undifferentiated, because nearly all Holland personality types are represented to varying degrees.

An important question from the perspective of Holland's theory is how much congruence exists between Leslie and her work environment. Leslie's type of investigative-social-conventional would seem to be congruent with the social nature of the high school environment, yet the more immediate environment of her math teacher colleagues presents a more incongruent environment. Furthermore, Leslie may feel somewhere in between the math teachers and the other teachers: She has more social interests than the math teachers yet more investigative interests than the other teachers, and she may feel that she does not really fit with either group. Thus, she may feel unappreciated in her environment.

An additional issue is whether Leslie's current dissatisfaction is related to a shift in her interests in terms of either absolute or relative strength. That is, she may have increased her interest in social activities relative to her investigative activities, or she may simply want more expression of long-standing social interests.

Questions for Discussion

1. What specific hypotheses would you develop about Leslie from Holland's theoretical perspective? How does using Holland's theory help you understand Leslie? How might it help Leslie understand herself?

2. How might the inconsistency in Leslie's typology have had an influence on her career decision making in the past? How might it be affecting her current career decision making?

3. What possible reasons might there be for Leslie's having similar areas of interest to some areas of her mother's and father's interests but not others? What type of influence or encouragement might they have provided her in these areas?

4. How could Leslie find expression for her diverse interests?

5. How might it be helpful for Leslie to conceptualize her current work environment in terms of person-environment congruence? From what does her dissatisfaction stem?

6. What other factors in Leslie's work situation, in addition to congruence, might be related to her dissatisfaction?

7. Leslie can be viewed as existing within multiple environments, such as with her husband, family of origin, and social and leisure activities. To what extent is she congruent with each of these environments? How might this congruence contribute to her overall satisfaction?

8. What types of occupations might offer a more congruent environment for Leslie?

9. What factors in Leslie's life are encouraging her to change occupational directions? What factors are discouraging her from doing so?

THE CASE OF JUDY

Judy (a 38-year-old Caucasian woman) was a successful attorney who recently became a partner in a medium-sized firm in Denver. Without warning, she tendered her resignation. She sought counseling for depression. She had quit because she was not enjoying her work; she resented the demands made by other partners, as well as the inordinately long hours. Her therapist suggested she also seek career counseling.

Judy finished her baccalaureate degree in psychology at a small midwestern liberal arts college. She had decided on psychology based on her interest in working with people, particularly children, and because her friends told her she was a good listener. She enjoyed her classes in psychology and volunteered at a crisis line during her sophomore year. She became a resident assistant her junior year and worked in the dorms for two years. She did well in college, and her adviser strongly encouraged her to apply to graduate programs in psychology. She considered doing so but was dating a young man who did not want her to pursue her doctorate.

She decided to become an attorney because her fiancé was in law school. She thought this would be a good way for them to be in the same geographic location, and she had some interest in the field of law. She was accepted into the same school and excelled. She was particularly interested in litigation, while her fiancé was interested in corporate law. She passed the bar exam on the first try, while her fiancé failed three times and finally chose another career. Their relationship ended. She was quite depressed about the termination of her engagement but decided to move to another city to work and, hopefully, to meet a new man.

Judy joined a law firm after law school and impressed the attorneys with her diligence and willingness to work extra hours. She soon became the associate that partners vied to have assigned to them. She worked hard and enjoyed some of the work she was assigned, though she also found some of it boring. The partners voted to make her partner a year earlier than she had expected. After Judy became a partner, she began to question her activities and values and, in general, became depressed. Although she had dated occasionally, she did not really have any time to devote to a relationship. She also did not have much time to make friends outside of the law firm, and she felt that her life was quite narrowly focused.

Questions for Discussion

1. How would you explain Judy's behavior from the perspective of Holland's theory? What specific hypotheses would you develop about Judy from Holland's theoretical perspective? How does using Holland's theory help you understand Judy? How might it help Judy understand herself?

2. What are Judy's interest themes?

3. How would you incorporate Judy's depression into career counseling through the perspective of Holland's theory?

4. How congruent has Judy been in her work as an attorney?

5. How would you evaluate Judy's person-environment fit in terms of her interests?

6. How do Judy's gender and race/ethnicity enter into her career decisions?

Directions and Implications
for Career Counseling

Holland's model has been extensively applied in career counseling, most notably in using the six-category typology to categorize individuals in the interpretation of interest inventories such as the Self-Directed Search (SDS) (Holland, Powell, & Fritzsche, 1994) or the SII (Harmon et al., 2005). In addition, Holland's typology has been used to classify occupational information, college majors, and so on in an attempt to facilitate the matching of individuals and environments.

Holland (1996b) attributed the enduring prominence of person-environment fit theories to their focus on two major questions in people's lives: At what kind of work will I be happy? Will I be able to perform the job well? These two questions are relevant to consider in working with both cases.

BOX 6.2

Counselor Cognitions

What is the client's interest type or combinations of types?

What is the client's pattern of congruence in his or her vocational environments?

How consistent are the client's interests?

How well differentiated are the client's interests?

How congruent are the client's occupational aspirations?

GOALS OF COUNSELING

From the perspective of Holland's theory, career interventions include using the typology to identify a client's typical mode of interacting with the world of work and using the constructs of differentiation, consistency, and congruence to predict the difficulty of the decision-making process. The typology provides a framework for clients to conceptualize their own vocational personalities and see how they may best fit with the world of work. Counseling is intended to "create self understanding and stimulate more insightful and constructive planning" (Holland, 1997, p. 199).

As an initial step, the counselor would listen carefully to Leslie's or Judy's concerns to clarify how the client sees her current situation and why she sought counseling. Leslie is unhappy with how she is being treated by her principal, whose behavior might be due to a number of factors, such as poor job performance on her part or poor management style on his part. A goal of counseling with either Leslie or Judy might be to examine the degree to which her current environment is congruent with her characteristics and to examine other careers or jobs that might provide a better match. In addition, counseling with Leslie may focus on the inconsistency of her investigative and social interests and the possible shifting of her primary interests in the social and investigative areas. Counseling with Judy may focus on whether law is a congruent choice for her and whether other options might be more congruent.

INTERVENTIONS

Knowing a client's type, in terms of Holland's theory, allows the counselor to make predictions about the manner in which counseling will proceed, such as the amount of interaction the client will have with the counselor and the attitude with which the client will approach counseling. How will Leslie behave in counseling as an investigative-social-conventional type? As an investigative type, Leslie will likely be quite invested in the exploratory activities of career counseling. She will enjoy researching occupations, will ask many questions about the details of her assessment results (including how scores are derived), and will engage in "making sense" of her career history and current dissatisfaction. She is likely to be quite comfortable with following through with assignments between sessions and bringing back new information to discuss with the counselor in the next session. Her secondary social type suggests that Leslie is likely to be verbally and socially skilled, and she is likely to be engaged during counseling sessions. Her tertiary conventional type suggests that she will appreciate and work well within structure and will enjoy organizing information about careers. She may prefer the counselor to provide structure and direction within counseling and may feel frustrated if she perceives an insufficient amount of direction. The counselor can thus view Leslie's interest profile and typology as a predictor of her in-session behavior.

Typically, a primary intervention is assessment, both of the client and of his or her environment. A counselor working within Holland's framework would use some assessment tool to determine Judy's primary, secondary, and tertiary types. Identification of type then would guide further interventions. A counselor working within Holland's theory may have used some alternative assessments to those provided in Chapter 3. First, the counselor would be likely to administer the SDS (Holland et al., 1994) rather than the SII. One unique feature of the SDS is that it elicits a client's vocational daydreams, which then would be classified and coded according to Holland's theory and examined to determine the coherence of her career aspirations. Eliciting Judy's early vocational daydreams and aspirations may provide a rich source of information, particularly given the decisions around work and family she has made over the past several years. These aspirations could also be elicited in session and used in conjunction with the SII results.

Second, the counselor may use the Career Attitudes and Strategies Inventory (CASI) (Holland & Gottfredson, 1994) to evaluate a range of factors related to the client's current career. The CASI was designed to address adult career issues and includes scales measuring job satisfaction, work involvement, and family commitment. For example, the counselor may use the CASI to explore Judy's career situation and her reasons for quitting her position.

Third, the counselor would examine the pattern of types on the assessment tool. As evidenced by the General Occupational Themes of the SII, Leslie's primary type is clearly investigative. Leslie exhibits intellectual curiosity and likes scientific activities, and she tends to use abstract reasoning to solve problems. Her secondary type is social. She is interested in helping others, particularly through teaching, and she values her relationships with others. She uses interpersonal skills to solve problems, such as through discussion with others. Conventional types like structured environments and attend well to detail. She may perceive herself as conforming and preferring to follow established rules.

Interpretation of Leslie's SII profile focuses on determining her three-letter Holland code. Her General Occupational Themes indicate a code of investigative-social-conventional (ISC), which also is reflected in the Basic Interest Scales. However, examination of the SII Occupational Scales shows that most of her high scores are for investigative occupations, followed by occupations in the conventional area; she has relatively few high scores on social occupations. The three-letter code resulting from the Occupational Scales portion, determined by the frequency of scales in the "similar" range, is investigative-conventional-social (ICS). Following interpretation of the SII, Leslie may consult the *Occupations Finder* (Holland, 1994) or the *Dictionary of Holland Occupational Codes* (Gottfredson & Holland, 1996) to explore occupations with various combinations of her three-letter Holland code, beginning with ISC and ICS.

Leslie's primary code of investigative is infrequent for women, while social and conventional are frequent types for women. One avenue to explore with Leslie is the gender traditionality of her interests. How did her family's expectations shape her interests? How do her husband's expectations shape her interests? What effect did discouragement during college have on her nontraditional (investigative) interests? Would she describe her interests, and her Holland type, as accurately reflecting her authentic self? These questions introduce a gendered context to interpretation of Leslie's SII profile.

Examination of Leslie's Skills Confidence Inventory supports her three-letter code as evidenced on the SII. Leslie indicates a high degree of confidence and a correspondingly high degree of interest in the three areas of investigative, social, and conventional.

Another important focus of counseling is the degree of incongruence that Leslie may experience with her current work environment. The counselor helps her to conceptualize her feeling that she "doesn't fit" in terms of the discrepancy in Holland's typology. This provides Leslie with a framework with which to think about her dissatisfaction that may provide some new clarification and insight.

Holland (1997) recommended using all six themes as part of an analysis of congruence, comparing the relative ordering of types for the individual to the time spent in job tasks or activities related to the six areas. Investigative activities are reflected in the content matter that she teaches, particularly the higher-level math courses where she engages students in abstract problem solving. Leslie engages in many social activities at work, primarily through teaching and through using her interpersonal problem-solving skills in interactions with students and teachers. She also incorporates conventional activities throughout her work day and frequently devises new ways of structuring or organizing her tasks. The remaining three types—artistic, enterprising, and realistic—all are infrequently occurring tasks in her current job.

Another issue to explore with Leslie in counseling relates to the potential change in her vocational aspirations—in particular, whether her expressed desire to consider other occupations is a by-product of the dissatisfaction she feels with the specific job she currently holds. Holland (1997) noted the reasons underlying stability of aspirations: "People trying to change themselves or their careers receive little environmental support and must overcome the cumulative learning associated with a particular job or self-concept" (p. 12). Individuals may remain in their initial vocational choices because their exploration of alternatives occurs within a circumscribed range and because environmental influences (employers and significant others) discourage change. These issues also could be addressed in counseling with Leslie.

Additional Cases

CASE 1: JOHNNY

Johnny is a 38-year-old Asian American man from a traditional Hmong family. Johnny has lived in the United States since the age of 10, growing up in a primarily White suburb of Atlanta. His parents came to the United States after the end of the Vietnam War, and his father was able to find work as a teacher, but they maintained traditional Hmong values, including a strong value of family. Johnny is the oldest of seven children, three of whom were born in the United States after his family immigrated. His parents were in a refugee camp in Laos and endured a number of hardships to come to the United States. He has a strong feeling of family obligation to succeed in his career. His family very much wanted him to be a doctor.

Johnny did well in high school and attended a large university where he majored in biology. He was admitted to a medical school, completed his residency in ophthalmology, and is now practicing in a town close to his parents. He is married to a European American woman, Janelle, and they are expecting their first child. His wife is also a physician and plans to take 6 weeks off when the baby is born. Johnny's parents are pressuring Janelle to stay home longer with the baby. Johnny is feeling caught between his desire to please his parents and his wife's commitment to her career and her expectations that they have an egalitarian balance of work and family responsibilities. He is also realizing that his work is not very satisfying, and this might be an opportunity to stay home with the baby and begin considering a new career. He has not enjoyed the patient contact he has had and is impatient with the marketing efforts he must do to attract new patients to the clinic. He is considering taking a position in a research laboratory, using his skills to investigate eye diseases, but he would need more schooling for this career. Janelle is supportive of his thinking about a new career, but his parents are very upset about it. His career as a doctor has brought great honor to them. They also think he should be the primary breadwinner in the family and are disappointed that he is thinking of staying home.

Questions for Discussion

1. What role has congruence played in Johnny's career decisions?

2. Examine Johnny's occupational environment from the perspective of Holland's theory. What would you predict about Johnny given this information?

(Continued)

(Continued)

3. Investigative and realistic interests are stereotypic of Asian males, and these also correspond to Johnny's initial career choice of medicine. How might you help Johnny determine if these are "true" interests, and if not, would it be appropriate for you to help him choose a more congruent environment?

4. How might you help Johnny sort out the expectations he feels from his parents? From Janelle? For himself?

5. What unique strengths and assets may Johnny have that were unappreciated in his various work environments? How might you help to identify the environment that would be most congruent?

CASE 2: SUSAN

Susan is a 17-year-old Caucasian high school junior. She has a 2.5 grade point average, and her favorite classes are drafting and shop. Susan is in a co-op program in which she attends school in the morning and works in the afternoon, which she enjoys because "it's more fun than sitting in class all day." Her father is a building contractor, and her mother is a homemaker.

Susan enjoys athletics and fixing and repairing things. She has no interest in going to college but is not sure what else she might do. She has been talking with her friends and parents about what she might do after graduating from high school. She doesn't know much about the range of job possibilities but thinks she would like to work with her hands. In her co-op program, she's seen the work of welders, tool-and-die makers, mechanics, and assembly line workers. Susan's brother is an electrician, and her older sister stays home with two young children. She also is familiar with the building trades by observing her father's work. Last summer, she asked her father if she could work with him, but he said she was too young. She has asked him again for the upcoming summer and is awaiting his answer.

Susan's parents have given her little guidance about work but do expect her to finish high school and, beyond that, "be happy." She really would like to try something related to building and construction but wonders how difficult it would be as a girl. Although her father has not overtly discouraged her interest in construction, he believes it is an inappropriate choice for her. He is concerned about her physical safety on the job site as well as whether she might be harassed by her coworkers.

Susan doesn't know what to do after high school and feels confused about how to even start choosing a direction. She secretly hopes that her father will hire her after graduation but is afraid to ask him directly about it.

Questions for Discussion

1. What is Susan's type likely to be, and in what type of environment might she be congruent?

2. How would you use Holland's framework to encourage Susan's exploration? How does Holland's theory assist you in understanding Susan's career dilemma? How might it help you in working with Susan?

3. What interventions might be effective to increase her career exploration and decision making?

4. How might you help Susan address her relationship with her parents, particularly with her father?

5. How would you address Susan's concerns about being a female in the building and construction trades?

CASE 3: CYNTHIA

Cynthia is a 42-year-old European American mother of three who is seeking career counseling because she is unhappy in her present job as a purchasing agent for a large furniture company. She took the job a year ago when her own interior design business failed. She started the business 10 years ago when her youngest child started first grade; it had been a dream of hers to own an interior design studio because her friends often told her how nicely decorated her house was. She did quite well in the business for a number of years; however, she developed multiple sclerosis 3 years ago and was increasingly unable to visit clients' homes and engage in the physical activity necessary to keep her business viable.

Cynthia's educational history includes 2 years of college immediately after high school and completion of a certificate program in design. She has taken a few adult education courses at a local community college, primarily to develop new computer skills.

Cynthia's husband died in a car accident 2 years ago. She has managed to save the bulk of an insurance settlement that she received and hopes to keep that money set aside for her inevitable medical expenses. She has been fortunate to have adequate health insurance, but she is concerned about what the future might hold. In addition, her oldest daughter is a sophomore at a state university, and her two younger daughters are planning to attend college if they are financially able to do so. She therefore has a number of practical concerns related to her career, such as maintaining her health insurance, providing for her children, and planning for retirement.

Cynthia took her current job because purchasing for a furniture company was in a similar area as being an interior designer and she believed that she would be able to continue to use her design skills. Unfortunately, in her year on the job, her activities have primarily entailed maintenance of purchasing and client records on the computer, making delivery arrangements, and occasionally dealing with customer complaints. The anticipated promotion to designer does not appear likely in the near future, and although her physical functioning is stabilized, she feels that she should make changes now before her condition deteriorates.

Questions for Discussion

1. Describe Cynthia's past and current work environments in terms of Holland's theory. In what ways do these environments allow her to express her type?

2. What are some alternate occupations that would allow Cynthia to be in a congruent environment and accommodate her disability?

3. What have been (and are) the factors involved in Cynthia's original career decision making? How does she balance her practical financial concerns with her dissatisfaction with her current job?

4. How would you incorporate a consideration of her health status into career counseling?

BOX 6.3

Summary of Key Constructs

Construct	Definition
Congruence	Fit between interests and work environment; the greater the congruence, the greater the predicted job satisfaction.
Consistency	How similar top interests are on the hexagon; consistent interests predict more stable occupational choices.
RIASEC interest types	Realistic, Investigative, Artistic, Social, Enterprising, and Conventional interest types.
Hexagon	RIASEC types arranged in a hexagonal pattern.
Calculus	Interest types are arranged equidistantly around the hexagon; opposing types are least similar and adjacent types most similar.
Differentiation	The difference between the highest and lowest interest types; well-differentiated interests predict more stable occupational choices.

References

Betz, N. E. (2008). Advances in vocational theories. In S. D. Brown & R. W. Lent (Eds.), *Handbook of counseling psychology* (4th ed., pp. 357–374). New York: Wiley.

Chartrand, J. M. (1991). The evolution of trait-and-factor career counseling: A person X environment fit approach. *Journal of Counseling and Development, 69*, 518–524.

Dawis, R. V. (2005). The Minnesota Theory of Work Adjustment. In S. D. Brown & R. W. Lent (Eds.), *Career development and counseling: Putting theory and research to work* (pp. 3–23). New York: Wiley.

Dawis, R. V., & Lofquist, L. H. (1984). *A psychological theory of work adjustment.* Minneapolis: University of Minnesota Press.

Gottfredson, G. D. (1999). John L. Holland's contributions to vocational psychology: A review and evaluation. *Journal of Vocational Behavior, 55*, 15–40.

Gottfredson, G. D., & Holland, J. L. (1996). *Dictionary of Holland occupational codes* (3rd ed.). Palo Alto, CA: Consulting Psychologists Press.

Harmon, L. W., Hansen, J. C., Borgen, F. H., & Hammer, A. C. (2005). *Strong Interest Inventory: Applications and technical guide.* Palo Alto, CA: Consulting Psychologists Press.

Holland, J. L. (1994). *The occupations finder.* Odessa, FL: Psychological Assessment Resources.

Holland, J. L. (1996a). Exploring careers with a typology: What we have learned and some new directions. *American Psychologist, 51*, 397–406.

Holland, J. L. (1996b). Integrating career theory and practice: The current situation and some potential remedies. In M. L. Savickas & W. B. Walsh (Eds.), *Handbook of career counseling theory and practice.* Palo Alto, CA: Davies-Black.

Holland, J. L. (1997). *Making vocational choices: A theory of vocational personalities and work environments* (3rd ed.). Odessa, FL: Psychological Assessment Resources.

Holland, J. L., & Gottfredson, G. D. (1994). *CASI: Career Attitudes and Strategies Inventory: An inventory for understanding adult careers.* Odessa, FL: Psychological Assessment Resources.

Holland, J. L., Powell, A. B., & Fritzsche, B. A. (1994). *The Self-Directed Search professional user's guide.* Odessa, FL: Psychological Assessment Resources.

Parsons, F. (1989). *Choosing a vocation.* Garrett Park, MD: Garrett Park Press. (Original work published in 1909)

Rounds, J. B., & Tracey, T. J. (1990). From trait-and-factor to person-environment fit counseling: Theory and process. In W. B. Walsh & S. H. Osipow (Eds.), *Career counseling: Contemporary topics in vocational psychology* (pp. 1–44). Hillsdale, NJ: Lawrence Erlbaum.

Sharf, R. S. (1997). *Applying career development theory to counseling* (2nd ed.). Pacific Grove, CA: Brooks/Cole.

Spokane, A. R. (1996). Holland's theory. In D. Brown, L. Brooks, & Associates (Eds.), *Career choice and development* (3rd ed., pp. 33–74). San Francisco: Jossey-Bass.

Spokane, A. R., & Cruza-Guet, M. C. (2005). Holland's theory of vocational personalities in work environments. In S. D. Brown & R. W. Lent (Eds.), *Career development and counseling: Putting theory and research to work* (pp. 24–41). New York: Wiley.

Swanson, J. L., & Chu, S. P. (2000). Applications of person-environment psychology to the career development and vocational behavior of adolescents and adults. In M. E. Martin Jr. & J. L. Swartz-Kulstad (Eds.), *Person-environment psychology and mental health: Assessment and intervention* (pp. 143–168). Mahwah, NJ: Lawrence Erlbaum.

Walsh, W. B., Price, R. H., & Craik, K. H. (1992). Person-environment psychology: An introduction. In W. B. Walsh, K. H. Craik, & R. H. Price (Eds.), *Person-environment psychology: Models and perspectives* (pp. vii–xi). Mahwah, NJ: Lawrence Erlbaum.

Additional Readings

Betz, N. E., Borgen, F. H., Kaplan, A., & Harmon, L. W. (1998). Gender and Holland type as moderators of the validity and interpretive utility of the Skills Confidence Inventory. *Journal of Vocational Behavior, 53,* 281–299.

Helwig, A. A. (2003). The measurement of Holland types in a 10-year longitudinal study of a sample of students. *Journal of Employment Counseling, 40,* 24–32.

Reardon, R. C., Vernick, S. H., & Reed, C. A. (2004). The distribution of the U.S. workforce from 1960 to 1990: A RIASEC perspective. *Journal of Career Assessment, 12,* 99–112.

Spokane, A. R., Meir, E. I., & Catalano, M. (2000). Person-environment congruence and Holland's theory: A review and reconsideration. *Journal of Vocational Behavior, 57,* 137–187.

Tracey, T. J. G. (2001). The development of structure of interests in children: Setting the stage. *Journal of Vocational Behavior, 59,* 89–104.

Wampold, B. E., Ankarlo, G., Mondin, G., Trinidad-Carrillo, M., Baumler, B., & Prater, K. (1995). Social skills of and social environments produced by different Holland types: A social perspective on person-environment fit models. *Journal of Counseling Psychology, 42,* 365–379.

The Theory of Work Adjustment 7

The theory of work adjustment (TWA) (Dawis, 2005; Dawis & Lofquist, 1984), like Holland's theory, is considered a theory of "person-environment fit." Although these two theories are quite similar in many respects, Holland's theory places greater emphasis on vocational choice, whereas the TWA emphasizes vocational adjustment (Dawis, 1994), thus providing complementary rather than competing views. TWA might be particularly helpful to use with clients who are not satisfied with their jobs, because they may be considering choosing an entirely new career or wondering whether to adjust to a current job.

The TWA consists of a number of formal propositions and their corollaries that address the process of adjustment to work (Dawis, 2005; Dawis & Lofquist, 1984). These propositions identify aspects of the individual (e.g., abilities) as well as of the work environment (e.g., rewards) that predict job satisfaction and tenure. In other words, the constructs in the TWA suggest whether an individual would be satisfied on the job and how long he or she might remain in the job. According to the TWA, the fit between the individual and the environment predicts the individual's satisfaction as well as his or her satisfactoriness as an employee.

As with Holland's theory, the concept of fit, or correspondence, in the TWA rests on using the same dimensions to describe both people and environments. Holland postulates six types of persons or environments; the TWA takes a different approach. Dawis (2005) describes two sets of common dimensions—namely, an individual's abilities in relation to those required by his or her job and an individual's needs and work values in relation to the rewards available on the job. Both of these are thought to reciprocally interact; in other words, the environment has requirements of the individual (his or her ability to do the job), and the individual has requirements of the environment (the environment's ability to satisfy his or her needs). For example, among the requirements of the occupation of truck driver are that employees be able to drive a truck, load the truck, and keep to a set schedule. Requirements of people who are truck drivers include that the job provide them with rewards such as secure employment, independence, and good working conditions.

The TWA stresses the importance of describing the individual's level of *satisfactoriness,* or how well his or her abilities and skills meet what the job or organization requires—literally how satisfactory an employee the individual is. In the preceding example, how well an individual can function as a truck driver is an indication of satisfactoriness. The TWA also stresses the individual's level of *satisfaction,* or how well his or her needs are met by the job. An individual with high security, autonomy, and good working condition needs would be predicted to be satisfied as a truck driver. Satisfactoriness and satisfaction are depicted in Figure 7.1.

As shown on the left of Figure 7.1, an individual has abilities, and the work environment has ability requirements. If abilities and ability requirements correspond, the individual is satisfactory. For example, if a woman has good interpersonal skills, can take measurements, report, and analyze results of medical tests, then she might meet the ability

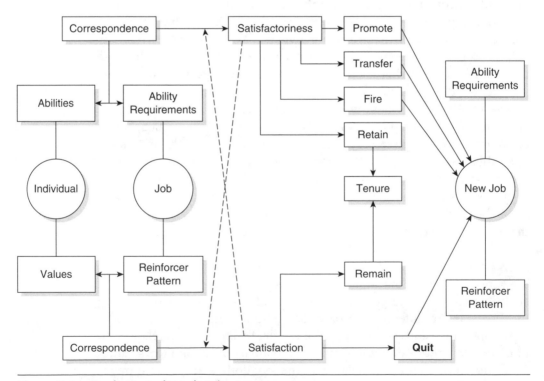

Figure 7.1   Prediction of Work Adjustment

SOURCE: Dawis and Lofquist (1984).

requirements of a medical sonographer. Once in the position, she may be promoted, transferred, or fired on the basis of her degree of satisfactoriness. The result of promotion, transfer, or termination may be a new job.

The path to satisfaction is portrayed at the bottom of Figure 7.1. An individual has values and needs, and the job has a reinforcer pattern, or pattern of rewards. If needs and reinforcers correspond, an individual is satisfied. The medical sonographer described above may require security and compensation in her work; she would be satisfied if her position in a hospital provides these. If she is not satisfied, she may quit, leading her to seek a new job. The middle of Figure 7.1 shows that if she is both satisfied and satisfactory she is predicted to be retained in the job. A central feature of the TWA is that both satisfaction and satisfactoriness are equally important components in the prediction of work adjustment.

Despite the dual focus on person and environment, the TWA clearly emphasizes what the person experiences and uses the word *satisfaction* for an individual's satisfaction with his or her job; the word *satisfactoriness* is used for the individual with whom the work environment is satisfied. Therefore, tenure occurs when an individual is both satisfied and has the abilities to do the job (Dawis, 2005). A further extension of these ideas, which is particularly important for career planning, is that length of time in a job depends on an individual's level of satisfaction and ability to do the job.

The TWA emphasizes the measurement of abilities and values to facilitate the match of an individual to a work environment. Abilities are viewed as "reference dimensions of skills" (Dawis, 2005, p. 13); that is, abilities are seen as general dimensions that underlie groupings of acquired skills. Similarly, values are viewed as representing a grouping of needs. Dawis defines six crucial values: achievement, comfort, status, altruism, safety, and autonomy. In terms of environment, research underlying the TWA has identified occupational ability patterns and occupational reward patterns to describe a wide variety of occupations. In other words, what abilities does an occupation require of an individual, and what needs or values of the individual can the occupation fulfill? In predicting career choice, abilities are compared with ability patterns required, and values are compared with value patterns supported. Occupations are compared according to how they predict satisfaction and satisfactoriness, and a cost-benefit analysis is conducted to predict the optimal choice for an individual.

Dawis (2005) proposes that satisfaction is predicted from the correspondence between an individual's values and the rewards available in the environment. Satisfaction is predicted to be negatively related to the probability of an individual's quitting a job. An individual's ability to carry out the duties of a job is predicted from the correspondence between his or her abilities and what the environment requires and is negatively related to an individual's being fired from a job. In other words, people are least likely to lose their jobs if they are able to do those jobs successfully. Adjusting to the job and staying in the job for some length of time (job tenure) results from both an individual's level of satisfaction and his or her ability to do the job at a specific time. Moreover, satisfaction and ability to do the job (satisfactoriness) influence the prediction of each other; that an individual is satisfied in a job helps to predict that she or he is able to do the job and vice versa.

The TWA postulates that four personality style variables are important in characterizing how an individual interacts with the environment: celerity, pace, rhythm, and endurance. *Celerity* refers to the speed with which an individual initiates interaction with his or her environment. An individual may have a high celerity—quickly, or perhaps impulsively, acting on the environment—or may have a very low celerity—moving slowly to action.

Pace indicates the intensity or activity level of one's interaction with the environment. Once the individual acts on the environment, pace indicates the rate of interaction. Individuals may, for example, be viewed as having very high energy; this is an indication of the pace of their interaction with the environment. A high-energy person, however, may have that high energy only when in front of a group of people or may be able to sustain it for only a short period of time. These are indications of his or her rhythm and endurance.

Rhythm is the pattern of the pace of interaction with the environment (steady, cyclical, or erratic), and *endurance* refers to the sustaining of interaction with the environment. These variables help explain why individuals with similar abilities and values may behave in different ways within a given work environment. Moreover, these constructs can be used to describe environments as well as people, and environments differ from one another in terms of celerity, pace, rhythm, and endurance.

In TWA terms, dissatisfaction serves a central motivational role. Dissatisfaction on the part of either the person or the environment represents disequilibrium in the system and is the impetus for adjustment to occur to restore equilibrium. "Satisfaction motivates 'maintenance' behavior; dissatisfaction motivates adjustment behavior" (Dawis, 1996, p. 87). Figure 7.2 depicts the postulated process of adjustment that occurs when there is discorrespondence between an individual's needs and values and the rewards provided by the job.

The TWA hypothesizes that the stylistic variables of flexibility and perseverance moderate the prediction of satisfaction, satisfactoriness, and work adjustment. The bottom point of the axis in Figure 7.2 indicates zero discorrespondence. *Flexibility* is the ability to tolerate a mismatch (discorrespondence) between needs and rewards offered by the environment before doing something to make an adjustment. However, at some point, the lack of correspondence between an individual's needs and the environmental rewards is too great, and the individual will move into an adjustment mode. This is shown as the lower horizontal line in Figure 7.2. The individual may strive to adjust himself or herself (reduce level of

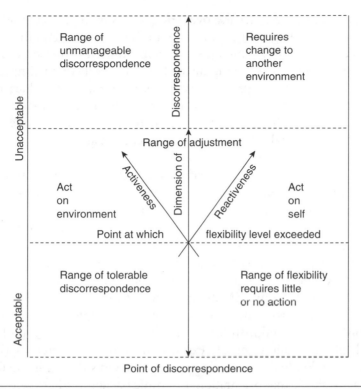

Figure 7.2 Relationships Between Adjustment-Style Dimensions

SOURCE: Lofquist and Dawis (1991).

needs) or may try to adjust the environment (increase rewards). These are depicted as the vectors in Figure 7.2; *activeness* is acting on the environment, and *reactiveness* is adjusting self.

Perseverance is continuing in the job after a mismatch is noted and the individual works to bring it into adjustment, shown as the upper horizontal line. For example, a man who needs autonomy will exhibit flexibility if he is able to tolerate some close supervision. There may be a point, however, when he no longer can tolerate the discrepancy between his need for autonomy and the supervision, and he will try to make an adjustment that reduces the discorrespondence. He will exhibit perseverance if he continues in the environment while he is in adjustment mode. At some point, of course, if he cannot successfully adjust the discorrespondence, he would then be predicted to terminate employment. Flexibility and perseverance are conceptualized as fluctuating constructs; an individual may be flexible and able to tolerate discorrespondence one day, then unable to tolerate it the next, at which point he or she moves into an adjustment mode.

As shown in Figure 7.2, adjustment can occur in two different modes. In the *active mode,* the individual attempts to change the work environment to reduce the amount of discorrespondence by changing the requirements of the environment or the rewards available in the environment. For example, in response to feeling overworked, an employee could ask for a reduction in job assignments or ask for a raise or promotion. In the *reactive mode*, the individual attempts to change himself or herself to reduce discorrespondence by changing his or her work skills or the importance attached to needs. In the previous example, an employee could learn time management skills to increase efficiency or shift priorities so that less focus is placed on work. Thus, adjustment behavior can be aimed at one of four targets: the individual's skills or need requirements and the environment's available ability requirements and rewards.

The concepts of active and reactive modes and of flexibility and perseverance are, thus, important predictors of what individuals are likely to do if they are dissatisfied (or if the environment is dissatisfied with their behavior). These concepts are also important considerations from a broader perspective: An individual develops a characteristic *adjustment style* over time, which is useful information in career counseling.

The TWA is heavily based on an individual differences premise—that is, that individuals differ in their abilities, needs, values, and interests, among other variables. This tradition views people as complex individuals who differ on a number of dimensions and believes that counseling needs to be individualized to allow for the expression of those differences (Dawis, 2005). The individual differences approach suggests that individuals' sex, national origin, sexual orientation, or ethnic background are not reliable bases for determining their abilities and needs.

However, Dawis (2005) notes that an individual's current situation is a product of the opportunities he or she has had to develop work skills and needs. Individuals who have experienced gender or racial discrimination have been restricted in their opportunities for development. The individual differences tradition acknowledges that one's sex or racial or cultural background does not necessarily restrict opportunities, for individuals of all groups and both sexes exist in all occupations. But Dawis (1996) notes that gender and racial and ethnic background "become important when they influence level, ranges, and patterns of work skills and work needs that are or are not developed . . . and when these person characteristics adversely affect employability" (pp. 95–96).

The TWA evolved from Dawis and Lofquist's research on how to help vocational rehabilitation clients adjust to work after a disability. Dawis (2005) notes that their team had collected a large amount of data and realized that a theoretical framework was needed to help organize the information. Thus, the foundation of the theory was a framework for research, and its evolution over the past 40 years has been empirically guided. Strongest support has been found for the aspects of the theory outlined in Figure 7.1 (Dawis, 2005). In other words, research has supported the TWA prediction of satisfaction, satisfactoriness, and tenure. There has been less examination and, therefore, less support for the personality style variables and their relationship to adjustment. There has also been limited support for the application of the theory to non-White populations (Betz, 2008).

> **Box 7.1**
>
> **Personal Reflection**
>
> Have I ever been in a job that was very dissatisfying?
>
> What needs were not met in this job?
>
> How did I adjust?
>
> Did I try to change myself or my job?

Applying the Theory of Work Adjustment

A counselor who uses the TWA approach would ask the sorts of questions that are outlined in Box 7.2. The counselor would wonder what the client's history might say about his or her abilities and needs/values, as well as what information may be gathered from the times the client has been dissatisfied.

> **Box 7.2**
>
> **Counselor Cognitions**
>
> What are the client's needs?
>
> What is the client's adjustment style?
>
> What are the client's abilities?
>
> Is there discorrespondence between the client's actual abilities and the job requirements?
>
> Is the client accurately perceiving his or her abilities?
>
> Is the client adequately doing the tasks on the job?

CONCEPTUALIZING LESLIE'S CAREER HISTORY

Leslie has high abilities in math and science and the ability to teach children. She did well in other subjects as well, indicating that her pattern of abilities was high. Leslie places a high value on achievement, as indicated by her frustration at the lack of challenge in her math classes. She also places a high value on helping others, such as by working as a middle school tutor, and on making decisions on her own rather than having others make them for her.

Leslie was a satisfactory employee in her first teaching position. Clearly, the job met some of her needs. Teaching challenged her; it met her achievement needs. She also was able to meet her responsibility needs, because she was able to make decisions in her own classroom. She felt she was able to help others and felt part of the larger community. However, many of her social needs were not met in the smaller town. Although the specific occupation of teaching was a good choice for Leslie, who was both satisfactory and satisfied in the occupation, the overall setting did not provide rewards for her.

CONCEPTUALIZING LESLIE'S PRESENT SITUATION

Leslie has been a satisfactory employee in her current job in that she has been in the same school for 10 years. However, she reported some dissatisfaction even before a new principal began to change the rewards in the job. Leslie enjoyed the interaction that teaching allowed her with the children, providing social service rewards. However, she reported that the long hours and the stress of the position frustrated her. The stress she reports may be a result of the lack of correspondence with her environment. This has been exacerbated by the new policies implemented by the principal, which have influenced her ability to get her autonomy and responsibility needs met. In addition, interactions with parents have left her feeling that she is not receiving adequate recognition for her work.

Questions for Discussion

1. What specific hypotheses would you develop about Leslie from the TWA? How does using the TWA help you understand Leslie? How might it help Leslie understand herself?

2. How would you incorporate the other assessment information that Leslie completed?

3. Leslie did not complete an ability assessment; the counselor inferred abilities from past achievements. What are other ways to assess ability information? Is it important for adults to have their abilities tested?

4. The counselor estimated Leslie's satisfactoriness from the length of her tenure in the same position. However, this information is from a single source—the client herself, who may have underestimated or overestimated her satisfactoriness. What are other ways you could assess satisfactoriness?

5. How might it be helpful for Leslie to conceptualize her current work environment in terms of person-environment correspondence or discorrespondence?

6. How would you incorporate other life issues into counseling? What is the degree of Leslie's correspondence with the other multiple environments in her life? How might these multiple environments interact with one another?

7. Working from the perspective of a TWA counselor, how would you incorporate Leslie's gender and cultural background into counseling?

THE CASE OF CHARLES

Charles is a European American man in his early 40s. He has a bachelor's degree in biology and has been employed as a biological technician for a pathology laboratory for 3 years. He seeks career counseling because he is not very satisfied with his work; he is not sure if he wants to find a new job in this field or if he wants to change careers.

Charles grew up as the youngest child of middle-class parents. His sisters are considerably older than he is and had left for college before he had finished grade school. His mother stayed home until he started high school and then went to work as a secretary. His father worked as an insurance salesperson and traveled a five-state region during Charles's childhood. His father has just retired after working for the same company his entire career.

Charles was a good student during high school and played a number of sports. He had a large circle of acquaintances but few close friends, because he was viewed as moody and temperamental. His parents had very high expectations of his achievements in school and in athletics and relatively rigid standards for his behavior. He did particularly well in math and science, and they thought he should be a physician. His father offered to pay for his college expenses if he pursued that degree but would not contribute if he went into another field.

Charles went to a state college and majored in biology. He enjoyed his time in college. He formed a close circle of friends and became engaged to a woman during his last year in college. He graduated with a 3.3 grade point average and scored about average on the Medical College Admissions Test (MCAT). However, Charles did not succeed in his application to medical school. He decided to graduate with a major in biology, seek a job in a laboratory as a biological technician, and apply to medical school the following year.

Charles ultimately unsuccessfully applied to medical school three times. The feedback he received on his lack of success varied from lack of distinguishing characteristics to mediocre MCAT scores to a poor interview. While he pursued this goal, he continued to work as a biological technician. He and his wife put off having children, hoping that he would be able to enter medical school.

Charles started his career as a biological technician in a hospital close to the college where he graduated, so his wife could pursue an advanced degree. He moved from that hospital to a hospital lab when he and his wife moved for her first postgraduate position. He left that hospital after 3 years due to a personality conflict with his supervisor. He took a position with a local clinic and was there for 3 years.

Charles had major life changes in his mid-30s. He decided to give up his goal of medical school, he and his wife divorced, and he moved to another city. He took a position in a pathology laboratory, where he began to conduct tests to diagnose cancer. He changed positions again about 3 years ago to a pathology laboratory that serves as a regional center for the diagnosis of cancer, particularly prostate cancer. He reports that he left that position because of personality clashes with his supervisor.

Currently, Charles is unhappy with his pay at the laboratory, dissatisfied with the lack of challenges in his work, and having interpersonal conflicts with his supervisor. He does, however, feel that he is doing work that is important and helping others. He is married again, to a woman about 15 years younger than he is, and they hope to have children soon. He expects that she will stay home when they do have children.

Questions for Discussion

1. What specific hypotheses would you develop about Charles from the TWA? How does using the TWA help you understand Charles?

2. What information about abilities do you infer from Charles's unsuccessful application to medical school?

3. Does Charles accurately perceive his abilities?

4. What role might Charles's temperament play in his work history? How might this relate to his adjustment style?

5. What are your hypotheses about Charles's dissatisfaction with work? Is it related to other areas of his life?

Directions and Implications for Career Counseling

Career counseling from the perspective of the TWA addresses both the client's satisfaction with the occupation and his or her satisfactoriness. TWA counselors assess a client's abilities and needs and evaluate them against the abilities required of and rewards provided by an occupation. As the name implies, however, the TWA is particularly well suited to counseling related to job adjustment. In helping clients with career concerns related to adjustment, counselors evaluate where they are in terms of their threshold of flexibility and evaluate their skills in reactive and active adjustment modes.

GOALS OF COUNSELING

Career counseling can serve many purposes, including identifying a career choice, clarifying decision making, helping a client identify opportunities for adjustment, and helping a client decide on various ways to change an environment. Fundamentally, person-environment correspondence counseling focuses on the discorrespondence clients experience in the environment. Counseling goals may include career choice, as well as examination of the possibility that the work environment will be adjusted or how likely it is that the client is able to engage in active adjustment.

INTERVENTIONS

A counselor who uses the TWA approach would first identify the needs and abilities of the client. Often this is done through the use of assessment tools. Lofquist and Dawis (1991) outline several hypotheses that counselors may entertain as they help clients identify the discorrespondence they are experiencing. These hypotheses, or the way that a counselor might conceptualize the client's concerns, are outlined in Box 7.2.

The first hypothesis concerns the match between abilities and the job requirements. Are the client's abilities too high or too low for the position? For example, a nurse may have more abilities than the job requires, or a secretary may not have the computer skills required by the job.

The second hypothesis focuses on the client's subjective evaluation of his or her abilities and discorrespondence with the environmental ability requirements. The client may perceive his or her abilities as higher or lower than they are in reality, or the environmental requirements may be perceived as more or less difficult than they actually are. Or perhaps the client is seeking counseling because the abilities and requirements correspond to each other but he or she is not performing well.

The counselor might also wonder about the correspondence in needs. Are the client's needs met by the job environment? Another question the counselor might have is whether the rewards are higher or lower than the needs. In the latter situation, a client's needs are not met by the job environment. Finally, the counselor may test the hypothesis that the client is both satisfactory and satisfied and is coping with problems in other domains. In this case, the client's concerns are less with the work environment than with possible dissatisfaction in other areas of life, such as in a marital relationship.

Assessment is critical to career counseling from the TWA perspective. Thus, TWA counselors set expectations that clients will participate in the assessment process and will complete all homework assignments: "The career counseling process that we will go through will include taking a variety of assessment tools to find out more about your abilities and needs. We will spend time talking about the results in here and which occupations best correspond to your needs and abilities. It will also be important for you to do some work outside of the session."

Counselors often explore the environments in which clients have experienced the most problems. This exploration helps the counselor identify situations and environments in which needs have not been met. For example, in the case of Leslie, the counselor may say, "Leslie, you have talked about teaching in a smaller school and teaching at your current school. Tell me about some of the problems you have encountered in these situations." Leslie's problems as a teacher in her first position included the stress of not feeling competent and of feeling isolated in the community; in her current position, she is frustrated with new policies imposed by the principal, not having the opportunity to teach advanced classes, discouraging interactions with parents, and student problems. The counselor could identify Leslie's needs for achievement and recognitions from her work history.

In the case of Charles, the counselor might hypothesize that Charles's work history includes a number of situations in which he has had conflicts with supervisors. Are these conflicts due to Charles's interpersonal style or his reaction to discorrespondence, or is Charles an unsatisfactory employee? Charles identified dissatisfaction with compensation, achievement, and his supervisor. The counselor would work with Charles to determine which of these are the most pressing of his concerns. The counselor would also help Charles to identify if he wants to adjust to his current position or find a new career. Perhaps Charles continues to be disappointed with a career as a biological technician because he was not able to pursue his goal to be a physician. Charles's history also indicates that he has changed positions every 3 years. Some of these changes might have been prompted by other life changes, but the counselor might also hypothesize that Charles does not adjust well to discorrespondence and does not persevere in the face of disscorrespondence. Thus, the counselor's goals might include exploring his pattern of adjustment in other areas of his life. The counselor will also assess the likely motivation to engage in adjustment and could ask Charles to take an environmental satisfaction questionnaire for his current work environment as homework.

A TWA counselor will also evaluate clients' needs and abilities. For example, Leslie's Minnesota Importance Questionnaire (MIQ) indicated that her highest values are achievement, altruism, and autonomy. Her most important rewards are moral values (doing the work without feeling it is morally wrong), ability utilization (doing something that makes use of her abilities), achievement (the job's giving her a feeling of accomplishment), and social service (doing things for others). She also indicated that coworkers (making friends with coworkers), autonomy (planning her work with little supervision), and responsibility (making decisions on her own) are important. Leslie did not take an ability assessment; therefore, she is inferred to be high in general cognitive ability and verbal ability, because she successfully completed her college degree, and, from her math background, high in numerical ability. No information is available on her perceptual or motor abilities. However, it should be noted that a TWA counselor would have asked Leslie to take an ability assessment in addition to the other instruments.

The TWA counselor would also assess Charles's work abilities and needs, as well as the abilities required and rewards provided by his environment. This is done through the use of expert ratings, previous research, or interpretation of the information Charles has provided. The occupational aptitude patterns indicate that Charles's work environment of biological technician has ability requirements of cognitive ability, verbal ability, and scientific reasoning. It appears that he has been a satisfactory employee able to do this work for nearly 20 years, although he has changed the specific environment in which he works. Rewards available in the job of biological technician have been found, through previous research, to be altruism, security, working conditions, and supervision. The work of technicians is relatively closely supervised and monitored. Other occupations that reward those needs are nurse, dietician, physical therapist, and firefighter.

Both Leslie and Charles indicate discorrespondence between the rewards in the environment and their needs. Leslie identified the discorrespondence between the environment and her needs for achievement, ability utilization, and autonomy. Although Charles noted that while his altruism needs are met, there is discorrespondence in his needs for achievement, compensation, and autonomy needs. It is possible that the close supervision he has had over the years did not correspond with his autonomy and achievement needs, leading to the clash with his supervisors.

It is critical to understand what a client means in responding to each MIQ statement. Thus, the counselor might ask Leslie, "Tell me what you mean by not doing work that you feel is morally wrong? What might be some examples of times that has occurred?" The counselor asks similar probes about feeling that the job would give Leslie a feeling of accomplishment, make use of her abilities, or allow her to help others. Leslie gives examples of times she felt that she was using her abilities, accomplishing things on the job, and helping others. Leslie also discusses how her needs for responsibility and autonomy are not being met with the new bureaucratic policies implemented by the principal. She acknowledges that the most important priority is to create more correspondence between the environment and her need for achievement and ability utilization.

The counselor would also identify actions to reduce the discorrespondence between the client and the environment, discussing this in terms of personality and adjustment styles. Charles's personality style appears to be characterized by a relatively steady rhythm but a low level of endurance, both of these inferred from his job changes every three years. It is more difficult to infer his celerity or pace from his employment history. The counselor uses a personality style checklist to aid in this discussion. In assessing Charles's adjustment style, the counselor finds that Charles has not adjusted reactively (changing himself), nor is there evidence that he has taken steps to change the environment. It appears that when he feels too discorrespondent with the environment, he leaves. The counselor identifies actions that Charles might take to adjust to his current position before leaving, also discussing the consequences of those actions. These actions may include identifying ways that he might change his environment to increase his feelings of accomplishment, autonomy, and ability utilization or ways that he might find other environments to meet those needs. For example, the counselor might want to know if Charles has ever talked to his supervisor about the level of autonomy he could build. He might also choose to reprioritize to increase the importance of rewards available in the environment, such as security or altruism.

Additional Cases

CASE 1: PHIL

Phil is a 48-year-old Caucasian man who is a foreperson in charge of shipping in a small manufacturing company. He sought career counseling at the urging of his wife, who is concerned that he is underemployed; she feels that he could be earning more money than in his current job. Phil had attended college briefly but did not complete a degree. He had planned to major in accounting, primarily because of his father's encouragement rather than as a reflection of his real interests. He was much more interested in fixing things and was particularly interested in anything related to cars.

Phil has worked at a variety of unskilled jobs. He did not want to enter schooling or work at a career, primarily because he did not want to climb a corporate ladder. Phil began working as an assembly line worker for a manufacturing company to support his family. He described this first job as "checking his brain at the door," but in reality, he was not overly concerned that the work did not engage him intellectually. He was able to use his abilities in a number of ways outside of work; he was active in chess and bridge clubs and was an avid reader of *Science* and *Scientific American* magazines.

Phil also enjoys building and repairing model trains and has an extensive model train collection that he inherited from his father. Both his father and grandfather had been railroad executives, and his only brother is a civil engineer who designs railroad bridges. Phil's family has a love of railroads in general and of the Burlington Northern railroads in particular. Phil's model railroad collection includes several antique engines; he has developed a small following as an antique model train expert.

Phil's first marriage ended in divorce, and he was left with financial obligations to his first wife and their daughter. He subsequently married again, and he and his second wife have two sons and are expecting a third child. Phil eventually worked his way from entry-level loading dock to foreperson of shipping. This advancement was primarily because his supervisors recognized his abilities. His tested abilities are uniformly high in all areas, and he places high value on security, compensation, and achievement. Phil is quite bright and capable of learning, but his lack of formal education has limited his options. His supervisor has told him he cannot expect any more promotions in the company because he would need a baccalaureate degree to be eligible.

Phil is not averse to returning to school to finish his degree, but his credits will not transfer, and he would have to start over. Meanwhile, he will soon have four children, and his wife is not currently working outside the home. He cannot afford to quit his job to go to school, and he is very unsure what he would major in if he did go back. Overall, Phil is satisfied with his job. He likes feeling that he can do the work without a lot of stress, likes the men and one woman he works with, likes the security of belonging to a union, and likes the benefits the company provides. He is dissatisfied with the amount of money he is making, however, and has a vague feeling that he could be doing more.

Questions for Discussion

1. Given the financial pressures that Phil feels, how does he balance his high need for achievement with his equally high need for security?

2. What are other possible environments that could provide achievement rewards for Phil?

3. How would you evaluate Phil's adjustment style?

4. Phil entered counseling at the urging of his wife. How would you handle this? How would you incorporate Phil's other life roles into counseling?

5. How would you incorporate Phil's avocational interests into counseling?

6. How do Phil's gender and race influence his career decisions?

CASE 2: MELISSA

Melissa is a 32-year-old Caucasian woman who is a midlevel executive working for a large firm that conducts marketing research. She holds a bachelor's degree in economics and an MBA in marketing. She is married to Kevin (a 42-year-old Caucasian man) who works for a similar company in another town; they met while they were attending a professional meeting. They have been married for 7 years and have two small children, ages 2 and 4. The children live primarily with Melissa; Kevin comes home each weekend. Melissa, then, has primary responsibility for the household and child rearing during the week, but she and Kevin share the tasks on the weekend.

Melissa sought career counseling because she was feeling anxious and resentful of the demands she was juggling at work and at home. She feels that she and Kevin are able to communicate very well; they talk and e-mail each other several times a day, and they maintain time for themselves on the weekends. She also feels that they both make time for their children. But she is frustrated that they live so far apart and that her job is not as rewarding as she hoped. She enjoys some aspects of her work, primarily the opportunity to create new research surveys, and she enjoys working with clients and with her colleagues in the company. Melissa does not feel, however, that she is able to use her skills most effectively and also feels that she does not receive adequate recognition for her work. She has been passed over for promotions, and she is not certain if this was due to her performance or her status as a working mother or because she is a woman. The last time she was passed over for a promotion, she seriously considered talking to her manager about it but decided against it because she did not want to "rock the boat."

She and Kevin have talked about opening their own marketing research firm; that is one option that she is considering. Kevin's company has no openings at her level, so it is not possible for her to move to join him at his firm. There is no real reason they need to stay in this geographic area, because they have no family obligations or ties other than their current jobs.

Questions for Discussion

1. What are the rewards in Melissa's environments?

2. How would the TWA characterize Melissa's satisfactoriness? How would you incorporate this into counseling?

3. What is Melissa's adjustment style, and how would you work with her to increase the correspondence with her environment?

4. How would you incorporate the personal issues that Melissa is facing into career counseling?

5. How would you incorporate Melissa and Kevin's work-family interface into counseling?

6. How do Melissa's gender and race influence her career decisions?

CASE 3: LINDA

Linda is an 18-year-old college freshman. Both of her parents are Korean and immigrated to the United States when Linda and her sisters were small children. Linda was 10 when they arrived in the United States; her sisters were 8, 5, and 2. She grew up in a primarily Korean community in Los Angeles, living with her parents, three sisters, and her paternal grandmother. Linda's parents both completed college degrees in Korea prior to the immigration. Linda's father was in business in Korea, and her mother was a teacher. However, when they came to the United States, neither was able to find work commensurate with their education and work experience. Her father worked for another Korean family in a grocery store, and her mother took in sewing and took care of the children. When Linda was 15, her parents were able to buy the grocery store. Since then, her mother has worked in the store with her father.

Linda's parents learned to speak English, though her grandmother refused to learn and only spoke Korean at home. Linda's parents spoke Korean at home as well, out of respect for her grandmother. Thus, Linda grew up speaking Korean and English. Her parents came in contact with individuals from many cultures in the grocery store, but their primary social network consisted of the Korean American community; much of this community was focused on involvement with the Korean Church. Linda and her sisters were expected to be very involved with the Korean community as well, participating in activities in the church and forming friendships with other Korean children.

Linda attended an elementary school that was predominantly Korean and African American. Her parents placed a very high emphasis on education, making sure that she and her sisters worked hard at their studies each evening. She made some friends at school but was discouraged from participating in afterschool activities, since those might interfere with her studies. She also was discouraged from making friends outside her parents' social circle. Eventually, she did not want to bring friends home, since she was embarrassed at her grandmother's inability to communicate with anyone who could not speak Korean.

Linda did well in school and was chosen to attend a high school known for its science and math instruction and college-preparatory curriculum. Linda's parents were very pleased at their daughter's accomplishment and wanted to ensure that she would do well enough to enter a very good university; they increased their expectations of the time she spent studying. The high school was a racially diverse school with many gifted students. Linda became friends with students from a wide geographic region and began to want to participate in more school and off-campus activities. Linda and her parents entered into many conflicts during her high school years: they expected her to be home, working on her schoolwork, but she wanted to have the same freedoms as her new friends. She was particularly interested in participating in theater and received much verbal encouragement to pursue her interest in acting from her teachers and drama coach.

Her grandmother was highly critical of her mother during this time, blaming her mother for what she perceived as Linda's disobedience and disrespect. Her mother expected her father to support her against his mother, but he also felt that Linda was disrespectful and selfish in her desire to be "more American." This led to increased conflict between her parents as well. They were very concerned that her sisters not learn "bad lessons" from Linda, wanting them to find their primary social relationships within their Korean community.

Linda finished high school with a 4.0 grade point average and won an academic scholarship to a prestigious university in the Los Angeles area. She enrolled as a biology major and did well in her classes during the first semester. The second semester, however, her grades began to slip. Linda was suddenly unsure of her decision to pursue a biology major and began to reconsider her interests in acting. She sought the help of a career counselor on campus to decide whether to change majors.

Questions for Discussion

1. How would you explain Linda's behavior from the perspective of a TWA counselor?

2. What is the correspondence between Linda's abilities and the requirements of her environment? Between her values and the reinforcers?

3. How would you incorporate Linda's feelings about her decisions into counseling through the perspective of the TWA?

4. What is Linda's adjustment style?

5. How would you evaluate Linda's person-environment fit in terms of true needs?

6. How do Linda's gender and race/ethnicity influence her decisions?

Box 7.3

Summary of Key Constructs

Construct	Definition
Values	Grouping of needs
Abilities	General dimensions that underlie groupings of acquired skills
Satisfaction	How well an individual's needs are met by the job
Satisfactoriness	How well an individual's abilities and skills meet what the job or organization requires
Reinforcer pattern	Pattern of rewards
Tenure	Length of time in a job
Celerity	Speed with which an individual initiates interaction with his or her environment
Pace	Intensity or activity level of one's interaction with the environment
Rhythm	Pattern of the pace of interaction with the environment
Endurance	Sustaining of interaction with the environment
Flexibility	Ability to tolerate a mismatch (discorrespondence) between needs and rewards
Perseverance	Continuing in the environment while in adjustment mode
Active adjustment	Acting on the environment
Reactive adjustment	Acting on self

References

Betz, N. E. (2008). Advances in vocational theory. In S. D. Brown & R. W. Lent (Eds.), *Handbook of counseling psychology* (4th ed., pp. 357–374). New York: Wiley.

Dawis, R. V. (1994). The theory of work adjustment as convergent theory. In M. L. Savickas & R. W. Lent (Eds.), *Convergence in career development theories* (pp. 33–43). Palo Alto, CA: Consulting Psychologists Press.

Dawis, R. V. (1996). The theory of work adjustment and person-environment-correspondence counseling. In D. Brown, L. Brooks, & Associates (Eds.), *Career choice and development* (3rd ed., pp. 75–120). San Francisco: Jossey-Bass.

Dawis, R. V. (2005). The Minnesota theory of work adjustment. In S. D. Brown & R. W. Lent (Eds.), *Career development and counseling: Putting theory and research to work* (pp. 3–23). New York: Wiley.

Dawis, R. V., & Lofquist, L. H. (1984). *A psychological theory of work adjustment.* Minneapolis: University of Minnesota Press.

Lofquist, L. H., & Dawis, R. V. (1991). *Essentials of person-environment-correspondence counseling.* Minneapolis: University of Minnesota Press.

Additional Readings

Eggerth, D. E. (2008). From theory of work adjustment to person-environment correspondence counseling: Vocational psychology as positive psychology. *Journal of Career Assessment, 16,* 60–74.

Griffin, B., Hesketh, B., Brown, S. D., & Lent, R. W. (2005). Counseling for work adjustment. In S. D. Brown & R. W. Lent (Eds.), *Career development and counseling: Putting theory and research to work* (pp. 483–505). Hoboken, NJ: Wiley.

Lyons, H. Z., Brenner, B. R., & Fassinger, R. E. (2005). A multicultural test of the theory of work adjustment: Investigating the role of heterosexism and fit perceptions in the job satisfaction of lesbian, gay, and bisexual employees. *Journal of Counseling Psychology, 52,* 537–548.

Lyons, H. Z., & O'Brien, K. M. (2006). The role of person-environment fit in the job satisfaction and tenure intentions of African American employees. *Journal of Counseling Psychology, 53,* 387–396.

Super's Developmental Theory

8

Developmental theories include Super's life-span, life-space approach and Gottfredson's theory of circumscription and compromise, which is discussed in the next chapter. Compared to the person-environment fit theories described in Chapters 6 and 7, Super's and Gottfredson's theories are characterized by viewing career choice as a process rather than an event and by incorporating developmental concepts into this process.

The developmental theory of Donald Super has been one of the most influential vocational theories of the 20th century (Borgen, 1991). Super died in 1994, and the last chapter with his 14 theoretical propositions was published posthumously (Super, Savickas, & Super, 1996). Savickas (2002, 2005) has continued to update Super's theory, incorporating the central constructs of the theory with a constructionist perspective. The constructionist perspective emphasizes a subjective view "that individuals actively create their own subjective and personal career realities" (Hartung & Taber, 2008). In other words, individuals actively interpret and construct the meaning of their experiences, rather than fit into a career created by an outside force.

Super (1953) introduced the propositions outlining his theory in his 1952 presidential address to the Division of Counseling Psychology of the American Psychological Association. Super continued to develop and refine his theory until his death in 1994 and was remarkable for his active scientific investigation of real-life phenomena, their eventual theoretical implications, and the application of his work in counseling (Herr, 1997; Savickas, 1997). Savickas has modified some of the original propositions and added others.

One of the hallmarks of Super's theory is that vocational development is a process of making several decisions, which culminate in vocational choices that represent an implementation of the self-concept. Vocational choices are viewed as successive approximations of a good match between the vocational self and the world of work.

Among the basic assumptions underlying the propositions is that development is a process. Three propositions focus on developmental contextualism, which is the process of developing a work identity that occurs within the individual's social context. This social context helps to create both opportunities and constraints. Five propositions indicate an underlying belief in the differences among people and among occupations. People differ in terms of their abilities, personalities, and values, as well as other variables. Occupations have distinctive combinations of required abilities and personality traits. Differences among individuals translate into suitability for a number of different occupations. Individuals may have characteristics appropriate for multiple occupations. Thus, no one occupation is the only possible fit for an individual, nor does only one individual fit a particular occupation. Work satisfaction is predicted to increase proportionately with self-concept implementation and is dependent on the importance of and satisfaction with other life roles. Super suggested that individuals hold various roles in their lives that vary in importance across the life span. Individuals may, in fact, find little satisfaction with the worker role but may be fully satisfied with another life role.

Eight additional propositions discuss development of the self-concept and its implementation in vocational choices, stages, and work roles. Embedded in these propositions are the notions that self-concepts are formed by vocational preferences and competencies, that these change and evolve over time in interaction with situations, that they are products of social learning, and that they are increasingly stable over the life span. Super proposed five distinct life stages, noting that each has unique developmental tasks. He also suggested that career patterns (the sequence of jobs or occupations held by individuals) are determined by a variety of personal and environmental characteristics. One proposition discusses the concept of career adaptability, which is the readiness of the individual to cope with the demands of the environment; another proposition focuses on career maturity, or the readiness and resources to cope with developmental tasks.

The five life stages, or "maxicycles," are Growth (ages 4 to 13), Exploration (ages 14 to 24), Establishment (ages 25 to 44), Maintenance or Management (ages 45 to 65), and Disengagement (over age 65). Super characterized the stages as linear and predictable but not invariant. In other words, he described a series of stages that individuals typically go through but was careful to note that not everyone progresses through these stages in the same manner or at fixed ages. Each transition between stages is characterized by a "minicycle," or a recycling through the stages of growth, reexploration, and reestablishment. The age ranges are the approximate ages at which most individuals encounter each stage.

Within each stage, Super proposed characteristic developmental tasks. Successful mastery of these tasks allows individuals to function effectively in their life roles within that stage and prepares them for the next task. Successful coping with the requirements of each stage is dependent on an individuals' career maturity. Career maturity—or readiness to master the developmental tasks of each stage effectively—involves both attitudinal factors and cognitive factors. Osipow and Fitzgerald (1996) note that "vocational maturity allows the observer to assess the rate and level of an individual's development with respect to career matters" (p. 114). In adults, however, the concept of maturation is less appropriate, and Super et al. (1996) and Savickas (1994) discuss *career adaptability*, defined as "readiness to cope with changing work and work conditions" (Savickas, 1994, p. 58).

Super considered the development of vocational choices within the context of other life roles: "While making a living, people live a life" (Super et al., 1996). He delineated six roles that individuals hold, sometimes concurrently: child, student, homemaker, worker, citizen, and leisurite. Individuals hold multiple roles, and those roles interact. The life-career rainbow schema in Figure 8.1 is a pictorial representation of the intersection of stages and roles and may be used to clarify the various roles for a particular client (Super, 1980). *Life space* corresponds to the roles that one fulfills at various times in life, and *life span* denotes the stages described earlier. An individual "lives in the intersection of the two dimensions" (Super et al., 1996, p. 128).

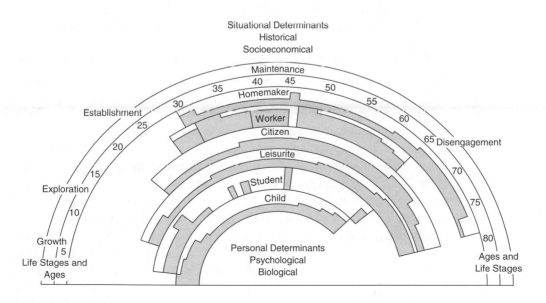

Figure 8.1   Super's Life-Career Rainbow

SOURCE: Super (1980).

A fundamental aspect of Super's theory is that vocational choice is an implementation of the self-concept. The self-concept includes the objective and subjective views of the self. Individuals construct their careers in a continuing self-evaluation within their social context. Individuals begin to consider work roles that fit their self-concepts. Their self-concepts are shaped by feedback from the external world (e.g., parents, teachers, employers), and in turn, the evolving self-concept begins to be implemented in different work roles. The implication for career counselors is that in addition to providing clients with objective information about the self (i.e., interests, values, abilities), counselors also need to integrate clients' subjective views of who they are and the role that they want work to play in their lives.

Salomone (1996) traces the development of Super's theory over 40 years and concludes that the theory did not change substantially over the years but that many of the propositions still needed to be empirically tested. Blustein (1997) and Herr (1997) both note that Super's theory was a framework flexible enough to be revised and refined as the context of working changed. Herr highlights the need for Super's theory to incorporate the impact of economic changes on careers, as well as the role of barriers due to gender and culture in career development. Blustein argues that a more contemporary understanding of Super's theory is best placed within a perspective that is broad and inclusive of the many contexts in which individuals function. Thus, a context-rich way of conceptualizing antecedents of career exploration helps to explain more fully how and why clients explore various aspects of work. A contextual view of the outcomes of career exploration may help to broaden our understanding of the ways in which exploratory behavior influences life roles and decisions.

The developmental theory has been very influential in helping to form the basis of activities related to career exploration in schools (Turner & Lapan, 2005). School counselors at the elementary, middle, and high school levels work individually, in small groups, and in classrooms to help students develop competencies to explore careers, learn more about themselves, and develop skills to plan and implement a future career. School-based career interventions focus on helping students learn more about themselves (e.g., exploring vocational interests and values), about the world of work (e.g., knowing about different types of engineering careers), and how to make career decisions. Lapan (2004) describes a number of different types of interventions that promote career development. Turner and Lapan reviewed research on school-based career counseling, concluding that "overall, analyses of such group-based interventions have shown that they are related to positive changes in . . . vocational identity, career maturity, reduced career indecision, and greater psychological development" (p. 429).

Box 8.1

Personal Reflection

What role does work play in my life now?

What balance do I want among the roles in my life?

How have I constructed the work role over my life span?

Applying Developmental Theory

Counselors who use the developmental approach would ask the sorts of questions that are outlined in Box 8.2. They would ask about the client's life roles and assess which roles are more important than others and how those life roles have evolved over the client's work history. They would ask questions to assess the client's life themes, and they would listen to the client's narrative story and assess how the client attaches meaning to the various events in his or her development. They would listen to how the client has constructed his or her career, including how the self-concept has been implemented in career decisions over time.

Box 8.2

Counselor Cognitions

What are the client's life themes?

What is the client's life structure?

What are the client's adaptive coping strategies?

What are the client's individual style characteristics, such as abilities, interests, and personality?

What are the client's narrative stories?

What is the relative importance of a client's life roles?

How does the client's context affect his or her decisions and developmental process?

How does the client's self-concept influence his or her vocational choices?

CONCEPTUALIZING LESLIE'S CAREER HISTORY

Developmental theorists would view Leslie's case as a series of decisions from childhood through adulthood. We will discuss Leslie's decisions using Super's stages as a framework. We will then discuss developmental career counseling and possible career interventions.

Childhood

Four tasks are addressed in the Growth stage (ages 4–13): becoming concerned about the future, increasing personal control over one's own life, convincing oneself to achieve in school and at work, and acquiring competent work habits and attitudes (Super et al., 1996).

Leslie consistently enjoyed school throughout her elementary and junior high years. Many subjects intrigued her, and she enjoyed the attention of good teachers who challenged her and sparked her interest in a variety of activities. She began to excel in math and science in elementary school and continued to take these courses in middle school.

Other influences on her developing self-concept included her mother, who was her primary role model during childhood. Her father, however, was her earliest occupational role model. As she progressed through elementary and middle school, additional role models were teachers. School in general played an important role in Leslie's life, and her teachers provided valuable support and encouragement.

Leslie's parents communicated their expectations to her about achievement, emphasizing that she should do her best. On the other hand, while her parents were happy that Leslie enjoyed and excelled in school, they did not expect work-related achievement to be a central focus in Leslie's life. She was not expected to work throughout her adult life but rather work until she married and had children, a pattern that was modeled by Leslie's mother and followed by her sister. Thus, she received messages to continue to achieve but not to place achievement as her top priority. These messages influenced the constructions of her developing sense of career.

Adolescence/Early Adulthood

During the Exploration stage (ages 14–24), the primary tasks are crystallizing, specifying, and implementing, or actualizing, a career choice (Super et al., 1996). Leslie experimented with a number of different options, and her difficulty in choosing was related to her ability to see many possible selves due to her wide-ranging interests and talents. Moreover, her indecision may have been exacerbated by the expectations that Leslie experienced from others, particularly her parents, about the importance of the work role in her life: it may have been difficult for her to be planful and decisive about something that others believed would not be important in her life. In contrast to Leslie's experience, her older brother was coached and encouraged by their parents to consider his career alternatives carefully, beginning in early adolescence. Leslie, on the other hand, received little guidance and direction about the process of planning for the future; consequently, she did not plan her entrance into college and had difficulty negotiating the tasks of the exploration stage. Within her family, then, Leslie experienced messages about career choice that differed by one's gender. As she moved into high school, her natural interest in math, particularly advanced math, carried her into a time when she enjoyed being recognized for her ability in math. She tutored other students while in high school and later in college. Thus, excelling at math became a central part of Leslie's developing self-concept. Leslie also developed conscientious study habits, and she took pride in her work.

These messages about career issues relative to gender issues were mirrored by other sources throughout Leslie's adolescence. She continued to receive mixed messages about the appropriate role that a career should play in her life, as well as the appropriateness of her interest in math-related activities and her pursuit of these activities as a career.

Leslie's subjective view of herself conformed to traditional gender-role socialization, in that she focused on marriage and family roles as opposed to long term investment in her work role. She therefore opted out of some career decisions because they were outside of her self-concept. For example, she decided against engineering because of her perceptions of the difficulty of combining work and family in that field, and she decided against math because of her disinterest in pursuing graduate-level education. Math education, on the other hand, represented a compromise between traditional and nontraditional options.

Readiness to make vocational decisions becomes central in Super's Exploration stage. Leslie's difficulty with making a decision about attending college and about her college major may have been related to slightly delayed career maturity—developmentally, she was not as ready to make a decision as she ideally might have been. This delay, in turn, may have been related to the issues just discussed: Leslie had little experience in making career plans prior to entering college because she was not encouraged or expected to do so. The "unreadiness" also led to some discomfort at not having a decision made, and she found herself comparing her progress in making a decision with her college friends, as well as with her brother, who teased her when she had difficulty with decision making. She at times agonized over the "right" choice of college major and career, and the actual decision point stretched over several semesters, as she struggled to keep her options open. Her salient life roles during this period included child and student, although she also was preparing for the homemaker role because she anticipated marrying after college.

In spite of the difficulty she experienced in making a decision, Leslie's choice of secondary education seemed to represent a good avenue for implementing her self-concept as it was developed to that point in her life. The salient parts of her self-concept included being good at math and being recognized for her achievements, as well as being responsible, conscientious, and caring. Teaching allowed her to express these elements of her identity.

CONCEPTUALIZING LESLIE'S PRESENT SITUATION

The Establishment stage (ages 25–40) entails entering and becoming established in one's career and work life, and the tasks of this stage include stabilizing, consolidating, and advancing. *Stabilizing* involves settling in and learning what needs to be done to perform one's job adequately. *Consolidating* occurs when an individual feels comfortable that he or she possesses the skills required by the job and feels secure that he or she is performing well in the eyes of supervisors and coworkers. *Advancing* refers to moving up within one's job, assuming greater responsibility at higher pay. Advancing can occur throughout the Establishment stage but is typically subsequent to stabilizing and consolidating.

Leslie entered teaching with much enthusiasm and experienced the transition into her full-time work role in a manner typical to many young adults; that is, she found it both satisfying and stressful. Despite her success as a teacher, she decided to leave her first position. This decision was primarily based upon a discrepancy between her work and nonwork roles. Leslie's feeling that she did not have enough time to spend with her parents and siblings and the termination of the relationship with her boyfriend led her to question her work-nonwork priorities. She hoped that the job change would provide a better balance between roles and, therefore, that she would feel less stressed and more satisfied. In Super's terms, Leslie spent most of the three years in her first job working on the task of stabilizing. Although from an objective perspective, she clearly possessed the necessary skills, her subjective view was that her skills were not sufficient to make her a good teacher. She wondered whether the amount of stress she was experiencing resulted from her being inadequate at her job, and she did not have any other new teachers to whom she could compare her job performance and stress level. In the absence of external feedback, her career construction was that she was a poor teacher.

Upon taking her new (current) job, Leslie was able to get a different perspective on her skills as a teacher, primarily because she noticed that other teachers seemed to experience a similar level of stress. She thus completed the process of stabilizing and moved on to the tasks related to consolidating in her career. Currently, however, Leslie's dissatisfaction with a number of factors in her job suggests that these tasks may need additional attention and exploration within counseling.

Leslie's current dissatisfaction can be viewed as related to career adaptation; namely, that she is struggling to adapt to changes in her work environment. These changes may be simply too extensive for her to address simultaneously, as she expressed dissatisfaction with the principal, her fellow teachers, the children, and their parents. An alternative hypothesis is that her dissatisfaction with one aspect may have spilled over into other areas and colored her view of the entire work situation. Moreover, a view consonant with developmental theory is that Leslie's dissatisfaction has escalated as her self-concept has become more refined and crystallized. Following this line of thought, the counselor might choose to affirm and validate Leslie's feelings of anger and dissatisfaction, as they may indicate an evolving clarity of who she is and who she wants to become.

Leslie has primarily focused on her student and worker roles. In addition, her role as "child" is still active, as her family of origin continues to be an important influence in her current career situation. Moreover, Leslie is considering a shift in the priority of her life roles, by becoming a parent. As with many people in early adulthood, Leslie has focused on entering and establishing her career and now is stopping to examine her decisions to date. Leslie could be viewed as experiencing an additional stage of midlife career renewal (Williams & Savickas, 1990).

In summary, Leslie can be conceptualized as being in the midst of the Establishment stage (stabilizing, consolidating, advancing). However, like many individuals who have entered career counseling at this point in their careers, she may be recycling back to a consideration of tasks in the Exploration stage (crystallizing, specifying, implementing).

Questions for Discussion

1. What specific hypotheses would you develop about Leslie from Super's theory? How does using Super's theory help you understand Leslie? How might it help Leslie understand herself?

2. What are the advantages of viewing Leslie as reentering the Exploration stage (minicycle within maxicycle)? What are the disadvantages?

3. How ready is Leslie to make a career decision right now? How does she feel about the prospect of making a decision, particularly of making a job or career change? How might her previous experiences with career decision making influence the process or content of this current decision?

4. Who is likely to influence her decision? How much pressure does she feel now? What types of pressure and from whom?

5. Which life roles seem most salient to Leslie? How can she balance the roles that she desires?

6. How might Leslie describe her self-concept and the narrative of her life? How does she make meaning from the interaction of her various life roles?

THE CASE OF KAREN

Karen is a 52-year-old European American living in the southwest United States. She seeks career counseling because she is struggling to understand how she can continue to advance in her career and still take care of her elderly mother. Karen is divorced, with two grown children who are starting careers of their own. Her mother, Irene, is in her early 80s and lives in an independent living apartment in a midsize town in Iowa. Irene recently fell and broke her hip. In the process of helping her mother, Karen discovered that her mother has several signs of advancing dementia. Karen is not sure that Irene can live on her own any more, but Irene refuses to move from her home or leave her friends.

Karen went to nursing school right after her high school graduation. She wanted to help others and liked her science courses in high school. Her original goal was to have a job that she could easily blend with her strong desire to stay home with children. She also hoped to meet a doctor and not have to work after she had children. She graduated with an RN and began working at a hospital in Iowa, where she met her future husband, a medical intern. They married and had two children in 3 years. Karen did not work after her children were born. She noted that her husband's career took precedence in their family and his hours as an internist were unpredictable. She stayed home with her children until they were in school full-time. She enjoyed being a doctor's wife in their community and was very involved in civic and political organizations. Soon, though, she realized that all her friends were returning to work, and she needed more to occupy her time.

She began to look for work but found that employers preferred nurses with a bachelor's degree rather than an RN. She went back to school to complete her bachelor's of science in nursing (BSN), and in the process of her schoolwork, realized she really enjoyed the role that information played in the work of medical professionals. She began to consider working in health information, but she was not sure if she would need more schooling for that career. As she was finishing her BSN degree, her husband accepted a position with a practice in Phoenix, Arizona, and, though their marriage was beginning to unravel, she moved with him. Her children did not join them; they were already in college and chose to stay with their grandmother during summers.

Karen's life roles shifted in Phoenix. Her children were not actively part of her household, her husband's work hours were long, and her role as a doctor's wife was very different in a big city than in a small town. She started to look for a job and found a position as a nursing supervisor in a hospital. She took the job in part because the hospital would give her an opportunity to work her way into health information systems. In fact, she was offered a position in the health information department within a year and quickly excelled, receiving three promotions within 5 years.

Karen's work became more important to her as she and her husband decided to divorce. She enjoyed the tasks in her work, enjoyed the challenges of solving technology problems, and enjoyed the recognition she was receiving. She liked having her own money and independence. She also felt that she was in the right place at the right time, because the health care industry was booming in Phoenix. She began to be recruited to work for other hospitals and firms and was considering an offer from a software company when her mother fell.

Currently, Karen is very torn about her future. She feels that she should go back to take care of Irene. Moving back to Iowa would also bring her closer to her children, who stayed in the Midwest. But the opportunities to work in health information systems are very limited in her mother's hometown. Karen feels that she has to choose between caring for her mother and her work and independence.

Questions for Discussion

1. What specific hypotheses would you develop about Karen from Super's theory? How does using Super's theory help you understand Karen? How might it help Karen understand herself?

2. What are the advantages of viewing Karen as reentering the Maintenance/Management stage? What are the disadvantages?

3. How ready is Karen to make a career decision right now? What alternatives might Karen consider?

4. Who is likely to influence her decision? How much pressure does she feel now? What types of pressure and from whom?

5. How can Karen balance the roles that she desires?

6. How might Karen describe her self-concept and the narrative of her life? How does she make meaning from the interaction of her various life roles?

Directions and Implications for Career Counseling

GOALS OF COUNSELING

From Super's framework, the goals of counseling for clients are as follows:

To (1) develop and accept an integrated and adequate picture of themselves and their life roles, (2) test the concept against reality, and (3) convert it into reality by making choices that implement the self-concept and lead to job success and satisfaction as well as benefit to society. (Super et al., 1996, pp. 158–159)

Savickas (2002) adds that the goal of constructivist counseling is to "help clients construct a career path that moves them toward the community, not climb a ladder that elevates them above it" (p. 185).

Super's theory also has been expanded into an explicit model of counseling, named the career development assessment and counseling model (C-DAC) (Osborne, Brown, Niles, & Miner, 1997; Super, 1983; Super, Osborne, Walsh, Brown, & Niles, 1992). The C-DAC model was developed to use concepts from Super's developmental theory to augment trait-and-factor approaches to career counseling. The model incorporates four phases of assessment: (1) life space and work-role salience; (2) career development status and resources, or career adaptability; (3) vocational identity, including values, interests, and abilities; and (4) vocational self-concepts and life themes. In each of these four phases, assessment can be accomplished either in session with the client or by using inventories developed by Super and his colleagues.

The first step, assessment of life space and work-role salience, begins by exploring the importance of the work role to the client, particularly in relation to the other potential roles in a client's life, such as child, student, homemaker, citizen, and leisurite. *Life structure* refers to the constellation of core and peripheral roles that define an individual's life. The degree to which the work role is salient will influence the weight placed on the three subsequent assessments, since these focus specifically on the work role and identity.

The second focus of assessment is career development status and resources, or the client's career adaptability. The counselor needs to determine which developmental tasks are of concern to the client. Identification of the client's concerns is followed by an assessment of the coping resources that he or she possesses to deal with those concerns. Coping resources are typically viewed as the attitudes and competencies that the client holds for dealing with the specific developmental tasks that he or she is facing. Hartung and Taber (2008) describe this as the focus on adaptive coping strategies that the client has, or needs to develop, to resolve career concerns.

Third, the assessment of vocational identity represents the "traditional trait-and-factor" portion of the C-DAC model (Super et al., 1996) and includes values, abilities, and interests. However, rather than the trait-factor view that assessment focuses on uncovering objective traits that a client may possess, career construction theory views this phase as assessing the client's way of coping with the world, or style (Hartung & Taber, 2008). The goal of this step is to develop a description of these aspects of the client's vocational identity, then explore how this identity might be expressed in the various roles in the client's life.

The fourth and final step in assessment focuses on occupational self-concepts and life themes. Here, the focus shifts from the "objective" assessment during the previous step to an assessment of the client's subjective self-concept. The C-DAC model recommends two methods, a cross-sectional method, which focuses on the client's current self-schema, and a longitudinal method, which focuses on themes that have developed throughout the client's life. Hartung and Taber (2008) describe this as helping the client to identify his or her career story. The career style interview (Savickas, 2005) may be used to assess life themes by assessing domains of role models, favorite television shows or magazines, leisure activities, favorite school subjects, early memories, and favorite sayings.

Following these four steps in assessment, the counselor then develops an "integrative interpretation which narrates the client's life story" (Super et al., 1996, p. 157) and serves as a transition from the assessment phase to the counseling phase. Super (1957) described a process of counseling that alternates between directive and nondirective techniques. For example, the counselor may begin with a nondirective exploration of Leslie's career concerns, followed by a directive setting of topics for further discussion, then nondirective clarification of Leslie's self-concept and life structure, directive discussion of assessment results, and nondirective discussion of her reactions to the assessment. This cyclical approach to career counseling offers a way to "balance attention to the objective and subjective dimensions of self and career" (Super et al., 1996, p. 162). Karen's counselor may be less directive than Leslie's counselor, because Karen appears to be more concerned with the salience of different life roles. Thus, her counselor may focus more on her life structure and on her life themes.

INTERVENTIONS

Consonant with the goals of developmental theory, Leslie's goals include achieving a better view of herself and what is causing her dissatisfaction at work and an understanding of the ways in which she can juggle the multiple roles of child, worker, and parent. She stated that she wants to decide whether to stay at her current job or move to a new field and that she wants to discuss incorporating possible shifts of roles. Karen's goals are to decide how to balance the roles of child, parent, and worker. She also needs to decide whether to move back to Iowa and, if she does not move, to determine how to take care of her mother.

Assessment of Life Space and Work-Role Salience

The interaction of primary roles has potential for either creating stress or reducing stress: "Multiple roles can enrich life or overburden it" (Super et al., 1996, p. 129). Further, the process of completing a career transition may lead to the evolution of roles and how roles interact in a client's life: roles may be added or deleted, or ongoing roles may be modified.

The counselor begins with a clarification of roles and their relative salience at this point. For example, how might Leslie characterize her current balance of roles? How might she construct an ideal balance of roles? How much discrepancy is there between her current balance of roles and her ideal balance? Moreover, Leslie is contemplating adding the role of "parent" to her life, and the interaction of that role with her work role needs to be examined.

Super's life-career rainbow suggests that Leslie is fulfilling a number of different social roles in her life and that she may be re-evaluating the relative priority or salience of these roles. An intervention that may help Leslie clarify her life roles is an "interrole assessment" technique (Brown & Brooks, 1991). This technique can be used to identify and clarify the interaction of work roles with other life roles. First, Leslie lists the life roles in which she currently is involved and estimates the amount of time spent in each role. Next, she ranks her life roles using values as the basis for ranking. Finally, she identifies roles that conflict with one another, roles that are compensatory with one another, and roles that complement one another (Brown & Brooks, 1991).

The life-career rainbow shows that Karen's current primary role is that of worker, but that is now in conflict with her child role. Karen has not often had to balance multiple roles. Early in her marriage, her role as parent was the most salient, with some importance given to the role of citizen. As her children grew and were home less, her primary role was that of student. After she moved and her marriage ended, her primary role was that of worker. Now, with her mother ill and needing her help while her career is advancing with many opportunities, she is struggling with the balance among roles.

Assessment of Career Adaptability

Assessment of career adaptability involves assessing the client's career concern, the developmental tasks the client is encountering, and the skills and resources the individual brings to resolving those tasks. Savickas (2002, 2005) conceptualizes the four dimensions of career adaptability as concern, control, curiosity, and confidence. Each task is proposed to have specific attitudes, competencies, and coping behaviors, as well as types of career interventions to address it. For example, the concern dimension is characterized by a concern about the future as a worker. Positive responses to this concern would be a planful attitude and developing competencies in planning. Coping behaviors would include becoming aware of the need for planning, becoming involved in exploring future options, and preparing for future decisions. Interventions for this concern would focus on helping clients have a future orientation, developing occupational daydreams, and developing planning skills.

To determine which developmental tasks are of concern to Leslie, a counselor might use results from the Adult Career Concerns Inventory (ACCI) (Super, Thompson, & Lindeman, 1988) as a guide. Leslie's highest score of the four stage scales is in Exploration, suggesting that her primary career concerns are tasks related to the Exploration stage (see Appendix A, Figure 4). This is particularly useful to note and to address in counseling, because Leslie may be feeling some discrepancy between her age and her expected career stage. That is, she may feel that she should be further along in her career path. Indeed, she expresses that she "should have figured this out by now." Moreover, Leslie's parents and siblings convey their amusement about her still being "undecided about what she wants to do."

The counselor also would examine the substage scores on the ACCI for further clues about Leslie's concerns. Her highest scores within the Exploration stage are on Specification and Crystallization, with a relatively lower score on Implementation. These scores suggest that Leslie is focused upon identifying and choosing a specific occupational direction, confirming what she has expressed to the counselor.

Given the career concerns that Leslie expresses, the counselor then may assess the coping resources available to Leslie. The first type of resource is positive attitudes toward career planning. Leslie is quite enthused about career counseling and feels ready to "make a career choice the right way this time." She is interested in researching different occupations, and her analytical skills would serve her well in this regard.

A second type of coping resource is Leslie's knowledge about herself and about the world of work. Her knowledge about herself appears appropriate to her age and experience, as indicated by her confidence in completing the assessment inventories, her ability to describe the positive and negative aspects of her current job, and her self-description of her strengths and weaknesses. The counselor, however, would remain attentive for areas in which Leslie could benefit from additional self-exploration, as well as areas in which Leslie underestimates her abilities and skills. Leslie's knowledge of occupational information also seems quite appropriate to her situation, and she clearly expresses specific occupations about which she would like additional information. Again, the counselor would be attentive to misinformation that Leslie might hold or areas in which she needs further information.

The final type of coping resource that the counselor assesses is decision-making skills. Because Leslie reports that she has "not made good decisions in the past," the counselor would attempt to make a careful and thorough assessment of her decision-making strategies and skills. The counselor would ask Leslie to describe the process that she uses to make decisions by analyzing several situations in which Leslie has made decisions in the past (e.g., changing jobs, buying a car). One hypothesis that the counselor may explore is whether Leslie's decision-making skills are truly inadequate or whether she only believes this to be true because her family has told her so.

In Karen's case, the career concern may be related to curiosity about her future self and how to resolve the dilemma of balancing multiple roles, but the counselor would go through very similar processes. The counselor would assess Karen's attitudes toward considering various ways to resolve her concerns. An open attitude to examining options leads to competence in exploring various alternatives. Karen's counselor might encourage her to experiment with a variety of solutions. The counselor would also help Karen identify factors that are inhibiting her from developing confidence in ways that she could blend multiple roles. Finally, the counselor would help Karen identify the resources she has to construct her future career, including her planning and decision-making skills, the strength of her relationship with her mother, and her vocational options as a professional in a growing field.

Assessment of Vocational Identity

Vocational identity, the focus of the third step, is described by integrating information about the client's interests, values, abilities, and personality. In Leslie's case, these would be seen in the inventories that she took prior to counseling. In Karen's case, this would be assessed in an interview focusing on the tasks and activities she does or does not enjoy at work.

Leslie is interested in working with and helping people, as evidenced by her scores on the SII and the MIQ, yet her confidence in Social activities does not match her interest; her lack of confidence may be due to her tendency to be introverted in nature. She also is quite comfortable working alone and may, in fact, be perceived by others as preferring to work alone. Leslie also is interested in mathematical and scientific activities, which is supported by her logical and analytical style and her valuing of achievement and the use of her abilities.

The counselor may explore how Leslie's vocational identity is expressed in her life through her work role and other life roles. One area for exploration is whether Leslie wishes to incorporate more Social-type activities into her work role or whether she can express those interests in her leisure pursuits.

Assessment of Occupational
Self-Concepts and Life Themes

In the final step of assessment in the C-DAC model, the client's subjective self-concept is explored. The focus in this step is on clients' self-schemas—how they "make sense" of themselves and their world. For example, Leslie's counselor would assess Leslie's self-concept by listening carefully to how she describes herself, both as she is today and as she has seen herself throughout her life. Leslie seems to view herself as capable and talented, yet she is self-critical and easily discouraged when she compares herself to others. She has internalized her family's perception of her as indecisive as well as their mixed messages about achievement, although she is beginning to examine these beliefs about herself. Leslie feels that she has much to offer, if only she could identify the best outlet for her talents.

Karen's counselor would also listen carefully to her stories and life themes. Karen's career concerns focus more on the balance of her roles as child and parent with her worker role. Her self-concept in early adulthood was shaped by her own expectations of her roles as a mother and doctor's wife, and her self-concept as a worker did not develop until she returned to school and realized she had interests in technology. She began to construct her career as a health information professional as her other roles began to be less demanding or not available to her. Now she is struggling between her self-concept as an independent professional woman and her self-concept as a caring daughter and mother. She does not know how—or even if—she can blend the roles.

Other Interventions

The cases of Leslie and Karen suggest the use of interventions related to exploratory behavior. The counselor would thoroughly examine career decisions up to this point in time. How did Leslie and Karen make earlier career decisions? What factors influenced the process and outcome of their decisions? What other career options had they considered and why? Why were the other options discarded?

Leslie's counselor would help her to acknowledge explicitly and accept her status in the Exploration stage. She may benefit from "making meaning" for herself about where she is in the career development process. For example, she may decide that she is "starting over" but this time possessing greater wisdom and self-knowledge and having different questions to answer for herself. The counselor would encourage Leslie to see herself as "recycling" through the Exploration stage with a description of the tasks of crystallizing, specifying, and implementing career choice. Super proposed that individuals go through a minicycle during career transitions; Leslie could be conceptualized as being in a career transition, although the extent of the transition is not yet clear.

Super et al. (1996) stated that "individuals eventually complete the task of specifying an occupational choice by translating the privately experienced occupational self-concept into educational/vocational choices" (p. 132). Leslie's self-concept continues to evolve, becoming more clearly defined with age and with experience. The counselor may help Leslie explore how her current self-concept fits with the career choice that she implemented immediately after college and whether her dissatisfaction with her current job may be related to changes in her self-concept. Have her job responsibilities kept up with her evolving self-concept? Are there opportunities where she is now or in a new teaching-related position, or is a career change indicated?

The construct of career maturity (or career adaptability) is particularly relevant in the Exploration stage, and the counselor would examine how ready Leslie is to make vocational decisions. The uncertainty of her future pregnancy plans adds another dimension to Leslie's readiness. How is she feeling about making a career decision? Moreover, Leslie's previous experiences with career decision making were associated with some anxiety related to time pressure, family expectations, and/or the decision-making process itself.

Additional Cases

CASE 1: WALTER

Walter is a 65-year-old Caucasian man who is a manufacturing representative for a large tractor company. He has worked for this company for almost 40 years and worked his way up to his current position of regional manager. Walter plans to retire within a year or two.

Walter married his wife, Martha, while he was in the Army. He had completed two years of college but discontinued his education when their first daughter was born. Walter did not pursue any further formal education and expresses regret that he did not complete his degree.

Walter and Martha have four children, all of whom are married and successfully employed. Walter and Martha have nine grandchildren, seven of whom live within a 30-mile radius. Martha has been a traditional homemaker, raising the children and supporting Walter's business activities. She is a very active civic volunteer and maintains a busy schedule.

Walter (and Martha) will be entering retirement with good health and financial security. He is preparing himself for voluntary retirement; he would prefer to continue working indefinitely, but Martha has encouraged him to retire so that they can do more traveling. Also, Walter is feeling some unspoken pressure to retire from the vice president of sales so that another individual can be promoted into Walter's position.

Walter typically worked 80 hours per week and spent a good deal of time on the road. Because of this very busy workload, he has not had time to develop many hobbies other than the golf he played as a business activity. His expressed plans for retirement include traveling, playing golf, and learning French. He also has expressed interest in taking college courses, perhaps to finish his degree. Martha has encouraged Walter to enter counseling because of her worry that he will not have enough to do and will "be underfoot" at home. He recently has experienced several anxiety attacks that were initially believed to be minor heart attacks, and his physician also has encouraged him to pursue counseling.

Another issue facing Walter and Martha is that his 87-year-old mother may need more daily living assistance than she currently is receiving in her apartment.

Questions for Discussion

1. How would you conceptualize the salience of roles in Walter's life? How might he be experiencing the shifting roles in his life with more emphasis on the grandparent, leisurite, student, and/or caretaking roles?

2. What issues would you encourage Walter to consider as he shifts into the Disengagement phase of his career? How might he use the remaining time in his work role to prepare for retirement?

3. In what specific activities could Walter engage to develop alternate roles?

4. Are there any unresolved tasks from earlier life/career stages that might need to be addressed in counseling?

5. How would you assess Walter's career adaptability?

6. What issues might be occurring between Martha and Walter? How might you address these issues?

CASE 2: MARIA JOSEFINA

Maria Josefina is a 16-year-old girl of Puerto Rican descent living in the Southeast. She is the oldest daughter of six children; her father is a skilled laborer in construction, and her mother is a homemaker. She has one older brother who attended a community college to learn how to be an electrician and is working for the same construction company as their father. Maria Josefina's family moved from Puerto Rico 8 years ago, when she was 10 and her older brother was 12 and her younger sisters and brothers were 8, 6, 4, and 2. Her family lives in a middle-class neighborhood that is ethnically diverse, and they get along well with their neighbors. They primarily socialize with other Puerto Ricans, though, and often spend time with members of their extended family in the area.

Maria Josefina feels that she lives in two worlds: school and home, each characterized by different languages, expectations, and relationships. At school, she speaks English and has many friends with whom she enjoys spending time talking about boys and clothes and the future. At home, she speaks Spanish, spends time with her brothers and sisters, and enjoys the support and warmth of having her aunts, uncles, grandparents, and cousins around her. They sing, talk, and dance together.

Maria Josefina has done well in school and is being encouraged by her high school teachers and guidance counselors to consider college. Her parents, though, do not want her to leave home and are encouraging her to consider attending the same community college that her brother attended. Maria Josefina knows that, as the oldest daughter, she is expected to be home to help her mother, but she would very much like to become a social worker. Her aunt, who is strongly encouraging her to attend one of the universities, has referred her for career counseling.

Questions for Discussion

1. How would you conceptualize Maria Josefina from a developmental framework?

2. What developmental tasks has she accomplished? What tasks does she yet have to accomplish?

3. How would you characterize her objective and subjective self-concepts?

4. What are the role interactions she is encountering?

5. How would you help her make a decision?

6. How do Maria Josefina's gender and race/ethnicity influence her decisions?

CASE 3: DEBORAH AND TRISH

Deborah (age 33) enters counseling at a community agency specializing in women's issues at the urging of her partner, Trish (age 38); both are of European American descent. Deborah has been depressed and irritable for the past few months, and Trish is concerned that Deborah is unhappy with their 5-year relationship, although Deborah has denied that this is the case.

Deborah is currently experiencing considerable dissatisfaction in her career. She is a lawyer in the district attorney's office in a medium-sized town in the Southwest. She views her work environment as undesirable for a number of reasons, including the lack of opportunities for advancement and her perception that she cannot disclose her sexual orientation at work. She frequently comes home from work depressed. Deborah recently had an offer from a law firm in San Francisco that was quite attractive; however, she did not accept the position because of the difficulty of relocating.

Trish is an associate professor of biology at a state university. She has successfully established herself and is happy in her profession and work environment. She supported Deborah's application for the San Francisco job, but she also made it clear that moving to another university might be difficult and would disrupt her career. Trish expresses skepticism that Deborah's depression could be the result of work factors and continues to believe that Deborah is dissatisfied with their relationship.

As is typical in their professions, Deborah and Trish both work many hours and frequently work at home in the evenings and weekends. This dedication to their respective careers was one of the aspects that first attracted them to one another, and they support one another's career advancement. However, lately Deborah has begun to wonder if there isn't more to life than work and has wished that she and Trish could spend more time together taking trips and just enjoying the weekends. Trish, however, easily gets absorbed in the work that she brings home and frequently stays up late at night working on projects.

Questions for Discussion

1. How might Deborah be conceptualized from the perspective of developmental theories? How might Trish be conceptualized?

2. With what developmental tasks might Deborah be struggling?

3. How could you help Deborah and Trish understand one another's career perspectives? What, if any, discrepancies exist between their respective career stages and issues?

4. How might you address their relationship issues? How might career and relationship concerns be connected for Deborah? For Trish?

5. How do Deborah's gender and race/ethnicity influence her decisions? How do gender and race/ethnicity influence Trish's decisions?

Box 8.3

Summary of Key Constructs

Construct	Definition
Career construction	Developing and implementing the self-concept through vocational choices.
Developmental contextualism	Belief that the process of developing a work identity occurs within the individual's social context.
Stages	Series of steps that individuals typically go through in constructing a career, though not everyone progresses through these stages in the same manner or at fixed ages.

(Continued)

(Continued)

Construct	Definition
Growth	Stage, typically occurring in childhood, whose primary tasks include becoming concerned about the future, learning more about self and the need to make future decisions.
Exploration	Stage, typically occurring in adolescence and early adulthood, whose primary tasks are crystallizing, specifying, and implementing, or actualizing, a career choice.
Establishment	Stage, typically occurring in adulthood, which entails entering and becoming established in one's career and work life. The tasks of this stage include stabilizing, consolidating, and advancing.
Maintenance/Management	Stage, typically occurring in middle adulthood, in which individuals are maintaining and advancing in their careers. Primary tasks are renewal, holding, updating, and innovating.
Disengagement	Stage, typically occurring in later adulthood, in which an individual retires or disengages from work.
Developmental tasks	Career concerns specific to each stage.
Career maturity	Readiness to master the developmental tasks of each stage effectively.
Career adaptability	Readiness and resources to cope with developmental tasks.
Life roles	Roles individuals have in their lives: child, student, homemaker, worker, citizen, leisurite. Roles may interact and hold different levels of importance throughout life span.
Work role salience	Importance of the work role in relation to the other potential roles in a client's life.
Vocational identity	An individual's work values, interests, and abilities.

References

Blustein, D. L. (1997). A context-rich perspective of career exploration across the life roles. *Career Development Quarterly, 45,* 260–274.

Borgen, F. H. (1991). Megatrends and milestones in vocational behavior: A 20-year counseling psychology retrospective. *Journal of Vocational Behavior, 39,* 263–290.

Brown, D., & Brooks, L. (1991). *Career counseling techniques*. Needham Heights, MA: Allyn & Bacon.

Hartung, P. J., & Taber, B. J. (2008). Career construction and subjective well-being. *Journal of Career Assessment, 16,* 75–85.

Herr, E. L. (1997). Super's life-span, life-space approach and its outlook for refinement. *Career Development Quarterly, 45,* 238–246.

Lapan, R. T. (2004). *Career development across the K–16 years: Bridging the present to satisfying and successful futures*. Alexandria, VA: American Counseling Association.

Osborne, W. L., Brown, S., Niles, S., & Miner, C. U. (1997). *Career development, assessment, and counseling: Applications of the Donald E. Super C-DAC approach*. Alexandria, VA: American Counseling Association.

Osipow, S. H., & Fitzgerald, L. (1996). *Theories of career development* (4th ed.). Needham Heights, MA: Allyn & Bacon.

Salomone, P. R. (1996). Tracing Super's theory of vocational development: A 40-year retrospective. *Journal of Career Development, 22,* 167–184.

Savickas, M. L. (1994). Measuring career development: Current status and future directions. *Career Development Quarterly, 43,* 54–62.

Savickas, M. L. (1997). Career adaptability: An integrative construct for life-span, life-space theory. *Career Development Quarterly, 45,* 247–259.

Savickas, M. L. (2002). A developmental theory of vocational psychology. In D. Brown (Ed.), *Career choice and development* (4th ed., pp. 149–205). San Francisco: Jossey-Bass.

Savickas, M. L. (2005). The theory and practice of career construction. In S. D. Brown & R. W. Lent (Eds.), *Career development and counseling: Putting theory and research to work* (pp. 42–70). Hoboken, NJ: Wiley.

Super, D. E. (1953). A theory of vocational development. *American Psychologist, 8,* 185–190.

Super, D. E. (1957). *The psychology of careers*. New York: HarperCollins.

Super, D. E. (1980). A life-span, life-space approach to career development. *Journal of Vocational Behavior, 13,* 282–298.

Super, D. E. (1983). Assessment in career counseling: Toward truly developmental counseling. *Personnel and Guidance Journal, 61,* 555–562.

Super, D. E., Osborne, W. L., Walsh, D. J., Brown, S. D., & Niles, S. G. (1992). Developmental career assessment and counseling: The C-DAC. *Journal of Counseling and Development, 71,* 74–80.

Super, D. E., Savickas, M. L., & Super, C. M. (1996). The life-span, life-space approach to careers. In D. Brown, L. Brooks, & Associates (Eds.), *Career choice and development* (3rd ed., pp. 121–178). San Francisco: Jossey-Bass.

Super, D. E., Thompson, A. S., & Lindeman, R. H. (1988). *Adult Career Concerns Inventory: Manual for research and exploratory use in counseling*. Palo Alto, CA: Consulting Psychologists Press.

Turner, S. L., & Lapan, R. T. (2005). Promoting career development and aspirations in school-age youth. In S. D. Brown & R. W. Lent (Eds.), *Career development and counseling: Putting theory and research to work* (pp. 417–440). Hoboken, NJ: Wiley.

Williams, C. P., & Savickas, M. L. (1990). Developmental tasks of career maintenance. *Journal of Vocational Behavior, 36,* 166–175.

Additional Readings

Blustein, D. L., Schultheiss, D. E. P., & Flum, H. (2004). Toward a relational per-
    spective of the psychology of careers and working: A social constructionist
    analysis. *Journal of Vocational Behavior, 64,* 423–440.

Flum, H. (2001). Relational dimensions in career development. *Journal of
    Vocational Behavior, 59,* 1–16.

Hartung, P. J. (2002). Cultural context in career theory and practice: Role salience
    and values. *Career Development Quarterly, 51,* 12–25.

Hartung, P. J. (2005). Integrated career assessment and counseling: Mindsets,
    models and methods. In W. B. Walsh & M. L. Savickas (Eds.), *Handbook of
    vocational psychology* (3rd ed., pp. 371–395). Mahwah, NJ: Lawrence
    Erlbaum.

Hartung, P. J., Porfeli, E. J., & Vondracek, F. W. (2005). Child vocational develop-
    ment: A review and reconsideration. *Journal of Vocational Behavior, 66,*
    385–419.

Savickas, M. L., Briddick, W. C., & Watkins, C. E. (2002). The relation of career
    maturity to personality type and social adjustment. *Journal of Career
    Assessment, 10,* 24–41.

Schultheiss, D. E. P., Palma, T. V., & Manzi, A. J. (2005). Career development in
    middle childhood: A qualitative inquiry. *Career Development Quarterly,
    53,* 246–262.

Gottfredson's Theory of Circumscription and Compromise

9

As noted in the previous chapter, Gottfredson's theory of circumscription and compromise is a developmental theory, characterized by viewing career choice as a process rather than an event and by incorporating developmental concepts into this process. Gottfredson (1996, 2005) developed her theory of circumscription and compromise to explain why individuals' vocational expectations, even when they are children, vary by sex, race, and social class. Gottfredson differs from Super in that she views vocational choice first as an implementation of the social self and only secondarily as an implementation of the psychological self. Inherent in this approach is the circumscription of psychological variables, such as interests or values, by social variables, such as gender or social class. Gottfredson focuses on cognitive development as children grow in awareness of themselves and their social place in the world and begin to eliminate vocational options that are not compatible with their evolving self-image.

In a recent description of her theory, Gottfredson (2005) poses the scenario of 1,000 newborns in their cribs. They are unaware of differences among themselves or among social or occupational options in the world. Yet, within 15 to 20 years, all will have developed similar perceptions of occupations and will have "reproduced most of the class and gender differences of the parent generation" (p. 72). How does this happen? Gottfredson proposes that four development processes provide an explanation: cognitive growth, self-creation, circumscription, and compromise.

COGNITIVE GROWTH

During the normal process of development, children develop increasingly complex cognitive structures. These structures allow the processing of occupational information and determining the quality of matches. As Gottfredson (2005) notes, children begin to narrow their options and make other decisions that directly affect their career choices long before they have developed sufficient cognitive complexity to do so satisfactorily. As children develop their cognitive abilities, they are increasingly able to think abstractly and to consider multiple dimensions when evaluating information. Further, cognitive growth affects two important components of vocational choice: the cognitive map of occupations and the self-concept. As in person-environment fit models, accurate perceptions of occupations and of oneself are crucial features in Gottfredson's model.

SELF-CREATION

An age-old question in psychology is the relative influence of nature (genetic factors) versus nurture (environmental influences) on human development. A corollary is whether individuals are passive recipients of either (or both) nature and nurture or if they have an active role in their own development. An early critique of Gottfredson's theory was that its use of genetic concepts gave it a deterministic flavor—that it implied individuals have little control over the course of their career lives. In her most recent writing, Gottfredson (2005) explicitly discusses the concept of self-creation, suggesting that although many characteristics of an individual are biologically based, the emergence and further development of these characteristics are shaped by the experiences that one chooses. Repeated experiences consolidate an individual's genetically based characteristics, turning them into "traits" that gain stability across a variety of situations. We come to realize our characteristics and traits through interactions with others, by observing ourselves and others' reactions to us, leading to the self-concept. Thus, a wealth or lack of exposure to a variety of experiences influences the expression of an individual's genetic makeup. Further, adolescents rarely have sufficient experiences to draw upon when they are making choices related to education and career.

Gottfredson (1996, 2005) also discusses "niche seeking," "birth niches," and "ecological niches," concepts derived from developmental psychology to explain how individuals find their place in the world. As social beings, we strive to find our place in society, and vocational choice is one way to announce our place.

CIRCUMSCRIPTION

The importance of our social nature becomes apparent in considering how children view the variety of occupations in their world. Circumscription is the process by which children narrow the "zone of acceptable alternatives" by progressive elimination of unacceptable alternatives, or those that conflict with one's self-concept (see Figure 9.1). Gottfredson's four-stage model of circumscription characterizes children as having an increasing capacity to think abstractly. She also suggests that elimination of alternatives is progressive and irreversible (except under unusual circumstances) and mostly occurs without conscious awareness of the process or of the details of the occupations that are being eliminated.

Gottfredson's four stages are as follows:

Stage 1 (ages 3–5): Children develop an orientation to size and power. They categorize people in simple ways, such as big versus little. Although they do not have firm ideas about sex differences or gender roles, they do recognize observable physical differences between men and women.

Stage 2 (ages 6–8): This recognition increases in Stage 2, when children develop an orientation to sex roles. They tend to use dichotomous thinking, characterize their own sex as superior to the other sex, and use sex-appropriateness to define their vocational aspirations. In this stage, children construct their tolerable-sex-type boundary (see Figure 9.1).

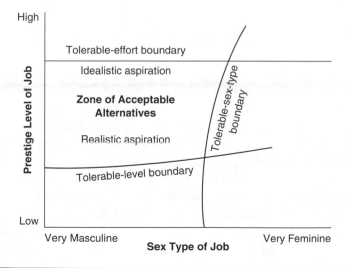

Figure 9.1   Gottfredson's Model of Circumscription and Compromise

SOURCE: Gottfredson (1996).

Stage 3 (ages 9–13): This stage entails orientation to social valuation, or sensitivity to prestige and status, whether by their peers or the larger society. Children become aware of status hierarchies among occupational choices and now view the range of occupations along the two dimensions of prestige level and sex type. Children establish their tolerable-level boundary to eliminate occupations that are unacceptably low in prestige and their tolerable-effort boundary to eliminate occupations that are too difficult to attain (see Figure 9.1). By the end of Stage 3, the full range of occupations has been whittled down to those that are of the appropriate sex type, that have high enough prestige, and that are not too difficult. What remains is a child's zone of acceptable alternatives (or social space). As Gottfredson (2005) notes, vocational choice to this point "seems to be mostly a by-product of wanting to belong, be respected, and live a comfortable life as defined by the individual's reference group" (p. 81), and vocational interest or personal fulfillment has not entered the equation.

Stage 4 (ages 14 and older): Adolescents become aware of the need to consider their vocational choices, and they develop their orientation to the internal, unique self. Here, interests, values, and abilities are clarified, and occupational exploration occurs within the zone of acceptable alternatives as circumscribed in earlier stages. Stages 1 through 3 are focused on rejecting unacceptable alternatives, with greater attention to the social self; Stage 4 is focused on identifying which of the acceptable alternatives are most preferred, with greater attention to the psychological self (Gottfredson, 1996). Stage 4 thus begins the process of compromise.

COMPROMISE

As the pressure to make vocationally relevant decisions intensifies, adolescents begin to consider more concrete aspects of different occupations. Vocational aspirations can be viewed as the product of accessibility (choices that are most realistic) and compatibility (person-environment fit), and idealistic aspirations may give way to realistic ones.

Compromise entails the modification of alternatives due to inaccessibility, leading to the acceptance of less attractive alternatives. Gottfredson (1996) suggests that sex type, prestige, and field of interest are the three dimensions considered in the process of compromise. She also discusses three factors pertinent to the compromise process (Gottfredson, 2005).

The first factor, "truncated search, limited knowledge," describes how people minimize their required effort by searching for information only for their most-preferred occupations, only when they need to make a decision, and only from sources that they already know. This strategy severely restricts the range of occupational information that adolescents gather, thus limiting their perceived opportunities.

Second, "bigger investment, better accessibility" refers to the important role that an individual's initiative has in exposing him or her to a broad range of opportunities; the more active an individual is in terms of creating his or her own options, the greater number of options that will be accessible.

Third, most individuals will settle for a "good enough or not too bad" choice rather than the best possible choice. People look for compatible career choices within those that seem accessible, or those that provide a good match with their three preferred dimensions of sex type, prestige level, and field of interest. However, these three dimensions are compromised in a specific order such that sex type is least likely and field of interest most likely to be compromised. In other words, the dimensions that are established first developmentally, those closest to the core of self-concept, are maintained longer. So individuals will choose an occupation from among those in their zone of acceptable alternatives on the basis of interest first. If none is accessible, they will sacrifice interest but maintain preferred prestige and sex type. Occupations outside the zone of acceptable alternatives will be considered only if those inside the zone are not perceived as accessible, and the zone will be expanded beyond the tolerable-level boundary (prestige) before the tolerable-sex-type boundary.

The order of compromise might also vary depending on the degree of compromise. Based on some initial research evidence, the theory was revised to take into account the discrepancy between one's ideal and realistic choices (Gottfredson, 1996; Gottfredson & Lapan, 1997). If the discrepancy is small, then interests are hypothesized to be the most influential; if the discrepancy is moderate, then prestige is hypothesized to be most influential; and, if the discrepancy is large, interests will be sacrificed before sex type or prestige (Betz, 2008).

Gottfredson's theory explicitly addresses the impact of sex-role socialization and other societal factors that influence the development of occupational aspirations. As such, it offers a complementary perspective to Super's theory. On the other hand, Super's theory was designed to span a much broader scope of career behavior than does Gottfredson's theory and, thus, is a more comprehensive theory of life span career development.

Gottfredson's theory has received relatively little attention from researchers, despite its intuitive appeal to practitioners. One reason for the minimal attention is likely related to the difficulty in assessing perceptions in early childhood and in measuring the important constructs in the theory (Fassinger, 2005; Swanson & Gore, 2000). Further, the dimensions of sex type, prestige, and interest are difficult to consider separately from one another (Phillips & Jome, 2005). Some support has been shown for the revised theory regarding different degrees of compromise (Blanchard & Lichtenberg, 2003).

> **Box 9.1**
>
> **Personal Reflection**
>
> How were my aspirations constrained by sex type? By prestige?
>
> Which occupations did I eliminate from my "zone of acceptable alternatives"?
>
> Have I reconsidered occupations previously outside the zone?

Applying Gottfredson's Theory

Counselors who use Gottfredson's theory would ask the sorts of questions that are outlined in Box 9.2. They would wonder what occupations clients have rejected earlier in their lives and for what reasons, the extent of information that clients have about themselves, and what level of complexity will best meet clients' current needs.

> **Box 9.2**
>
> **Counselor Cognitions**
>
> How does the client view his or her available alternatives?
>
> What alternatives has the client eliminated due to sex type or prestige?
>
> In what ways has the client compromised his or her preferred alternatives?

CONCEPTUALIZING LESLIE'S CAREER HISTORY

As noted in the previous chapter, developmental theorists such as Super and Gottfredson would view Leslie as having made a series of decisions from childhood through adulthood. We will discuss Leslie's decisions using Gottfredson's stages as a framework.

Childhood

Gottfredson's (1996, 2005) theory places greater emphasis on childhood and early adolescence than do other theories. She suggests that children ages 3 to 5 (Stage 1) recognize that there is an adult world and that occupations are part of that adult world. Stage 2 (ages 6 to 8) is characterized by a child's increasing awareness of gender-appropriate roles and by dichotomous thinking. Children are motivated by choices that they believe are socially appropriate, particularly focusing on sex-typed choices. During ages 9 to 13, children begin to incorporate prestige as a factor in consideration of acceptable alternatives (Stage 3).

Leslie's early childhood experiences may not be readily accessible to either the counselor or to Leslie, but she appears to have had a typical and relatively uneventful time as a young child. The period during which she was aged 3 to 5 coincided with her brother starting elementary school, so she was home alone with her mother until her sister was born when Leslie was 5. Leslie's mother has told stories about how much Leslie missed her brother when he went to school; she would wait for him at the bus stop at the end of the day. Leslie also has heard family stories about how excited she was to help with "the new baby" when her sister was born. Leslie looked forward to starting kindergarten but also didn't want to leave her mother and sister. After a brief period of adjustment, she loved going to school.

Leslie's elementary school experience was very positive. As noted in the previous chapter, she enjoyed a variety of subjects and responded to attention and praise from her teachers. Since her brother attended the same school, she frequently was referred to as "Scott's sister." Even though she demonstrated the same level of math ability as her brother, he received more encouragement; even in elementary school, teachers and parents suggested that Scott might pursue engineering, whereas they did not suggest that path for Leslie. Leslie's early interest in teaching continued into elementary school, and she would come home from school and "teach" her younger sister what she had learned that day. It was Leslie who taught her younger sister how to read, and she identified more closely with her sister than with her older brother.

The middle school years correspond to the third stage of Gottfredson's theory, and Leslie became more aware of the status of different occupational choices, partly by observing her older brother. Scott had a passionate childhood interest in trucks and construction equipment, which their parents channeled into the higher-prestige occupational fields of engineering and architecture. Leslie also became more aware of the social status of their family and understood that they were more well off financially than some of her friends. She knew that she was expected to choose an occupation that was "important" enough and that would use her abilities.

Adolescence and Early Adulthood

Gottfredson proposes that the occupational alternatives adolescents consider are circumscribed by options considered appropriate for their sex and within the range acceptable for their social class and self-perceived abilities. The fourth stage in Gottfredson's theory begins around age 14, which corresponds to transition from middle school to high school. As Gottfredson (2005) notes, this is a time when "vocational development erupts into conscious awareness" (p. 81).

In this stage, Leslie began to pay more attention to who she was and what she liked to do—and how she was different from her brother and from other adolescents. She had heard clear statements from her parents to Scott about how he needed to be able to support a family in the future and to her about how she could rely on a husband's financial support. These messages were mirrored by what she heard from her friends and at school. Leslie took a mandatory career exploration class during high school and learned more about her interests and skills and the range of occupational options. In retrospect, she doesn't remember much detail from the class other than feeling a bit lost. At the same time, her parents worked closely with Scott to plan his choices about college and career, and Leslie both envied the attention but was happy not to feel the pressure.

Completion of the last stage of circumscription ushers in the process of compromise, which entails relinquishing one's most preferred alternatives for ones that are more realistic. Leslie continued to excel at math throughout high school, but the career options that built upon her strengths were already circumscribed in accordance with acceptable levels of sex type and prestige. She occasionally considered a number of other occupations, such as physician, engineer, computer programmer, and math professor; however, these seemed less accessible to her than being a high school math teacher.

CONCEPTUALIZING LESLIE'S PRESENT SITUATION

Unlike Super's theory, Gottfredson's theory does not contain stages that extend into adulthood, although compromise is a process that may continue throughout one's career. Leslie's current feelings about her job and/or career could present an opportunity for her to investigate the choices made earlier in her life, most of which were not in her conscious awareness at the time. Although some of her current dissatisfaction is likely due to changes in the work environment, it also may be related to the way in which she circumscribed her options earlier in her life. Her choice of teaching, rather than engineering or other occupations that would utilize her math abilities, has its roots in early childhood and in the subsequent decisions later in her life.

Questions for Discussion

1. What specific hypotheses would you develop about Leslie from Gottfredson's theory? How does using Gottfredson's theory help you understand Leslie? How might it help Leslie understand herself?

2. What are the advantages of viewing Leslie as being in her current occupation as a result of the processes of circumscription? Of compromise?

3. How ready is Leslie to make a career decision right now? How does she feel about the prospect of making a decision, particularly of making a job or career change? How might her previous experiences with career decision making influence the process or content of this current decision?

4. Who is likely to influence her decision? How much pressure does she feel now? What types of pressure and from whom?

5. What kind of career life does Leslie seem to be envisioning? How can she optimize her chance of achieving that career life?

6. How might Leslie describe her social self-concept? How does she see her occupational social space?

7. How has Leslie circumscribed and compromised her occupational aspirations?

THE CASE OF GARY

Gary is a 16-year-old Caucasian high school sophomore in a small town in rural Georgia. Both of his parents worked in a furniture mill in a nearby town until its closure last year; Gary's father now works at a hardware store, and his mother works part-time in a nursing home after a brief stint at an administrative aide in a local real estate office. Gary's 20-year-old brother went to work at the furniture mill right after high school and, after the mill's closure, now spends much of his time working on cars in the family's yard; he also does some part-time work as an auto mechanic. Gary's 14-year-old sister is very active in drama and choir activities in her school, and she is thinking about a career in nursing.

The closing of the furniture mill has had a subtle but pervasive impact on Gary's family. Although his parents were able to find other employment, the pay and benefits are far below what they had received at the mill, and they have had to cut back substantially on their spending. His mom's first job after the mill closed, at the real estate office, did not last long because of cutbacks in the office due to slowing sales. The economic climate of the entire community has been affected. In addition to these tangible changes, Gary's family also has experienced other consequences: his parents are worried about money and anxious about the future, and there is more tension in the household.

Gary doesn't see many employment options in his community, particularly given his parents' recent experience in losing their jobs. He perceives an increasingly strong message to pursue some type of postsecondary training or education from his family, as well as from his high school teachers. His father has encouraged him to consider joining the military, and his mother has suggested some health care occupations. Gary spends much of his free time playing video games and would like to be a video software designer. The community college in his area offers courses in Web design, animation, and digital media technology. He has little motivation to explore career options and, other than hearing radio commercials about the community college offerings, has not received much information about possible careers or educational choices. His contact with the high school guidance counselor has been mostly to schedule classes, in which he has been getting Bs and Cs without too much effort or interest. His science teacher has encouraged Gary to go to a summer camp sponsored by the community college, but Gary isn't sure he wants to break his summer video game routine, and his parents are pushing him to look for a job at a fast-food restaurant.

Questions for Discussion

1. What specific hypotheses would you develop about Gary from Gottfredson's theory? How does using Gottfredson's theory help you understand Gary? How might it help Gary understand himself?

2. What is Gary's status in terms of the processes of circumscription? Of compromise?

3. How ready is Gary to make a career decision right now? How could you engage him in the process?

4. Who is likely to influence Gary's decision? How much pressure does he feel now? What types of pressure and from whom?

5. What kind of career life does Gary seem to be envisioning? What kinds of messages is he receiving from his parents and community?

6. How would you describe Gary's "zone of acceptable alternatives"?

Directions and Implications for Career Counseling

GOALS OF COUNSELING

Gottfredson (2005) describes the traditional goal of career counseling as helping individuals "clarify and implement their visions of a satisfying career life, even if parents or social engineers might prefer something different" (p. 85). She suggests that the similarity of assumptions among theories leads to similar strategies for counseling but that her theoretical perspective may require some rethinking of how to assist clients. For example, she cites several issues that present challenges to counselors, such as helping adolescents reexamine their childhood choices without undermining these choices, encouraging realism of choice without placing limits on clients' dreams, and presenting complex information without overwhelming clients (Gottfredson, 2005). All of these dilemmas arise from the specific focus within the theory on circumscription and compromise.

INTERVENTIONS

Meta-analytic evidence produced by Brown and Ryan Krane (2000) suggests that there are five critical components in effective career interventions: (1) written exercises to enhance personal reflection, (2) individualized interpretation and feedback, (3) practical information about the world of work, (4) opportunities to observe role models who are successful in career exploration and decision making, and (5) attention to building social support for choices. Gottfredson (2005) incorporates these five elements into her proposed career guidance and counseling system. Her system addresses each of the four developmental processes outlined in her theory, as described earlier—cognitive growth, self-creation, circumscription, and compromise—and matches them with the counseling strategies aimed at optimizing a set of client behaviors of learning, experience, self-insight, and self-investment, respectively.

Optimize Learning

Adolescents may not gain sufficient knowledge to make good career decisions because it is cognitively demanding to do so. But inadequate knowledge then contributes to the processes of circumscription and compromise, limiting occupational alternatives. How can counselors optimize clients' learning? As Gottfredson (2005) notes, vocational psychology has long valued the role of gathering information about oneself and the world of work, yet it is important to not exceed an individual's cognitive capacity at any given time. She suggests two specific counseling strategies: reducing task complexity to meet clients' needs and accommodating cognitive diversity among individuals by tailoring information.

Leslie exhibits substantial cognitive complexity and ability to deal with abstract ideas; she enjoys putting new information together in meaningful ways. For her, the counselor might provide some general direction in terms of useful resources and then encourage Leslie to explore and gather information on her own, assigning homework between sessions to assess how she is progressing.

In Gary's case, most of his exposure to occupational information and to career planning has been in classes at school, in which he has not been very engaged. A counselor working individually with Gary would need to gauge how he is processing occupational information and adjust accordingly. For example, the counselor might explore a Web site with Gary and ask him to think aloud as he's reading the information. What does he gain from the Web site's information? Does he seem to be attending to the most important information? How would he summarize what he has read? The counselor, in class or individually, could use some structured worksheets to help Gary gather information. A good place to start might be with something that grabs his attention, even if it might not be Gary's most realistic option, such as video software developer.

Optimize Experience

Adolescents may not experience a sufficient variety of activities to understand their own career-related traits, such as interests, values, and skills. How can counselors optimize clients' experience? Gottfredson (2005) suggests two counseling strategies: providing "broad menus of experience" (p. 87) by systematically exposing students to a wide variety of occupations and promoting awareness of the active role that clients may take in shaping their own experience.

Leslie has entered counseling to focus on the pros and cons of staying in her current position, and she appears to be ready and willing to explore a broad range of options. Although she did not have the kind of early broad exposure that Gottfredson promotes, the counselor could help Leslie systematically explore the full range of options now. Further, Leslie and the counselor could identify areas in which she has not had experience, such as administration, leadership, or writing.

Gary clearly could benefit from systematic exposure to "broad menus of experience." His actual experience has been fairly limited, and the vicarious exposure through his parents' experience has not been positive or encouraging. The counselor could address this lack of (or negative) exposure directly and encourage Gary to engage in the available career exploration in his school.

Optimize Self-Insight

Adolescents may prematurely eliminate occupations that could be good choices if they lack self-knowledge. How can counselors optimize clients' self-insight? Gottfredson (2005) suggests that counselors first encourage clients to "take stock" of what they already know about themselves, then encourage clients to think of making the choice of an occupation within the broader context of other factors (in other words, choosing an occupation entails commitment to a "career life" that encompasses other life roles).

Leslie's entry into counseling signals her readiness to take stock of herself and her situation, and the counselor can help with this process. She also is acutely aware of the impact of the broader context of her choices, given her work and life experience, and is likely to benefit from an extended discussion of these factors in her current career dilemma. Gary, on the other hand, does not currently demonstrate much insight about himself or his future. The counselor may use formal assessment to help Gary learn more about himself and also may walk him through the long-term implications of making an informed career decision.

Optimize Self-Investment

Adolescents (and other clients) may compromise in implementing a career choice due to perceived inaccessibility or unrealism of the choice. However, such compromise may be unnecessary. How can counselors help clients increase the chances that they will achieve their choice? Gottfredson (2005) suggests the two strategies of assessing the accessibility of clients' choices and promoting awareness of enhancing one's own qualifications, as well as creating one's own opportunities and support.

Leslie is at a crossroads in her career and life, and choosing and implementing a new direction may be difficult. The counselor would support and encourage Leslie's ability to pursue new options and help her determine the next steps and how to overcome challenges she might encounter. A counselor working with Gary would emphasize the importance of his investment in the process of career exploration and in the actions he needs to take to achieve goals that he defines.

Additional Cases

CASE 1: DORECE

Dorece is a 21-year-old African American woman who is a student at a major urban university on the East Coast. She was referred to career counseling by her academic adviser, because she had not yet declared a major despite accumulating enough credits to be considered a junior. Dorece presents herself as quite self-assured yet seems unnerved by the prospect of making a decision. She comes to counseling each week with a different idea of what she might choose, which she states with considerable enthusiasm. However, she does not complete the tasks assigned by her counselor, such as investigating the requirements of the major or what the job might entail, nor does her enthusiasm carry into the following week.

Dorece is the youngest child of four and grew up in an upper-middle-class home in suburban Washington, D.C. Her father is an advertising manager for a radio station, and her mother is a government attorney. Dorece attended an exclusive all-girls private high school, where she excelled in all her courses and graduated with a 3.8 grade point average. She enjoyed choir, French club, and the sailing club. Her older siblings have successfully completed graduate or professional degrees and are working in the Washington, D.C., area.

When she entered college, Dorece was encouraged by her parents not to choose a major too hastily but, rather, to explore various opportunities before she settled on the "right choice." She initially enrolled in standard freshman year courses and did well in all of them. She particularly enjoyed her English classes and found that she appreciated the challenge of creative writing. Despite this, however, she did not declare English as a major because her father expressed concerned about what she could "do" with a degree in English. After rejecting English as a major, she experienced similar concerns with other majors and soon found herself ruling out most of the possibilities. She has considered becoming a broadcast journalist, because many have told her that she her good looks and presentation style would serve her well in that field. She has considered nursing, because she enjoys caring for others and has considered teaching for the same reason. Her sisters, however, were horrified when she mentioned these possibilities, claiming that she would disgrace the family if she entered such a gender-stereotypic occupation. She continued to search for the "right choice" for a major.

Dorece is in a serious relationship with an African American man who is attending graduate school at the same university. He is completing his doctorate in political science and has some aspirations to a political career; if that is not possible, he would like an academic career. He and Dorece have discussed her lack of decision making; he thinks she should become an English major. He also has expressed concern that it may be detrimental to his future political career if she were to enter broadcast journalism.

Questions for Discussion

1. What specific hypotheses would you develop about Dorece from Gottfredson's theory?

2. How has Dorece circumscribed her career options? How has she compromised her choices?

3. What interventions might be effective in addressing her current career status?

4. What would you do as a counselor from the perspective of Gottfredson's theory to help Dorece make a career decision?

5. Who is likely to influence Dorece's decision? How much pressure does she feel now? What types of pressure and from whom?

CASE 2: STEVE

Steve is a Caucasian man, aged 39, and a divorced father of an 8-year-old son. He is employed as a writer for a greeting card company. He seeks career counseling because he is not satisfied as a greeting card writer but is not sure he wants to continue his original goal of becoming a college professor. Steve majored in English as an undergraduate and pursued a doctorate in American literature. However, he dropped out of his graduate program in the middle of his third year and has not returned to finish his degree.

Steve met his ex-wife, Mariela, while he was an undergraduate. She had already finished her degree and was working as a secretary. She worked while he finished his undergraduate degree and continued supporting him while he was in his first year of graduate school. In his second year, however, she quit working when she became pregnant with their son. He took out loans to support them but realized in the third year of his graduate program that he needed to leave school and work while she stayed home with their child. Their plan was that she would return to work when their son was 3 years old, at which point Steve would return to finish his degree and pursue a career as a college professor.

Their marriage, however, failed, and Steve's financial obligations for child support and alimony are significant enough that he feels he cannot quit his job to return to school to finish his degree. He is also questioning his original plans to get a doctorate and become a professor. He is the oldest son of eight children born to lower-working-class parents; his mother stayed home with the children, and his father worked in a factory. His father often worked two jobs to make ends meet. Steve is the first child in his entire extended family to attend college, much less graduate and enter graduate school. His parents are disappointed that his marriage failed but have been very supportive of his decision to quit school to support his family.

When he took the job as a greeting card writer, he anticipated that he would be with the company only temporarily. However, he has now worked there for over 5 years and has worked his way up to increased levels of responsibility. He enjoys some aspects of the greeting card business, or at least some parts of business decisions. He does not like having to create trite greeting card phrases but does enjoy the marketing meetings that he attends.

Questions for Discussion

1. How does using Gottfredson's theory help you understand Steve? How might it help Steve understand himself?

2. How would you describe Steve's zone of acceptable alternatives?

3. What interventions might be effective in dealing with his decision making?

4. How has Steve's family influenced his decision making?

5. How might you help Steve with his career concerns?

CASE 3: LORI

Lori is referred for career counseling by a good friend who is a social worker and is concerned about Lori's lack of energy and possible depression.

Lori is a 45-year-old Caucasian woman. She is married to John, who is running his family's farm in southeastern Iowa. Lori met John when they were both in college, where John was studying agricultural economics and Lori was studying home economics. They both finished their bachelor's degrees and moved to John's hometown, a small farming community. When they were first married, they lived in town while John's parents lived on the farm. John worked with his father, incorporating more modern agricultural practices into the farm operation, and gradually took over the farm business from his father. John's mother was a very traditional farm wife, raising chickens and helping her husband on the farm when necessary but primarily taking care of her seven children.

Lori and John have two children, both daughters. They moved to the farm when John's father had a stroke; they needed to take care of him and John's mother, who also was in poor health. Lori had worked as a home economist for the local extension office after she and John married, but at the encouragement of her husband and mother-in-law, she quit her job when her first daughter was born. She had enjoyed working, especially the teaching aspects of her work, as well as meeting lots of new people.

Lori's daughters are now in high school, and the older one just received her driver's license. Her daughters have been spending more time away from home than in the past with activities in town and at the consolidated school several miles away. The oldest daughter's newly acquired driver's license means that Lori is not asked to drive the girls to and from their activities as often as she had previously done. Her father-in-law died the previous month, and Lori and John are struggling with decisions about caring for her mother-in-law, who requires daily assistance from Lori due to deteriorating health.

Lori feels quite isolated on the farm. She would like to return to work but does not know what she wants to do or even what options are open to her. Lori and John are not able to relocate, because John is committed to maintaining the family farm for their daughters. She had enjoyed her work as a home economist, but because women are now less often at home, Lori doesn't know if that job even exists anymore.

Questions for Discussion

1. How have Lori's early experiences affected her career decision making, and how have her life circumstances affected her current situation?

2. How would you incorporate the personal issues that Lori is facing into career counseling?

3. How would you incorporate Lori's possible depression into career counseling from Gottfredson's perspective?

4. How has Lori circumscribed her career options? How has she compromised her choices?

5. What would you do as a counselor from the perspective of Gottfredson's theory to help Lori?

BOX 9.3

Summary of Key Constructs

Construct	Definition
Circumscription	Process by which children narrow their occupational alternatives by eliminating those that are not acceptable in prestige or sex type.
Compromise	Process by which preferred alternatives are sacrificed because they are inaccessible.
Cognitive growth	Development of increasingly complex cognitive ability during childhood, which influences the cognitive occupational map and the self-concept.
Self-creation	How the experiences that one chooses build upon biologically based characteristics of an individual.
Zone of acceptable alternatives	The occupations remaining after an individual eliminates occupations due to sex type, intolerably low prestige, or intolerably high effort.
Tolerable-effort boundary	The lowest level of prestige considered acceptable among occupational alternatives.
Tolerable-level boundary	The highest level of effort considered acceptable among occupational alternatives.
Sex type	A limiting boundary within one's zone of acceptable alternatives; it emerges as an influence in Stage 2, where children become aware of the sex-appropriateness of different occupations.
Prestige	A limiting floor and ceiling boundary within one's zone of acceptable alternatives; it emerges as a factor in Stage 3, where children become aware of the differential prestige of occupations within society.

References

Betz, N. E. (2008). Advances in vocational theories. In S. D. Brown & R. W. Lent (Eds.), *Handbook of counseling psychology* (4th ed., pp. 357–374). New York: Wiley.

Blanchard, C. A., & Lichtenberg, J. W. (2003). Compromise in career decision making: A test of Gottfredson's theory. *Journal of Vocational Behavior, 62,* 250–271.

Brown, S. D., & Ryan Krane, N. E. (2000). Four (or five) sessions and a cloud of dust: Old assumptions and new observations about career counseling. In S. D. Brown & R. W. Lent (Eds.), *Handbook of counseling psychology* (3rd ed., pp. 740–766). Hoboken, NJ: Wiley.

Fassinger, R. E. (2005). Theoretical issues in the study of women's career development: Building bridges in a brave new world. In W. B. Walsh & M. L. Savickas (Eds.), *Handbook of vocational psychology* (3rd ed., pp. 85–124). Mahwah, NJ: Lawrence Erlbaum.

Gottfredson, L. S. (1996). A theory of circumscription and compromise. In D. Brown & L. Brooks (Eds.), *Career choice and development: Applying contemporary theories to practice* (3rd ed., pp. 179–232). San Francisco: Jossey-Bass.

Gottfredson, L. S. (2005). Applying Gottfredson's theory of circumscription and compromise in career guidance counseling. In S. D. Brown & R. W. Lent (Eds.), *Career development and counseling: Putting theory and research to work* (pp. 71–100). New York: Wiley.

Gottfredson, L. S., & Lapan, R. T. (1997). Assessing gender-based circumscription of occupational aspirations. *Journal of Career Assessment, 5,* 419–441.

Phillips, S. D., & Jome, L. M. (2005). Vocational choices: What do we know? What do we need to know? In W. B. Walsh & M. L. Savickas (Eds.), *Handbook of vocational psychology* (3rd ed., pp. 127–153). Mahwah, NJ: Erlbaum.

Swanson, J. L., & Gore, P. A. (2000). Advances in vocational psychology theory and research. In S. D. Brown & R. W. Lent (Eds.), *Handbook of counseling psychology* (3rd ed., pp. 233–269). New York: Wiley.

Additional Readings

Hartung, P., Porfeli, E., & Vondracek, F. (2005). Child vocational development: A review and reconsideration. *Journal of Vocational Behavior, 66,* 385–419.

Lapan, R. T., Adams, A., Turner, S. L., & Hinkelman, J. M. (2000). Seventh graders' vocational interest and efficacy expectation patterns. *Journal of Career Development, 26,* 215–229.

Leung, S. A. (1993). Circumscription and compromise: A replication study with Asian Americans. *Journal of Counseling Psychology, 40,* 188–193.

Leung, S. A., & Harmon, L. W. (1990). Individual and sex differences in the zone of acceptable alternatives. *Journal of Counseling Psychology, 37,* 153–159.

Leung, S. A., & Plake, B. S. (1990). A choice dilemma approach for examining the relative importance of sex type and prestige preferences in the process of career choice compromise. *Journal of Counseling Psychology, 37,* 399–406.

Vandiver, B. J., & Bowman, S. L. (1996). A schematic reconceptualization and application of Gottfredson's model. In M. L. Savickas & W. B. Walsh (Eds.), *Handbook of career counseling theory and practice* (pp. 155–168). Palo Alto, CA: Davies-Black.

Whiston, S. C., & Oliver, L. W. (2005). Career counseling process and outcome. In W. B. Walsh & M. L. Savickas (Eds.), *Handbook of vocational psychology* (3rd ed., pp. 155–194). Mahwah, NJ: Lawrence Erlbaum.

Social Cognitive
Career Theory 10

The theoretical approaches we have examined thus far have been well-established theories that have shaped vocational psychology for several decades. However, the theory we will discuss in this chapter is relatively new. The concepts were first introduced in 1981 (Hackett & Betz, 1981), and a complete description of the theory wasn't published until 1994 (Lent, Brown, & Hackett, 1994). We include this theory because of its utility and because of the impact this theory has already had on the field. It differs from the other theories in its focus on the personal constructions that people place on events related to career decision making (Lent, Brown, & Hackett, 2002).

Social cognitive theory (Bandura, 1977, 1986, 1997) has been recently applied in vocational psychology to help explain how individuals' career interests develop, how they make career choices, and how they determine their level of performance. Bandura hypothesizes that individuals' conception of their confidence to perform tasks (self-efficacy) mediates between what they know and how they act and that people's beliefs in their ability to accomplish things helps to determine the actions they will take. Self-efficacy comes from individuals' previous performance accomplishments, vicariously by observing others, from verbal persuasion, and from physiological states and arousal.

Bandura also postulates that self-efficacy is distinct from outcome expectancies, or the expectations one has of the result of behavior. Bandura (1986) notes that self-efficacy and "outcome expectancies judgments are differentiated because individuals can believe that a particular course of action will produce certain outcomes, but they do not act on that outcome belief because they question whether they can actually execute the necessary activities" (p. 392). The constructs of self-efficacy and outcome expectancies are an individual's perceptions of reality; as such, those perceptions may or may not be realistic. It is important to note that in decision making, individuals' perceptions of reality are hypothesized to be greater determinants of their behavior than objective reality.

Hackett and Betz (1981) were the first to apply Bandura's social cognitive theory, with its emphasis on the role of self-efficacy, to career choices. They focused on self-efficacy theory to explain women's traditional career choices, suggesting that low self-efficacy may explain the restricted range of women's career options. Their work led to investigations of the role self-efficacy may play in a variety of career-related behaviors, and the constructs of self-efficacy and outcome expectancies were then incorporated into a theoretical framework related to career decisions. Lent et al. (1994, 2002) developed a social cognitive framework to explain and predict career behavior. Specifically, their three-part model links interests, choices, and performance based on Bandura's social cognitive model.

Basic to all three of the segments of the model, Lent et al. (1994, 2002) propose that performance accomplishments, verbal persuasion, vicarious learning, and physiological states and arousal forge an individual's self-efficacy expectations. For example, a young woman who does well in French class, is persuaded by others that she could be mistaken for a native French speaker, observes others speaking French, and is mildly anxious about performing well would be expected to have high self-efficacy beliefs for speaking French. It is important to note that Bandura's conceptualization of self-efficacy is situation-specific. In the example above, the young woman may have high self-efficacy for speaking French but lower self-efficacy beliefs for speaking German or Russian.

Lent et al. (1994, 2002) also propose that demographic and individual difference variables (such as sex, race/ethnicity, and socioeconomic status) interact with background and contextual variables to influence learning experiences that play a role in forming self-efficacy beliefs. Those self-efficacy expectations, in turn, are related to outcome expectations that individuals have about the outcomes of behavior. In the earlier example of the young, French-speaking woman, a high socioeconomic status may have provided her with opportunities to learn French and may lead to her outcome expectations of speaking French, such as opportunities to travel or live in France.

In the *interest* segment (see Figure 10.1), outcome expectancies and self-efficacy beliefs both predict interests (Lent et al., 2002). Interests (together with self-efficacy beliefs and outcome expectancies) predict goals, which in turn lead to behaviors related to choosing and practicing activities, which then lead to performance attainments. For example, a young man may have developed an interest in playing the drums based on his self-efficacy beliefs that he is competent as a drum player. He also expects positive

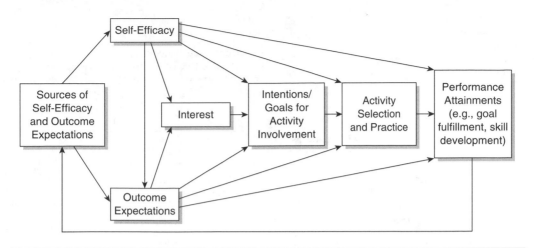

Figure 10.1 Predicting Interest Development in Social Cognitive Career Theory
SOURCE: Lent, Brown, and Hackett (1994).

outcomes out of playing the drums, such as social interaction with friends or enjoying the music, as well as verbal reinforcement from his family. He then is predicted to intend to continue to play the drums and perhaps to form a goal to join a band. This leads to his increased choice to practice the drums and eventually to his skill development in drum playing.

Lent et al. (2000, 2002) also propose that background and contextual variables, termed *contextual affordances,* help to explain why an individual does not pursue an area in which he or she has strong interest. Background and contextual variables may serve as perceived barriers, or supports, to entry or to outcome expectations. For example, a young man with high interests in helping others and in medical fields may not go into nursing because of his perception that nursing is not an appropriate occupation for a man. He may further perceive weak support from others to enter that occupation, support that might have helped him to overcome that barrier. Similarly, a young woman who has strong parental and teacher support to achieve in math courses may choose to major in engineering.

Lent et al. (2000, 2002) conceptualize two types of contextual affordances, those that are much earlier (distal) than the choice and those that are closer in time (proximal) to the choice. Examples of distal influences may be factors that either constrict or facilitate the development of self-efficacy and outcome expectations (e.g., gender-role socialization, impoverished learning environments), while proximal barriers and supports affect the implementation of choices (e.g., anxiety about moving, financial support to go to college). Barriers may be objective or subjective; what is important is an individual's perception of the barrier (Kenny, Blustein, Chaves, Grossman, & Gallagher, 2003; McWhirter, 1997; Swanson, Daniels, & Tokar, 1996).

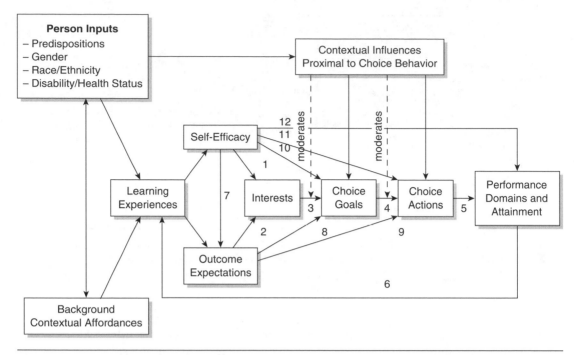

Figure 10.2   Predicting Vocational Choice in Social Cognitive Career Theory

SOURCE: Lent, Brown, and Hackett (1994).

The *choice* model (Lent et al., 2002) proposes that person inputs (e.g., gender, race, disability, personality, and predispositions) and background context together influence learning experiences, which influence self-efficacy beliefs and outcome expectancies (see Figure 10.2). As already described, these influence interests, which influence choice goals; goals influence actions, and actions influence performance attainments. For example, a young girl from an affluent background is taken to science museums, encouraged to read and learn about science and famous scientists, and given opportunities to take science classes and to attend summer science camp. These learning experiences, afforded by her socioeconomic status, influence the development of her beliefs in her ability to do well in science. Her performance in science and her knowledge that doing well in science will lead to positive outcomes, such as good grades, parental approval, and time spent with friends, lead to the development of her interest in science. She believes she can do well in science in college, she learns that science is a field that is well compensated and one that is not typical for women, and she develops an intention to enter a science major in college. Lent (2005) notes that the process of making a career choice involves choosing a goal (e.g., becoming a scientist), taking action to implement that goal (completing courses in a biology major), and the subsequent consequences of those actions (successful graduation in biology).

The *performance* model predicts the level of performance as well as the persistence an individual has in pursuing goals (Lent et al., 2002). This segment (see Figure 10.3) proposes that past performance accomplishments

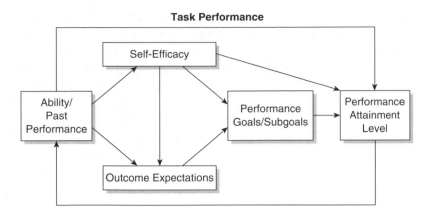

Figure 10.3   Predicting Task Performance in Social Cognitive Career Theory
SOURCE: Lent, Brown, and Hackett (1994).

influence self-efficacy and outcome expectancies, which in turn influence performance goals; these lead to performance attainment level. In other words, past performance influences self-efficacy beliefs along with the expectations individuals have about the outcomes of their future behavior. These expectations affect the goals that people set for themselves. These goals then affect the level of performance they may attain. Thus, a woman who did well in basketball while in high school has confidence in her ability to play and decides to try out for the basketball team in college. After making the team, she sets challenging goals for her offensive and defensive performance (e.g., averaging at least 12 points a game), based on her past successes and current self-efficacy and outcome beliefs. Lent et al. differentiate their choice and interest models from the performance model. The former involve the content of career choices, such as the field or specific occupation in which one would like to work, while the performance model predicts the level of performance toward which one aspires within one's chosen field.

Bandura (1997) comments that "in making career decisions, people must come to grips with uncertainties about their capabilities, the stability of their interests, . . . the prospects of alternative occupations, . . . and the type of identity they seek to construct for themselves" (p. 422). Individuals' perceptions of their own efficacy in mastering various skills and tasks play an important role in predicting their choices as well as their perseverance to accomplish their goals. Social cognitive theory thus is readily applicable to development of interventions targeted at increasing individuals' self-efficacy in a variety of areas (Betz & Schifano, 2000). Other areas for intervention include expanding career choice options, fostering positive and realistic outcome expectations, setting specific goals, coping with barriers and building supports, and increasing coping self-efficacy and strong performance skills. Interventions may be targeted at expanding vocational interests, at increasing decision-making skills and exploratory behavior, at helping clients explore various careers, and at increasing consideration of nontraditional careers.

The social cognitive career model has generated a great deal of interest among researchers in vocational psychology. Roughly 20% of the articles published in vocational psychology in the past 10 years have emphasized some aspect of the social cognitive career theory (SCCT). Research has demonstrated support for the relationship between self-efficacy and interests, between self-efficacy and outcome expectations, and the influence of the model in predicting occupational choices (Betz, 2008; Lent, 2005; Lent et al., 2002). Donnay and Borgen (1999) demonstrate that self-efficacy helps to explain vocational choice over and above vocational interests. Finally, performance accomplishments have been shown to be the most powerful influence on self-efficacy. Research on SCCT has also supported the model across racial/ethnic groups, across many developmental levels, and for both men and women. Betz concludes her review of the research on SCCT by noting that "the theory has relevance for understanding a wide range of vocational behaviors relevant to both career choice and adjustment" (p. 365).

Box 10.1

Personal Reflection

Have I ever thought, "I can't do that career!"?

What factors have influenced my self-efficacy about the career?

What outcomes did I expect?

Applying Social Cognitive Career Theory

Counselors who use a social cognitive theoretical model would wonder about their clients' learning experiences, their self-efficacy to approaching various choice options, their career decision-making self-efficacy, how realistic their outcome expectations are, and the barriers or supports for their career decisions. They would also question which options their clients have foreclosed and how to help them expand their career options (Lent, 2005). Counselors' cognitions from an SCCT perspective are presented in Box 10.2.

CONCEPTUALIZING LESLIE'S CAREER HISTORY

In conceptualizing Leslie's career history, counselors using a social cognitive model (Lent et al., 1996) would focus on the learning experiences Leslie has had. They would examine how those learning experiences may

---

Box 10.2

Counselor Cognitions

What is the client's self-efficacy for various career options?

What are the client's outcome expectations for various career options?

What are the client's interests?

What is the client's career decision-making self-efficacy?

What learning experiences does the client have?

What choices has the client foreclosed?

Are the client's outcome expectations realistic?

How do barriers and supports influence the client's vocational choices?

---

relate to the self-efficacy beliefs and outcome expectations Leslie had as an adolescent, how those may have influenced her interests, and, in turn, how those affected performance and choices as she grew older.

Leslie's family had the resources to expose her to a variety of opportunities when she was a child. Her mother was very involved in the arts in their community, and thus Leslie visited the art museum with her mother, took art or music classes, and attended symphony concerts with her family. Leslie also had significant learning experiences while in school; her active roles as a math tutor, as a leader in the French club, and her successful participation in her school's science fair were opportunities for her to learn about herself and to gain confidence in her skills. Leslie did well academically, as well as socially, in high school. Others perceived her as a leader, though she did not view herself as a leader, since she did not seek out leadership positions.

Leslie's learning experiences were related to her eventual occupational choice. In other words, the activities in which Leslie was engaged as a child and adolescent, such as becoming a tutor, helped in preparation for a career as a teacher. However, there were barriers to her translation of her learning experiences into a major occupational direction. She knew she was going to attend college, consistent with her parents' expectations, but did not declare a major until well into her sophomore year. She took general courses in the community college she attended after high school and then was "undecided" for several semesters after she transferred to a larger university.

In the performance model proposed by Lent et al. (1994), the level of goals toward which Leslie aspired was influenced by her self-efficacy beliefs and the outcomes she expected would result from pursuing her goals. Leslie did very well academically in high school yet chose to attend a community college rather than a university. Leslie set lower goals for herself than were consistent with her level of performance. This may have been due to faulty self-efficacy beliefs about her ability to do well academically; this is evidenced in her uncertainty about being successful in college. Such lowered self-efficacy beliefs may have been due to a lack of role models or verbal encouragement to seek an academically challenging curriculum. Leslie also may not have had a good knowledge of the outcomes associated with attending a community college versus the university, although she did expect that her parents would approve of her decision to pursue some postsecondary education. Once she was enrolled in the community college, however, she was frustrated by the lack of challenge. This may have led to increased self-efficacy beliefs about her ability to do well academically and to her decision to transfer to the university.

Even after she enrolled in the university, Leslie still struggled with making a career decision. She did well in many of her classes, though she did not do well in mechanical drawing, which led her to conclude that she would not do well in engineering. Her overall self-efficacy beliefs in her ability to do well academically were relatively high; however her self-efficacy beliefs in her ability to do well in the specific areas related to engineering were low. She also appeared to have low self-efficacy beliefs related to advanced training, or she may have had low self-efficacy beliefs in her ability to juggle the multiple roles required of balancing career and family obligations. These beliefs led her to foreclose career options that required postgraduate training.

Leslie did not want to consider options that were nontraditional for a woman. This was influenced by the outcomes she expected of entering a nontraditional career, such as continuing to be among the few women in her area or having difficulty in combining her career with raising a family. Leslie also received little encouragement to consider nontraditional careers; in fact, she was at times actively discouraged by her professors.

Leslie's learning experiences led her to know that she was proficient in math and that she was interested in teaching and in helping others. She had developed self-efficacy beliefs in her ability to teach when she was a math tutor in high school. Leslie's decision to major in secondary math education was influenced by her self-efficacy beliefs in her math and teaching abilities and her lower self-efficacy beliefs about advanced training, since teaching did not require a graduate degree. Her student teaching experience gave her a sense of accomplishment and verbal encouragement, which led to increased self-efficacy beliefs in her teaching ability, which led to greater interest in being a teacher and then to her subsequent implementation of that choice. Her choice also was influenced by the outcomes she expected of a teaching career: She would have a career that she could combine with raising a family, as well as a career in which she would not be singled out as one of the few women. In addition, Leslie expected that the choice of teaching would meet with her family's approval. Leslie's decision, then, was strongly influenced by her pattern of self-efficacy and outcome beliefs, which perhaps led to her setting a lower performance goal than she was capable of (Lent et al., 1996). However, her decision to be a math teacher was a choice consonant with her self-efficacy beliefs and with her outcome expectations.

Leslie's early career years were a time of increasing her self-efficacy beliefs in her teaching ability. Lent et al. (1996) note that the social cognitive model "asserts that people form an enduring interest in an activity when they view themselves as competent at it and when they anticipate that performing it will produce valued outcomes" (p. 383). Leslie viewed herself as a good, perhaps even very good, teacher. She also began to anticipate that being a teacher would have outcomes that she enjoyed and appreciated. The outcomes included approval from her family, approval from her students and peers, and feeling competent as a teacher. Leslie also enjoyed the challenge of teaching a variety of math classes and being able to be autonomous and creative in her own classroom.

Lent et al.'s (1996) performance model suggests that Leslie's performance accomplishments as a teacher and positive outcome expectations of a teaching career would lead her to set higher accomplishment goals. However, Leslie made a lateral move to a teaching position in a larger city to be closer to her family. This change of environment brought with it some unwelcome changes in the rewards of her work and, subsequently, her outcome expectations. She did not pursue a graduate degree, even though she took several continuing education classes, thus suggesting that she may have low outcome expectancies about the student role or the rewards that an advanced degree may bring her. She may also have anticipated barriers to pursuing a graduate degree, either from her family or from her husband.

CONCEPTUALIZING
LESLIE'S PRESENT SITUATION

Leslie has been a teacher for over 13 years, suggesting that she has high self-efficacy beliefs in her ability to teach, that she expects positive outcomes from the occupation, and that she has formed long-lasting interest in the occupation. However, Leslie is reporting considerable dissatisfaction with her job. Some of her concerns may be related to changes in outcomes she has come to expect from the job; others may be related to her own changing self-efficacy beliefs regarding certain aspects of her current teaching role. Or, conversely, she may have developed interests in another field in which she has higher self-efficacy beliefs and higher outcome expectancies.

Leslie states that she is a good teacher, suggesting high teaching efficacy overall. She enjoys the outcomes associated with direct interactions with her students. However, she also notes frustration in not reaching some students, and this may be threatening her self-efficacy beliefs about her teaching ability. She has had some difficult interactions with parents as well, which led her to question her teaching efficacy, at least within the context of her current school and teaching assignment.

Some of the outcomes associated with being a teacher, such as approval from parents and students, autonomy in her classroom, and ability to challenge herself through teaching advanced classes, have recently diminished for Leslie. She reports frustration with the principal's new accountability measures. She may perceive this as feedback on her teaching, interpreting that the principal does not trust her ability to teach, which in turn may lead to lower teaching efficacy. She also is distrustful of participating in reporting on her teaching goals and activities. She may fear, for example, that she will be evaluated negatively or that she may lose her ability to set her own goals and activities in the class. Other outcomes that Leslie has expected of teaching have changed, as well. Approval from students and parents is not as frequent as it once was for Leslie. She has had fewer opportunities to teach challenging courses, even though she has been at this high school for 10 years.

One of the outcomes that Leslie expected from her teaching was the ability to combine teaching with raising a family. However, she is having difficulty having children, which may lead her to question the premise on which that expectancy was based. She also reports some dissatisfaction with the division of labor in her marriage, suggesting that she may be questioning the way in which she had intended to combine work and family.

Leslie reports that she is willing to consider graduate school at this point, indicating that her efficacy beliefs in her academic skills have become more congruent with her documented skills in doing well academically and/or that her expectations of the outcomes of attending graduate school have changed. Leslie is considering a wide range of occupational areas, though she continues to have weak self-efficacy beliefs in her ability to make a career decision. Her family has given her little encouragement in her career exploration; her brother has actively discouraged her from changing careers, and her mother and sister feel that she should quit work to concentrate on having a family. It is not known whether Leslie has had any role models of individuals who have changed careers in midlife. It would appear that Leslie is less inclined than earlier in her life to foreclose options that are nontraditional for women; she indicated, for example, that she would consider engineering as a career. Leslie may perceive the relatively traditional division of labor in her marriage as a barrier to choices, however, particularly since she reports that her husband and family expect her to stay home if and when she does have children.

Questions for Discussion

1. What specific hypotheses would you develop about Leslie from SCCT? How does using social cognitive theory help you understand Leslie? How might it help Leslie understand herself?

2. Leslie appears to be struggling to make some midlife career changes. How would you address the issues that Leslie is dealing with regarding her career from a social cognitive career model perspective? How would you address the issues that she is dealing with in her marriage?

3. How may Leslie's efficacy beliefs be influenced by the messages she has received from her husband and family about the role of work in her life?

4. How might you incorporate information from the additional inventories that Leslie completed?

5. What interventions or techniques from social cognitive theory might you use with Leslie?

6. What role did Leslie's gender socialization play in her career decisions as an adolescent? What role is her gender socialization playing in her career decisions as an adult?

7. What additional barriers may Leslie encounter if she decides to stay in her current profession of teaching? What barriers may she encounter if she chooses to become a social worker? Engineer? Minister? Technical writer?

THE CASE OF RON

Ron, a 57-year-old Caucasian male, has been employed as a mechanical assembler for a large manufacturing company for the last 38 years. His company, which has been in business in his hometown for 100 years, has just announced a major restructuring to cut costs. The company says that these changes are necessary to remain competitive in the global market. To achieve its ends, it is offering a buyout for all employees who have been with the company for at least 30 years. Ron needs to decide whether to take the buyout offer and seek a new job or to stay in the position. The buyout offer includes a lump sum of $42,000, health insurance for 2 years, and a guarantee that he will receive the pension he has earned to this point if he begins drawing it when he turns 62. If he stays in the position, his income will continue to go up, and he will contribute more to his pension, but he risks being laid off. He has 45 days to decide whether to take the offer. If he does not take the buyout offer and is laid off later, he will not get the lump sum payout or health insurance. His company has offered career counseling, and he seeks help to make the decision.

Ron grew up in a working-class family, the oldest of five children. His father worked for a company that supplied parts to the company where Ron is currently employed. There were no family expectations of schooling beyond high school. Ron's father had graduated from high school, and his mother had a year of secretarial school but did not work after she had children. Both grandfathers had been farmers, and none of his grandparents finished high school. There was a strong expectation that men were the primary breadwinners while women stayed home to take care of children.

Ron was an average student in high school and had no interest in going to college or to a technical school. He did well in high school shop classes, so he decided to apply to the manufacturing company in his hometown. Two of his uncles worked there and recommended he apply. He felt lucky to be hired right after graduation and has worked there for nearly 40 years. During those years, he has worked on many products. Each time there was a change in production, he was able to adjust to the needs of the new process. Although the company has had tuition reimbursement programs, Ron has never taken any outside coursework. He has, however, learned a number of skills, including running computer-controlled equipment, while he rotated through several tasks. He has enjoyed the security of working for a company that had been in business for over 100 years.

Ron married his high school sweetheart shortly after he began working. They had three children. All are grown; two are married and have children of their own. One grandchild lives in Washington, D.C., and the other set of grandchildren live in Oregon. His youngest son has moved back home following a layoff. Ron's wife has not worked during their marriage. It has been important to Ron to be the sole provider for his family.

Ron has worked steadily for nearly 40 years. Although he reports that there have been several periods of layoffs over the years, his assembly job has always been safe. He credits the union for this security. Although his job has been secure, he feels his wages have not kept up with his family's needs. He and his wife recently refinanced their home to add an extra room for the son who moved home. They help support his mother-in-law, who is now in a nursing home. They travel as often as they can to see their grandchildren who live at opposite ends of the country. These expenses have led to a substantial amount of credit card debt. Ron and his wife have no savings set aside for retirement because they had been told, and witnessed through friends, that the company pension was excellent.

Ron was aware that the company had been losing market share, and he had seen several product lines move to Mexico. He felt, though, that his position would not be affected because assemblers had always been needed. He was stunned when the union agreed to the buyout offer. He is angry, scared of his financial obligations, and worried about supporting his family. His pride in this company has shaped his identity for nearly 40 years. He also is very unsure of how to go about making a career decision.

Questions for Discussion

1. What specific hypotheses would you develop about Ron from SCCT? How does using social cognitive theory help you understand Ron? How might it help Ron understand himself?

2. How would you address Ron's dilemma about choosing the buyout option or not from a social cognitive career model perspective?

3. How may Ron's efficacy beliefs be influenced by the messages he has received from his family about his role as a breadwinner?

4. What interventions or techniques from social cognitive theory might you use with Ron?

5. What additional barriers may Ron encounter if he decides to stay in his current job? What barriers may he encounter if he chooses to leave his career as an assembler? What supports does Ron have?

Directions and Implications for Career Counseling

Career counseling within the framework of the social cognitive career model focuses on helping clients identify faulty efficacy beliefs and unrealistic outcome expectations that have led them to make poor career decisions or, as in Ron's case, helping clients expand career options. Brown and Lent (1996) and Lent (2005) suggest three basic tenets inherent in career counseling from a social cognitive framework:

1. Help clients explore options and identify those options that they have foreclosed because they have unrealistic or faulty self-efficacy beliefs or outcome expectancies.

2. Identify and evaluate barriers to, and supports for, various career choices, particularly barriers that may have led clients to eliminate a career possibility prematurely from consideration.

3. Help clients modify and counteract faulty efficacy beliefs and faulty occupational information.

These interventions are not necessarily done in a linear order. For example, it may be necessary to work with clients to identify options that they have eliminated from consideration. It may be important then to help clients modify efficacy beliefs or to correct their occupational information so that they can consider careers that seem to be particularly appropriate choices. It may be important finally to help them identify supports and eliminate barriers to implementing that choice.

GOALS OF COUNSELING

The overarching goal of the social cognitive career model is to help clients make a career choice that "correspond[s] well with important aspects of their work personality" (Lent et al., 1996, p. 402). In other words, the goal of career counseling within this framework is to help clients find a career that matches their interests, values, and skills. An important part of this process is to help clients explore possibilities that are a good match but were discarded from consideration due to poor self-efficacy perceptions or inaccurate outcome expectations.

IDENTIFY FORECLOSED OPTIONS

Career counseling begins with helping clients clarify their goals for career counseling. For example, the career counselor works with Leslie to help her identify whether she was seeking counseling to help her choose an entirely new career path or whether she wanted to make some changes to be more satisfied in her current position. Ron's counselor helps him clarify if career counseling will focus on the decision to stay in his position or if he wants to identify new career paths. Initially, the counselor works to help Leslie or Ron clarify goals. The counselor asks the question "When will you know counseling has been successful?" Clarifying the counseling goals helps the client and counselor focus the assessments and interventions toward that goal and helps clients and counselors evaluate the process and result of counseling.

Once the client and counselor have clarified the goals for counseling, the counselor focuses on exploring those paths the client has dropped from consideration and to expand the possibilities that he or she could consider. In Leslie's case, the counselor also encourages Leslie to explore options to become more satisfied with her current career. The counselor might say, "Leslie, I noticed that you were considering the occupations of engineering, psychology, and medicine. Let's examine why you decided those weren't for you. We can also spend some times looking at ways to make teaching a more viable career option for you." In Ron's case, the counselor might begin by asking Ron to consider the outcomes expected of the various options. What outcomes would Ron expect if he stayed in the job? What outcomes might occur if he took the buyout, and what career paths might he consider if he chose this option? The counselor might also ask Ron what career options he has foreclosed by choosing a career so quickly out of high school and by not seeking additional training over the years.

Brown and Lent (1996) identify three approaches to identifying specific foreclosed options. One is to focus on the results from an interest inventory, using both high-scoring interests as well as those interest scales on which clients scored lower. In the latter case, the counselor incorporates an analysis of the basis of those areas of less interest. This approach may also include an analysis of the relationship between areas of interest and level of confidence in that area, such as that provided by the Skills Confidence Inventory (SCI). Thus, Ron's counselor would suggest that Ron take the Strong Interest Inventory (SII) and the SCI to help identify possible career options.

Leslie's results on the SII indicated high interest in the Investigative, Social, and Conventional General Occupational Themes and the Research, Teaching, Mathematics, Taxes and Accounting, and Science Basic Interest Scales. Leslie had much less interest in the Enterprising and Artistic General Occupational Themes and indicated low interest in the Basic Interest Scales associated with the Artistic General Occupational Theme, such as Performing Arts, Visual Arts, Culinary Arts, and Writing. She also indicated little interest in Military, Healthcare Services, Law, Sales, Management, Politics, Marketing, and Entrepreneurship. The counselor explores these areas to examine the basis for a low level of interest in the areas. For example, as noted earlier, Leslie had a variety of opportunities to be exposed to careers related to the arts through her mother's work in community arts organizations. The basis for her lack of interest in the arts area may be due to a realistic appraisal of her skills in the area. However, Leslie also may have decided early in her adolescence that she did not want to pursue careers in the arts areas for reasons unrelated to her skills. For example, she may have decided that she did not want to pursue a path followed by her mother, she may have negative outcome expectations associated with entering the arts field, or she may have erroneously decided that she did not have the skills to pursue an arts career further. The counselor spends some time exploring this as a possible avenue for further consideration: "Leslie, the Strong Interest Inventory results indicate that, compared to a large group of women, you aren't very interested in the areas represented in the Artistic General Occupational Theme. Can you think back to a time when you may have been interested in this area? Perhaps there are some occupations that you would like to explore for further consideration?"

The counselor also discusses the scales on which Leslie scored high but that she has not pursued in her career, specifically the areas indicated by the Science, Research, Mathematics, and Tax and Accounting Basic Interest Scales, as well as those related to the Religion and Spirituality Basic Interest Scale. Occupations on which Leslie scored high include mathematician, software developer, actuary, financial analyst, biologist, financial manager, university professor, and medical technologist. She also scored high on the Mathematics Teacher Occupational Scale, indicating that she is a good match for her own career. The latter may indicate that career counseling should focus on helping her to find a different occupational environment rather than a different career. However, the counselor may also encourage her to explore the occupations on which she scored similarly to women in that occupation: "Leslie, your pattern of likes and dislikes was similar to that of women who are school counselors and special education teachers; these two are in the Social General Occupational Theme area. Tell me what you think of these occupations."

Leslie's Learning Environment Scale score on the SII indicates that she enjoys learning through lectures and books, which may help the counselor to explore her reluctance to pursue a graduate degree. Her decision not to seek advanced training may have been related to her negative outcome expectations related to the type of learning required in graduate school, rather than to her low self-efficacy beliefs related to graduate training.

Examination of the comparison between Leslie's interests and skills confidence on the SCI lends some support for the counselor to encourage Leslie to explore options in both the Investigative and Social General Occupational Theme areas. Interventions for areas in which a client has lower interest than confidence would target outcome expectancies. Self-efficacy beliefs would be the target of interventions in areas in which confidence is lower than interest. Leslie's results indicate that Leslie has more confidence in her skills than interest in the Conventional area and more interest than skill confidence in the Investigative and Social areas. The lower confidence in the Conventional theme may be due to her lower outcome expectations in this area. The counselor explores this with Leslie: "I notice that the Strong and SCI results indicate that you have more confidence in your ability to do the tasks related to the Conventional area than you have interests in the area. This may be related to the outcomes you would expect from tasks and occupations in this area. Tell me what you would expect if you were to pursue the occupation of financial analyst or actuary." The counselor then helps Leslie to determine if this is related to her negative outcome expectations related to further education. The counselor helps her to re-evaluate those outcome expectations or to determine if other Investigative occupations are more consonant with her educational goals.

The difference in Leslie's confidence and interest in the Social area may be due to lack of learning opportunities available to Leslie in the areas tapped by the Social Skills Confidence scale, such as directly working to help people with their problems or counseling an unhappy couple. The counselor works with Leslie to assess areas that she wants to consider, particularly focusing on those areas that might be fruitful for further investigation but that Leslie is not considering due to poor self-efficacy beliefs or low outcome expectations. If, for example, Leslie indicates that she might be interested in being a social worker but does not feel she could actually help people, social work would be an area the counselor would target for further exploration.

A second approach for identifying foreclosed options is to analyze discrepancies between occupations identified on an interest inventory and those identified on an aptitude inventory or on a needs inventory, such as the Minnesota Importance Questionnaire (MIQ). The assumption behind the latter analysis is that occupations predicted to be satisfying based on needs would also be predicted to be satisfying based on interests, unless faulty efficacy or outcome perceptions have prevented the development of interest in that area. Identifying those discrepant occupations may help the client to expand the possible range of occupations she or he is considering. This should be used only as a guide, however, since the occupations on each inventory do not overlap entirely (i.e., not all occupations on the MIQ are found on the Strong and vice versa). It is important to note that SCCT views needs and values as outcome expectations and would consider the MIQ as providing information related to the outcome expectations (i.e., rewards) a client may have about an occupation.

Occupations on which Leslie had high scores in both the SII and MIQ included secondary teacher, speech pathologist, engineer, and programmer. Occupations in which Leslie was predicted to be satisfied based on her needs results but in which she did not indicate an interest included architect, interior designer, librarian, technical writer, minister, occupational therapist, social worker, real estate agent, and law enforcement officer. These provide additional areas for the counselor to explore with Leslie: "Leslie, I note that several occupations may provide the rewards you would expect from an occupation, but you did not indicate you were interested in that occupation. In particular, I wonder what you think of those occupations in the Social area, such as nurse and occupational therapist, as well as in the Artistic area, such as librarian and architect." Two occupations may deserve further discussion. Leslie's interests in religious activities suggest that the occupation of minister may be an occupation worthy of in-depth consideration, particularly if her lack of efficacy beliefs regarding helping others has caused her to preclude it as an option. The other occupation to discuss is technical writing, since she entered counseling having listed that as an option. She may have low efficacy beliefs in her writing ability that have led to low interests in this area; these merit further investigation to determine the accuracy of those efficacy beliefs.

A third approach to identifying foreclosed options is to use a card sort (Dewey, 1974; Dolliver, 1969). In this strategy, the counselor gives Leslie a set of cards with an occupation listed on each card and asks her to sort them into three piles. The first pile consists of occupations she might choose, the second pile is occupations she would not choose, and the last pile consists of occupations "in question." The counselor then focuses on the occupations in the "in question" and "would not choose" piles. Leslie is asked to further sort these occupations into occupations she might choose if she felt she had the skills to do the job well, those she might choose if she felt the occupation would result in positive outcomes, and occupations she would not ever choose. The counselor then focuses on occupations targeted either for further skill development, if in fact Leslie does not have the skills to accomplish the job, or for modification of efficacy beliefs, if her perceptions of her skills is inaccurate. The latter may be the case if Leslie feels she could not enter engineering because she does not have the skills to take advanced math courses such training would require. The counselor then focuses on the "might choose if result in positive outcomes" pile. The counselor asks Leslie: "Tell me what you would expect from the occupations in this pile. How accurate do you think your perceptions of the outcomes might be?" The counselor also encourages Leslie to obtain more information if her knowledge of outcomes expected of various occupations is incomplete or inaccurate. For example, if Leslie still believed that she would not be able to combine work as an engineer with a family, the counselor refers her for informational interviewing to women engineers who are combining both.

REEVALUATE AND MODIFY EFFICACY BELIEFS

A second tenet of the social cognitive career model is that counselors need to help their clients modify faulty self-efficacy beliefs that are preventing them from considering viable career options. Lent et al. (1996) suggest that counselors working with clients who have evidence of skills but who have weak self-efficacy develop strategies that promote efficacy. These strategies may be designed specifically to encourage performance accomplishments, to rethink previous performance accomplishments, or "to interpret their past and present successes in a manner that promotes, rather than discounts, perceived competence" (p. 406). Ron, for example, might have no confidence in his ability to make a career decision and, thus, might believe that he cannot take the buyout option. He might also have low self-efficacy beliefs in pursuing careers other than factory work. The counselor would work to counteract these weak career decision-making self-efficacy beliefs.

Brown and Lent (1996) and Lent (2005) identify several strategies to help clients modify their efficacy beliefs, including helping clients create opportunities to experience successful performance accomplishments. One strategy is to give Leslie additional opportunities to form efficacy beliefs about her ability to do graduate work, for example, encouraging her to talk to current graduate students or to examine syllabi for graduate courses. The counselor also needs to help her to attribute her performance correctly as related to her abilities when she performs well, as opposed to attributing it to some other external source, such as ease of the test or mere effort on her part. It is important that Leslie gain a more accurate view of her abilities to raise her efficacy beliefs.

Additionally, the counselor works with Leslie to help her further reanalyze previous experiences that led her to conclude she would not do well in school. For example, the counselor encourages Leslie to identify the faulty efficacy beliefs she had as an adolescent that led her to choose entering a community college instead of a university or that led her to close off a number of options that required graduate training. The counselor helps Leslie analyze which of those efficacy beliefs are still operating and helps her identify methods to change those beliefs. The counselor could, for example, encourage Leslie to gather more information about how she compares with others. Her beliefs in her ability to perform well in graduate school may have been due to inaccurate perceptions of the performance level required of graduate students. Gathering more accurate information of graduate school expectations, as well as gaining a more accurate picture of herself, may help Leslie modify her efficacy beliefs.

IDENTIFY BARRIERS AND SUPPORTS

The third tenet in career counseling from a social cognitive model is that counselors need to work with clients to help them identify barriers and supports to implementing career options. Once barriers are identified, counselors need to help clients to evaluate whether the perceptions of barriers are based on a realistic appraisal of the environment and to help clients evaluate how likely they are to encounter those barriers. For example, Ron has financial barriers that influence either option he is considering. His considerable debt affects his decisions. On the one hand, the $42,000 lump sum payout would help his immediate financial burdens, but the buyout option would reduce his company pension. On the other hand, staying at the company could give him more income and a greater contribution to his pension, but he would run the risk of being laid off with no lump sum payout.

Leslie's greatest barriers in making a career decision appear to be related to her focus on others' approval and involvement in her decisions, as well as what appears to be her lack of willingness to take risks. The counselor works to help Leslie identify strategies to overcome the identified barriers. One strategy identified by Brown and Lent (1996) is to ask clients to complete a decisional balance sheet (Janis & Mann, 1977) for each career alternative under consideration. Clients are asked to indicate positive and negative consequences related to each alternative; they identify consequences anticipated for themselves and for others in both the short and long term.

Leslie's counselor asks her to complete a decisional balance sheet for staying in her current occupation and for each alternative career she was considering. Leslie may, for example, identify her husband's and mother's traditional views of women's role in child rearing as a barrier to pursuing a career as an engineer, or she may identify her own discomfort with being in a nontraditional field as a barrier. She may identify her lack of confidence in helping others as a barrier to entering ministry, also perhaps voicing a fear that her family would not support such a choice. She may also identify her anger at the principal and lack of challenge as barriers to continuing in her current position.

Leslie's counselor then helps her to identify how realistic each of those barriers may be: "Leslie, you indicated that your family may not approve of your pursuing a degree in engineering. What information have they given you that has led you to this conclusion? What might happen if you discussed the possibilities of further education with your husband or if you talked about engineering as a possible option with your family?" Her fears of their reaction may, in fact, be well grounded, or they may be inaccurate. If her fears were realistic barriers to her pursuing these options, the counselor would encourage her to identify possible ways to manage or prevent those barriers. For example, the counselor may encourage her to talk further with her husband to enlist his help in a more role-sharing model of child rearing. Leslie may, however, also decide that the consequence of losing familial support is too great, and that may help her decide to stay in her current position as a teacher.

If Leslie decides to remain a math teacher, identification of the barriers associated with that position might help her to determine specific actions to make her more satisfied in that occupation. For example, she may decide that the barriers include her principal and that she has little power to change his specific actions. This may lead her to seek a position as a math teacher in another school, knowing that she would be happier in a smaller school system in which she could teach a greater variety of classes.

Additional Cases

CASE 1: JERRY

Jerry is a 32-year-old gay Caucasian man who is seeking career counseling because he was diagnosed as HIV-positive several years ago. When he was first diagnosed, he expected his health to deteriorate rapidly, initially thinking he had only 4 years to live, and he decided to continue working as a hair stylist. However, his regimen of treatments has enabled him to be well enough to work, and he is in a position of facing that he never really liked his work as a stylist. He continued to do that work because it paid the bills. Now he is seeking career counseling because he is ready to make a different career choice.

Jerry is a licensed hair stylist working in a suite of hair salons; he shares his leased space with another stylist, Latasha. Jerry initially became a hair stylist because he enjoyed the creativity of working with different styles and liked helping people look better; he also was "sick of school," so he did not want an occupation that entailed a college degree. Jerry had been struggling with his sexual identity through high school and did not do well in his high school classes, precluding options for postsecondary training. He had taken drafting in high school and enjoyed that, as well as a shop class he took as a senior. Jerry was also on the basketball team during his first two years in high school but dropped out during his junior year. He came out to his parents during his senior year in high school; they were initially unhappy but were eventually supportive of his orientation. His decision to become a stylist was also influenced by his perception that it was an occupation in which others would be supportive of a gay man.

His counselor began to clarify Jerry's goals and found that Jerry also had some interpersonal conflicts in his current work environment with Latasha. Jerry complained that Latasha was stealing his items and was forming alliances with others in the suite against him. Jerry was reluctant to confront her directly, however, suggesting that if he ignored the problems, they would go away. However, Latasha had informed him that she was breaking their agreement and moving to a salon by herself, leaving Jerry solely responsible for the rent on their shared suite. Again, Jerry was reluctant to confront the issue, choosing not to take legal action against her. His career decisions then included whether he should quit being a hair stylist altogether, declare bankruptcy, and move back to his parents' home while he considered what to do; expand his services to make more money to cover the rent in the salon; or seek and train another partner.

Jerry indicated that he really "got sick of hearing people talk all day" and did not enjoy the interpersonal conflicts that others seemed to create. He was frustrated at having to be inside a lot, when he would rather be outside. He did enjoy being able to work with his hands and still enjoyed some of the creative aspects of his job. He appreciated some of the flexibility of his work as well, since it enabled him to schedule around days when he was not feeling well.

Jerry's SII indicated that his highest interests were in the Realistic and Social General Occupational Themes, with high Counseling & Helping, Culinary Arts, Mechanics & Construction, Athletics, Teaching, and Mathematics Basic Interest Scales. He was most similar to men who are law enforcement officers, auto mechanics, athletic trainers, and occupational therapists. Jerry's MIQ indicated that it was very important for him to get along well with his coworkers, do things for other people, and do something that made use of his abilities. His scores on the General Aptitude Test Battery indicated that he was at least 1 standard deviation above the mean in all tested areas and had particularly high level of ability in verbal reasoning, numerical reasoning, and general learning ability.

Questions for Discussion

1. How might Jerry's self-efficacy beliefs or outcome expectations have foreclosed his options? What are specific examples of options he may have foreclosed?

2. What barriers is Jerry facing in his career alternatives?

3. What are Jerry's likely outcome expectations about his various career alternatives?

4. How would you incorporate the information presented by Jerry's career history and his assessment results?

5. How might Jerry's learning opportunities have been partly shaped by his sexual orientation?

6. How might you modify Jerry's self-efficacy beliefs?

7. How may Jerry's interpersonal conflicts affect his career decisions? What role might have self-efficacy beliefs and/or outcome expectancies played in his interpersonal conflicts?

8. How do Jerry's gender and race/ethnicity influence his decisions?

CASE 2: KAMISHA

Kamisha is a 21-year-old African American woman in her third year of college. She is seeking counseling because she is undecided about her college major. She is attending a private liberal arts college and has done very well in all of her courses. She originally declared a major in chemistry, then changed to English during her second year, and finally changed to psychology. However, although she is getting an A in the class, she does not like the psychology course she is currently taking and has begun to have doubts about her entry into the field. She knows she will need to continue on to graduate school if she wishes to be a psychologist. She is confident she would do well if she would choose to pursue this avenue; she is concerned, however, that psychology may not be the right choice for her.

Kamisha is the daughter of two successful corporate lawyers; she is the older of two sisters. Her parents, though busy with their careers while she was growing up, were able to provide her with numerous educational opportunities. She attended a prestigious private high school, traveled abroad extensively with her family, and spent her junior year in high school studying in France. Kamisha also attended various summer camps, as well as participating in several classes provided by the local university specifically targeting African American girls. She particularly enjoyed her classes in science, in English, in math, and in social studies. The latter area included courses in political science, sociology, and psychology.

Kamisha's parents have high expectations for their daughters. They believe that they both should not only finish college but should seek some additional postgraduate training, such a law degree or a doctorate. They provided them both with many opportunities, and they also feel that their daughters "owe it to their race" to do well. Kamisha's parents have worked hard also to shield their daughters from overt discrimination, sending them to private educational institutions known for their racially egalitarian policies and practices. Kamisha's sister is currently on an athletic scholarship at another private university, where she is excelling as a soccer player and doing well in her premedical studies.

Although Kamisha has done well in all her courses and is interested in most of the material she has studied, she is genuinely confused about which avenue to pursue. She has changed her major so often because she has been pressured by the college to declare a major, but she does not feel that she can determine which one is best for her. Her interest inventory results indicate that she is interested in Artistic, Investigative, and Social areas and that she is similar to women who are psychologists, college professors, mathematicians, biologists, chemists, and English teachers.

Questions for Discussion

1. How may Kamisha have foreclosed her career options? What are specific examples of options she has foreclosed, if any?

2. What barriers is Kamisha encountering, if any?

3. What might be Kamisha's outcome expectations about her college major decision?

4. How may a counselor incorporate Kamisha's assessment results into counseling?

5. What additional information may the counselor seek?

6. How have Kamisha's learning opportunities been shaped by her socioeconomic status and by her cultural background?

7. What social cognitive strategies would you employ to help Kamisha make a career choice?

CASE 3: JIM

Jim is a 27-year-old Caucasian male who suffered a spinal cord injury in the neck area 4 years ago, which has severely limited his mobility. How his injury occurred is unknown to Jim. He related that he was attending a party in honor of his completion of the Reserve Officer's Training Corp (ROTC), and the last thing he remembers is opening the bathroom door and closing it behind him. The next thing he knew, he was lying on the bathroom floor and could not move. He underwent 6 months of hospitalization and therapy. Jim returned to finish his baccalaureate degree, is currently enrolled in a graduate program, and is seeking counseling because he has begun to have doubts about whether or not he is taking the right career path.

During his high school years, Jim was involved in volunteer work at two schools for children with physical and cognitive disabilities. He enjoyed working with the kids individually and in groups. One of the things that he liked most was seeing the progression that the children made over time. He also enjoyed sports and being active. The aspects of sports he enjoyed the most were the teamwork, motivation, and the sense of achievement he received after successfully accomplishing a goal. He wanted to incorporate both of these factors in choosing a career and chose to pursue physical education with an adaptive emphasis to include children with special needs.

Jim was very active in college, becoming involved in many campus activities, such as student government, intramural sports, and ROTC. He also continued to volunteer working with children. After 4 years in college, he was a year and a half from finishing his degree, a well-respected student leader on campus, and near completion of the ROTC program, when the accident occurred.

Following the accident, Jim knew he could no longer pursue physical education and decided to major in recreation therapy, because it involved actively participating with a client or groups and also might include sporting activities. He completed his degree three and half years later and decided to enroll in graduate school. He hoped one day to pursue a doctorate and decided first to enroll in a master's program. He also hoped to move away from home and establish his independence.

Jim found a few things that were difficult in going to a school out of state. Two roadblocks were a lack of wheelchair-accessible housing accommodations and insurance and medical benefits. After researching the possibility of a move, he found that it would be more difficult than it was worth, and, feeling pressured by the time constraints of the deadlines for applications, he applied to a local graduate program in rehabilitation counseling. He chose rehabilitation counseling as a good complement to his bachelor's degree in recreation therapy. He was admitted and began to take classes.

Although his conflict had been solved, Jim felt rushed by the decision and was not 100% sure this was the right direction for him. He took one class in the summer session to ease himself into attending classes again, to get familiar with the campus, and establish himself in the program. This class was a basic introductory counseling class that exposed him to a few different aspects of counseling he had not considered. He now wants to determine whether to leave rehabilitation counseling and enter a more general counseling curriculum for his master's work or finish his master's and seek a doctorate in clinical or counseling psychology.

Questions for Discussion

1. How may Jim have foreclosed his career options? What are specific examples of options he has foreclosed, if any?

2. What barriers is Jim encountering, if any?

3. What might be Jim's outcome expectations about his decisions about graduate training?

4. How would you incorporate Jim's disability into your approach to counseling?

5. What additional information would you seek?

6. How have Jim's learning opportunities been shaped by his disability and by his cultural background?

7. What social cognitive strategies would you employ to help Jim make a career choice?

Box 10.3

Summary of Key Constructs

Construct	Definition
Self-efficacy	Confidence in ability to accomplish tasks in a particular domain
Outcome expectations	Outcomes expected of domain-specific actions
Interests	Preference for activities
Distal barriers and supports	Factors that hinder or facilitate the development of learning experiences and self-efficacy
Proximal barriers and supports	Factors that hinder or facilitate implementation of career choices that are close in time to the choice
Contextual affordances	Environmental resources and obstacles that shape career development

References

Bandura, A. (1977). Self-efficacy: Toward a unifying theory of behavioral change. *Psychological Review, 84,* 191–215.

Bandura, A. (1986). *Social foundations of thought and action.* Englewood Cliffs, NJ: Prentice Hall.

Bandura, A. (1997). *Self-efficacy: The exercise of control.* New York: Freeman.

Betz, N. E. (2008). Advances in vocational theories. In S. D. Brown & R. W. Lent (Eds.), *Handbook of counseling psychology* (4th ed., pp. 357–374). New York: Wiley.

Betz, N. E., & Schifano, R. S. (2000). Evaluation of an intervention to increase realistic self-efficacy and interests in college women. *Journal of Vocational Behavior, 56,* 35–52.

Brown, S. D., & Lent, R. W. (1996). A social cognitive framework for career choice counseling. *Career Development Quarterly, 44,* 354–366.

Dewey, C. R. (1974). Exploring interests: A nonsexist method. *Personnel and Guidance Journal, 52,* 311–315.

Dolliver, R. H. (1969). An adaptation of the Tyler Vocational Card Sort. *Personnel and Guidance Journal, 45,* 916–920.

Donnay, D. A. C., & Borgen, F. H. (1999). The incremental validity of vocational self-efficacy: An examination of interest, self-efficacy, and occupation. *Journal of Counseling Psychology, 46,* 432–447.

Hackett, G., & Betz, N. E. (1981). A self-efficacy approach to the career development of women. *Journal of Vocational Behavior, 18,* 326–339.

Janis, I. L., & Mann, L. (1977). *Decision making: A psychological analysis of conflict, choice, and commitment.* New York: Free Press.

Kenny, M. E., Blustein, D. L., Chaves, A., Grossman, J. M., & Gallagher, L. A. (2003). The role of perceived barriers and relational support in the educational and vocational lives of urban high school students. *Journal of Counseling Psychology, 50,* 142–155.

Lent, R. W. (2005). A social cognitive view of career development and counseling. In S. D. Brown & R. W. Lent (Eds.), *Career development and counseling: Putting theory and research to work* (pp. 101–127). Hoboken, NJ: Wiley.

Lent, R. W., Brown, S. D., & Hackett, G. (1994). Toward a unifying social cognitive theory of career and academic interest, choice, and performance. *Journal of Vocational Behavior, 45,* 79–122.

Lent, R. W., Brown, S. D., & Hackett, G. (1996). Career development from a social cognitive perspective. In D. Brown, L. Brooks, & Associates (Eds.), *Career choice and development* (3rd ed., pp. 373–422). San Francisco: Jossey-Bass.

Lent, R. W., Brown, S. D., & Hackett, G. (2000). Contextual supports and barriers to career choice: A social cognitive analysis. *Journal of Counseling Psychology, 47,* 36–49.

Lent, R. W., Brown, S. D., & Hackett, G. (2002). Social cognitive career theory. In D. Brown (Ed.), *Career choice and development* (4th ed., pp. 255–311). San Francisco: Jossey-Bass.

McWhirter, E. H. (1997). Perceived barriers to education and career: Ethnic and gender differences. *Journal of Vocational Behavior, 50,* 124–140.

Swanson, J. L., Daniels, K. K., & Tokar, D. M. (1996). Assessing perceptions of career-related barriers: The Career Barriers Inventory. *Journal of Career Assessment, 4,* 219–244.

Additional Readings

Anderson, S. L., & Betz, N. E. (2001). Sources of social self-efficacy expectations: Their measurement and relation to career development. *Journal of Vocational Behavior, 58,* 98–117.

Bandura, A., Barbaranelli, C., Vittorio Caprara, G., & Pastorelli, C. (2001). Self-efficacy beliefs as shapers of children's aspirations and career trajectories. *Child Development, 72,* 187–206.

Diegelman, N. M., & Subich, L. M. (2001). Academic and vocational interests as a function of outcome expectancies in social cognitive career theory. *Journal of Vocational Behavior, 59,* 394–405.

Hackett, G., & Byars, A. M. (1996). Social cogntive theory and the career development of African American women. *Career Development Quarterly, 44,* 322–340.

Tang, M., Fouad, N. A., & Smith, P. L. (1999). Asian Americans' career choices: A path model to examine factors influencing their career choices. *Journal of Vocational Behavior, 54,* 142–157.

Turner, S. L., & Lapan, R. T. (2005). Evaluation of an intervention to increase non-traditional career interests and career-related self-efficacy among middle-school adolescents. *Journal of Vocational Behavior, 66,* 516–531.

Summary and Integration 11

We wrote this book to give students an understanding of how theories of career development could be applied in career counseling. Our intent in each chapter was to give a brief overview of the theory, apply it to a client (Leslie) as well as to another case, and then discuss how a career counselor with that theoretical perspective would work with these two clients. We also used additional case studies at the end of each chapter to encourage readers to develop hypotheses about a wide variety of clients and to practice applying each theory to realistic cases. In the process, we ourselves were frequently reminded how focusing on one theoretical perspective very much influenced the course of counseling. It determined the questions we asked about Leslie, it determined the behavior that was examined and brought into counseling, and it determined the goals we imagined Leslie would set for herself. We realized that in our own career counseling, neither of us uses a single theory. Although we were both trained initially in the theory of work adjustment at the University of Minnesota, our approaches stem from a combination of theoretical perspectives and interventions.

At this point, many readers may ask: How do these theories compare? What are the strengths and weaknesses of each? How well do they apply to clients with whom I work (or will work in the future)? Is there any empirical support for these theories? How can I combine the theories in my own work? These are the questions we hope to begin to answer in this chapter. We will first summarize and compare each of the major theoretical approaches we examined in the book. As we did in Chapter 1, we then ask readers to stop and think about how each perspective applies to their own lives. Theories were designed to represent reality and help us understand and predict behavior, and it is helpful to think of how each has contributed to a greater understanding of our own career history and decision making.

Consistent with the format of the rest of the book, we examine how each theory or approach contributes to our understanding of Leslie. We will explicate the contributions of each theory to career counseling with Leslie and examine what may be the unique contributions of each theory to conceptualizing the case. Then, just as we have used cases throughout the book to exemplify the application of theories and approaches, we will present two cases to illustrate the integration of theoretical perspectives. We ask readers to consider thoroughly how each theoretical perspective would approach the new cases.

In the first case, George, we will discuss our view of what a counselor from each perspective would do. We summarize by outlining what we would do as counselors and identifying the theoretical approaches on which we are drawing. We hope, in doing so, that we are modeling the integrative perspective that we discussed in Chapter 1. In the second case, Tom, we present the case and follow-up stimulus questions and then leave it to readers to consider how each theoretical perspective would approach Tom.

We then turn our attention to the questions readers may have about support for these theories. As strong proponents of the scientist-practitioner model, we believe it is important to evaluate the research foundation underlying each theory. We briefly examine the empirical support available for the constructs delineated in each theory and the empirical support for the application of the theory to a broad range of populations, regardless of sex, racial and ethnic background, socioeconomic level, disability, or sexual orientation. Because no theory has been empirically supported for every construct and every population, we will also identify some areas we would encourage researchers to examine in the future. Finally, we will finish by suggesting areas for further training and skill development.

Summary and Comparison of the Theories

Recall from Chapter 1 that it is useful to think of theories as road maps. We use maps to plan a trip, considering alternate routes to a final destination and locating interesting sights to visit along the road. Maps prevent us from arriving at the wrong destination (or not arriving at all) and from taking circuitous routes when more direct ones are available. Likewise, theories offer us alternate views of reality, of explaining human behavior, and of conducting counseling to assist clients with their concerns. Each of the five theories discussed in this book has many areas in which it overlaps with other theories. For example, each attempts to predict optimal situations for clients, whether good career choices or satisfying work environments. Each uses a variety of ways to help clients learn more about themselves, and although each theory uses different language to describe it, each assumes that individuals interact with their environment in some way. However, a review of the major constructs reveals that each theory does more than use different labels for the same behavior; rather, each focuses on a unique perspective of vocational behavior.

We summarize the major constructs for each theory in Table 11.1, along with the outcomes that each theory predicts. This information will aid readers in keeping track of which construct is used by which theory and which theoretical perspective is most likely to be used in helping clients make career choices or adjustments. We will discuss the last two columns of Table 11.1 in later sections.

Holland's theory describes vocational personalities and work environments and how they fit together. Individuals differ in their vocational personalities and seek out the environments that fit with their personality types. Outcomes predicted by Holland's theory include vocational choice as well as vocational adjustment; both of these are predicted by congruence with the environment. The theory of work adjustment (TWA) also describes individual differences, although this theory highlights individuals' abilities and needs. The environmental focus is on ability requirements and rewards rather than on vocational personality. The TWA delineates processes postulated to occur as an individual tries to decrease job dissatisfaction. Similar to Holland's theory, outcomes predicted by the TWA also include vocational choice and adjustment, although the focus is much more on adjustment and behavior within a work setting.

The developmental theories of Super and Gottfredson describe the development of an individual's career over the life span. Super's theory puts more emphasis on later life stages, ranging from implementing a career choice to retirement, than does Gottfredson's, which places more emphasis on childhood and adolescence. Developmental models explain how choices are made and implemented more than the other theories discussed in this book. Both theories predict vocational choice and development; Super's outcomes also include implementation of the self-concept and delineation of work as one of many life roles.

Social cognitive career theory also focuses on how individuals learn from others, but this model emphasizes the personal construction that individuals place on what they have learned. This model also highlights how interests develop and how choices develop, with an emphasis on an individual's beliefs about his or her competence in the related abilities and the outcomes expected of pursuing that field. The social cognitive model is the most explicit in its consideration of environmental conditions and events.

As we noted in Chapter 1, the counselor's theoretical perspective helps to determine the way clients and their concerns are conceptualized, the most appropriate tools to use with clients, and the overall goals of counseling. Choosing which theory to incorporate into your own map of your

Table 11.1 Comparison of Theories

Theories	Constructs	Outcome	Understanding Leslie	Support
Holland	Personality types (RIASEC) Environmental type (RIASEC) Congruence Consistency Differentiation Identity	Congruence Satisfaction	Congruence between her personality type and current work environment	Well researched Empirically supported Evidence of support for women and racial/ethnic minority groups
Theory of Work Adjustment	Abilities Ability requirements Needs Rewards (need reinforcers) Satisfaction Satisfactoriness Reactive adjustment Active adjustment Person-environment correspondence Flexibility Perseverance	Satisfaction Tenure Work adjustment	Dissatisfaction due to discorrespondence between her needs and environmental rewards	Well researched Well supported for some constructs, less supported for personality style variables Some evidence of support for women and racial/ethnic minority groups

Theories	Constructs	Outcome	Understanding Leslie	Support
Developmental (Super)	Life stages Career adaptability Developmental tasks Career maturity Implementation of the self-concept Career construction Life roles Salience	Vocational choice Life role balance	Recycling through exploration tasks Balancing roles in her life	Well researched Well supported for some constructs, less supported for newer constructs Some evidence of support for women and racial/ethnic minority groups
Gottfredson	Circumscription Compromise Vocational aspirations Life stages	Vocational choice	Circumscription of Investigative aspirations	Not fully empirically examined Limited evidence of support for women and racial/ethnic minority groups
Social Cognitive Career Theory	Self-efficacy beliefs Outcome expectations Choice model Performance model Interest model Identifying barriers Foreclosure of options	Interests Vocational choice Level of performance	Self-efficacy beliefs for math and teaching Changing outcome expectations	Well researched Substantial empirical support for constructs and model Substantial evidence of support for women and racial/ethnic minority groups

client's career behavior will depend on your own experiences as well as on the client's presenting problem. Osipow's (1996) description of the focus of theoretical perspectives may be helpful as readers evaluate which of these theories they will use in their own counseling, for which theory you use will depend on what you want to emphasize. Osipow summarizes the theories by noting that Holland's theory identifies *what happens,* developmental theories describe *how it happens,* and the TWA depicts *how it happens and the outcome.* He did not include social cognitive career theory in his discussion, but that model would describe how an individual's perceptions of reality help to make career outcomes happen.

APPLYING THEORIES TO YOUR OWN CAREER DEVELOPMENT

Before reading the subsequent section on applying theoretical perspectives, use the personal reflections throughout the book and the following questions to evaluate how each theory may contribute to a greater understanding of your own career history.

1. What insights have you gained about your own career history from each of the theories?

2. Is one theory more applicable to your own career decision making than others?

3. How might a combination of two or more theories be more applicable than just one? Which parts of the theories would be more applicable?

4. How can you use the major concepts from each theory to explain your career history?

5. What aspects of your career history and decision making are not explained by the theories?

6. What role has your culture and gender played in your own career decisions?

Integrating Theoretical Perspectives

We have summarized the major constructs of each theory and discussed how they may shape a counselor's perspective in conducting career counseling. The manner in which that can happen is what we have tried to illustrate throughout the book as we have applied each theory to Leslie's situation (presented in Chapter 3). We have conceptualized her career history and present situation from each perspective and conducted career counseling with her from each theoretical viewpoint. In this section, we connect these pieces to examine what we believe has been each theory's contribution to a fuller understanding of Leslie's history, her expectations, and her career goals. This understanding is summarized in the fourth column of Table 11.1. We then apply each theoretical focus to a new case, George. Following our discussion of each theory's perspective on George, we share how we would integrate theoretical approaches in career counseling with him.

CONTRIBUTIONS OF DIFFERENT THEORIES TO UNDERSTANDING LESLIE

The models of culturally appropriate counseling and gender-aware and feminist approaches remind us to consider the multiple contextual factors that exert influence in Leslie's life. Her educational and career experiences have been shaped by societal expectations for her as a White, middle-class, heterosexual woman, regardless of her level of awareness of these expectations. Exploring these contextual factors will help Leslie realize the influence that they have had on her choices and help her make future decisions with a clearer sense of who she is and who she wants to be. Moreover, the counselor's own contextual experiences might influence his or her interaction with Leslie in counseling.

The two theories of person-environment fit help us understand the sources of satisfaction and dissatisfaction that Leslie perceives in her current job and in her career. Holland's theory does so by suggesting that her type (investigative-social-conventional) is relatively congruent with her occupation as a math teacher (coded on the Strong Interest Inventory [SII] profile as CIR for women). Furthermore, many other types of high school teachers are primarily social types, so the individuals in her environment are likely to be social types. Her dissatisfaction, therefore, is probably not due to being in an occupation that is incongruent with her type. This understanding helps the counselor to look at other factors that might contribute to her dissatisfaction, such as people and policies in her specific job environment.

The TWA also offers a perspective on how Leslie corresponds to her environment, this time in terms of her satisfaction and her satisfactoriness. Here, her dissatisfaction is conceptualized as related to whether her values and needs are being met by the reward structure available in her work environment. We know that part of her dissatisfaction is likely due to her frustrated needs for autonomy, even as her other needs continue to be met on the job. An important feature that the TWA adds to our understanding is the explicit attention to determining if she has been a satisfactory employee. We have some information that she has performed well on the job, but the TWA helps us to focus more specifically on her job performance.

Both of these theories also suggest other alternatives, should Leslie decide that she wants to change jobs or occupations. In the case of Holland's theory, Leslie's type of investigative, social, and conventional can be used as a guide for identifying other occupations with which she might be congruent. In the TWA, her identified values and needs, as well as her identified dissatisfactions with her current job, provide the avenue for exploring new occupational choices. Her needs to achieve and to use her talents, as well as her need to help others, are important to consider in occupational exploration.

Developmental theories provide a life span perspective in understanding Leslie. Her career concerns are not atypical for someone of her age and career stage, as she is trying to determine the role of work in her life, particularly in relation to her other current (and desired) life roles. She has established herself as a teacher, yet she is still struggling with Super's developmental tasks of consolidating and advancing in her career, and she is questioning whether she wants to continue in this occupation or move into a new career. Considering the totality of Leslie's life space allows the counselor to incorporate an explicit discussion of her various life roles and their relation to one another. Leslie's other life roles undoubtedly interact with how she experiences her work role; for example, her dissatisfaction with her job may influence or be influenced by her desire to have children. Super's focus on career choice as an implementation of the self-concept thus helps us to understand Leslie's life in context.

Furthermore, Gottfredson's theory adds hypotheses about how Leslie may have circumscribed her occupational aspirations as a child and adolescent and then compromised her choices from those remaining acceptable alternatives. Leslie's compromises corresponded to those predicted by Gottfredson, in that she chose an occupation that appeared to preserve her sex-typed aspirations (teaching), perhaps at the expense of her interests (engineering, math, and science).

Social cognitive career theory also uses learning experiences in understanding Leslie, with a particular focus on her self-efficacy for specific activities and the expected outcomes she anticipates from performing these activities. Leslie has considerable self-efficacy about mathematics and about teaching, and she also values the outcomes provided by doing well in math and teaching. Social cognitive career theory also suggests that her job dissatisfaction might be due to changing self-efficacy or outcome expectations, particularly as related to her desire to have children.

The Case of George

We will use the case of George to demonstrate the way in which different theoretical perspectives inform how career counseling might proceed with another client. Assume that the following information was gathered during an intake interview with George; as you read, think about each of the theoretical approaches described in this book.

George is a 54-year-old Caucasian male of German and English descent. He is seeking counseling because he is becoming increasingly dissatisfied with his career as a financial planner. George lives in a semirural area in the Northeast. He is married with two college-aged children, and his wife is a special education teacher.

George has a bachelor's degree in industrial engineering. He had been accepted at several major universities after high school graduation and chose the one he attended because of its reputation for engineering and because it was his father's alma mater (who also received a degree in industrial engineering). George knew at that time that math and science were his "strong suits" and that he had interest and skills in working with people. However, he states now that he "never felt engineering was the right fit" but that industrial engineering was the best fit of the possible specialties within engineering.

After college graduation, he sought a position in engineering sales; after interviewing with several firms, he was hired by a company that manufactured french fryers to sell to fast food restaurants. George reported that he enjoyed this job and was very good at it. After 5 years, however, he tired of the constant travel, and he did not like some of the company's policies or some of the customers with whom he had to deal routinely. He quit the job with no plans for what he might do next and despite the company's efforts to retain him.

While on a vacation shortly after he quit his job, George bought a large quantity of Oriental rugs and returned home to open a retail store in a historic district of his small town that was undergoing redevelopment. The business flourished for several years, until an economic recession dried up the market. A friend asked for his assistance in setting up a food business in another town, and when George visited him to help, he decided to close his own business and join with his friend. This business grew rapidly, and George and his friend split into two independent operations so that George was managing a restaurant on his own.

George thoroughly enjoyed managing the restaurant. He handled all catering sales, hired and trained personnel, and managed the orders and accounts. The restaurant was very successful for several years until a highway was rerouted, which caused the traffic into the restaurant to drop off precipitously. George then found himself somewhat stranded, and he worried that he would need to move elsewhere to find a sales job with a corporation. However, one of his customers at the restaurant had been recruiting him to join his life insurance office as a financial planner, and George decided to give it a try.

George felt out of place with the other agents and planners at first but quickly "learned the ropes." He felt that it was the first time in his life that he was doing something to help other people. He has been working in life insurance and financial planning for 11 years; as he stated, "I took the job because I had to, and I've continued because I'm good at it." However, lately he's been feeling like "it's not fun anymore." He enjoys meeting with clients, but he finds it harder to make the phone calls necessary to set up the meetings and to solicit new sales prospects. He also finds himself more consciously aware that he benefits from each sale and wonders whether that awareness affects how he works with clients. He's worried that he is not doing as good a job for his clients as he would like.

When asked what he would do if he could change careers, he answered without hesitation: "Teach." He has had some experience teaching basic insurance courses to new agents, which he enjoyed. He is interested in teaching math but is unsure about the practicality of doing so at his age.

Seven years ago, George took the SII as part of a continuing education workshop sponsored by his office. His highest General Occupational Theme scores were social (very high), enterprising (high), and artistic (high), and his investigative score was moderately high. Other notable features of his SII profile are high Basic Interest Scale scores in Athletics, Military, Medical Science, Teaching and Education, Counseling and Helping, Religion and Spirituality, Politics and Public Speaking, Law, Marketing and Advertising, and Sales, and he had a very high score on the Risk-Taking Personal Style Scale. High Occupational Scale scores include law enforcement officer, dentist, optometrist, registered nurse, parks and recreation manager, community service director, school administrator, life insurance agent, purchasing agent, nursing home administrator, real estate agent, and credit manager.

WORKING WITH GEORGE

Before we turn to a consideration of George from the various theoretical perspectives, consider the following questions:

1. What are your impressions of George?

2. What more would you like to know about him?

3. What hypotheses would you develop about George from the perspective of each approach, including gender-aware and culturally appropriate career counseling?

4. How will you gather information to test your hypotheses?

5. How does each of these theoretical approaches influence the next step in counseling? What direction would you take from the perspective of each, including gender-aware and culturally appropriate career counseling?

CONSIDERING GEORGE FROM VARIOUS THEORETICAL PERSPECTIVES

We will begin with gender-aware (Chapter 4) and culturally appropriate (Chapter 5) approaches and work through the theories (Chapters 6–10). We will consider George from each approach or theoretical perspective, highlighting the unique contributions of each perspective.

Gender-Aware and Feminist Approaches

Several aspects of George's career history seem pertinent to a gender analysis. First, George clearly identified with his father early in his career: His decision of university and major were both influenced by his father's choices, and although engineering did not seem like a good fit at the time, he pursued it anyway. More information about George's father would be helpful, particularly related to how George perceived his father's expectations for him generally and for his career success specifically.

Second, there is a theme in George's career history of working hard at building businesses but also having an underlying interest in and concern for people. The latter interest seems to be increasing in strength, as evidenced by George's expressed desire to teach. The interest in people may be an area that he did not feel encouraged to express earlier in his life.

Culturally Appropriate Approaches

George is a White, middle-class, heterosexual male, possibly belonging to the upper middle class. He is of German and English descent. It is not indicated to what ethnic group his wife belongs, nor is his religious background noted. One more aspect of his context is given in the case study; he is from the Northeast and lives in a small town.

The culturally appropriate approach would assume that as a heterosexual White male, George had a great deal of privilege in his life. His options appear not to have been restricted by racism or sexism. He was able twice to open a new business impulsively and was successful at it, apparently without a barrier due to his race or sex. He was affected when the highway was rerouted, but there is no indication that he construed that as anything other than a neutral environmental event. However, George may have felt restricted due to the cultural messages he received about appropriate behavior for men.

The culturally appropriate approach would examine what George's multiple cultural contexts have conveyed to him. For example, George attended his father's alma mater, following his father's footsteps into a career that was not necessarily a good fit for him. Did his family expect him to carry on a family tradition? If so, are there other similar expectations? What expectations did George have in terms of being a financial provider for his family? George's ethnic background was German and English; how were those different ethnic backgrounds integrated into his upbringing? How may they affect him now?

Holland's Theory

A counselor working from the perspective of Holland's theory would examine George's aspirations from early in his life and the relation between George's personality type and the environments in which he has worked. Clearly, George has had entrepreneurial aspirations and has always excelled at occupations that require persuasive abilities and sales skills—enterprising-type occupations. According to the General Occupational Themes of the SII, George is an SEA type, and the work environments in which he has thrived have been predominantly enterprising and social in nature.

George's decisions to change jobs relatively frequently may not be viewed as an unstable pattern, because he remained in occupations with the same environmental type. In fact, he probably has moved into more congruent occupations, incorporating increasingly more of his social interests.

The Theory of Work Adjustment

George has indicated that he is not satisfied in his occupation. The TWA would conceptualize George as a satisfactory employee whose abilities have matched the job requirements for the past 11 years. However, George's needs have not been met by the job. He would appear to have high compensation and social service needs as well as achievement needs. It would also seem that his social service needs at times interfere with his compensation needs, and when they do, the social service needs are stronger. George's adjustment style would appear to have a relatively high level of flexibility but a low level of perseverance (he stayed in a job he did not like for 5 years, then quit with no other plans in place). He seems to have a high level of pace.

His counselor would begin by examining whether George can increase the correspondence with his environment, either by changing his needs or by changing the environment. George may, for example, work to resolve the conflict between his social service needs and his compensation needs, perhaps finding ways to meet his social service needs by volunteering for a local youth group. Alternatively, he may work to change the environment, perhaps by taking on different aspects of financial planning within the organization or by encouraging his firm to offer more free seminars and workshops so that he can feel he is helping others.

If George decides that he would rather explore new occupations than make his current occupation a better fit, the counselor would give George additional assessments, particularly the Minnesota Importance Questionnaire (MIQ) to help identify occupations in which he would be predicted to fit. He would be assumed to have high abilities in a variety of areas, including math, reasoning, and interpersonal communication. Occupations that dovetail between the SII and the MIQ would be good options for more exploration.

Developmental Theories

Developmental theories add explicit attention to how George's self-concept has evolved throughout his life. He seems to have longstanding interests both in entrepreneurial and social service activities, but perhaps the relative importance of these two areas has shifted with time. George's self-concept thus has remained stable throughout his life, with a clear sense of what he is good at doing and what is important to him.

In Super's formulation, George is in the age range corresponding to Maintenance stage career tasks; however, he has made enough career shifts that he could be conceptualized as being in the Establishment stage. In fact, his current career dissatisfaction seems to be related to his transition into Maintenance: He seems to be asking, "Should I do something new or continue with this until retirement?"

Gottfredson's Theory

George's current interest in teaching may be an example of an occupation eliminated during the process of circumscription earlier in his life. When George was a child, being a teacher may have fallen outside of his tolerable sex-type boundary; being a teacher also may have not been prestigious enough, given his family background and expectations, therefore falling below his tolerable-level boundary. Engineering, on the other hand, clearly was within the zone of acceptable alternatives that he developed during childhood and adolescence.

Social Cognitive Career Theory

The social cognitive theoretical perspective would focus on George's self-efficacy beliefs and his outcome expectations. He has been in an occupation for several years that he feels he is good at but that he does not want to continue doing. George would appear to have high self-efficacy beliefs about his abilities as a financial planner, but the outcomes he is expecting from his occupation are not as positive as perhaps they once were. He does not like cold sales calls and would like to feel that he is of more help to people than he may be. He expects better outcomes from being a teacher.

George appears to have high self-efficacy beliefs related to change, including changing careers. He has changed careers several times and been successful at it. He has a large number of diverse interests, indicating a variety of areas that may be options for him to examine. A career counselor working from a social cognitive perspective would help George examine the option of becoming a teacher, identifying possible barriers he may have. The counselor would also examine whether George has prematurely foreclosed other options, many of which may be identified by the SII results.

Our Own Approach to Conceptualizing George

We blend a variety of approaches when we do career counseling, based on our own experiences of using different career counseling approaches with diverse clients. We have tried to show how that may be done in this section. However, it is important to note that this is just an example and certainly not a prescription for working with all clients. There are many ways to blend and integrate various theoretical approaches, and these will vary both with the counselor and the concern brought by the client.

George may be seeking career counseling for help adjusting to his current occupation or for help choosing a new career. He has an idea of an area that he might like to explore—teaching—but is not certain that it is a viable option for him. George has a large number of strengths: He appears to have high abilities in a variety of areas, including general intellectual ability and strong interpersonal skills; he has been successful in a number of ventures; he has the skills and confidence to initiate and adapt to change; and he has interests in diverse areas.

We would use a combination of person-environment fit theories (Holland's and the TWA), as well as Super's developmental theory, to begin to conceptualize hypotheses about George's current career concerns. We would use a combination of social cognitive theory and Super's developmental theory to conceptualize his career history.

His career history would appear to include increasing knowledge in high school about his abilities but perhaps not about his interests. For example, he notes that he knew he excelled in math and science and chose to enter an engineering curriculum, but he does not say why he chose engineering; he does not indicate whether this was based on an examination of his interests and abilities. Nonetheless, by the end of high school, he had crystallized an occupation (engineering), and by the time he had graduated from college, he had specified an occupation (industrial engineering). When he implemented that choice, however, he did not decide to pursue a traditional industrial engineering job; rather, he implemented his choice in engineering sales. It would seem that George was implementing a self-concept that combined engineering knowledge with greater use of interpersonal skills than a traditional engineering position would involve.

Developmental theory does not entirely explain some of George's decisions, however. Why did he choose industrial engineering, even though he felt engineering was not a good fit for him? Why did he continue in it, and how did he decide to go into engineering sales? Examining George's decisions from a social cognitive perspective may be useful in formulating hypotheses about his early choices. George reported that he knew he was good in math and science, thus indicating that he had high self-efficacy beliefs about his abilities in these areas. He attended his father's alma mater, majoring in the same field as his father. It may be that George expected very positive outcomes from pursuing this avenue, such as strong approval from his father or other family members. What other occupations did George consider, and what were the barriers to pursuing those occupations?

Social cognitive theory may help to explain George's decisions when he quit his first job in engineering sales. He had high self-efficacy beliefs in his ability to find another job, and his outcome expectancies for leaving the position and finding a new job were more positive than the outcomes expected of staying. The TWA would explicate this further.

His correspondence with the first job was very poor; he may have tried to adjust himself or his environment, but despite being a satisfactory employee, his needs were not met and he chose to leave the environment. What may have been his adjustment style in that job? Has that been consistent in other jobs?

The TWA would suggest that George's subsequent jobs of owning an Oriental rug store and managing a restaurant were more correspondent occupations for him. Both of those jobs ended for reasons outside his control; there is no indication that he was dissatisfied in either position. In fact, he notes that he enjoyed them very much. It would appear that managing a restaurant met his compensation, social service, and achievement needs and that he was well able to do it, because the restaurant was quite successful. George is less correspondent with the occupation of financial planner. He complains that it is "no longer any fun," connoting that his needs are not being met. We would hypothesize that his social service needs, in particular, are not being met, as well as, perhaps, his achievement needs.

George's current dilemma is what to do about his dissatisfaction with his job. Should he change jobs? The first approach we would take would be to talk with George about the context of this decision. What other factors does George need to consider? He has two college-aged children; what responsibilities does he have for their education? How would a change in jobs or in life circumstances affect George's wife, and are there concomitant dual career concerns? Does he have aging parents for whom he is responsible? In other words, does this decision affect others? What about the context of his decision within the other roles George plays in his life? What role does he want work to have at this point? Are there other roles (e.g., leisurite, student, citizen) that may be just as salient for George or that he would like to make more salient? What cultural messages does George have about the role of work in a man's life? Which of those messages would he like to include in the way he lives his life? He may, for example, decide that he likes to be the major breadwinner and provider in the family. On the other hand, he may choose to share this role with his wife if he returns to school.

We would incorporate the developmental perspective in examining George's life roles and the context of the decision. Another aspect of the developmental perspective we would include is encouraging George to talk about the development of his career as a financial planner. He has worked as a financial planner for 11 years; he may be moving out of the establishment stage into the maintenance stage and using this transition point to stop and examine his options.

One of the questions we would want to explore with George is whether he is dissatisfied with the occupation of financial planner or if he is feeling dissatisfaction with the specific job environment. This question is from the TWA approach. He is a satisfactory employee, but his needs and the rewards provided by the job do not correspond. Three options or combinations of options are possible. First, counseling may focus on either adjusting himself or his environment. Is it very important to him that his social service needs are met in the work environment, or can he meet those needs in other domains of his life? How amenable is the work environment to being adjusted? Is it possible to increase the social service activities he does as part of his job and reduce the activities he finds aversive? If this is not possible in this job, the second option is to determine if he would be more satisfied as a financial planner in another firm or agency.

The third option is that the activities he finds aversive are integral to the occupation of financial planner and he will have to change his occupation to find a better fit. We would turn to Holland's theory to help George find a new occupational area. His General Occupational Theme code is SEA, with some moderate interest in Investigative. This code illuminates the lack of fit for George as an engineer, an environment characterized as realistic and investigative. It also may illuminate why he has enjoyed a variety of enterprising types of occupations over the course of his career that capitalized on his experience in sales and his enterprising interests, such as owning a store and managing a restaurant. Financial planner is not an occupation included on the SII, nor is it included in the *Dictionary of*

Holland Occupational Codes (Gottfredson & Holland, 1996). However, George is in an office that combines life insurance agents and financial planners, and life insurance agents have a Holland code of E on the SII. This would indicate that George has some interests that are congruent with his work environment but that he may be seeking an environment more congruent with his social interests. We would encourage George to begin to examine the occupations with a strong social component from the SII, such as nurse, parks and recreation leader, community service organization director, and special education teacher.

We would return to the questions raised earlier about context and life roles as George moves toward making a decision first about whether he would like to adjust to the occupation, move to another company, or choose a new career. Are these options that George would like to pursue, how do they fit in his life right now, and what would he need to do differently to fit them into his life in the future? How does this fit with the developmental stage he is in right now and how he feels about the role of work in his life? How does he feel about taking on the role of student if he decides to go back to school for a teaching degree? How can George find out more information about the occupations he is considering?

Summary

Each of the theoretical perspectives offers a different perspective about George's career history and his current career concerns. The theories also suggest different hypotheses and directions for counseling. As we just demonstrated, the theories are not necessarily incompatible or mutually exclusive, and there are benefits to using multiple approaches to conceptualize a single client. This is particularly true when the client has had considerable life and career experience. Now consider the case of Tom, who is a traditional college-aged student.

The Case of Tom

Tom is a 21-year-old Caucasian man of Irish descent and the younger of two brothers from a medium-sized town in the southern United States. He grew up in a lower-middle-class neighborhood; his mother works as a postal clerk, and his father is an airplane mechanic. They live near many relatives, and much of the family's social life revolves around family celebrations and events.

Tom enjoyed high school. He was an average student. He enjoyed the material he learned in school, but his main goal in high school was to be with his friends. He was very social, and he participated in as many activities as he could while still playing football and basketball. He was an average athlete in high school, and he knew he could not compete athletically at the college level, but he had fun being a part of the team and playing when he could.

In contrast to Tom, his older brother, Jeff, was an outstanding student. He graduated from high school with a 4.0 grade point average, took several advanced placement courses, and received scholarships to many universities. He ended up attending a prestigious school about 70 miles away from his parents. Jeff is able to come home frequently and still participates in the family activities.

Tom and Jeff are 3½ years apart in age but are very close emotionally. Jeff was eager to give Tom advice about attending college and was very disappointed when Tom's grades were not high enough to enable him to attend the same university. Tom was unsure of whether to go to college or not. His parents, aunts, and uncles had not graduated from college, and he thought they were successful and happy. He is happy at home, enjoys his family, and enjoys his friends. Tom feels no particular need to leave his hometown or to move far away from his family. But his brother told him that increasingly, more jobs require college degrees and he would be severely hampered in the future if he did not go to college.

Tom enrolled in a college close to his hometown. He lived in a dorm with his cousin as his roommate. They went home frequently to be part of family gatherings. He had to declare a major when he enrolled, and he decided to major in police science. He thought it sounded good, and one of his friends was majoring in it. He had never really given much thought to choosing a major; his primary decision was whether to attend college or not. He had not had much career guidance in high school, so he really did not have a very clear idea of his interests or his alternatives.

Tom loved college life and became heavily involved in many of the social aspects of a residential college environment. He pledged a fraternity, made many friends, and decided to run for student government office. But he did not do well in his studies. His first-year grades were slightly below a C average. He did even more poorly his second year. He had not realized that police science required such a strong math and science background; math was his weakest subject in high school. At the end of the first semester of his second year, Tom flunked out of college.

WORKING WITH TOM

Use the following questions to consider how you are viewing Tom and how you might work with him in career counseling:

1. What are your impressions of Tom?

2. What more would you like to know about him?

3. What hypotheses would you develop about Tom from the perspective of each theory, including gender-focused and culturally appropriate approaches?

4. How will you gather information to test your hypotheses?

5. How does each of these theoretical approaches influence the next step in counseling? What direction would you take from the perspective of each, including gender-focused and culturally appropriate approaches?

Evaluation of the Major Theories

One of the most important questions that readers should ask as they consider each of the theories presented in this book is "How well does it work?" The next most important question should be "For whom does it work?" These are critical questions and are answered by the research conducted on each theory by its author(s) and others in the field. The last column of Table 11.1 includes a brief evaluation of the level of empirical support for each theory. This is an overly simplistic summary evaluation, for space does not allow a comprehensive review of the empirical support for each theory. Readers are referred to Brown and Lent (2005) and Brown (2002) for extensive reviews of the empirical bases for these theories. However, this summary will provide some basis for evaluating the theories. We examined the literature related to each theory on the following criteria: how well the theoretical constructs have been operationalized, how much support those constructs have received, and how applicable each theory is across a wide variety of populations.

The theories in this book have all been developed by scholars dedicated to testing and revising their theories. Consequently, all have stimulated research in an attempt to support their constructs and the relationships among them. It is not surprising that the oldest theories (Holland's, the TWA, and Super's) are the most well researched and, consequently, are the most well established of the theories.

Holland's theory has been operationalized in a number of instruments, among them the SII (Harmon, Hansen, Borgen, & Hammer, 2005) and the Self-Directed Search (Holland, Powell, & Fritzsche, 1994). With over 500 research studies conducted on it, Holland's theory has been the most extensively examined career theory (Osipow & Fitzgerald, 1996). One reason is how clearly and easily its constructs have been operationalized; Borgen (1991) notes that "its simplicity makes it eminently useful" (p. 274). For example, research has determined that the RIASEC types exist in both individuals and environments (Holland et al., 1994). Hypothesized relationships among constructs also have been supported. For example, congruence is related to satisfaction (Spokane, 1996), and the types appear to be related to each other as predicted by the theory (e.g., Day & Rounds, 1998; Fouad, Harmon, & Borgen, 1997).

The TWA also has received empirical support, although the constructs have not stimulated as much research as has Holland's theory. Several of the constructs are well operationalized, and one of the hallmarks of TWA is that the authors have developed tools to measure the constructs (e.g., Lofquist & Dawis, 1991). Support for the constructs is somewhat equivocal, although more support has been found for correspondence, satisfaction, and satisfactoriness than for the adjustment style and personality variables. Osipow and Fitzgerald (1996) note that, unlike the extensive research on Holland's theory, empirical support for the TWA has come mostly from its authors and their students with little independent verification. Betz (2008), however, reviews more recent literature on applications of TWA across cross-cultural populations, concluding that the constructs may be useful across developmental stages, including in understanding college retention.

Super's theory has been generally supported in over five decades of studies. As noted by Borgen (1991), "Super's comprehensive conceptual work has splendidly stood the test of time" (p. 278). Individuals' careers do develop as predicted by Super, and research supports the construct of self-concept implementation (Betz, 2008). Gottfredson's theory is the newer of the two developmental theories discussed here and is less well operationalized than Super's theory. It has received mixed empirical support, although Gottfredson (2005) notes that research has not tested many areas of the model. Hartung, Porfeli, and Vondracek (2005) reviewed literature in child vocational development and concluded that all four areas (gender, prestige, interests, and socioeconomic status) influence children's vocational choices.

Social cognitive theory, through the newest model in the book, has received a substantial amount of support. It is well operationalized and has stimulated quite a bit of research since Hackett and Betz's (1981) initial introduction and Lent, Brown, and Hackett's (1994) publication of the full social cognitive career theory. Self-efficacy, in particular, has received a great deal of attention and support, as has the application of the theory to diverse groups (Betz, 2008; Swanson & Gore, 2000).

All of the theories were developed with the intention of being applied across a wide variety of populations. However, all have been criticized (e.g., Fouad & Bingham, 1995; Hackett & Lent, 1992; Leong & Brown, 1995; Worthington, Flores, & Navarro, 2005) for not incorporating gender and culture explicitly in the theory. All are equally open to criticism for not thoroughly examining how well the theory applies to various populations. In fact, most were originally developed based on research conducted on White, middle-class men. We simply do not know if the theories operate similarly for women and men, for individuals of different racial and ethnic groups, or for gay and lesbian individuals. If they do differ, we do not know specifically how, nor do we know how to incorporate that knowledge into more effective practice.

It is incumbent on researchers and practitioners alike to work together to create a joint research agenda that will more effectively inform practice. First, more research needs to be conducted on the theories themselves and whether the constructs in fact reflect reality. Second, we need to know if the theoretical relationship among constructs differs across populations. Third, we need to know what works for whom and when; in other words, we need to know which particular interventions are effective with specific individuals at distinct times in their lives.

Revisiting Counselor Cognitions

We would like to return to the three cases at the very beginning of Chapter 1: Ruth, Harry, and Joel. Ruth is returning to the workforce but is unsure of her options, Harry is worried about losing his job, and Joel is uncertain what he will do after high school. All three are at different stages of their work lives, but all three seek career counseling for help making work and career decisions. And each of these three cases could be viewed as simply helping a client make a work-related decision. However, as we pointed out in Chapter 1, to be effective, career counseling and personal counseling are often integrated. If we look at each case more holistically, we can see that an integrated perspective may be more helpful to the client. A counselor working with Ruth might want to help her brainstorm options to use her medical technology degree or may help her explore other options, but the counselor might also help her think through how she can adapt to her new role as worker and how her family may react. Harry's counselor would want to help Harry work through his depression and would most likely confront Harry with potential alcohol abuse. The counselor would also help Harry think through how he is doing at work and how he could change his work tasks or change work environments to use his skills better. Joel's counselor might help him consider post–high school options but also help him consider how to talk to his parents about not wanting to go to school.

Each of these three cases, indeed all of the cases in this book, highlight how important it is to understand the context in which decisions are made, how race and gender influence decisions, and what work means to each individual. Blustein (2006) argues that work can have three main purposes in people's lives: survival, relationships, and identity. It is important for career counselors to understand what purpose work plays in clients' lives in helping them make decisions but also what role they want work to play. For example, a client may have worked to earn money for his or her family but may want a future career to have a stronger identity purpose. It is important to look at the context from the clients' perspectives to understand how to help them effectively. We have discussed counselor cognitions throughout this book, using this discussion as a way to highlight the differences among approaches. In this chapter, we have provided an example of a way to integrate those cognitions, and we want to encourage readers to extend their cognitions to reflect this perspective on context.

In Chapter 1, we described how to use career theories to guide your work with clients, primarily through generating and testing hypotheses about clients, and we hope that working with the cases in this text has convinced you of the value of doing so. Developing and implementing a theoretical approach to working with clients involves learning a set of skills. Just like the process of learning any other counseling-related skills, it takes conscious attention and practice.

We recommend that you continue to hone your conceptualization skills by explicitly using them. Only with continued exercise does conceptualization become second nature. Consider the three cases of Ruth, Harry, and Joel. For each case, ask the following questions:

1. How and what am I thinking about this client?

2. What assumptions am I making about the client's career history? What assumptions am I making about the client's current career concerns?

3. How might personal concerns influence the client's career concerns?

4. How does the client's current context (gender, race, family, disability, social class, sexual orientation) influence his or her perceptions of opportunities or barriers of options?

5. Which theoretical approaches are most useful in thinking about this client, and what hypotheses do the approaches suggest?

6. What specific cultural and gender issues are relevant with this client?

7. How do my culture and gender influence how I am thinking about this client?

8. Am I imposing my values on the client?

Parting Words

Finally, we want to return to the fundamental purpose of this book. We continue to be fascinated by the study of career development and by the career issues that clients bring to counseling. We sincerely hope that we have conveyed our excitement and enthusiasm in the pages of this book. We encourage you to allow yourself to be fascinated by career stories. Understanding the role that work plays in individuals' lives will serve to make you a better counselor and will help you assist the clients that come to you for counseling.

References

Betz, N. E. (2008). Advances in vocational theories. In S. D. Brown & R. W. Lent (Eds.), *Handbook of counseling psychology* (4th ed., pp. 357–374). New York: Wiley.

Blustein, D. L. (2006). *Psychology of working: A new perspective on career development, counseling, and public policy.* Mahwah, NJ: Lawrence Erlbaum.

Borgen, F. H. (1991). Megatrends and milestones in vocational behavior: A 20-year counseling psychology retrospective. *Journal of Vocational Behavior, 39,* 263–290.

Brown, D. (Ed.). (2002). *Career choice and development* (4th ed.). San Francisco: Jossey-Bass.

Brown, S. D., & Lent, R. W. (Eds.). (2005). *Career development and counseling: Putting theory and research to work.* New York: Wiley.

Day, S. X., & Rounds, J. (1998). Universality of vocational interest structure among racial and ethnic minorities. *American Psychologist, 53,* 728–736.

Fouad, N. A., & Bingham, R. (1995). Career counseling with racial/ethnic minorities. In W. B. Walsh & S. H. Osipow (Eds.), *Handbook of vocational psychology* (2nd ed., pp. 331–366). Hillsdale, NJ: Lawrence Erlbaum.

Fouad, N. A., Harmon, L. W., & Borgen, F. H. (1997). Structure of interests of employed male and female members of U.S. racial-ethnic minority and nonminority groups. *Journal of Counseling Psychology, 44,* 339–345.

Gottfredson, G. D., & Holland, J. L. (1996). *Dictionary of Holland occupational codes* (3rd ed.). Palo Alto, CA: Consulting Psychologists Press.

Gottfredson, L. S. (2005). Applying Gottfredson's theory of circumscription and compromise in career guidance counseling. In S. D. Brown & R. W. Lent (Eds.), *Career development and counseling: Putting theory and research to work* (pp. 71–100). New York: Wiley.

Hackett, G., & Betz, N. E. (1981). A self-efficacy approach to the career development of women. *Journal of Vocational Behavior, 18,* 326–339.

Hackett, G., & Lent, R. W. (1992). Theoretical advances and current inquiry in career psychology. In S. D. Brown & R. W. Lent (Eds.), *Handbook of counseling psychology* (pp. 419–451). New York: Wiley.

Harmon, L. W., Hansen, J. C., Borgen, F. H., & Hammer, A. C. (2005). *Strong Interest Inventory: Applications and technical guide.* Palo Alto, CA: Consulting Psychologists Press.

Hartung, P. J., Porfeli, E. J., & Vondracek, F. W. (2005). Child vocational development: A review and reconsideration. *Journal of Vocational Behavior, 66,* 385–419.

Holland, J. L., Powell, A. B., & Fritzsche, B. A. (1994). *The Self-Directed Search professional user's guide.* Odessa, FL: Psychological Assessment Resources.

Lent, R. W., Brown, S. D., & Hackett, G. (1994). Toward a unifying social cognitive theory of career and academic interest, choice, and performance. *Journal of Vocational Behavior, 45,* 79–122.

Leong, F. T. L., & Brown, M. T. (1995). Theoretical issues in cross-cultural career development: Cultural validity and cultural specificity. In W. B. Walsh & S. H. Osipow (Eds.), *Handbook of vocational psychology* (2nd ed., pp. 143–180). Hillsdale, NJ: Lawrence Erlbaum.

Lofquist, L. H., & Dawis, R. V. (1991). *Essentials of person-environment-correspondence counseling.* Minneapolis: University of Minnesota Press.

Osipow, S. H. (1996). Does career theory guide practice or does career practice guide theory? In M. L. Savickas & W. B. Walsh (Eds.), *Handbook of career counseling theory and practice* (pp. 403–409). Palo Alto, CA: Davies-Black.

Osipow, S. H., & Fitzgerald, L. (1996). *Theories of career development* (4th ed.). Needham Heights, MA: Allyn & Bacon.

Spokane, A. R. (1996). Holland's theory. In D. Brown, L. Brooks, & Associates (Eds.), *Career choice and development* (3rd ed., pp. 33–74). San Francisco: Jossey-Bass.

Swanson, J. L., & Gore, P. A. (2000). Advances in vocational psychology theory and research. In S. D. Brown & R. W. Lent (Eds.), *Handbook of counseling psychology* (3rd ed., pp. 233–269). New York: Wiley.

Worthington, R. L., Flores, L. Y., & Navarro, R. L. (2005). Career development in context: Research with people of color. In S. D. Brown & R. W. Lent (Eds.), *Career development and counseling: Putting theory and research to work* (pp. 225–252). New York: Wiley.

Appendix A:
Leslie's Profiles

Strong Interest Inventory® Profile   LESLIE MORENO | Page 2

GENERAL OCCUPATIONAL THEMES   SECTION 1

The General Occupational Themes (GOTs) measure six broad interest patterns that can be used to describe your work personality. Most people's interests are reflected by two or three Themes, combined to form a cluster of interests. Work activities, potential skills, and values can also be classified into these six Themes. This provides a direct link between your interests and the career and education possibilities likely to be most meaningful to you.

Your *standard scores* are based on the average scores of a combined group of working adults. However, because research shows that men and women tend to respond differently in these areas, your *interest levels* (Very Little, Little, Moderate, High, Very High) were determined by comparing your scores against the average scores for your gender.

THEME DESCRIPTIONS

THEME	CODE	INTERESTS	WORK ACTIVITIES	POTENTIAL SKILLS	VALUES
Investigative	I	Science, medicine, mathematics, research	Performing lab work, solving abstract problems, conducting research	Mathematical ability, researching, writing, analyzing	Independence, curiosity, learning
Social	S	People, teamwork, helping, community service	Teaching, caring for people, counseling, training employees	People skills, verbal ability, listening, showing understanding	Cooperation, generosity, service to others
Conventional	C	Organization, data management, accounting, investing, information systems	Setting up procedures and systems, organizing, keeping records, developing computer applications	Ability to work with numbers, data analysis, finances, attention to detail	Accuracy, stability, efficiency
Realistic	R	Machines, computer networks, athletics, working outdoors	Operating equipment, using tools, building, repairing, providing security	Mechanical ingenuity and dexterity, physical coordination	Tradition, practicality, common sense
Enterprising	E	Business, politics, leadership, entrepreneurship	Selling, managing, persuading, marketing	Verbal ability, ability to motivate and direct others	Risk taking, status, competition, influence
Artistic	A	Self-expression, art appreciation, communication, culture	Composing music, performing, writing, creating visual art	Creativity, musical ability, artistic expression	Beauty, originality, independence, imagination

YOUR HIGHEST THEMES	YOUR THEME CODE
Investigative, Social, Conventional	**ISC**

THEME	CODE	STANDARD SCORE & INTEREST LEVEL	STD SCORE
Investigative	I	VERY HIGH	74
Social	S	HIGH	64
Conventional	C	MODERATE	54
Realistic	R	LITTLE	38
Enterprising	E	VERY LITTLE	36
Artistic	A	VERY LITTLE	34

The charts above display your GOT results in descending order, from your highest to least level of interest. Referring to the Theme Descriptions provided, determine how well your results fit for you. Do your highest Themes ring true? Look at your next highest level of interest and ask yourself the same question. You may wish to highlight the Theme descriptions on this page that seem to fit you best.

Figure 1   Leslie's Strong Interest Inventory Profile   (Continued)

BASIC INTEREST SCALES   SECTION 2

The Basic Interest Scales represent specific interest areas that often point to work activities, projects, course work, and leisure activities that are personally motivating and rewarding. As with the General Occupational Themes, your interest levels (Very Little, Little, Moderate, High, Very High) were determined by comparing your scores against the average scores for your gender.

As you review your results in the charts below, note your top interest areas and your areas of least interest, and think about how they relate to your work, educational, and leisure activities. Take time to consider any top interest areas that are not currently part of your work or lifestyle and think about how you might be able to incorporate them into your plans.

YOUR TOP FIVE INTEREST AREAS	Areas of Least Interest
1. Research (I)	Culinary Arts (A)
2. Teaching & Education (S)	Writing & Mass Communication (A)
3. Mathematics (I)	Visual Arts & Design (A)
4. Taxes & Accounting (C)	
5. Science (I)	

INVESTIGATIVE — Very High

BASIC INTEREST SCALE	STD SCORE & INTEREST LEVEL	STD SCORE
Research	VH	78
Mathematics	VH	73
Science	VH	71
Medical Science	M	54

SOCIAL — High

BASIC INTEREST SCALE	STD SCORE & INTEREST LEVEL	STD SCORE
Teaching & Education	VH	76
Religion & Spirituality	VH	71
Human Resources & Training	M	56
Counseling & Helping	M	56
Social Sciences	M	54
Healthcare Services	L	38

CONVENTIONAL — Moderate

BASIC INTEREST SCALE	STD SCORE & INTEREST LEVEL	STD SCORE
Taxes & Accounting	VH	72
Programming & Information Systems	M	50
Finance & Investing	M	49
Office Management	M	47

REALISTIC — Little

BASIC INTEREST SCALE	STD SCORE & INTEREST LEVEL	STD SCORE
Computer Hardware & Electronics	H	54
Mechanics & Construction	M	50
Nature & Agriculture	M	45
Athletics	M	42
Protective Services	L	40
Military	VL	36

ENTERPRISING — Very Little

BASIC INTEREST SCALE	STD SCORE & INTEREST LEVEL	STD SCORE
Law	L	41
Sales	L	40
Management	L	40
Politics & Public Speaking	L	39
Marketing & Advertising	L	39
Entrepreneurship	L	38

ARTISTIC — Very Little

BASIC INTEREST SCALE	STD SCORE & INTEREST LEVEL	STD SCORE
Performing Arts	VL	36
Visual Arts & Design	VL	35
Writing & Mass Communication	VL	35
Culinary Arts	VL	31

INTEREST LEVELS: VL = Very Little | L = Little | M = Moderate | H = High | VH = Very High

Figure 1 (Continued)

OCCUPATIONAL SCALES   SECTION 3

This section highlights your Profile results on the Occupational Scales of the *Strong*. On the next three pages you will find your scores for 122 occupations. The 10 occupations most closely aligned with your interests are listed in the summary chart below. Keep in mind that the occupations listed in your Profile results are just *some* of the many occupations linked to your interests that you might want to consider. They do not indicate those you "should" pursue. It is helpful to think of each occupation as a single example of a much larger group of occupational titles to consider.

Your score on an Occupational Scale shows how similar your interests are to those of people of your gender who have been working in, and are satisfied with, that occupation. The higher your score, the more likes and dislikes you share with those individuals. The Theme Codes associated with each occupation indicate the GOTs most commonly found among people employed in that occupation.

YOUR TOP TEN STRONG OCCUPATIONS

1. Actuary (CI)
2. Mathematician (IRC)
3. Software Developer (IR)
4. Financial Analyst (CE)
5. Mathematics Teacher (CIR)
6. University Professor (IAR)
7. Medical Technologist (IRC)
8. Biologist (IRA)
9. Bookkeeper (C)
10. Financial Manager (CE)

Occupations of Dissimilar Interest

Public Relations Director (AE)

Graphic Designer (ARI)

Medical Illustrator (AIR)

Art Teacher (ASE)

Advertising Account Manager (AE)

As you read through your Occupational Scales results on this and the following pages, note the names of those occupations for which you scored "Similar." Those are the occupations you might want to explore first. If you have no scores in this range, take a look at those in the midrange and begin there. You might also consider occupations of least interest or for which you scored "Dissimilar"; however, keep in mind that you are likely to have little in common with people in those types of work and probably would contribute to such occupations in a unique way. Your career professional can guide you further in this process.

You can learn about occupations from information found in a public library, in the career library of a college or university near you, in a professional career center, or on the Internet. A recommended online source for occupational information is the O*NET™ database at http://online.onetcenter.org. You can also learn a lot about an occupation by talking to people who are working in that particular occupation. These people can describe their day-to-day work and tell you what they like and dislike about it.

Figure 1 (Continued)

Strong Interest Inventory® Profile

OCCUPATIONAL SCALES

INVESTIGATIVE – Researching, Analyzing, Inquiring

THEME CODE	OCCUPATIONAL SCALE	DISSIMILAR / MIDRANGE / SIMILAR	STD SCORE
IRC	Mathematician		65
IR	Software Developer		64
IAR	University Professor		62
IRC	Medical Technologist		61
IRA	Biologist		60
IRA	Physicist		59
IRA	Geologist		57
IR	Chemist		55
IR	R&D Manager		52
IRC	Computer Scientist		51
IR	Optometrist		51
IRS	Science Teacher		51
IRA	Respiratory Therapist		46
IAR	Physician		45
IRC	Medical Technician		44
ICR	Pharmacist		44
IA	Geographer		41
IA	Psychologist		39
IES	Dietitian		37
IRA	Chiropractor		36
IAR	Sociologist		36
IRA	Veterinarian		36
IRA	Dentist		22

Similar results (40 and above)
You share interests with women in that occupation and probably would enjoy the work.

Midrange results (30–39)
You share some interests with women in that occupation and probably would enjoy some of the work.

Dissimilar results (29 and below)
You share few interests with women in that occupation and probably would not enjoy the work.

For more information about any of these occupations, visit O*NET™ online at http://online.onetcenter.org.

SOCIAL – Helping, Instructing, Caregiving

THEME CODE	OCCUPATIONAL SCALE	DISSIMILAR / MIDRANGE / SIMILAR	STD SCORE
SE	Special Education Teacher		42
SE	School Counselor		38
S	Elementary School Teacher		36
SA	College Instructor		35
SAI	Rehabilitation Counselor		35
SA	Speech Pathologist		35
SI	Registered Nurse		34
SAE	Foreign Language Teacher		32
SA	Recreation Therapist		30
SCE	Licensed Practical Nurse		28
SA	Social Worker		27
SRC	Physical Education Teacher		26
SEA	Social Science Teacher		26
SEA	School Administrator		25
SAR	Occupational Therapist		24
SAR	Minister		22
SE	Community Service Director		20
SE	Parks & Recreation Manager		17
SIR	Physical Therapist		9

Figure 1 (Continued)

Strong Interest Inventory® Profile

OCCUPATIONAL SCALES

CONVENTIONAL – Accounting, Organizing, Processing Data

THEME CODE	OCCUPATIONAL SCALE	DISSIMILAR / MIDRANGE / SIMILAR	STD SCORE
CI	Actuary		71
CE	Financial Analyst		62
CIR	Mathematics Teacher		62
C	Bookkeeper		60
CE	Financial Manager		59
CE	Accountant		58
CE	Credit Manager		53
CES	Production Worker		50
C	Computer Systems Analyst		49
CE	Banker		46
C	Health Information Specialist		43
CES	Food Service Manager		42
CES	Business Education Teacher		40
CS	Administrative Assistant		37
C	Computer & IS Manager		37
CSE	Farmer/Rancher		37
CES	Nursing Home Administrator		36
CE	Paralegal		35
CRE	Military Enlisted		27

Similar results (40 and above)
You share interests with women in that occupation and probably would enjoy the work.

Midrange results (30–39)
You share some interests with women in that occupation and probably would enjoy some of the work.

Dissimilar results (29 and below)
You share few interests with women in that occupation and probably would not enjoy the work.

For more information about any of these occupations, visit O*NET™ online at http://online.onetcenter.org.

REALISTIC – Building, Repairing, Working Outdoors

THEME CODE	OCCUPATIONAL SCALE	DISSIMILAR / MIDRANGE / SIMILAR	STD SCORE
RIC	Technical Support Specialist		55
RI	Forester		53
RIC	Network Administrator		52
RI	Engineer		50
RIC	Engineering Technician		45
RSI	Vocational Agriculture Teacher		37
REI	Horticulturist		34
RIS	Radiologic Technologist		29
REI	Military Officer		27
R	Automobile Mechanic		26
RCI	Emergency Medical Technician		26
RC	Landscape/Grounds Manager		24
RIA	Carpenter		22
RIA	Electrician		22
RE	Law Enforcement Officer		19
RIS	Athletic Trainer		12
RIS	Firefighter		11

Figure 1 (Continued)

OCCUPATIONAL SCALES

ENTERPRISING – Selling, Managing, Persuading

THEME CODE	OCCUPATIONAL SCALE	DISSIMILAR / MIDRANGE / SIMILAR	STD SCORE
EIR	Investments Manager		38
ECS	Housekeeping/Maintenance Manager		37
ECS	Operations Manager		33
ECR	Optician		28
E	Top Executive		26
E	Retail Sales Representative		22
E	Sales Manager		22
EC	Cosmetologist		21
EAI	Technical Sales Representative		19
EAS	Human Resources Manager		18
ECA	Retail Sales Manager		16
ECA	Travel Consultant		16
EA	Marketing Manager		13
ECR	Purchasing Agent		13
E	Life Insurance Agent		10
EC	Buyer		8
EAC	Florist		8
ECR	Restaurant Manager		8
EAS	Flight Attendant		7
E	Realtor		5
EAS	Elected Public Official		4
ERA	Chef		-4
EA	Interior Designer		-5

Similar results (40 and above)
You share interests with women in that occupation and probably would enjoy the work.

Midrange results (30–39)
You share some interests with women in that occupation and probably would enjoy some of the work.

Dissimilar results (29 and below)
You share few interests with women in that occupation and probably would not enjoy the work.

For more information about any of these occupations, visit O*NET™ online at http://online.onetcenter.org.

ARTISTIC – Creating or Enjoying Art, Drama, Music, Writing

THEME CODE	OCCUPATIONAL SCALE	DISSIMILAR / MIDRANGE / SIMILAR	STD SCORE
A	Librarian		31
AI	Urban & Regional Planner		27
A	Musician		26
ASI	ESL Instructor		23
A	Translator		22
AES	Corporate Trainer		19
AR	Artist		18
AIR	Technical Writer		13
ARI	Architect		10
A	Attorney		10
AER	Public Administrator		9
AI	Editor		8
ARE	Photographer		7
AE	Broadcast Journalist		2
ASE	English Teacher		0
A	Reporter		-8
AE	Advertising Account Manager		-9
ASE	Art Teacher		-10
AIR	Medical Illustrator		-10
ARI	Graphic Designer		-13
AE	Public Relations Director		-21

Figure 1 (Continued)

PERSONAL STYLE SCALES   SECTION 4

The Personal Style Scales describe different ways of approaching people, learning, leading, making decisions, and participating in teams. Personal Style Scales help you think about your preferences for factors that can be important in your career, enabling you to more effectively narrow your choices and examine your opportunities. Each scale includes descriptions at both ends of the continuum, with scores indicating your preference for one style versus the other.

Your scores on the Personal Style Scales were determined by comparing your responses to those of a combined group of working men and women.

YOUR PERSONAL STYLE SCALES PREFERENCES

1. **You are likely to prefer a balance of working alone and working with people**
2. **You seem to prefer to learn through lectures and books**
3. **You probably prefer to lead by example**
4. **You may dislike taking risks**
5. **You probably enjoy participating in teams**

Clear Scores
(Below 46 and above 54)
You indicated a clear preference for one style versus the other.

Midrange Scores (46–54)
You indicated that some of the descriptors on both sides apply to you.

PERSONAL STYLE SCALE						STD SCORE
Work Style	Prefers working alone; enjoys data, ideas, or things; reserved		◆		Prefers working with people; enjoys helping others; outgoing	54
Learning Environment	Prefers practical learning environments; learns by doing; prefers short-term training to achieve a specific goal or skill			◆	Prefers academic environments; learns through lectures and books; willing to spend many years in school; seeks knowledge for its own sake	56
Leadership Style	Is not comfortable taking charge of others; prefers to do the job rather than direct others; may lead by example rather than by giving directions		◆		Is comfortable taking charge of and motivating others; prefers directing others to doing the job alone; enjoys initiating action; expresses opinions easily	45
Risk Taking	Dislikes risk taking; likes quiet activities; prefers to play it safe; makes careful decisions	◆			Likes risk taking; appreciates original ideas; enjoys thrilling activities and taking chances; makes quick decisions	34
Team Orientation	Prefers accomplishing tasks independently; enjoys role as independent contributor; likes to solve problems on one's own			◆	Prefers working on teams; enjoys collaborating on team goals; likes problem solving with others	60

Figure 1 (Continued)

Figure 1 (Continued)

Strong Interest Inventory® Profile — LESLIE MORENO | Page 9

PROFILE SUMMARY — SECTION 5

YOUR HIGHEST THEMES
Investigative, Social, Conventional

YOUR THEME CODE
ISC

YOUR TOP FIVE INTEREST AREAS
1. Research (I)
2. Teaching & Education (S)
3. Mathematics (I)
4. Taxes & Accounting (C)
5. Science (I)

Areas of Least Interest
Culinary Arts (A)
Writing & Mass Communication (A)
Visual Arts & Design (A)

YOUR TOP TEN STRONG OCCUPATIONS
1. Actuary (CI)
2. Mathematician (IRC)
3. Software Developer (IR)
4. Financial Analyst (CE)
5. Mathematics Teacher (CIR)
6. University Professor (IAR)
7. Medical Technologist (IRC)
8. Biologist (IRA)
9. Bookkeeper (C)
10. Financial Manager (CE)

Occupations of Dissimilar Interest
Public Relations Director (AE)
Graphic Designer (ARI)
Medical Illustrator (AIR)
Art Teacher (ASE)
Advertising Account Manager (AE)

YOUR PERSONAL STYLE SCALES PREFERENCES
1. You are likely to prefer a balance of working alone and working with people
2. You seem to prefer to learn through lectures and books
3. You probably prefer to lead by example
4. You may dislike taking risks
5. You probably enjoy participating in teams

RESPONSE SUMMARY — SECTION 6

This section provides a summary of your responses to the different sections of the inventory for use in interpretation by your career professional.

ITEM RESPONSE PERCENTAGES

Section Title	Strongly Like	Like	Indifferent	Dislike	Strongly Dislike
Occupations	25	3	12	6	55
Subject Areas	35	0	13	17	35
Activities	38	8	8	15	31
Leisure Activities	39	4	0	21	36
People	31	0	6	0	63
Characteristics	56	11	11	0	22
TOTAL PERCENTAGE	33	4	10	11	42

Total possible responses: 291   Your response total: 290   Items omitted: 1   Typicality index: 16—Combination of item responses appears inconsistent

Note: Due to rounding, total percentage may not add up to 100%.

Skills Confidence Inventory®
Profile

LESLIE MORENO

F

LEVELS OF SKILLS CONFIDENCE BY THEME

Your *Skills Confidence Inventory* results describe how you perceive your own capabilities in performing activities related to the same six broad areas represented by the General Occupational Themes. Keep in mind that these results may not reflect your actual abilities; the results reflect how you rate yourself. Your own rating may influence what kinds of activities you try or avoid and may determine what occupations or educational programs you consider as possibilities for exploration.

Your confidence in each of the six areas is shown below in rank order. Your Skills Confidence Theme code summarizes the areas in which you feel most confident performing particular activities. Your Skills Confidence Theme code is ISC.

THEME	CODE	CONFIDENCE SCORE & LEVEL	SCORE (1–5)	TYPICAL SKILL AREAS
Investigative	I	VERY HIGH	4.6	Research, math, science
Social	S	HIGH	3.7	Education, counseling, social service
Conventional	C	HIGH	3.6	Finance, computers, organization
Enterprising	E	LITTLE	2.4	Sales, speaking, management
Artistic	A	VERY LITTLE	1.6	Creative expression, music, design
Realistic	R	VERY LITTLE	1.2	Outdoor work, construction, repair

COMPARISON OF LEVELS OF SKILLS CONFIDENCE AND INTEREST

The chart below compares your skills confidence levels with your interest levels as measured by the *Strong*. Your Skills Confidence Theme code is ISC. Your *Strong* Theme code is ISC. Use this comparison to help you select Themes you'd like to explore further to find satisfying career, educational, and leisure options. Also, refer to Understanding Your Results on the *Skills Confidence Inventory*, available from your career professional, for more information.

THEME	CODE	FURTHER EXPLORATION if highest level of confidence is moderate	FURTHER EXPLORATION	PRIORITIES FOR CAREER EXPLORATION
		Less →	→ More	
Investigative	I		CONFIDENCE / INTEREST	High priority
Social	S		CONFIDENCE / INTEREST	High priority
Conventional	C		CONFIDENCE / INTEREST	High priority
Enterprising	E	CONFIDENCE / INTEREST		Low priority
Artistic	A	CONFIDENCE / INTEREST		Low priority
Realistic	R	CONFIDENCE / INTEREST		Low priority

Total responses out of 60: 60

Figure 2   Leslie's Skills Confidence Inventory Profile

SOURCE: Adapted and reproduced by special permission of the Publisher, CPP, Inc., Mountain View, CA 94043 from Skills Confidence Inventory. Copyright 1996, 2005, by CPP, Inc. All rights reserved. Further reproduction is prohibited without the publisher's written consent.

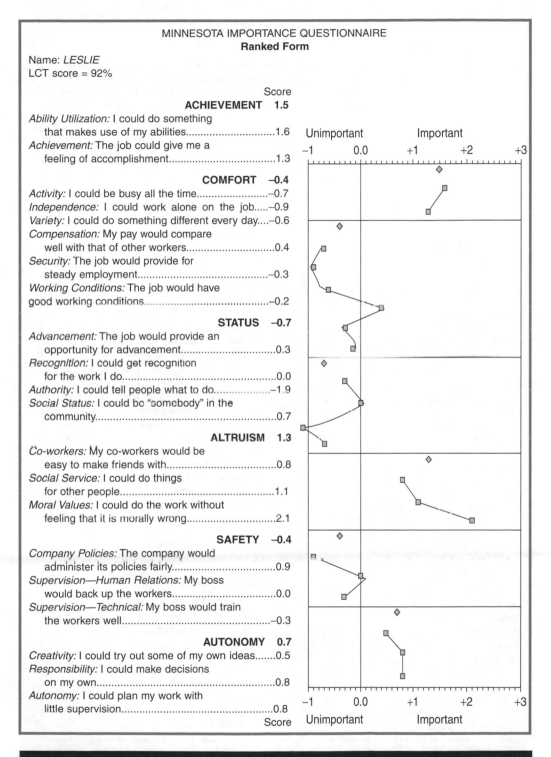

MINNESOTA IMPORTANCE QUESTIONNAIRE
Ranked Form

Name: *LESLIE*
LCT score = 92%

Score
ACHIEVEMENT   1.5

Ability Utilization: I could do something
that makes use of my abilities.............................1.6
Achievement: The job could give me a
feeling of accomplishment....................................1.3

COMFORT   −0.4

Activity: I could be busy all the time.........................−0.7
Independence: I could work alone on the job.....−0.9
Variety: I could do something different every day....−0.6
Compensation: My pay would compare
well with that of other workers.............................0.4
Security: The job would provide for
steady employment..−0.3
Working Conditions: The job would have
good working conditions..−0.2

STATUS   −0.7

Advancement: The job would provide an
opportunity for advancement................................0.3
Recognition: I could get recognition
for the work I do..0.0
Authority: I could tell people what to do..................−1.9
Social Status: I could be "somebody" in the
community..0.7

ALTRUISM   1.3

Co-workers: My co-workers would be
easy to make friends with.....................................0.8
Social Service: I could do things
for other people...1.1
Moral Values: I could do the work without
feeling that it is morally wrong.............................2.1

SAFETY   −0.4

Company Policies: The company would
administer its policies fairly....................................0.9
Supervision—Human Relations: My boss
would back up the workers....................................0.0
Supervision—Technical: My boss would train
the workers well..−0.3

AUTONOMY   0.7

Creativity: I could try out some of my own ideas.......0.5
Responsibility: I could make decisions
on my own...0.8
Autonomy: I could plan my work with
little supervision...0.8
Score

Unimportant   Important
−1   0.0   +1   +2   +3

Figure 3   Leslie's Minnesota Importance Questionnaire Profile   (Continued)

Minnesota Importance Questionnaire

Correspondence report for *LESLIE*

The MIQ profile is compared with Occupational Reinforcer Patterns (QRPS) for 90 representative occupations. Correspondence is indicated by the C index. A prediction of *Satisfied (S)* results from C values greater than .49, *Likely Satisfied (L)* for C values between .10 and .49, and *Not Satisfied (N)* for C values less than .10. Occupations are clustered by similarity of Occupational Reinforcer Patterns.

	C Index	Pred. Sat.		C Index	Pred. Sat.
CLUSTER A (ACH-AUT-Alt)	.68	S	CLUSTER B (ACH-Com)	.51	S
Architect	.62	S	Bricklayer	.43	L
Dentist	*.58*	S	Carpenter	.31	L
Family Practitioner (M.D.)	.45	L	Cement Mason	.42	L
Interior Designer/Decorator	.63	S	Elevator Repairer	.31	L
Lawyer	.48	L	Heavy Equipment Operator	.48	L
Minister	*.52*	S	Landscape Gardner	.49	L
Nurse, Occupational Health	*.58*	S	*Lather*	*.55*	S
Occupational Therapist	.68	S	*Millwright*	.54	S
Optometrist	.54	S	Painter/Paperhanger	.38	L
Psychologist, Counseling	*.72*	S	Patternmaker, Metal	.33	L
Recreation Leader	.63	S	Pipefitter	.43	L
Speech Pathologist	.67	S	Plasterer	.37	L
Teacher, Elementary School	.65	S	Plumber	.54	S
Teacher, Secondary School	.66	S	Roofer	.46	L
Vocational Evaluator	.60	S	*Salesperson, Automobile*	.50	S
CLUSTER C (ACH-Aut-Com)	.60	S	CLUSTER D (ACH-STA-Com)	.48	L
Alteration Tailor	*.57*	S	Accountant, Certified Public	.49	L
Automobile Mechanic	.47	L	*Airplane Co-Pilot, Commercial*	*.32*	L
Barber	.60	S	Cook (Hotel-Restaurant)	.32	L
Beauty Operator	.68	S	Department Head, Supermarket	.19	L
Caseworker	.66	S	Drafter, Architectural	.46	L
Claim Adjuster	*.50*	S	Electrician	.44	L
Commercial Artist, Illustrator	.46	L	Engineer, Civil	.47	L
Electronics Mechanic	.32	L	*Engineer, Time Study*	.51	S
Locksmith	.40	L	Firm-Equipment Mechanic I	.33	L
Maintenance Repairer, Factory	.40	L	Line-Installer-Repairer (Telephone)	.08	N
Mechanical-Engineering Technician	.60	S	Machinist	.29	L
Office-Machine Servicer	.41	L	Programmer (Business,		
Photoengraver (Stripper)	.42	L	Engineering, Science)	.54	S
Sales Agent, Real Estate	.70	S	Sheet Metal Worker	.44	L
Salesperson, General Hardware	.40	L	Statistical-Machine Servicer	.28	L
CLUSTER E (COM)	.24	L	Writer, Technical Publication	.57	S
Assembler, Production	−.05	N	CLUSTER F (Alt-Com)	.54	S
Baker	.18	L	*Airplane-Flight Attendant*	.57	S
Bookbinder	.22	L	Clerk, General Office, Civil Service	.30	L
Bookkeeper I	.28	L	Dietitian	.40	L
Bus Driver	.22	L	Fire Fighter	.35	L
Key-Punch Operator	.25	L	*Librarian*	.65	S
Meat Cutter	.10	L	*Medical Technologist*	.61	S
Post-Office Clerk	.19	L	Nurse, Professional	.46	L
Production Helper (Food)	.35	L	Orderly	.38	L
Punch-Press Operator	.20	L	*Physical Therapist*	.58	S

Figure 3 (Continued)

	C Index	Pred. Sat.		C Index	Pred. Sat.
CLUSTER E (COM)	.24	L	CLUSTER F (Alt-Com)	.54	S
Sales, General (Department Store)	.35	L	Police Officer	.48	L
Sewing-Machine Operator,			Receptionist, Civil Service	.42	L
Automatic	.23	L	Secretary (General Office)	.46	L
Solderer (Production Line)	.11	L	Taxi Driver	.35	L
Telephone Operator	.19	L	Telephone Installer	.41	L
Teller (Banking)	.24	L	Waiter-Waitress	.51	S

Vocational Psychology Research, Department of Psychology
University of Minnesota, Minneapolis MN 55455

Figure 3 (Continued)

SOURCE: Rounds, J. B., Henley, G. A., Dawis, R. V., Lofquist, L. H., & Weiss, D. J. (1981). *Manual for the Minnesota Importance Questionnaire.* Minneapolis: University of Minnesota. Used with permission.

Individual Analysis of Career Concerns

Name **Leslie** _____ Age _____

Compared with _____ Date _____

Ⓥ Consulting Psychologists Press, Inc.
Palo Alto, CA 94303

The ACCI can be self-scored to yield a profile based on the clusters of career development tasks of most concern to you. The procedures for self-scoring and profile analysis are:

1. On the Career Concerns Chart below, enter the distribution of ratings for each of the groups of 5 items in each substage. For example, if for items 1 to 5, you marked 1 for two items, 2 for two items, and 3 for one item, you would enter those numbers in the appropriate spaces on the Crystallization line.

2. Then compute the average score for the substage by dividing the weighted sum by the number of items in the group. For the above example, the weighted sum would be 2+4+3=9, divided by 5, equals 1.8. Enter the weighted sum and average in the appropriate columns. Follow the same procedure for each substage and stage.

3. Circle the number of the response you chose for Item 61.

4. Plot your Career Stage and Substage Profile below by marking with a capital X on the appropriate line the location of each of the four Stage averages, and with a small x each of the Substage averages. Connect the small x's in each Stage to draw the four profiles of your current career concerns. Intraindividual interpretations of average Substage scores are usually more insight-producing than are Stage scores because of present and future orientations and recycling.

5. Convert the raw scores (5-point ratings) into percentiles with the appropriate table in the Manual or from local norms. Percentiles make it possible to compare one person with a group of relevant people, and average ratings on the 5-point scale help when a person compares him or herself using the profile.

6. Record for each Substage the number of items rated either 4 or 5 to show the clustering of major concerns and to help interpret Stage and Substage averages in the Career Concerns Chart below.

CAREER CONCERNS CHART

Items	Career Concerns	None 1	Little 2	Some 3	Cons. 4	Great 5	Weighted Sum	Average
	A: EXPLORATION STAGE							
1–5	Crystallization		1	1	3		17	3.4
6–10	Specification			2		3	21	4.2
11–15	Implementation		2	3	3?		13	2.6
1–15	TOTAL EXPLORATION		3	6	3	3	51	3.4
	B: ESTABLISHMENT STAGE							
16–20	Stabilizing	1	2		1	1	14	2.8
21–25	Consolidating		4	1			11	2.2
26–30	Advancing		3	2			12	2.4
16–30	TOTAL ESTABLISHMENT	1	9	3	1	1	37	2.5
	C: MAINTENANCE STAGE							
31–35	Holding	1	4				9	1.8
36–40	Updating	3	1	1			8	1.6
41–45	Innovating		1	1	3		17	3.4
31–45	TOTAL MAINTENANCE	4	6	2	3		34	2.3
	D: DISENGAGEMENT STAGE							
46–50	Deceleration	5					5	1.0
51–55	Retirement Planning	5					5	1.0
56–60	Retirement Living	5					5	1.0
46–60	TOTAL DISENGAGEMENT	15					15	1.0
61	CAREER CHANGE STATUS	1	2	③	4	5 (Circle Response)		

CAREER STAGE AND SUBSTAGE PROFILE

%ile	Amount of Current Concern None 1.0 Little 2.0 Some 3.0 Cons. 4.0 Great 5.0	Substages	Number of Concerns Rated 4 (Considerable) or 5 (Great)
		Crystallization	3
		Specification	3
		Implementation	–
79			
		Stabilizing	1
		Consolidating	1
		Advancing	–
25			
		Holding	–
		Updating	–
		Innovating	3
23			
		Deceleration	–
		Retirement Planning	–
		Retirement Living	–
1			

0383

97 96 95 94   13 12 11

Figure 4   Leslie's Adult Career Concerns Inventory Profile

Appendix B:
National Career
Development Association
Code of Ethics

National Career Development Association

Code of Ethics
Revised May 2007

The NCDA Ethics Committee gratefully acknowledges the American Counseling Association (ACA) and its Ethics Committee for permission to adapt their 2005 Code of Ethics. NCDA, one of the founding associations of ACA in 1952, is a current division of ACA. The NCDA Ethics Committee endeavored to follow the structure of ACA's Code so that the two codes would be compatible with each other, while developing, adding, and enhancing profession-specific guidelines for NCDA's membership. More information on ACA's Ethics Code can be found on their website (see the attached web references section).

The NCDA Ethics Committee gratefully acknowledges Cassandra Smisson for her assistance in reviewing the final draft of this code. As of June 2006, Ms. Smisson was pursuing a Ph.D. in Counseling Psych at Florida State University.

2005-2007 NCDA Ethics Committee Members

David M. Reile, Chair, Cheri Butler (Board Liaison) ;Greta Davis; Dennis Engels; Janice Guerriero; Janet Lenz; Julia Makela; Kristin M. Perrone-McGovern; James Sampson; Donald Schutt; Keley Smith-Keller

Nondiscrimination Statement
NCDA opposes discrimination against any individual based on age, culture, mental/physical disability, ethnicity, race, religion/spirituality, creed, gender, actual or perceived gender identity or expression, actual or perceived sexual orientation, marital/partnership status, language preference, socioeconomic status, any other characteristics not specifically relevant to job performance. (Statement adopted by the NCDA Board of Directors, May 2007)

1

2007 NCDA Code of Ethics

Introduction & Purpose

While there are many ways to define and think about *ethics*, ethics and ethical behavior are basically about professionalism and transparency. The NCDA Ethics Code has been designed as a guide and resource for career practitioners. While it offers a set of principles that can be applied to wide range of settings and situations, it is not (nor can it be) comprehensive. If you are concerned about whether or not a particular practice is ethical, then you should not engage in that behavior without getting competent advice. More succinctly, when in doubt—don't; at least not without discussing the situation with others. Peer review isn't always going to give you perfect advice; but you can take comfort in knowing that you questioned your behavior before proceeding and allowed others to comment before taking action. There is safety and strength in the depth and breadth of opinions you seek before engaging in activity which may be untried or questionable. The Ethics Committee Members do not hold themselves up as definitive experts in all ethical matters. Further, we are not experts with regard to legal issues and cannot give legal advice. However, we encourage members of the National Career Development Association to contact us with questions. We are committed to working collaboratively to provide guidance where we can and to provide referrals as appropriate. You may reach us at ethics@ncda.org.

The *National Career Development Association (NCDA) Code of Ethics* serves five main purposes:

1. The *Code* enables NCDA to clarify to current and future members, and to those served by their members, the nature of ethical responsibilities held in common by its members.
2. The *Code* helps support the mission of NCDA.
3. The *Code* establishes principles that define ethical behaviors and practices of association members.
4. The *Code* serves as an ethical guide designed to assist members in constructing a professional course of action that best serves those utilizing career services and best promotes the values of the career profession.
5. The *Code* serves as a guide for those receiving career services so that they may understand what to expect from working with a career professional and to understand their rights and responsibilities as consumers of these services.

The *NCDA Code of Ethics* contains nine main sections that address the following areas:
> Section A: The Professional Relationship
> Section B: Confidentiality, Privileged Communication, and Privacy
> Section C: Professional Responsibility
> Section D: Relationships with Other Professionals
> Section E: Evaluation, Assessment, and Interpretation
> Section F: Use of the Internet in Career Services
> Section G: Supervision, Training, and Teaching
> Section H: Research and Publication
> Section I: Resolving Ethical Issues

2

Each section of the *NCDA Code of Ethics* begins with an Introduction. The Introduction helps set the tone for that particular section and provides a starting point that invites reflection on the ethical guidelines contained in each part of the *NCDA Code of Ethics*. When career professionals are faced with ethical dilemmas that are difficult to resolve, they are expected to engage in a carefully considered ethical decision-making process. Reasonable differences of opinion can and do exist among career professionals with respect to ways in which values, ethical principles, and ethical standards would be applied when they conflict. While there is no specific ethical decision-making model that is most effective, career professionals are expected to be familiar with a credible model of decision-making that can bear public scrutiny and its application. (For one example of an ethical decision-making model from the Ethics Resource Center, see the attached web references section). Through a chosen ethical decision-making process and evaluation of the context of the situation, career professionals are empowered to make decisions that help expand the capacity of people to grow and develop.

NCDA has members in various career services positions (see Career Professionals), as well as in instructional (counselor educators, counseling psychology professors, etc.) and supervisory roles (Director, Associate Director, Career Supervisor, etc.). The term "career professional" will be used throughout this document both as a noun and as an adjective to refer to anyone holding NCDA membership and who is therefore expected to abide by these ethical guidelines. Additionally, a brief glossary is given (see end of document) to provide readers with a concise description of some of the terms used in the *NCDA Code of Ethics*. NCDA Members who are affiliated with other professional associations (i.e., psychologists, school counselors, etc.) should also consult the ethics codes from those organizations and adhere to the highest standard of professional practice.

NCDA acknowledges and supports its members in their quest to achieve the highest academic and professional credentials appropriate to their work. Many NCDA members are trained credentialed counselors, psychologists, and/or educators with masters and/or doctoral-level degrees in counseling, psychology, or related disciplines. NCDA does not encourage or condone replacing these professionals with individuals who have lesser education, training, and/or credentials. However, NCDA acknowledges, respects, and welcomes individuals regardless of their training and educational backgrounds and recognizes the valuable contribution that all of its members make in the field of career development. Thus, NCDA opposes any statement, action, or activity, which implies a "second-class" status to any individuals within our association.

Section A: The Professional Relationship

Introduction
Career professionals encourage client growth and development in ways that foster the interest and welfare of clients and promote formation of healthy relationships. Career professionals actively attempt to understand the diverse cultural backgrounds of the individuals they serve. Career professionals also explore their own cultural identities and how one's cultural identity affects one's values and beliefs about the working relationship.

Career professionals are encouraged to contribute to society by devoting a portion of their professional activity to services for which there is little or no financial return (pro bono publico).

A.1. Welfare of Those Served by Career Professionals
A.1.a. Primary Responsibility
The primary responsibility of career professionals is to respect the dignity and to promote the welfare of the individuals to whom they provide service.

A.1.b. Differentiation Between Types of Services Provided
"Career planning" services are differentiated from "career counseling" services. Career planning services include an active provision of information designed to help a client with a specific need, such as review of a resumé; assistance in networking strategies; identification of occupations based on values, interests, skills, prior work experience, and/or other characteristics; support in the job-seeking process; and assessment by means of paper-based and/or online inventories of interest, abilities, personality, work-related values, and/or other characteristics. In addition to providing these informational services, "career counseling" provides the opportunity for a deeper level of involvement with the client, based on the establishment of a professional counseling relationship and the potential for assisting clients with career and personal development concerns beyond those included in career planning. All career professionals, whether engaging in "career planning" or "career counseling", provide only the services that are within the scope of their professional competence and qualifications. *(See C.2., C.4., E.2.a., F.7.)*

A.1.c. Records
Career professionals maintain records necessary for rendering professional services as required by laws, regulations, or agency or institution procedures. Career professionals include sufficient and timely documentation in their records to facilitate delivery and continuity of services. Career professionals take reasonable steps to ensure that documentation in records accurately reflects client progress and the services provided. If errors are made in records, career professionals take steps to properly note the correction of such errors according to agency or institutional policies. Career professionals are encouraged to purge their files according to the time frame required by federal, state, local, and/or institutional statute, law, regulation, or procedure, particularly when there is no reasonable expectation that a client will benefit from maintaining the records any longer than required. Career professionals are expected to know and abide by all applicable federal, state, local, and/or institutional statutes, laws, regulations, and procedures regarding record keeping. *(See B.6., B.6.g., H.2.j.)*

A.1.d. Career Services Plans
Career professionals and their clients work jointly in devising integrated career services plans (in writing or orally) that offer reasonable promise of success and are consistent with the abilities and circumstances of clients. Career professionals and clients regularly review career plans to assess their continued viability and effectiveness, respecting the freedom of choice of clients. *(See A.2.a., A.2.d.)*

A.1.e. Support Network Involvement
Career professionals recognize that support networks hold various meanings in the lives of clients and consider enlisting the support, understanding, and involvement of others (e.g., family members, friends, and religious/spiritual/community leaders) as positive resources, when appropriate and with client consent.

A.2. Informed Consent in the Professional Relationship
(See B.5., B.6.b., E.3., E.13.b., G.1.c., H.2.a.)
A.2.a. Informed Consent
Clients have the freedom to choose whether to enter into or remain in a professional relationship. To make informed choices, clients need adequate information about the working relationship and the career professional. Career professionals have an obligation to review in writing and orally the rights and responsibilities of both the career professional and the recipient of services prior to the beginning of the working relationship. Further, informed consent is an ongoing part of the professional relationship, and career professionals appropriately document discussions of informed consent throughout the working relationship.

A.2.b. Types of Information Needed
Career professionals clearly explain to clients the nature of all services provided. They inform clients about issues such as, but not limited to, the following: the purposes, goals, techniques, procedures, limitations, potential risks, and benefits of services; the career professional's qualifications, credentials, and relevant experience; continuation of services upon the incapacitation or death of the career professional; and other pertinent information. Career professionals take steps to ensure that clients understand the implications of diagnosis (if applicable), the intended use of tests/assessments and reports, fees, and billing arrangements. Clients have the right to confidentiality and to be provided with an explanation of its limitations (including how supervisors and/or treatment team professionals are involved); to obtain clear information about their records; to participate in the ongoing career services plans; and to refuse any services or modality change and to be advised of the consequences of such refusal.

A.2.c. Developmental and Cultural Sensitivity
Career professionals communicate information in ways that are both developmentally and culturally appropriate. Career professionals use clear and understandable language when discussing issues related to informed consent. When clients have difficulty understanding the language used by career professionals, they provide necessary services (e.g., arranging for a qualified interpreter or translator) to ensure comprehension by clients. The cost for such services, however, may be passed onto clients in accordance with federal, state, local, and/or institutional statute, law, regulation, or procedure. Thus clients should be given the opportunity to seek another career professional or to employ an interpreter or translator of their own

5

choosing. In collaboration with clients, career professionals consider cultural implications of informed consent procedures and, where possible, career professionals adjust their practices accordingly.

A.2.d. Inability to Give Consent
When providing career services to minors or persons unable to give voluntary consent, career professionals seek the assent of clients to services, and include them in decision making as appropriate. Career professionals recognize the need to balance the ethical rights of clients to make choices, their capacity to give consent or assent to receive services, and parental or familial legal rights and responsibilities to protect these clients and make decisions on their behalf.

A.3. Clients Served by Others
When career professionals learn that their clients are in a professional relationship with another mental health professional, they request a written release from clients to inform the other professionals and strive to establish positive and collaborative professional relationships, when necessary and appropriate.

A.4. Avoiding Harm and Imposing Values
A.4.a. Avoiding Harm
Career professionals act to avoid harming their clients, students, trainees, and research participants and to minimize or to remedy unavoidable or unanticipated harm.

A.4.b. Personal Values
Career professionals are aware of their own values, attitudes, beliefs, and behaviors and avoid imposing values that are inconsistent with clients' goals. Career professionals respect the diversity of clients, students, trainees, and research participants.

A.5. Roles and Relationships with Clients
(See G.3., G.10., H.3.)
A.5.a. Current Clients
Sexual or romantic interactions or relationships with current clients, their romantic partners, or their family members are prohibited.

A.5.b. Former Clients
Sexual or romantic interactions or relationships with former clients, their romantic partners, or their family members are prohibited for a period of 5 years following the last professional contact. Career professionals, before engaging in sexual or romantic interactions or relationships with clients, their romantic partners, or client family members after 5 years following the last professional contact, demonstrate forethought and document (in written form) whether the interactions or relationship can be viewed as exploitive in some way and/or whether there is still potential to harm the former client. In cases of potential exploitation and/or harm, the career professional does not enter into such an interaction or relationship.

A.5.c. Nonprofessional Interactions or Relationships (Other Than Sexual or Romantic Interactions or Relationships)

Nonprofessional relationships with clients, former clients, their romantic partners, or their family members should be avoided by career professionals, except when the interaction is potentially beneficial to the client. *(See A.5.d.)*

A.5.d. Potentially Beneficial Interactions

When a nonprofessional interaction with a client or former client may be potentially beneficial to the client or former client, the career professional must document in case records, prior to the interaction (or as soon as feasible), the rationale for such an interaction, the potential benefit, and anticipated consequences for the client or former client and other individuals significantly involved with the client or former client. Such interactions should be initiated with appropriate client consent. Where unintentional harm occurs to the client or former client, or to an individual significantly involved with the client or former client, due to the nonprofessional interaction, the career professional must show evidence of an attempt to remedy such harm. Examples of potentially beneficial interactions include, but are not limited to, attending a formal ceremony (e.g., a wedding/commitment ceremony or graduation); purchasing a service or product provided by a client or former client (excepting unrestricted bartering); hospital visits to an ill family member; and mutual membership in a professional association, organization, or community. *(See A.5.c.)*

A.5.e. Role Changes in the Professional Relationship

When a career professional changes a role from the original or most recent contracted relationship, s/he obtains informed consent from the client and explains the right of the client to refuse services related to the change. Examples of role changes include, but are not limited to:
1. changing from providing individual career services to therapy, relationship or family counseling, or vice versa;
2. changing from a non-forensic evaluative role to a therapeutic role, or vice versa;
3. changing from a career professional to a researcher role (i.e., enlisting clients as research participants), or vice versa; and/or
4. changing from a career professional to a mediator role, or vice versa.

Clients must be fully informed of any anticipated consequences (e.g., financial, legal, personal, or therapeutic) of role changes with a career professional.

A.6. Roles and Relationships at Individual, Group, Institutional, and Societal Levels
A.6.a. Advocacy

When appropriate, career professionals advocate at individual, group, institutional, and societal levels to examine potential barriers and obstacles that inhibit access and/or the growth and development of clients.

A.6.b. Confidentiality and Advocacy

Career professionals obtain consent prior to engaging in advocacy efforts on behalf of a client to improve the provision of services and to work toward removal of systemic barriers or obstacles that inhibit client access, growth, and development.

7

A.7. Multiple Clients

When a career professional agrees to provide career services to two or more persons who have a relationship, the career professional clarifies at the outset which person or persons are clients and the nature of the relationships the career professional will have with each involved person. If it becomes apparent that the career professional may be called upon to perform potentially conflicting roles, the career professional will clarify, adjust, or withdraw appropriately from one or more roles. *(See A.8.a., B.4.)*

A.8. Group Work *(See B.4.a.)*
A.8.a. Screening

Career professionals screen prospective group participants. To the extent possible, career professionals select members whose needs and goals are compatible with goals of the group, who will not impede the group process, and whose well-being will not be jeopardized by the group experience.

A.8.b. Protecting Clients

In a group setting, career professionals take reasonable precautions to protect clients from physical, emotional, or psychological trauma.

A.9. Fees and Bartering
A.9.a. Accepting Fees From Agency Clients

Career professionals refuse a private fee or other remuneration for rendering services to persons who are entitled to such services through the career professional's employing agency or institution. The policies of a particular agency may make explicit provisions for agency clients to receive career services from members of its staff in private practice. In such instances, the clients must be informed of other options open to them should they seek private career services.

A.9.b. Establishing Fees

In establishing fees for professional career services, career professionals consider the financial status of clients and the locality in which they practice. In the event that the established fee structure is inappropriate for a client, career professionals assist clients in attempting to find comparable services of acceptable cost.

A.9.c. Nonpayment of Fees

If career professionals intend to use collection agencies or take legal measures to collect fees from clients who do not pay for services as agreed upon, they first inform clients of intended actions and offer clients the opportunity to make payment.

A.9.d. Bartering

Career professionals may barter only if the relationship is not exploitive or harmful and does not place the career professional in an unfair advantage, if the client requests it, and if such arrangements are an accepted practice among professionals in the community. Career professionals consider the cultural implications of bartering and discuss relevant concerns with clients and document such agreements in a clear written contract. Career professionals must also be aware of local, state, and/or federal laws, including the tax implications of such an arrangement. Further, career professionals must make the recipients of their services aware of all applicable federal, state, local, and/or institutional statutes, laws, regulations, and procedures and should direct them to seek qualified counsel (i.e., attorney and/or accountant) in determining if such an arrangement is in their best interest.

A.9.e. Receiving Gifts
Career professionals understand the challenges of accepting gifts from clients and recognize that in some cultures, small gifts are a token of respect and a way of showing gratitude. When determining whether or not to accept a gift from clients, career professionals take into account the nature of their relationship, the monetary value of the gift, a client's motivation for giving the gift, and the career professional's motivation for wanting or declining the gift.

A.10. Termination and Referral
A.10.a. Abandonment Prohibited
Career professionals do not abandon or neglect clients to whom they provide career services. Career professionals assist in making appropriate arrangements for the continuation of treatment, when necessary, during interruptions such as vacations, illness, and following termination.

A.10.b. Inability to Assist Clients
If career professionals determine an inability to be of professional assistance to clients, they avoid entering into or continuing the relationship. Career professionals are knowledgeable about culturally and clinically appropriate referral resources and suggest these alternatives. If clients decline the suggested referrals, career professionals may discontinue the relationship.

A.10.c. Appropriate Termination
Career professionals terminate a professional relationship when it becomes reasonably apparent that the client no longer needs assistance, is not likely to benefit from, or is being harmed by continued service provision. Career professionals may terminate the working relationship when in jeopardy of harm by the client, or another person with whom the client has a relationship, or when clients do not pay agreed upon fees. Career professionals provide pre-termination career services and recommend other providers when feasible and necessary.

A.10.d. Appropriate Transfer of Services
When career professionals transfer or refer clients to other practitioners, they ensure that appropriate clinical and administrative processes are completed and open communication is maintained with both clients and practitioners.

Section B: Confidentiality, Privileged Communication, and Privacy

Introduction
Career professionals recognize that trust is a cornerstone of the professional relationship. Career professionals work to earn the trust of clients by creating an ongoing partnership, establishing and upholding appropriate boundaries, and maintaining confidentiality. Career professionals communicate the parameters of confidentiality in a culturally competent manner.

B.1. Respecting Client Rights
B.1.a. Multicultural/Diversity Considerations
Career professionals maintain awareness and sensitivity regarding cultural meanings of confidentiality and privacy. Career professionals respect differing views toward disclosure of information. Career professionals hold ongoing discussions with clients as to how, when, and with whom information is to be shared.

B.1.b. Respect for Privacy
Career professionals respect client rights to privacy. Career professionals solicit private information from clients only when it is beneficial to the working relationship.

B.1.c. Respect for Confidentiality
Career professionals do not share confidential information without client consent or without sound legal or ethical justification.

B.1.d. Explanation of Limitations
At initiation and throughout the professional relationship, career professionals inform clients of the limitations of confidentiality and seek to identify foreseeable situations in which confidentiality must be breached. *(See A.2.b.)*

B.2. Exceptions
B.2.a. Danger and Legal Requirements
The general requirement that career professionals keep information confidential does not apply when disclosure is required to protect clients or identified others from serious and foreseeable harm or when legal requirements demand that confidential information must be revealed. Examples of when career professionals may divulge confidential information may include, but not be limited to, mandated reporting in cases of suspected or actual child or elder abuse, when a client has a communicable and life threatening disease or condition and may infect an identifiable third party, or when notifying a collection agency to recover unpaid fees from a client. Career professionals consult with other professionals, include attorneys, when in doubt as to the validity of an exception. *(See A.9.c., B.2.b., B.2.c & B.2.d.)*

B.2.b. Contagious, Life-Threatening Diseases
When clients disclose that they have a disease commonly known to be both communicable and life threatening, career professionals may be justified in disclosing information to identifiable third parties, if they are known to be at demonstrable and high risk of contracting the disease. Prior to making a disclosure, career professionals confirm that there is such a diagnosis and

assess the intent of clients to inform the third parties about their disease or to engage in any behaviors that may be harmful to an identifiable third party. *(See B.2.a.)*

B.2.c. Court-Ordered Disclosure
When subpoenaed to release confidential or privileged information, career professionals endeavor to inform the client and to obtain written consent from the client or take steps to prohibit the disclosure, or have it limited as narrowly as possible, to minimize potential harm to the client. *(See B.2.d.)*

B.2.d. Minimal Disclosure
To the extent possible, clients are informed before confidential information is disclosed and are involved in the disclosure decision-making process. When circumstances require the disclosure of confidential information, only essential information is revealed. *(See B.2.c.)*

B.3. Information Shared With Others
B.3.a. Subordinates
Career professionals make every effort to ensure that privacy and confidentiality of clients are maintained by subordinates, including employees, supervisees, students, clerical assistants, and volunteers. *(See G.1.c.)*

B.3.b. Treatment Teams
When client treatment involves a continued review or participation by a treatment team, the client will be informed of the team's existence and composition, information being shared, and the purposes of sharing such information.

B.3.c. Confidential Settings
Career professionals discuss confidential information only in settings in which they can reasonably ensure client privacy.

B.3.d. Third-Party Payers
Career professionals disclose information to third-party payers only when clients have authorized such disclosure and in accordance with federal, state, local, and/or institutional statute, law, regulation, or procedure.

B.3.e. Transmitting Confidential Information
Career professionals take precautions to ensure the confidentiality of information transmitted through the use of computers, electronic mail, facsimile machines, telephones, voicemail, answering machines, and other electronic or computer technology.

B.3.f. Deceased Clients
Career professionals protect the confidentiality of deceased clients, consistent with legal requirements and agency or institutional policies.

B.4. Groups and Families
B.4.a. Group Work

In group work, career professionals clearly explain the importance and parameters of confidentiality for the specific group being entered.

B.4.b. Providing Career Services to Multiple Family Members

When providing career services to multiple family members (e.g., spouses/partners, parent and child, etc.), career professionals clearly define who is considered "the client" and discuss expectations and limitations of confidentiality. Career professionals seek agreement and document in writing such agreement among all involved parties having capacity to give consent concerning each individual's right to confidentiality and any obligation to preserve the confidentiality of information known.

B.5. Clients Lacking Capacity to Give Informed Consent
B.5.a. Responsibility to Clients

When providing career services to minor clients or adult clients who lack the capacity to give voluntary, informed consent, career professionals protect the confidentiality of information received in the professional relationship as specified by federal and state laws, written policies, and applicable ethical standards.

B.5.b. Responsibility to Parents and Legal Guardians

Career professionals inform parents and legal guardians about the role of career professionals and the confidential nature of the professional relationship. Career professionals are sensitive to the cultural diversity of families and respect the inherent rights and responsibilities of parents/guardians over the welfare of their children/charges according to law. Career professionals work to establish, as appropriate, collaborative relationships with parents/guardians to best serve the needs and welfare of their clients.

B.5.c. Release of Confidential Information

When providing career services to minor clients or adult clients who lack the capacity to give voluntary consent to release confidential information, career professionals seek permission from an appropriate third party to disclose information. In such instances, career professionals inform clients consistent with their level of understanding and take culturally appropriate measures to safeguard client confidentiality.

B.6. Records
B.6.a. Confidentiality of Records

Career professionals ensure that records are kept in a secure location and that only authorized persons have access to records.

B.6.b. Permission to Record

Career professionals obtain permission from clients prior to recording sessions through electronic or similar means (i.e., audio or video recording).

B.6.c. Permission to Observe

Career professionals obtain permission from clients prior to allowing observation of sessions, review of session transcripts, or viewing recordings of sessions with supervisors, subordinates, faculty, peers, or others within a training environment.

B.6.d. Client Access

Career professionals provide reasonable access to records and copies of records when requested by competent clients. Career professionals limit the access of clients to their records, or portions of their records, only when there is compelling evidence that such access would cause harm to the client and in accordance with federal, state, local, and/or institutional statute, law, regulation, or procedure. Career professionals document the request of clients and the rationale for withholding some or all of the record in the files of clients. In situations involving multiple clients, career professionals provide individual clients with only those parts of records that related directly to them and do not include confidential information related to any other client.

B.6.e. Assistance with Records

When clients request access to their records, career professionals provide assistance and consultation in interpreting such records.

B.6.f. Disclosure or Transfer

Unless exceptions to confidentiality exist, career professionals obtain written permission from clients to disclose or transfer records to legitimate third parties. Steps are taken to ensure that receivers of career services records are sensitive to their confidential nature. *(See A.3., E.4.)*

B.6.g. Storage and Disposal After Termination

Career professionals store records following termination of services to ensure reasonable future access, maintain records in accordance with all applicable federal, state, local, and/or institutional statutes, laws, regulations, and procedures governing records, and dispose of client records and other sensitive materials in a manner that protects client confidentiality. When records are of an artistic nature, career professionals obtain client (or guardian) consent with regard to handling of such records or documents. Career professionals are encouraged to purge their files according to the time frame required by federal, state, local, and/or institutional statute, law, regulation, or procedure, particularly when there is no reasonable expectation that a client will benefit from maintaining the records any longer. Career professionals are expected to know and abide by all applicable federal, state, local, and/or institutional statutes, laws, regulations, and procedures regarding record keeping and disposal. *(See A.1.c.)*

B.6.h. Reasonable Precautions

Career professionals take reasonable precautions to protect client confidentiality in the event of the career professional's termination of practice, incapacity, or death. *(See C.2.h.)*

B.7. Research and Training
B.7.a. Institutional Approval

When institutional approval is required, career professionals provide accurate information about their research proposals and obtain approval prior to conducting their research. They conduct research in accordance with the approved research protocol.

B.7.b. Adherence to Guidelines

Career professionals are responsible for understanding and adhering to state, federal, agency, or institutional policies or applicable guidelines regarding confidentiality in their research practices.

13

B.7.c. Confidentiality of Information Obtained in Research
Violations of participant privacy and confidentiality are risks of participation in research involving human participants, however, investigators maintain all research records in a secure manner. They explain to participants the risks of violations of privacy and confidentiality and disclose to participants any limits of confidentiality that can reasonably be expected. Regardless of the degree to which confidentiality will be maintained, investigators must disclose to participants any limits of confidentiality that can reasonably be expected. *(See H.2.e.)*

B.7.d. Disclosure of Research Information
Career professionals do not disclose confidential information that reasonably could lead to the identification of a research participant unless they have obtained prior consent of the person. Use of data derived from professional relationships for purposes of training, research, or publication is confined to content that is disguised to ensure the anonymity of the individuals involved. *(See H.2.a., H.2.d.)*

B.7.e. Agreement for Identification
Identification of clients, students, or supervisees in a presentation or publication is permissible only when they have reviewed the material and agreed to its presentation or publication. *(See H.4.d.)*

B.8. Consultation
B.8.a. Agreements
When acting as consultants, career professionals seek agreements among all parties involved concerning each individual's rights to confidentiality, the obligation of each individual to preserve confidential information, and the limits of confidentiality of information shared by others.

B.8.b. Respect for Privacy
Information obtained in a consulting relationship is discussed for professional purposes only with persons directly involved with the case. Written and oral reports present only data germane to the purposes of the consultation, and every effort is made to protect client identity and to avoid undue invasion of privacy.

B.8.c. Disclosure of Confidential Information
When consulting with colleagues, career professionals do not disclose confidential information that reasonably could lead to the identification of a client or other person or organization with whom they have a confidential relationship unless they have obtained the prior consent of the person or organization or the disclosure cannot be avoided. They disclose information only to the extent necessary to achieve the purposes of the consultation. *(See D.2.d.)*

14

Section C: Professional Responsibility

Introduction
Career professionals provide open, honest, and accurate communication in dealing with the public and other professionals. They practice in a nondiscriminatory manner within the boundaries of professional and personal competence and have a responsibility to abide by the *NCDA Code of Ethics*. Career professionals actively participate in local, state, and national associations that foster the development and improvement of the provision of career services. Career professionals promote change at the individual, group, institutional, and societal levels that improves the quality of life for individuals and groups and removes potential barriers to the provision or access of appropriate services being offered. Career professionals have a responsibility to the public to engage in ethical practice. In addition, career professionals engage in self-care activities to maintain and promote their emotional, physical, mental, and spiritual well-being to best meet their professional responsibilities.

C.1. Knowledge of Standards
Career professionals have a responsibility to read, understand, and follow the *NCDA Code of Ethics* and adhere to all applicable federal, state, local, and/or institutional statutes, laws, regulations, and procedures.

C.2. Professional Competence

C.2.a. Boundaries of Competence
Career professionals practice only within the boundaries of their competence, based on their education, training, supervised experience, state and national professional credentials, and appropriate professional experience. Career professionals gain knowledge, personal awareness, sensitivity, and skills pertinent to working with a diverse client population. *(See E.2., G.2., G.11.c.)*

C.2.b. New Specialty Areas of Practice
Career professionals practice in specialty areas new to them only after obtaining appropriate education, training, and supervised experience. While developing skills in new specialty areas, career professionals take steps to ensure the competence of their work and to protect others from possible harm. *(See G.6.e.)*

C.2.c. Qualified for Employment
Career professionals accept employment only for positions for which they are qualified by education, training, supervised experience, state and national professional credentials, and appropriate professional experience. Career professionals hire for professional positions only individuals who are qualified and competent for those positions.

C.2.d. Monitor Effectiveness
Career professionals continually monitor their effectiveness as professionals and take steps to improve when necessary. Career professionals in private practice take reasonable steps to seek peer supervision, as needed, to evaluate their efficacy as career professionals.

15

C.2.e. Consultation on Ethical Obligations

Career professionals take reasonable steps to consult with other career professionals or related practitioners when they have questions regarding their ethical obligations or professional activities.

C.2.f. Continuing Education

Career professionals recognize the need for continuing education to acquire and maintain a reasonable level of awareness of current scientific and professional information in their fields of activity. They take steps to maintain competence in the skills they use, are open to new procedures, and keep current with the populations with whom they work.

C.2.g. Impairment

Career professionals are alert to the signs of impairment from their own physical, mental, or emotional problems and refrain from offering or providing professional services when such impairment is likely to harm a client or others. They seek assistance for problems that reach the level of professional impairment, and, if necessary, they limit, suspend, or terminate their professional responsibilities until such time as it is determined that they may safely resume their work. Career professionals assist colleagues or supervisors in recognizing their own professional impairment. They provide consultation and assistance, when warranted, with colleagues or supervisors showing signs of impairment and intervene as appropriate to prevent imminent harm to clients. *(See A.10.b., G.8.b.)*

C.2.h. Incapacitation or Termination of Practice

When career professionals leave a practice, they follow a prepared plan for transfer of clients and files. Career professionals prepare and disseminate to an identified colleague or "records custodian" a plan for the transfer of clients and files in case of their incapacitation, death, or termination of practice. *(See A.1.c., A.10., B.6.g.)*

C.3. Advertising and Soliciting Clients

C.3.a. Accurate Advertising

When advertising or otherwise representing their services to the public, career professionals identify their credentials in an accurate manner that is not false, misleading, deceptive, or fraudulent. *(See C.4.)*

C.3.b. Testimonials

Career professionals who use testimonials do not solicit them from individuals who may be vulnerable to undue influence.

C.3.c. Statements by Others

Career professionals make reasonable efforts to ensure that statements made by others about them or the services they provide are accurate.

C.3.d. Recruiting Through Employment

Career professionals do not use their places of employment or institutional affiliations to recruit or gain clients, supervisees, or consultees for their private practices, unless they have permission.

If permitted to solicit for their private practices, career professionals must make potential clients, supervisees, or consultees aware of the free or low-cost services already provided by them or others through their place of employment or institutional affiliation. *(See A.9.a)*

C.3.e. Products and Training Advertisements
Career professionals who develop products related to their profession or conduct workshops or training events ensure that the advertisements concerning these products or events are accurate and disclose adequate information for consumers to make informed choices.

C.3.f. Promoting to Those Served
Career professionals do not use individual consultation, teaching, training, or supervisory relationships to promote their products or training events in a manner that is deceptive or would exert undue influence on individuals who may be vulnerable. However, educators may adopt textbooks and/or other materials they have authored or developed for instructional purposes.

C.4. Professional Qualifications

C.4.a. Accurate Representation
Career professionals claim or imply only professional qualifications actually completed and correct any known misrepresentations of their qualifications by others. Career professionals truthfully represent the qualifications of their professional colleagues. Career professionals clearly distinguish between paid and volunteer work experience and accurately describe their continuing education and specialized training. *(See A.1.b, C.2.a, E.9.c.)*

C.4.b. Credentials
Career professionals claim only licenses or certifications that are current and in good standing.

C.4.c. Educational Degrees
Career professionals clearly differentiate between earned and honorary degrees.

C.4.d. Implying Doctoral-Level Competence
Career professionals clearly state their highest earned degree in counseling or a closely related field. Career professionals do not imply doctoral-level competence when possessing only a master's degree in counseling or a related field. Career professionals do not use the title "Dr." nor refer to themselves as "Dr." in a counseling or career services context when their doctorate is not in counseling or a related field.

C.4.e. Program Accreditation Status
Career professionals clearly state the accreditation status of their degree programs at the time the degree was earned.

C.4.f. Professional Membership
Career professionals clearly differentiate between current, active memberships and former memberships in associations.

17

C.5. Nondiscrimination

Career professionals do not condone or engage in discrimination against any individual based on age, culture, mental/physical disability, ethnicity, race, religion/spirituality, creed, gender, gender identity, sexual orientation, marital/partnership status, language preference, socioeconomic status, any other characteristics not specifically relevant to job performance, or any basis prohibited by law. Career professionals do not discriminate against clients, students, employees, supervisees, or research participants in a manner that has a negative impact on these persons.

C.6. Public Responsibility

C.6.a. Sexual Harassment

Career professionals do not engage in or condone sexual harassment. Sexual harassment is defined as sexual solicitation, physical advances, or verbal or nonverbal conduct that is sexual in nature, that occurs in connection with professional activities or roles, and that either

1. is unwelcome, is offensive, or creates a hostile workplace or learning environment, and career professionals know or are told this; or
2. is sufficiently severe or intense to be perceived as harassment to a reasonable person in the context in which the behavior occurred. Sexual harassment can consist of a single intense or severe act or multiple persistent or pervasive acts.

C.6.b. Reports to Third Parties

Career professionals are accurate, honest, and objective in reporting their professional activities and judgments to appropriate third parties, including courts, health insurance companies, those who are the recipients of evaluation reports, and others. *(See B.3., E.4.)*

C.6.c. Media Presentations

When career professionals provide advice or comment by means of public lectures, demonstrations, radio or television programs, prerecorded tapes, technology-based applications, printed articles, mailed material, or other media, they take reasonable precautions to ensure that

1. the statements are based on appropriate professional literature and practice,
2. the statements are otherwise consistent with the *NCDA Code of Ethics,* and
3. the recipients of the information are informed that a professional relationship has not been established.

C.6.d. Exploitation of Others

Career professionals do not exploit others in their professional relationships. *(See A.5.b., A.9.d.)*

C.6.e. Scientific Bases for Treatment Modalities

Career professionals use techniques/procedures/modalities that are grounded in theory, are generally considered to be established professional practice in the fields of counseling and career development, and/or have an empirical or scientific foundation. Career professionals who do not must define the techniques/procedures as "unproven" or "developing" and explain the potential risks and ethical considerations of using such techniques/procedures and take steps to protect clients from possible harm. *(See A.4.a.)*

C.7. Responsibility to Other Professionals

C.7.a. Personal Public Statements
When making personal statements in a public context, career professionals clarify that they are speaking from their personal perspectives and that they are not speaking on behalf of all career professionals or the profession. *(See C.6.c.)*

Section D: Relationships with Other Professionals

Introduction
Career professionals recognize that the quality of their interactions with colleagues can influence the quality of services provided to clients. They work to become knowledgeable about colleagues within and outside the profession. Career professionals develop positive working relationships and systems of communication with colleagues to enhance services to clients.

D.1. Relationships with Colleagues, Employers, and Employees

D.1.a. Different Approaches
Career professionals are respectful of approaches to career services that differ from their own. Career professionals are respectful of traditions and practices of other professional groups with which they work.

D.1.b. Forming Relationships
Career professionals work to develop and strengthen interdisciplinary relations with colleagues from other disciplines to best serve clients.

D.1.c. Interdisciplinary Teamwork
Career professionals who are members of interdisciplinary teams delivering multifaceted services to clients keep the focus on how to best serve the clients. They participate in and contribute to decisions that affect the well-being of clients by drawing on the perspectives, values, and experiences of the profession and those of colleagues from other disciplines. *(See B.3.b.)*

D.1.d. Confidentiality
When career professionals are required by law, institutional policy, or extraordinary circumstances to serve in more than one role in judicial or administrative proceedings, they clarify role expectations and the parameters of confidentiality with their colleagues. *(See A.5.e, B.1.c., B.1.d., B.2.c., B.2.d., B.3.b.)*

D.1.e. Establishing Professional and Ethical Obligations
Career professionals who are members of interdisciplinary teams clarify professional and ethical obligations of the team as a whole and of its individual members. When a team decision raises ethical concerns, career professionals first attempt to resolve the concern within the team. If they cannot reach resolution among team members, career professionals pursue other avenues to address their concerns consistent with client well-being.

D.1.f. Personnel Selection and Assignment
Career professionals select competent staff and assign responsibilities compatible with their knowledge, skills, and experiences.

D.1.g. Employer Policies
The acceptance of employment in an agency or institution implies that career professionals are in agreement with its general policies and principles. Career professionals strive to reach agreement

20

with employers as to acceptable standards of conduct that allow for changes in institutional policy conducive to the growth and development of clients.

D.1.h. Negative Conditions
Career professionals alert their employers of inappropriate policies and practices. They attempt to effect changes in such policies or procedures through constructive action within the organization. When such policies are potentially disruptive or damaging to clients or may limit the effectiveness of services provided and change cannot be achieved, career professionals take appropriate further action. Such action may include referral to appropriate certification, accreditation, or state licensure organizations, or voluntary termination of employment.

D.1.i. Protection from Punitive Action
Career professionals take care not to harass or dismiss an employee who has acted in a responsible and ethical manner to expose inappropriate employer policies or practices.

D.2. Consultation

D.2.a. Consultant Competency
Career professionals take reasonable steps to ensure that they have the appropriate resources and competencies when providing consultation services. Career professionals provide appropriate referral resources when requested or needed. *(See C.2.a.)*

D.2.b. Understanding Consultees
When providing consultation, career professionals attempt to develop with their consultees a clear understanding of problem definition, goals for change, and predicted consequences of interventions selected.

D.2.c. Consultant Goals
The consulting relationship is one in which consultee adaptability and growth toward self-direction are consistently encouraged and cultivated.

D.2.d. Informed Consent in Consultation
When providing consultation, career professionals have an obligation to review, in writing and orally, the rights and responsibilities of career professionals and consultees. Career professionals use clear and understandable language to inform all parties involved about the purpose of the services to be provided, relevant costs, potential risks and benefits, and the limits of confidentiality. Working in conjunction with the consultee, career professionals attempt to develop a clear definition of the problem, goals for change, and predicted consequences of interventions that are culturally responsive and appropriate to the needs of consultees. *(See A.2.a., A.2.b.)*

Section E: Evaluation, Assessment, and Interpretation

Introduction
Career professionals use assessment instruments as one component of the career services process, taking into account the client's personal and cultural context. Career professionals promote the well-being of individual clients or groups of clients by developing and using appropriate career, educational, and psychological assessment instruments.

E.1. General

E.1.a. Assessment
The primary purpose of educational, psychological, and career assessments is to provide measurements that are valid and reliable in either comparative or absolute terms. These include, but are not limited to, measurements of ability, personality, interest, intelligence, achievement, skills, values, and performance. Career professionals recognize the need to interpret the statements in this section as applying to both quantitative and qualitative assessments.

E.1.b. Client Welfare
Career professionals do not misuse assessment results and interpretations, and they take reasonable steps to prevent others from misusing the information these tools provide. They respect the client's right to know the results, the interpretations made, and the bases for career professionals' conclusions and recommendations.

E.2. Competence to Use and Interpret Assessment Instruments

E.2.a. Limits of Competence
Career professionals utilize only those testing and assessment services for which they have been trained and are competent in administering and interpreting. Career professionals using technology-assisted test interpretations are trained in the construct being measured and the specific instrument being used prior to using its technology-based application. Career professionals take reasonable measures to ensure the proper use of psychological and career assessment techniques by persons under their supervision. *(See G.1.)*

E.2.b. Appropriate Use
Career professionals are responsible for the appropriate application, scoring, interpretation, and use of assessment instruments relevant to the needs of the client, whether they score and interpret such assessments themselves or use technology or other services.

E.2.c. Decisions Based on Results
Career professionals responsible for decisions involving individuals or policies that are based on assessment results have a thorough understanding of educational, psychological, and career measurement, including validation criteria, assessment research, and guidelines for assessment development and use.

E.3. Informed Consent in Assessment

E.3.a. Explanation to Clients
Prior to assessment, career professionals explain the nature and purposes of assessment and the specific use of results by potential recipients. The explanation will be given in the language of the client (or other legally authorized person on behalf of the client), unless an explicit exception has been agreed upon in advance. Career professionals consider the client's personal or cultural context, the level of the client's understanding of the results, and the impact of the results on the client. *(See A.2.)*

E.3.b. Recipients of Results
Career professionals consider the examinee's welfare, explicit understandings, and prior agreements in determining who receives the assessment results. Career professionals include accurate and appropriate interpretations with any release of individual or group assessment results. *(See B.2.c., B.5.)*

E.4. Release of Data to Qualified Professionals
Career professionals release assessment data in which the client is identified only with the consent of the client or the client's legal representative. Such data are released only to persons recognized by career professionals as qualified to interpret the data and in accordance with all applicable federal, state, local, and/or institutional statutes, laws, regulations, and procedures. *(See B.1., B.3., B.5.c., B.6.e.)*

E.5. Diagnosis

E.5.a. Proper Diagnosis
Career professionals take special care to provide proper diagnosis and do so only when making a diagnosis is appropriate and when properly trained. Assessment techniques (including personal interview) used to determine client care (e.g., locus of treatment, type of treatment/services, or recommended follow-up) are carefully selected and appropriately used.

E.5.b. Cultural Sensitivity
Career professionals recognize that culture affects the manner in which clients' problems are defined. Clients' socioeconomic and cultural experiences are considered when making a diagnosis. *(See A.2.c.)*

E.5.c. Historical and Social Prejudices in the Diagnosis of Pathology
Career professionals recognize historical and social prejudices in the misdiagnosis and pathologizing of certain individuals and groups and the role career professionals can play in avoiding the perpetuation of these prejudices through proper diagnosis and provision of services.

E.5.d. Refraining From Diagnosis
Career professionals may refrain from making and/or reporting a diagnosis if they believe it would cause harm to the client or others.

23

E.6. Instrument Selection

E.6.a. Appropriateness of Instruments
Career professionals carefully consider the validity, reliability, psychometric limitations, and appropriateness of instruments when selecting assessments.

E.6.b. Referral Information
If a client is referred to a third party for assessment, the career professional provides specific referral questions and sufficient objective data about the client to ensure that appropriate assessment instruments are utilized. *(See B.3.)*

E.6.c. Culturally Diverse Populations
Career professionals are cautious when selecting assessments for culturally diverse populations to avoid the use of instruments that lack appropriate psychometric properties for the client population. *(See A.2.c., E.5.b.)*

E.7. Conditions of Assessment Administration

E.7.a. Administration Conditions
Career professionals administer assessments under the same conditions that were established in their standardization. When assessments are not administered under standard conditions, as may be necessary to accommodate clients with disabilities, or when unusual behavior or irregularities occur during the administration, those conditions are noted in interpretation, and the results may be designated as invalid or of questionable validity.

E.7.b. Technological Administration
Career professionals ensure that administration programs function properly and provide clients with accurate results when technological or other electronic methods are used for assessment administration.

E.7.c. Unsupervised Assessments
Unless the assessment instrument is designed, intended, and validated for self-administration and/or scoring, career professionals do not permit inadequately supervised use of any assessment.

E.7.d. Disclosure of Favorable Conditions
Prior to administration of assessments, conditions that produce the most favorable assessment results are made known to the examinee.

E.8. Multicultural Issues/Diversity in Assessment
Career professionals use, with caution, assessment techniques that were normed on populations other than that of the client. Career professionals recognize the possible effects of age, color, culture, disability, ethnic group, gender, race, language preference, religion, spirituality, sexual orientation, and socioeconomic status on test administration and interpretation, and place test results in proper perspective with other relevant factors. *(See A.2.c., E.5.b.)*

24

E.9. Scoring and Interpretation of Assessments

E.9.a. Reporting
In reporting assessment results, career professionals indicate reservations that exist regarding validity or reliability due to circumstances of the assessment or the inappropriateness of the norms for the person tested.

E.9.b. Research Instruments
Career professionals exercise caution when interpreting the results of research instruments not having sufficient technical data to support respondent results. The specific purposes for the use of such instruments are stated explicitly to the examinee.

E.9.c. Assessment Services
Career professionals who provide assessment scoring and interpretation services to support the assessment process confirm the validity of such interpretations. They accurately describe the purpose, norms, validity, reliability, and applications of the procedures and any special qualifications applicable to their use. The public offering of an automated test interpretation service is considered a professional-to-professional consultation. The formal responsibility of the career professional is to the individual/ organization requesting the assessment, but the ultimate and overriding responsibility is to the client. *(See E.1.b., E.2.)*

E.10. Assessment Security
Career professionals maintain the integrity and security of tests and other assessment techniques consistent with legal and contractual obligations. Career professionals do not appropriate, reproduce, or modify published assessments or parts thereof without acknowledgment and permission from the publisher.

E.11. Obsolete Assessments and Outdated Results
Career professionals do not use data or results from assessments that are obsolete or outdated for the current purpose. Career professionals make every effort to prevent the misuse of obsolete measures and assessment data by others.

E.12. Assessment Construction
Career professionals use established scientific procedures, relevant standards, and current professional knowledge for assessment design in the development, publication, and utilization of educational and psychological assessment techniques.

E.13. Forensic Evaluation: Evaluation for Legal Proceedings

E.13.a. Primary Obligations
When providing forensic evaluations, the primary obligation of career professionals is to produce objective findings that can be substantiated based on information and techniques appropriate to the evaluation, which may include examination of the individual and/or review of records. Career professionals are entitled to form professional opinions based on their professional knowledge and expertise that can be supported by the data gathered in evaluations. Career

25

professionals will define the limits of their reports or testimony, especially when an examination of the individual has not been conducted.

E.13.b. Consent for Evaluation
Individuals being evaluated are informed in writing that the relationship is for the purposes of an evaluation, not to provide career services. Entities or individuals who will receive the evaluation report are identified. Written consent to be evaluated is obtained from those being evaluated unless a court orders evaluations to be conducted without the written consent of individuals being evaluated. When children or vulnerable adults are being evaluated, informed written consent is obtained from a parent or guardian. *(See A.2. B.2.c., B.5.)*

E.13.c. Client Evaluation Prohibited
Career professionals do not evaluate current or former clients for forensic purposes. Career professionals do not accept as clients, individuals they are evaluating or have previously evaluated for forensic purposes.

E.13.d. Avoid Potentially Harmful Relationships
Career professionals who provide forensic evaluations avoid potentially harmful professional or personal relationships with family members, romantic partners, and close friends of individuals they are evaluating or have evaluated in the past. *(See A.5.)*

Section F: Use of the Internet in the Provision of Career Services

Introduction
Career professionals have always been at the forefront in using new technologies to assist in serving clients. More and more, technology (and specifically the Internet) is being used to provide and/or support services offered by career professionals. However, the Internet should typically be only one component of the career services process and then its use must be evaluated based on the client's personal and cultural context. Above all, career professionals must practice ethically and continually promote the well-being of individual clients or groups of clients.

F.1. General

F.1.a. Benefits and Limitations
Career professionals inform clients of the benefits and limitations of using information technology applications in their professional relationship and in business/billing procedures. Such technologies include but are not limited to computer hardware and software, telephones, the Internet, online assessment instruments, and other communication devices.

F.1.b. Capability to Utilize and Benefit from Technology-Assisted Services
When providing technology-assisted distance career services, career professionals determine that clients are intellectually, emotionally, and physically capable of using, and are likely to benefit from, the application and that the application is appropriate for the needs of clients. Where possible, career professionals utilize multiple methods of contact (i.e., telephone, video conference, and email), in assessing the best means of providing career services to a particular client.

F.2. Technology Applications

F.2.a. Types of Technology-Assisted Services
Multiple means of online provision of career services currently exist, the most common of which are email, newsgroups, bulletin boards, instant messaging, chat rooms, blogs (web logs), web cams (video cameras) and websites offering a wide variety of services. Telephone or audiovisual linkages supported by the Internet continue to grow in popularity as the technology improves and the costs decline. Based on readily-available capabilities at the time of this writing, the Internet could be used in at least four ways to provide and/or support career services. These include:

1. Delivering information about occupations, the world of work, career planning, and job searching. This may include occupational/job descriptions, employment prospects, skills requirements, estimated salary, resume writing, job interviewing techniques, etc. Delivery may come through one or a combination of media including text, still images, graphics, and/or video. In providing these services, the standards for information development and presentation are the same as those for other print and audiovisual materials as stated in other NCDA documents.
2. Providing assessments and/or online searches of academic, occupational, or other databases to identify career, educational, or other alternatives. In providing these

27

services, other standards developed by NCDA (i.e., *Section E of this Code*) and the Association of Computer-based Systems for Career Information (ACSCI) apply.

3. Delivering interactive career services. This use assumes that clients, either as individuals or as part of a group, have intentionally placed themselves in direct communication with a career professional. Standards for using the Internet for these purposes are addressed in this section.
4. Providing a database of job openings. Guidelines for this application are included in this section as well.

F.2.b. Alternative Services
When technology-assisted distance career services are deemed inappropriate by the career professional or client, career professionals provide appropriate alternatives, including face to face service and/or a referral to career professionals who can provide in person services. *(See A.10)*

F.2.c. Access
Career professionals ensure reasonable access to computer applications when providing technology-assisted distance career services. If they are unable to do so they provide an alternative method of service delivery, including referrals to career professionals who would be able to provide face-to-face services. *(See A.10)*

F.2.d. Laws and Statutes
Career professionals ensure that the use of technology services with clients is in accordance with all applicable federal, state, local, and/or institutional statutes, laws, regulations, and procedures, particularly when the services offered via technology cross state and/or national boundaries.

F.2.e. Outside Assistance
Career professionals seek business, legal, and technical assistance (when necessary and appropriate) when using technology applications, particularly when the use of such applications crosses state or national boundaries.

F.2.f. Informed Consent & Confidentiality
As part of the process of establishing informed consent and defining confidentiality and its limits, career professionals who provide technology-assisted distance career services:

1. Provide information to clients about their credentials.
2. Work with clients to establish goals and determine if a technology-assisted distance modality is appropriate.
3. Where applicable, define the fees for service and billing procedures.
4. Provide clients with information regarding where and how they can report any behavior on the part of the career professional that they consider unethical.
5. Where feasible, address issues related to maintaining the confidentiality of electronically transmitted communications (e.g., the use of encryption).
6. Inform clients of the inherent difficulty of maintaining absolute confidentiality when conducting electronically transmitted communication.

7. Urge clients to be aware of all authorized or unauthorized users (including family members and fellow employees) who may have access to any technology clients use in the professional relationship.
8. Inform clients of pertinent legal rights and limitations governing the practice of a profession over state lines or international boundaries, when necessary and appropriate.
9. Inform clients if and for how long archival storage of transaction records will be maintained.
10. Discuss the possibility of technology failure and alternate methods of service delivery.
11. Inform clients of emergency procedures, such as calling 911 or a local crisis hotline, when the career professional is not available, should circumstances warrant.
12. Discuss time zone differences, local customs, and cultural or language differences that might impact service delivery.
13. Establish a method for verifying identity.
14. Obtain the written consent of the legal guardian or other authorized legal representative prior to rendering services in the event the client is a minor child, an adult who is legally incompetent, or an adult incapable of giving informed consent.

F.3. Qualifications of Developer or Provider
Websites and other services designed to assist clients with career planning and job searching should be developed with content input from career professionals. The service should clearly state the qualifications and credentials of the developers.

F.4. Access and Understanding of Environment
Career professionals have an obligation to be aware of free and/or low cost public access points to the Internet within the community, so that a lack of financial resources does not create a significant barrier to clients accessing career services or information, assessments, or instructional resources over the internet.

F.5. Content of Career Services on the Internet

F.5.a. Appropriateness of Internet Content
The content of a website or other online career information or planning services should be reviewed for the appropriateness of offering the material in this medium. Some types of content have been extensively tested for online delivery including searching databases by relevant variables; displaying occupational information; developing a resumé; assessing interests, abilities, personality, and other characteristics and linkage of these to occupational titles; relating school majors to occupational choices; and the completing of forms such as a financial needs assessment questionnaire or a job application.

When a website offers content or a service that has not been extensively tested for online delivery, is not grounded in theory, is not generally considered to be established professional practice in the fields of counseling and career development, and/or does not have an empirical or scientific foundation, career professionals must define the content or service as "unproven" or "developing" and explain the potential risks and ethical considerations of using such content or service and take steps to protect clients from possible harm.

29

F.5.b. Maintaining Internet Sites
Career professionals maintaining sites on the Internet do the following:

1. Regularly check that electronic links are working and are professionally appropriate.
2. Provide electronic links to relevant state licensure and professional certification boards to protect consumer rights and facilitate addressing ethical concerns.
3. Provide a site that is accessible to persons with disabilities, when feasible.
4. Provide translation capabilities (when feasible) for clients who have a different primary language while also acknowledging the imperfect nature of such translations.
5. Assist clients in determining the validity and reliability of information found on the Internet and in other technology applications.
6. If a website includes links to other websites, the career professional who creates this linkage is responsible for ensuring that the services to which the site is linked meet all applicable ethical standards. If this is not possible, career professionals should post a disclaimer explaining that the linked site may not meet all applicable ethical standards and (if known) which standards are not met by the site.

F.6. Ongoing Client Support
When providing technology-assisted distance career services, career professionals periodically monitor clients' progress. Should career professionals determine that little or no progress is being made toward stated goals, career professionals will discuss the need for a referral to a face-to-face service provider. Career professionals will assist clients in identifying appropriate providers and will facilitate the transition. *(See A.10., E.6.b., F.2.b.)*

F.7. Use of Assessment
When using assessments on the Internet, career professionals are responsible for knowing and abiding by other standards developed by NCDA (i.e., *Section E of this Code*) and the Association of Computer-based Systems for Career Information (ACSCI). Where applicable and possible, career professionals should:

1. determine if the assessments have been tested for online delivery and ensure that their psychometric properties are the same as in print form; or the client must be informed that the assessments have not yet been tested for this mode of delivery.
2. abide by the same ethical guidelines as if administering and interpreting these assessments in person or in print form.
3. make every effort to protect the confidentiality of client results.
4. refer clients to qualified career professionals in his or her geographic area, if there is evidence that the client does not understand the assessment results.
5. determine if the assessments have been validated for self-help use or that appropriate counseling intervention is provided before and after completion of the assessment resource if the resource has not been validated for self-help use.

F.8. Internet Job Posting and Searching
All job postings must represent a valid opening for which those searching on the Internet have an opportunity to apply. It is encouraged that job postings be removed from the database within 48 hours of the time that the announced position is filled. Names, addresses, resumés, and other

information that may be gained about individuals should not be used for any purposes other than provision of further information about job openings.

F.9. Unacceptable Behaviors on the Internet
Career professionals have a responsibility to act in an ethical manner at all times. Because a behavior is not expressly prohibited, this does not imply that it is ethical. The following behaviors are deemed unacceptable for career professionals:

1. Use of a false e-mail identity when interacting with clients and/or other professionals. When acting in a professional capacity on the Internet, career professionals have a duty to identify themselves honestly.
2. Accepting a client who will not identify him/herself and/or is unwilling to arrange for a telephone conversation as well as online interchange.
3. Anonymously monitoring chat rooms, web logs (blogs), bulletin board services, and/or other web-based communities and offering career planning and related services when no request has been made for such services. This includes sending out mass unsolicited e-mails to individuals with whom you do not have an already established professional relationship. Career professionals may advertise their services but must do so observing proper online "netiquette" and standards of professional conduct.

Section G: Supervision, Training, and Teaching

Introduction
Career professionals foster meaningful and respectful professional relationships and maintain appropriate boundaries with supervisees and students. Career professionals have theoretical and pedagogical foundations for their work and aim to be fair, accurate, and honest in their assessments of students.

G.1. Supervision and Client Welfare

G.1.a. Client Welfare
A primary obligation of supervisors is to monitor the services provided by other career professionals or students for whom they have responsibility. Supervisors also monitor client welfare and supervisee performance and professional development. To fulfill these obligations, supervisors meet regularly with supervisees to review case notes, samples of work, or live observations. Supervisees have a responsibility to understand and follow the *NCDA Code of Ethics*.

G.1.b. Credentials
Supervisors work to ensure that clients are aware of the qualifications of the supervisees who render services to clients. *(See A.2.b.)*

G.1.c. Informed Consent and Client Rights
Supervisors make supervisees aware of client rights including the protection of client privacy and confidentiality in the professional relationship. Supervisees provide clients with professional disclosure information and inform them of how the supervision process influences the limits of confidentiality. Supervisees make clients aware of who will have access to records of the professional relationship and how these records will be used. *(See A.2.a., A.2.b., B.1.d. D.3.)*

G.2. Supervisor Competence

G.2.a. Supervisor Preparation
Prior to offering supervision services, career professionals are trained in supervision methods and techniques. Career professionals who offer supervision services regularly pursue continuing education activities including both career services and supervision topics and skills. *(See C.2.a., C.2.f.)*

G.2.b. Multicultural Issues/Diversity in Supervision
Supervisors are aware of and address the role of multiculturalism/diversity in the supervisory relationship.

G.3. Supervisory Relationships

G.3.a. Relationship Boundaries with Supervisees
Supervisors clearly define and maintain ethical professional, personal, and social relationships with their supervisees, although they avoid and/or keep to a minimum nonprofessional

relationships with current supervisees. If supervisors must assume other professional roles (e.g., clinical and administrative supervisor, instructor, etc.) with supervisees, they work to minimize potential conflicts and explain to supervisees the expectations and responsibilities associated with each role. They do not engage in any form of nonprofessional interaction that may compromise the supervisory relationship.

G.3.b. Sexual Relationships
Sexual or romantic interactions or relationships with current supervisees are prohibited.

G.3.c. Harassment
Supervisors do not condone or subject supervisees to harassment, sexual or otherwise. *(See C.6.a.)*

G.3.d. Close Relatives and Friends
Supervisors avoid accepting close relatives, romantic partners, or friends as supervisees.

G.3.e. Potentially Beneficial Relationships
Supervisors are aware of the power differential in their relationships with supervisees. If they believe nonprofessional relationships with a supervisee may be potentially beneficial to the supervisee, they take precautions similar to those taken by career professionals when working with clients. Examples of potentially beneficial interactions or relationships include attending a formal ceremony; hospital visits; providing support during a stressful event; or mutual membership in a professional association, organization, or community. Supervisors engage in open discussions with supervisees when they consider entering into relationships with them outside of their supervisory roles. Before engaging in nonprofessional relationships, supervisors discuss with supervisees and document the rationale for such interactions, potential benefits or drawbacks, and anticipated consequences for the supervisee. Supervisors clarify the specific nature and limitations of the additional role(s) they will have with the supervisee. *(See A.5.d.)*

G.4. Supervisor Responsibilities

G.4.a. Informed Consent for Supervision
Supervisors are responsible for incorporating into their supervision the principles of informed consent and participation. Supervisors inform supervisees of the policies and procedures to which they are to adhere and the mechanisms for due process appeal of individual supervisory actions.

G.4.b. Emergencies and Absences
Supervisors establish and communicate to supervisees procedures for contacting them or, in their absence, alternative on-call supervisors to assist in handling crises.

G.4.c. Standards for Supervisees
Supervisors make their supervisees aware of professional and ethical standards and legal responsibilities. Supervisors of post-degree career professionals encourage these individuals to adhere to professional standards of practice. *(See C.1.)*

33

G.4.d. Termination of the Supervisory Relationship

Supervisors or supervisees have the right to terminate the supervisory relationship with adequate notice. Reasons for withdrawal are provided to the other party. When cultural, professional, or other issues are crucial to the viability of the supervisory relationship, both parties make efforts to resolve differences. When termination is warranted, supervisors make appropriate referrals to possible alternative supervisors.

G.5. Supervision Evaluation, Remediation, and Endorsement

G.5.a. Evaluation

Supervisors document and provide supervisees with ongoing performance appraisal and evaluation feedback and schedule periodic formal evaluative sessions throughout the supervisory relationship.

G.5.b. Limitations

Through ongoing evaluation and appraisal, supervisors are aware of the limitations of supervisees that might impede performance. Supervisors assist supervisees in securing remedial assistance when needed. They recommend dismissal from training programs, applied practice settings, or state or voluntary professional credentialing processes when those supervisees are unable to provide competent professional services. Supervisors seek consultation and document their decisions to dismiss or refer supervisees for assistance. They ensure that supervisees are aware of options available to them to address such decisions. *(See C.2.g.)*

G.5.c. Multiple Roles/Relationships with Supervisees

If supervisees request counseling, career services, or any other professional service which a supervisor may ordinarily offer, the supervisor will provide the supervisee with acceptable referrals. Career professionals do not typically engage in multiple roles/relationships with supervisees. If supervisors must provide a service to a supervisee in addition to providing supervision, they work to minimize potential conflicts and explain to supervisees the expectations and responsibilities associated with each role. In addition, the supervisor must address participation in multiple roles/relationships with the supervisee in terms of the impact of these issues on clients, the supervisory relationship, and professional functioning. *(See G.3.a.)*

G.5.d. Endorsement

Supervisors endorse supervisees for certification, licensure, employment, or completion of an academic or training program only when they believe supervisees are qualified for the endorsement. In addition, supervisors do not withhold endorsement of qualified supervisees for certification, licensure, employment, or completion of an academic or training program for any reason unrelated to their fitness as a student or professional. Regardless of qualifications, supervisors do not endorse supervisees whom they believe to be impaired in any way that would interfere with the performance of the duties associated with the endorsement.

G.6. Responsibilities of Educators

G.6.a. Educators
Educators who are responsible for developing, implementing, and supervising educational programs are skilled as teachers and practitioners. They are knowledgeable regarding the ethical, legal, and regulatory aspects of the profession, are skilled in applying that knowledge, and make students and supervisees aware of their responsibilities. Educators conduct education and training programs in an ethical manner and serve as role models for professional behavior. *(See C.1., C.2.a., C.2.c.)*

G.6.b. Integration of Study and Practice
Educators establish education and training programs that integrate academic study and supervised practice.

G.6.c. Teaching Ethics
Educators make students and supervisees aware of the ethical responsibilities and standards of the profession and the ethical responsibilities of students to the profession. Educators infuse ethical considerations throughout the curriculum. *(See C.1.)*

G.6.d. Peer Relationships
Educators make every effort to ensure that the rights of peers are not compromised when students or supervisees lead career groups or provide supervision. Educators take steps to ensure that students and supervisees understand they have the same ethical obligations as educators, trainers, and supervisors.

G.6.e. Innovative Theories and Techniques
When educators teach techniques/procedures that are innovative, without an empirical foundation, or without a well-grounded theoretical foundation, they define the techniques/procedures as "unproven" or "developing" and explain to students the potential risks and ethical considerations of using such techniques/procedures. *(See C.6.e.)*

G.6.f. Field Placements
Educators develop clear policies within their training programs regarding field placement and other clinical experiences. Educators provide clearly stated roles and responsibilities for the student or supervisee, the site supervisor, and the program supervisor. They confirm that site supervisors are qualified to provide supervision and inform site supervisors of their professional and ethical responsibilities in this role. In addition, educators do not accept any form of professional services, fees, commissions, reimbursement, or remuneration from a site for student or supervisee placement.

G.6.g. Professional Disclosure
Before initiating career services in a field placement, students disclose their status and explain how this status affects the limits of confidentiality. Educators ensure that the clients at field placements are aware of the services rendered and the qualifications of the students and supervisees rendering those services. Students and supervisees obtain client permission before

35

they use any information concerning the professional relationship in the training process. *(See A.2.b.)*

G.7. Student Welfare

G.7.a. Orientation
Educators recognize that orientation is a developmental process that continues throughout the education and training of students. Faculty provide prospective students with information about the educational program's expectations including but not necessarily limited to:

1. the type and level of skill and knowledge acquisition required for successful completion of the training;
2. training program goals, objectives, and mission, and subject matter to be covered;
3. bases for evaluation;
4. training components that encourage self-growth or self-disclosure as part of the training process;
5. the type of supervision settings and requirements of the sites for required clinical field experiences;
6. student and supervisee evaluation and dismissal policies and procedures; and
7. up-to-date employment prospects for graduates.

G.7.b. Self-Growth Experiences
Education programs delineate requirements for self-disclosure or self-growth experiences in their admission and program materials. Educators use professional judgment when designing training experiences they conduct that require student and supervisee self-growth or self-disclosure. Students and supervisees are made aware of the ramifications their self-disclosure may have when career professionals whose primary role as teacher, trainer, or supervisor requires acting on ethical obligations to the profession. Evaluative components of experiential training activities explicitly delineate predetermined academic standards that are separate from and do not depend on the student's level of self disclosure. Educators may require trainees to seek professional help to address any personal concerns that may be affecting their competency.

G.8. Student Responsibilities

G.8.a. Standards for Students
Students have a responsibility to understand and follow the *NCDA Code of Ethics* and adhere to all applicable federal, state, local, and/or institutional statutes, laws, regulations, and procedures governing professional staff behavior at the agency or placement setting. Students have the same obligation to clients as those required of career professionals. *(See C.1.)*

G.8.b. Impairment
Students refrain from offering or providing career services when their physical, mental, or emotional problems are likely to harm a client or others. They are alert to the signs of impairment, seek assistance for problems, and notify their program supervisors when they are aware that they are unable to effectively provide services. In addition, they seek appropriate

professional services for themselves to remediate the problems that are interfering with their ability to provide services to others. *(See A.1.a., C.2.d., C.2.g.)*

G.9. Evaluation and Remediation of Students

G.9.a. Evaluation

Career professionals clearly state to students, prior to and throughout the training program, the levels of competency expected, appraisal methods, and timing of evaluations for all areas of competency. Educators provide students with ongoing performance appraisal and evaluation feedback throughout the training program.

G.9.b. Limitations

Educators, through ongoing evaluation and appraisal, are aware of and address the inability of some students to achieve the level of competencies needed for successful continued performance. Educators

1. assist students in securing remedial assistance when needed,
2. seek professional consultation and document their decision to dismiss or refer students for assistance, and
3. ensure that students have recourse in a timely manner to address decisions to require them to seek assistance or to dismiss them and provide students with due process according to institutional policies and procedures.

G.9.c. Counseling for Students

If students request counseling or if counseling services are required as part of a remediation process, educators provide acceptable referrals.

G.10. Roles and Relationships Between Educators and Students
G.10.a. Sexual or Romantic Relationships

Sexual or romantic interactions or relationships with current students are prohibited.

G.10.b. Harassment

Educators do not condone or subject students to harassment, sexual or otherwise. *(See C.6.a.)*

G.10.c. Relationships with Former Students

Educators are aware of the power differential in the relationship between faculty and students. Faculty members foster open discussions with former students when considering engaging in a social, sexual, or other intimate relationship. Faculty members discuss with the former student how their former relationship may affect the change in relationship.

G.10.d. Nonprofessional Relationships

Educators avoid nonprofessional or ongoing professional relationships with students in which there is a risk of potential harm to the student or that may compromise the training experience or grades assigned.

37

G.10.e. Career Services
Educators do not serve as career professionals to current students unless this is a brief role associated with a training experience or in their role as an academic advisor.

G.10.f. Potentially Beneficial Relationships
Educators are aware of the power differential in the relationship between faculty and students. If they believe a nonprofessional relationship with a student may be potentially beneficial to the student, they take precautions similar to those taken by career professionals when working with clients. Examples of potentially beneficial interactions or relationships include, but are not limited to, attending a formal ceremony; hospital visits; providing support during a stressful event; or mutual membership in a professional association, organization, or community. Educators engage in open discussions with students when they consider entering into relationships with students outside of their roles as teachers and supervisors. They discuss with students the rationale for such interactions, the potential benefits and drawbacks, and the anticipated consequences for the student. Educators clarify the specific nature and limitations of the additional role(s) they will have with the student prior to engaging in a nonprofessional relationship. Nonprofessional relationships with students should be time-limited and initiated with student consent. *(See G.3.e)*

G.11. Multicultural/Diversity Competence in Education and Training Programs

G.11.a. Faculty Diversity
Educators are committed to recruiting and retaining a diverse faculty. Additionally, educators do not condone or engage in discrimination based on age, culture, mental/physical disability, ethnicity, race, religion/spirituality, creed, gender, actual or perceived gender identity or expression, actual or perceived sexual orientation, marital/partnership status, language preference, socioeconomic status, any other characteristics not specifically relevant to job performance, or any basis prohibited by law.

G.11.b. Student Diversity
Educators actively attempt to recruit and retain a diverse student body. Educators demonstrate commitment to multicultural/diversity competence by recognizing and valuing diverse cultures and types of abilities students bring to the training experience. Educators provide appropriate accommodations that enhance and support diverse student well-being and academic performance.

G.11.c. Multicultural/Diversity Competence
Educators actively infuse multicultural/diversity competency in their training and supervision practices. They actively train students to gain awareness, knowledge, and skills in the competencies of multicultural practice. Educators include case examples, role-plays, discussion questions, and other classroom activities that promote and represent various cultural perspectives.

Section H: Research and Publication

Introduction
Career professionals who conduct research are encouraged to contribute to the knowledge base of the profession and promote a clearer understanding of the conditions that lead to a healthy and more just society. Career professionals support efforts of researchers by participating fully and willingly whenever possible. Career professionals minimize bias and respect diversity in designing and implementing research programs.

H.1. Research Responsibilities

H.1.a. Use of Human Research Participants
Career professionals plan, design, conduct, and report research in a manner that is consistent with pertinent ethical principles, all applicable federal, state, and local statutes, laws, regulations, and/or procedures, host institutional regulations, and scientific standards governing research with human research participants. For one source of online training regarding information about the rights and welfare of human participants in research, see the attached web references section.

H.1.b. Need for Research and Review
Career professionals have an obligation to contribute to periodic evaluations of the services they provide to their clients. The interventions, techniques, and methods of service delivery they use should be evaluated to establish evidence-based practice. Career professionals also have an obligation to periodically review the evaluation and research literature in their area of expertise so that the career services they provide to their clients reflect established best practice.

H.1.c. Deviation from Standard Practice
Career professionals seek consultation and observe stringent safeguards to protect the rights of research participants when a research problem suggests a deviation from standard or acceptable practices.

H.1.d. Independent Researchers
When independent researchers do not have access to an Institutional Review Board (IRB), they should consult with researchers who are familiar with IRB procedures to provide appropriate safeguards.

H.1.e. Precautions to Avoid Injury
Career professionals who conduct research with human participants are responsible for the welfare of participants throughout the research process and should take reasonable precautions to avoid causing injurious psychological, emotional, physical, or social effects to participants.

H.1.f. Principal Researcher Responsibility
The ultimate responsibility for ethical research practice lies with the principal researcher. All others involved in the research activities share ethical obligations and responsibility for their own actions.

H.1.g. Minimal Interference
Career professionals take reasonable precautions to avoid causing disruptions in the lives of research participants that could be caused by their involvement in research.

H.1.h. Multicultural/Diversity Considerations in Research
When appropriate to research goals, career professionals are sensitive to incorporating research procedures that take into account cultural considerations. They seek consultation when appropriate.

H.2. Rights of Research Participants *(See A.2)*

H.2.a. Informed Consent in Research
Individuals have the right to consent to become research participants. In seeking consent, career professionals use language that

1. accurately explains the purpose and procedures to be followed.
2. identifies any procedures that are experimental or relatively untried.
3. describes any attendant discomforts and risks.
4. describes any benefits or changes in individuals or organizations that might be reasonably expected.
5. discloses appropriate alternative procedures that would be advantageous for participants.
6. offers to answer any inquiries concerning the procedures.
7. describes any limitations on confidentiality.
8. describes the format and potential target audiences for the dissemination of research findings.
9. instructs participants that they are free to withdraw their consent and to discontinue participation in the project at any time without penalty.

H.2.b. Deception
Career professionals do not conduct research involving deception unless alternative procedures are not feasible and the prospective value of the research justifies the deception. If such deception has the potential to cause physical or emotional harm to research participants, the research is not conducted, regardless of prospective value. When the methodological requirements of a study necessitate concealment or deception, the investigator explains the reasons for this action as soon as possible during the debriefing.

H.2.c. Student/Supervisee Participation
Researchers who involve students or supervisees in research make clear to them that the decision regarding whether or not to participate in research activities does not affect one's academic standing or supervisory relationship. Students or supervisees who choose not to participate in educational research are provided with an appropriate alternative to fulfill their academic or other requirements.

H.2.d. Client Participation
Career professionals conducting research involving clients make clear in the informed consent process that clients are free to choose whether or not to participate in research activities. Career

professionals take necessary precautions to protect clients from adverse consequences of declining or withdrawing from participation.

H.2.e. Confidentiality of Information
Information obtained about research participants during the course of an investigation is confidential. When the possibility exists that others may obtain access to such information, ethical research practice requires that the possibility, together with the plans for protecting confidentiality, be explained to participants as a part of the procedure for obtaining informed consent.

H.2.f. Persons Not Capable of Giving Informed Consent
When a person is not capable of giving informed consent, career professionals provide an appropriate explanation to, obtain agreement for participation from, and obtain the appropriate consent of a legally authorized person.

H.2.g. Commitments to Participants
Career professionals take reasonable measures to honor all commitments to research participants.

H.2.h. Explanations After Data Collection
After data are collected, career professionals provide participants with full clarification of the nature of the study to remove any misconceptions participants might have regarding the research. Where scientific or human values justify delaying or withholding information, career professionals take reasonable measures to avoid causing harm.

H.2.i. Informing Sponsors
Career professionals inform sponsors, institutions, and publication channels regarding research procedures and outcomes. Career professionals ensure that appropriate bodies and authorities are given pertinent information and acknowledgment.

H.2.j. Disposal of Research Documents and Records
Within a reasonable period of time following the completion of a research project or study, career professionals take steps to destroy records or documents (audio, video, digital, and written) containing confidential data or information that identifies research participants in accordance with all applicable federal, state, local, and/or institutional statutes, laws, regulations, and procedures. When records are of an artistic nature, researchers obtain participant consent with regard to handling of such records or documents. Career professionals are encouraged to purge their files according to the time frame required by federal, state, local, and/or institutional statute, law, regulation, or procedure, particularly when there is no reasonable expectation that anyone will benefit from maintaining the records any longer. *(See B.6.a, B.6.g.)*

H.3. Relationships with Research Participants (When Research Involves Intensive or Extended Interactions)

H.3.a. Nonprofessional Relationships
Nonprofessional relationships with research participants should be avoided as these interactions may set up dual relationships and role confusion that may be harmful to the emotional health of participants.

H.3.b. Relationships with Research Participants
Sexual or romantic interactions or relationships between career professionals/researchers and current research participants are prohibited.

H.3.c. Harassment and Research Participants
Researchers do not condone or subject research participants to harassment, sexual or otherwise. *(See C.6.a.)*

H.3.d. Potentially Beneficial Interactions
When a nonprofessional interaction between the researcher and the research participant may be potentially beneficial, the researcher must document, prior to the interaction (when feasible), the rationale for such an interaction, the potential benefit, and anticipated consequences for the research participant. Such interactions should be initiated with appropriate consent of the research participant. Where unintentional harm occurs to the research participant due to the nonprofessional interaction, the researcher must show evidence of an attempt to remedy such harm.

H.4. Reporting Results

H.4.a. Accurate Results
Career professionals plan, conduct, and report research accurately. They provide thorough discussions of the limitations of their data and alternative hypotheses. Career professionals do not engage in misleading or fraudulent research, distort data, misrepresent data, or deliberately bias their results. They explicitly mention all variables and conditions known to the investigator that may have affected the outcome of a study or the interpretation of data. They describe the extent to which results are applicable for diverse populations.

H.4.b. Obligation to Report Unfavorable Results
Career professionals report the results of any research of professional value. Results that reflect unfavorably on institutions, programs, services, prevailing opinions, or vested interests are not withheld.

H.4.c. Reporting Errors
If career professionals discover significant errors in their published research, they take reasonable steps to correct such errors in a correction erratum, or through other appropriate publication means.

H.4.d. Identity of Participants
Career professionals who supply data, aid in the research of another person, report research results, or make original data available take due care to disguise the identity of respective participants in the absence of specific authorization from the participants to do otherwise. In situations where participants self-identify their involvement in research studies, researchers take active steps to ensure that data is adapted/changed to protect the identity and welfare of all parties and that discussion of results does not cause harm to participants.

H.4.e. Replication Studies
Career professionals are obligated to make available sufficient original research data to qualified professionals who may wish to replicate a study.

H.5. Publication

H.5.a. Recognizing Contributions
When conducting and reporting research, career professionals are familiar with and give recognition to previous work on the topic, observe copyright laws, and give full credit to those to whom credit is due.

H.5.b. Plagiarism
Career professionals do not plagiarize; that is, they do not present another person's work as their own.

H.5.c. Review/Republication of Data or Ideas
Career professionals fully acknowledge and make editorial reviewers aware of prior publication of ideas or data where such ideas or data are submitted for review or publication.

H.5.d. Contributors
Career professionals give credit through joint authorship, acknowledgment, footnote statements, or other appropriate means to those who have contributed significantly to research or concept development in accordance with such contributions. The principal contributor is listed first, and minor technical or professional contributions are acknowledged in notes or introductory statements.

H.5.e. Agreement of Contributors
Career professionals who conduct joint research with colleagues or students/supervisees establish agreements in advance regarding allocation of tasks, publication credit, and types of acknowledgment that will be received.

H.5.f. Student Research
For articles that are substantially based on students' course papers, projects, theses, or dissertations, and on which students have been the primary contributors, they are listed as principal authors.

H.5.g. Duplicate Submission
Career professionals submit manuscripts for consideration to only one journal at a time. Manuscripts that are published in whole or in substantial part in another journal or published work are not submitted for publication without acknowledgment and permission from the previous publication.

H.5.h. Professional Review
Career professionals who review material submitted for publication, research, or other scholarly purposes respect the confidentiality and proprietary rights of those who submitted it. Career professionals use care to make publication decisions based on valid and defensible standards. Career professionals review article submissions in a timely manner and based on their scope and competency in research methodologies. Career professionals who serve as reviewers at the request of editors or publishers make every effort to review only materials that are within their scope of competency and use care to avoid personal biases.

Section I: Resolving Ethical Issues

Introduction
Career professionals behave in a legal, ethical, and moral manner in the conduct of their professional work. They are aware that client protection and trust in the profession depend on a high level of professional conduct. They hold other career professionals to the same standards and are willing to take appropriate action to ensure that these standards are upheld. Career professionals work to resolve ethical dilemmas with direct and open communication among all parties involved and seek consultation with colleagues and supervisors when necessary. Career professionals incorporate ethical practice into their daily work. They engage in ongoing learning and development regarding current topics in ethical and legal issues in the profession.

I.1. Standards and the Law

I.1.a. Knowledge
Career professionals understand the *NCDA Code of Ethics* and other applicable ethics codes from professional organizations or from certification and licensure bodies of which they are members and/or which regulate practice in a state or territory. Career professionals ensure that they are knowledgeable of and follow all applicable federal, state, local, and/or institutional statutes, laws, regulations, and procedures. Lack of knowledge or misunderstanding of an ethical responsibility is not a defense against a charge of unethical conduct.

I.1.b. Conflicts Between Ethics and Laws
If ethical responsibilities conflict with laws, regulations, or other governing legal authorities, career professionals make known their commitment to the *NCDA Code of Ethics* and take steps to resolve the conflict. If the conflict cannot be resolved by acknowledging and discussing the pertinent principles in the *NCDA Code of Ethics*, career professionals must adhere to the requirements of all applicable federal, state, local, and/or institutional statutes, laws, regulations, and procedures.

I.2. Suspected Violations

I.2.a. Ethical Behavior Expected
Career professionals expect colleagues to adhere to the *NCDA Code of Ethics*. When career professionals possess knowledge that raises doubts as to whether another career professional is acting in an ethical manner, they take appropriate action, as noted in I.2.b-I.2.g.

I.2.b. Informal Resolution
When career professionals have reason to believe that another career professional is violating or has violated an ethical standard, they attempt first to resolve the issue informally with the other career professional if feasible, provided such action does not violate confidentiality rights that may be involved.

I.2.c. Reporting Ethical Violations
If an apparent violation has substantially harmed, or is likely to substantially harm, a person or organization and is not appropriate for informal resolution or is not resolved properly, career

professionals take further action appropriate to the situation. Such action might include referral to state or national committees on professional ethics, voluntary national certification bodies, state licensing boards, law enforcement or other appropriate institutional authorities. This standard does not apply when an intervention would violate confidentiality rights or when career professionals have been retained to review the work of another career professional whose conduct is in question.

I.2.d. Consultation
When uncertain as to whether a particular situation or course of action may be in violation of the *NCDA Code of Ethics,* career professionals consult with others who are knowledgeable about ethics and the *NCDA Code of Ethics,* with colleagues, and/or with appropriate authorities.

I.2.e. Organizational Conflicts
If the demands of an organization with which career professionals are affiliated pose a conflict with the *NCDA Code of Ethics,* career professionals specify the nature of such conflicts and express to their supervisors or other responsible officials their commitment to the *NCDA Code of Ethics.* When possible, career professionals work toward change within the organization to allow full adherence to the *NCDA Code of Ethics.* In doing so, they are mindful of and address any confidentiality issues.

I.2.f. Unwarranted Complaints
Career professionals do not initiate, participate in, or encourage the filing of ethics complaints that are made with reckless disregard or willful ignorance of facts that would disprove the allegation.

I.2.g. Unfair Discrimination Against Complainants and Respondents
Career professionals do not deny persons employment, advancement, admission to academic or other programs, tenure, or promotion based solely upon their having made or their being the subject of an ethics complaint. This does not preclude taking action based upon the outcome of such proceedings or considering other appropriate information.

I.3. Cooperation with Ethics Committees
Career professionals assist in the process of enforcing the *NCDA Code of Ethics.* Career professionals cooperate with investigations, proceedings, and requirements of the NCDA Ethics Committee or ethics committees of other duly constituted associations or licensing/certifications boards having jurisdiction over those charged with a violation. Career professionals are familiar with the *NCDA Policy and Procedures for Processing Complaints of Ethical Violations* and use it as a reference for assisting in the enforcement of the *NCDA Code of Ethics.*

Glossary of Terms

NOTE: NCDA has members in various career services positions (see Career Professionals), as well as in instructional (counselor educators, counseling psychology professors, etc.) and supervisory roles (Director, Associate Director, Career Supervisor, etc.). The term "career professional" will be used throughout this document both as a noun and as an adjective to refer to anyone holding NCDA membership and who is therefore expected to abide by these ethical guidelines.

Advocacy – promotion of the well-being of individuals and groups, and the career counseling profession within systems and organizations. Advocacy seeks to remove barriers and obstacles that inhibit access, growth, and development.

Assent – to demonstrate agreement, when a person is otherwise not capable or competent to give formal consent (e.g., informed consent) to a career counseling service or plan.

Career Counselor – a professional (or a student who is a career counselor-in-training) engaged in a career counseling practice or other career counseling-related services. Career counselors fulfill many roles and responsibilities such as career counselor educators, researchers, supervisors, practitioners, and consultants.

Career Professionals – this term includes career counselors, career coaches, career consultants, career development facilitators, and anyone else who is a member of NCDA and provides career counseling, career advice/advising, career coaching, career planning, job search assistance, and/or related services.

Career Services – all activities delivered by career professionals to individuals, groups and organizations. Services may include, but are not necessarily limited to, career counseling, career planning, assessment, job search assistance, skills practice, workshops and training, homework assignments, bibliographies, journaling, and overall career program development.

Career Services Plan – a document created by a career professional and a client that outlines goals, steps, time frames and outcome measures whereby a client can learn and apply an orderly process for reaching career goals.

Client(s) – individuals seeking or referred to the services of a career professional. Clients willfully enter into a defined professional relationship with a career professional or are included by means of informed consent by a parent or guardian.

Educator – a professional engaged in developing, implementing, and supervising the educational preparation of students and/or supervisees.

Supervisor – a professional who engages in a formal relationship with a practicing career professional or a student for the purpose of overseeing that individual's career services work and/or clinical skill development.

Culture – membership in a socially constructed way of living, which incorporates collective values, beliefs, norms, boundaries, and lifestyles that are co-created with others who share similar worldviews comprising biological, psychosocial, historical, psychological, and other factors.

Distance Career Services – The use of technology (including but are not limited to computer hardware and software, telephone, the Internet, online assessment instruments, and other communication devices) to provide career services to clients who are not located in the same room with the career professional.

Diversity – the similarities and differences that occur within and across cultures, and the intersection of cultural and social identities.

Documents – any written, digital, audio, visual, or artistic recording of the work within the career services relationship between career professional and client.

Dual Relationships – relationships and/or interactions with clients, students, supervisees, and/or research participants that involve the career professional in more than one professional role or a combination of professional and nonprofessional roles.

Examinee – a recipient of any professional career service that includes educational, psychological, and career appraisal utilizing qualitative or quantitative techniques.

Forensic Evaluation – any formal assessment conducted for court or other legal proceedings.

Multicultural/Diversity Competence – a capacity whereby career professionals possess cultural and diversity awareness and knowledge about self and others, and how this awareness and knowledge is applied effectively in practice with clients and client groups.

Netiquette – the etiquette of online/internet communication.

Professional Relationship – a relationship in which the roles of client and career professional are defined, activities and services are selected, and fees are charged to a client, an employer, or a referring organization.

Student – an individual engaged in formal educational preparation as a career professional.

Supervisee – a career professional or student whose career services work and/or clinical skill development is being overseen in a formal supervisory relationship by a qualified trained professional.

Supervisor – Career professionals who are trained to oversee the work of other career professionals and students/supervisees.

Teaching – all activities engaged in as part of a formal educational program for career professionals.

Training – the instruction and practice of skills related to the work of career professionals. Training contributes to the ongoing proficiency of students and career professionals.

Working Relationship – a current agreement between a career professional and a client in which the roles, responsibilities and activities of both career professional and client are clearly defined.

49

Web References

ACA's Ethics Code: http://www.counseling.org/Resources

Introduction: An ethical decision-making model from the Ethics Resource Center
http://www.ethics.org/resources/decision-making-model.asp

H.1.a. Use of Human Research Participants
http://cme.cancer.gov/clinicaltrials/learning/humanparticipant-protections.asp

Index

Acculturation, role in career counseling, 78
Adult Career Concerns Inventory (ACCI), 28,
    44–45, 95, 159, 252 (figure)
Alpha bias, 52–53, 72
American Counseling Association, 26
American Psychological Association,
    26–28, 56, 58
American School Counselor Association, 9–10
Amundson, N., 8, 15
Assessment:
    abilities and skills, 24
    career counseling use of, 21
    choosing and evaluating, 22–23, 26–29, 68
    ethical use of, 22, 26–30
    gender and, 55–57
    interests, 23–24
    needs and values, 24
    personality, 24
    psychometric characteristics of, 22
    sources of sex bias in, 55–56
    types of, 23
    qualitative, 25

Bandura, A., 187–188, 191
Barriers to career development, 14–15, 58, 67, 69,
    81–82, 189–191, 193, 199, 205–206, 211,
    219 (table), 228–229, 236
Beta bias, 52–53, 72
Betz, N. E., 53, 57–58, 77–78,110, 188, 192, 234
Bingham, R. P, 76, 79–84, 93–96, 100
Blustein, D. L., 16, 78, 148, 235
Borgen, F. H., 192, 233–234
Bowman, S. L., 80, 83
Brooks, L., 17, 56–57, 66–69, 158
Brown, D., 17, 66, 69, 158, 233
Brown, L. S., 56–57, 66
Brown, S. D., 13, 179, 187–193, 195, 199–200, 201,
    204–205, 233, 234

Card sort, 25, 69, 203
Career Attitudes and Strategies Inventory
    (CASI), 117
Career Checklist, 95
Career counseling:
    definition of, 13
    goals in, 14–15, 55, 64–65, 68, 84, 92–96,
        115–116, 135–136, 155–157, 178–179, 200
    mental health and, 16–17
    models of, 14–16, 14 (figure). *See also* Gysbers,
        Heppner, and Johnston's model
    personal counseling and, 16–17
    settings, 8–10
Career maturity:
    applied to Leslie, 151, 162
    definition of, 146–148, 166, 219 (table)
    See also Super's theory
Career adaptability:
    applied to Leslie, 162
    definition of, 146–147, 156, 158–160, 166,
        219 (table)
    See also Super's theory
C-DAC (Career Development Assessment and
    Counseling) model, 156–161. *See also* Super's
    theory
Chronister, K. M., 54, 65
Circumscription, 171–172, 171 (figure), 185,
    219 (table), 222. *See also* Gottfredson's theory
Code of Fair Testing Practices, 26
Collective values, 78, 84
Compromise, 171 (figure), 172–173, 185, 219 (table),
    222. *See also* Gottfredson's theory
Congruence:
    definition of, 109, 122
    Leslie's interests and, 112–113, 116–118
    outcomes of, 109–110
    relation to hexagon, 110
    See also Holland's theory

Consistency:
    definition of, 109, 122
    Leslie's interests and, 111–113, 116
    relation to hexagon, 110
    outcomes of, 109–110
    See also Holland's theory
Cook, E. P., 55
Correspondence,
    definition of, 125
    for Leslie, 132, 137–138
    prediction of, 127
    See also theory of work adjustment
Counselor cognitions:
    culturally appropriate career counseling, 85
    gender-aware and feminist approaches, 64
    Gottfredson's theory, 174
    Holland's theory, 115
    social cognitive career theory, 193
    summary of, 235–246
    Super's developmental theory, 149
    theory of work adjustment, 131
Counselor roles, 8–10
Cramer, S. H., 148
Cultural context in career counseling, 77–78
Culturally appropriate career counseling model,
        80–84, 100
    applied to George, 225–226, 230
    applied to Leslie, 85–89, 92–96, 221
    counselor cognitions, 85
    goal setting in, 92, 94
    identification of career issues in, 93
    impact of cultural variables in, 80–82
    interventions in, 83–84
    key constructs in, 100

Dawis, R. V., 125–130, 126 (figure), 129 (figure),
        135, 234
Demographic changes, 75–76
Developmental theories, 145–149, 219 (table),
        222, 227–229, 234. *See also* Gottfredson's
        theory; Super's theory
Dictionary of Holland Occupational Codes, 117, 231
Differentiation:
    definition of, 109, 122
    Leslie's interests and, 112–113
    outcomes of, 109–110
    See also Holland's theory
Disability issues in cases, 121–122, 210–211
Discarded dreams technique, 69
Discorrespondence,
    definition of, 128
    focus in counseling, 135–138
    for Leslie, 132, 137–138

motivational role of, 128–130
    See also theory of work adjustment
Disengagement stage, 146–147, 166. *See also*
        Super's theory
Dissatisfaction, 128. *See also* theory of work
        adjustment
Donnay, D. A. C., 192

Egalitarianism in counseling relationship,
        54–55, 68
Environment, assessment of, 112–113, 118, 136
Environmental typology, 108. *See also* Holland's
        theory
Establishment stage, 146, 152–153, 166. *See also*
        Super's theory
Ethical decision making, 27–29
Ethical vignettes, 29–30
Exploration stage, 146, 150–151, 153, 159,
        161–162, 166. *See also* Super's theory

Feminist counseling/therapy:
    applied to career counseling, 51, 55, 64–69
    applied to Leslie, 59–62, 64–69
    assessment in, 55–57
    counselor cognitions, 64
    definition, 72
    goals of, 55, 64–65
    interventions in, 64–69
    key constructs in, 72
    tenets of, 54–55, 64–69
Figler, H., 9
Fitzgerald, L. F., 68, 78, 147, 233–234
Flores, L. Y., 83
Forrest, L., 54, 65
Fouad, N. A., 75–76, 79–83

Gay/lesbian issues in cases, 164–165, 206–208
Gender:
    social construction of, 51–53
    theories of career development and, 57–58
Gender-aware counseling and therapy:
    applied to career counseling, 55
    applied to George, 225
    applied to Leslie, 59–62, 64–69, 221
    counselor cognitions, 64
    definition, 72
    gender-role socialization and, 53
    key constructs in, 72
    principles of, 53
Gender-role analysis technique, 66–67, 205
Gender-role socialization:
    assessing, 56, 66–67
    counselor reaction to, 57

definition of, 53
effects on perceived options, 57
expectations regarding work, 53
influence on counseling process, 53–54
interests and, 66–67, 118, 120–121, 172–173
See also Leslie
Gendered context, 55, 60–61, 65–68, 118
Genograms, 25–26, 96
Gilbert, L. A., 52–53
Giordano, J., 86
Goals of counseling, 14–15, 55, 64–65, 68, 84,
    92–96, 115–116, 135–136, 155–157,
    178–179, 200
Good, G. E., 52–53
Gottfredson, L. S., 169–174, 171 (figure), 176,
    178–181, 234
Gottfredson's theory 169–173, 217, 219 (table)
  applied to George, 227
  applied to Leslie, 174–176, 178–181,
      219 (table), 222
  circumscription, 171–172, 171 (figure),
      185, 219 (table), 222
  cognitive growth, 170, 185
  compromise, 171 (figure), 172–173, 185,
      219 (table), 222
  counselor cognitions, 174
  evaluation of, 219 (table), 234
  key constructs in, 185
  prestige, 185
  self-creation, 170, 185
  sex type, 185
  stages of development, 171–172
  tolerable-effort boundary, 171 (figure),
      172, 185
  tolerable-level boundary, 171 (figure),
      172, 185
  tolerable-sex-type boundary, 171 (figure),
      171, 185
  vocational aspirations, 171–173, 219 (table)
  zone of acceptable alternatives, 171–174, 185
Growth stage, 146–147, 150, 166. *See also* Super's
    theory
*Guidelines for Psychological Practice With Girls and
    Women*, 58
Gysbers, Heppner, and Johnston's model of career
    counseling, 14 (figure), 14–16
Gysbers, N. C., 14 (figure), 14–16, 25, 52, 55, 60,
    66, 84–85

Hackett, G., 16, 56, 179, 187–193, 195, 200,
    204, 234
Hare-Mustin, R. T., 52–53, 57
Harmon, L. W, 57

Harris-Bowlsbey, J. G., 8, 15
Hartung, P. J., 79–80, 145, 148, 156–157
Haverkamp, B. E., 16
Heppner, M. J., 14 (figure), 14–16, 25, 52, 55, 60,
    66, 83–85
Heppner, P. P., 84
Herr, E. L., 148
Holland, J. L., 105–109, 106–107 (table),
    111, 109 (figure), 115, 117–118
Holland's theory, 105–110, 217, 218 (table)
  applied to George, 226, 228–231
  applied to Leslie, 110–113, 116–118,
      218 (table), 221
  calculus, 108 122
  characteristics of RIASEC types, 106–107 (table),
      218 (table)
  congruence, 109–110, 112–113, 115, 122, 217,
      218 (table), 226
  consistency, 109–110, 116, 122, 218 (table)
  counselor cognitions, 115
  development of types in, 108
  differentiation, 109–110, 112,
      122, 218 (table)
  evaluation of, 218 (table), 233–234
  hexagonal arrangement of types in, 108,
      109 (figure), 122
  identity and, 109–110, 112, 218 (table)
  key constructs in, 122
  Leslie's RIASEC type, 112, 116–118
  typology of persons and environments,
      108–110, 217, 233–234
  use in counseling, 115–118
Hypotheses about clients, 10–13, 135–136
  communicating, 11–12
  definition of, 10
  learning how to develop, 235–236
  sources of information for, 11
  using theories to guide, 10
  See also Leslie

Identity:
  definition of, 109, 122
  Leslie's interests and, 112
  outcomes of, 109–110
  See also Holland's theory
Ihle, K. H., 84
Integrative-sequential model, 79–80
Interrole assessment technique, 158. *See also*
    Super's theory

Johnston, J. A., 14 (figure), 14–16, 25, 52, 55,
    60, 66, 84–85
Joint Committee on Testing Practices, 22, 26

Katz, J. H., 81
Key theoretical constructs of:
    culturally appropriate career counseling, 100
    gender-aware and feminist approaches, 72
    Gottfredson's theory, 185
    Holland's theory, 122
    social cognitive career theory, 211
    Super's developmental theory, 165
    theory of work adjustment, 143
Krumboltz, J. D., 5

Lapan, R. T., 148
Lent, R. W., 179, 187–193, 195, 199–200, 201,
    204, 233, 234
Leong, F. T. L., 79–80, 100
Leslie, case information about:
    assessment, 39–46, 65–67, 95–96, 112, 136–137,
        159, 201–203, 221
    childhood activities, 110–111, 150, 175, 193
    decision making, 34–36, 111–112, 151,
        162, 194, 205
    desire for child, 38, 61, 153, 196, 222
    dissatisfaction with current job, 33, 60–61,
        112–113, 132, 153, 195–196, 221–222
    educational history, 34–35, 59–60, 111–112, 222
    expectations and goals for counseling, 38–39,
        93, 64–65, 68, 92–93, 115–116, 135, 200
    family of origin, 36–37, 86–88, 111, 150–151,
        196, 196
    gender-role expectations, 59–62, 118, 150–151,
        175, 194, 221
    hobbies and leisure activities, 35–36, 110
    hypotheses, 39, 46–50
    interests, 65–67, 95, 110–111, 201–203, 221
    marital relationship, 37–38, 61–62, 68–69,
        88–89
    needs and values, 95, 131–132, 136–137, 203
    perceived career options, 33–34, 221
    presenting issue, 33–34
    racial/ethnic background, 37–38, 86–89, 221
    satisfactoriness, 132
    work environment, 33–34, 60–61, 66, 68–69,
        112–113, 132, 135–138, 221
    work experience, 34–36, 60–61, 152, 195–196
Leung, A., 79–80, 100
Lofquist, L. H., 125, 126 (figure), 129 (figure), 130,
    135, 234
Lonborg, S. D., 56
Lucas, M. S., 8

Maintenance stage, 146–147, 166. See also Super's
    theory
Marecek, J., 52–53, 57

Maxicycles, 45, 146–147. See also Super's theory
McGoldrick, M., 86
McWhirter, E. H., 54, 65
Minicycles, 45, 146. See also Super's theory
Minnesota Importance Questionnaire (MIQ), 24,
    39, 43–44, 43–44, 95, 136–137, 160, 203, 207,
    227, 249–251 (figure)
Mintz, L. B., 53
Moore, D., 16
Multicultural career counseling tenets, 84–85
Myers-Briggs Type Indicator (MBTI), 24

National Career Development Association,
    13, 26–28, Appendix B
Neville, H. A., 84–85
Niles, S. G., 8, 15, 148
Nonsexist counseling, 52, 55, 72

O*NET, 24, 110
Occupations Finder, 117
Osipow, S. H., 7–8, 147, 220, 233–234
Outcome expectancies, 187–191, 195, 199, 202

Personal is political, in feminist therapy,
    54, 67–68
Personal reflections:
    culture, 79
    explanation of, 2, 3, 17, 220
    gender, 59
    Gottfredson's theory, 174
    Holland's theory, 110
    introductory, 18
    social cognitive career theory, 192
    Super's developmental theory, 149
    theory of work adjustment, 131
Person-environment fit, 105, 112, 125, 172, 212
Power analysis, 68
Power-sharing techniques, 68

Race/ethnicity in cases, 71–72, 90–92, 96–100,
    119–120, 141–142, 163–164, 181–182,
    208–209
Racial discrimination, role in career decisions,
    77–78
Rahardja, D., 14
Remer, P., 55–56, 68
RIASEC. See Holland's theory
Ryan Krane, N. E., 13, 179

Satisfaction, 126–128
    definition of, 126, 143
    prediction of, 126–127
    See also theory of work adjustment

Satisfactoriness, 126–127
  definition of, 126, 143
  Leslie's, 132
  prediction of, 126–127
  See also theory of work adjustment
Savickas, M. L., 5, 7, 45, 145–147, 150, 156–158, 161
Scher, M., 52–53
Self-determination, as goal of feminist therapy,
      68–69
Self-Directed Search (SDS), 115, 117, 233
Self-efficacy, 187–196, 204–205, 211
  antecedents of, 187–188
  definition of, 187
  See also social cognitive career theory
Seligman, L., 21
Sex bias in assessment, 55–57
Skills Confidence Inventory (SCI), 39, 42–43, 95,
      118, 201, 202, 248 (figure)
Social cognitive career theory, 187–192, 217,
      219 (table)
  applied to George, 228–229
  applied to Leslie, 192–197, 200–206,
      219 (table), 222
  card sort intervention, 203–204
  contextual affordances, 189, 211
  counselor cognitions, 193
  development of interventions, 191
  evaluation of, 219 (table), 234
  goals of counseling, 200
  identifying barriers, 140–142, 211,
      219 (table), 228
  identifying foreclosed options, 200–204,
      219 (table), 228
  key constructs in, 211
  modifying efficacy beliefs, 204–205
  outcome expectancies, 188–191, 211,
      219 (table), 222, 228–229, 234
  prediction of career choice, 128–129,
      219 (table)
  prediction of interest development, 191
  prediction of performance level, 189–191,
      219 (table)
  self-efficacy, 187–192, 211, 217, 219 (table),
      222, 228–229
Sociocultural conditions, in feminist therapy,
      54, 65–67
Spengler, P. M., 16
Spokane, A. R., 15, 109
Strong Interest Inventory (SII), 19, 28–31, 50, 96,
      112–113, 136–139, 144, 160–161, 202, 204,
      211, 217, 240 (figure)
Subich, L. M., 83
Super, C. M., 5, 145, 147, 150, 156–157, 161

Super, D. E., 5, 44–45, 147, 150, 156–157, 159, 161
Super's theory, 145–147, 217, 219 (table)
  applied to George, 227, 228–230
  applied to Leslie, 150–153, 157–162
      219 (table), 222
  career development status, 156
  career maturity and career adaptability,
      146–148, 158–160, 219 (table)
  C-DAC model and, 156–161
  counselor cognitions, 149
  developmental tasks, 146–147, 156,
      158–159 (table)
  evaluation of, 218–219 (table), 234
  goals of counseling, 155–157
  interrole assessment technique, 158
  key constructs in, 165
  life-career rainbow, 147 (figure), 158
  life roles, 146–148, 151, 153, 219 (table)
  life stages, 146–147, 219 (table)
  maxicycles and minicycles, 45, 146–147
  role salience, 156–157, 166
  self-concept in, 146, 148–152, 156–157,
      160–162, 219 (table)
  vocational identity, 148, 156, 160, 166
Stages of development. *See* Gottfredson's theory;
      Super's theory; theory of work adjustment
Swanson, J. L., 13, 23–24, 67

Techniques:
  card sort, 25, 69, 203
  career adaptability, assessment of, 156, 158–160
  Career Checklist, 95
  career development status, assessment of, 156
  C-DAC model, 156–161
  coping resources, assessment of, 156, 159
  culturally appropriate interventions, 94–96
  discarded dreams, 69
  environment, assessment of, 112–113,
      117–118, 136
  feminist interventions, 64–69
  gender-role analysis, 66–67, 205
  gender-role socialization, 56, 65–67
  genograms, 25–26, 96
  identifying barriers, 205–206, 219 (table), 228
  identifying foreclosed options, 192–195,
      219 (table), 228
  interrole assessment, 158
  life-role assessment, 156–158
  modifying efficacy beliefs, 204–205
  nonsexist card sort, 69
  occupational self-concept, assessment of,
      160–161
  power analysis, 68

power-sharing, 68
vocational identity, assessment of, 160
work-role salience, assessment of, 157–158
Theoretical orientation, 7–8, 10–12, 217, 220–221
Theories:
    applied to George, 225–231
    applied to Leslie, 59–62, 64–69, 85–89, 92–96,
        110–113, 116–118, 131–132, 134–138,
        150–153, 157–162, 174–176, 178–181,
        192–197, 200–206, 218–219 (table),
        221–222
    career counseling vs. career
        development, 7–8
    categories of, 6
    comparison among, 216–220, 225–231
    definition of, 4
    evaluation of, 218–219 (table), 233–235
    integration of, 2–3, 6, 215–216, 221, 222, 225–231
    purpose of, 5, 215–217
    types of, 4–6
Theory of work adjustment, 125–130, 217,
    218 (table)
    abilities and ability requirements, 126–127, 143,
        217, 218 (table)
    active adjustment, 128–129, 143, 218 (table)
    applied to George, 226–230
    applied to Leslie, 131–132, 134–138, 218 (table),
        221–222
    career choice, 127
    correspondence, 125–126, 127–130, 135–137,
        218 (table), 226, 234
    counselor cognitions, 131
    discorrespondence, 128–130, 135,
        136–138, 218 (table)

dissatisfaction, 128, 132, 217, 221
evaluation of, 218 (table), 222
flexibility, 128–130, 134, 143, 218 (table), 226
goals of counseling, 135
individual differences perspective, 130, 217
key constructs in, 143
Minnesota Importance Questionnaire (MIQ),
    43–44, 95, 136–137, 160, 203, 207, 227,
    249–251 (figure)
needs, 24, 125–127, 203, 218 (table), 227,
    229–230
perseverance, 128–130, 143, 218 (table), 226
personality style variables, 128, 130, 143,
    218 (table)
person-environment interaction, 126, 128
reactive adjustment, 129–130, 134, 138,
    143, 218 (table)
rewards, 125–139, 143, 217, 218 (table), 230
satisfaction, 126–127, 143, 217, 218 (table), 221
satisfactoriness, 125–127, 143, 218 (table), 229
tenure, 125–127, 143, 218 (table)
values, 125–127, 143, 222
Trait-and-factor approaches to career counseling,
    105, 156

Walborn, F. S., 10–13
Ward, C., 80, 93, 95
Welfel, E. R., 27–28
Whiston, S. C., 14
Working alliance, 14–15
Worrell, J., 55–56, 68

Zone of acceptable alternatives, 86–88. *See also*
    Gottfredson's theory

About the Authors

Jane L. Swanson, PhD, is Professor of Psychology and Chair of the Department at Southern Illinois University at Carbondale. She received her PhD from the University of Minnesota in 1986. She is a Fellow of the Society of Counseling Psychology (Division 17) of the American Psychological Association and has served as Chair of the Society for Vocational Psychology and on the boards of the Society of Counseling Psychology and the Association for Assessment in Counseling. Dr. Swanson has served on several journal editorial boards and as Associate Editor of the *Journal of Vocational Behavior.* She has published extensively on topics related to career and vocational psychology, such as career assessment, career barriers, measurement of vocational interests, and career interventions. Dr. Swanson also is experienced as a career counselor and facilitator, including founding and directing a university career counseling agency, developing and delivering a six-session high school career intervention, and providing career seminars to workers displaced due to a large industrial plant closing.

Nadya A. Fouad, PhD, is a Distinguished Professor in the Department of Educational Psychology at the University of Wisconsin–Milwaukee and Training Director of the Counseling Psychology program there. She is editor of *The Counseling Psychologist.* In 2003, she received the John Holland Award for Outstanding Achievement in Career and Personality Research. President of Division 17 (Counseling Psychology) from 2000 to 2001, she previously served as Vice President for Diversity and Public Interest (1996–1999). She is also a past Chair of the Council of Counseling Psychology Training Programs (2003–2007). She sits on the editorial boards of the *Journal of Vocational Behavior* and the *Journal of Career Assessment* and has published articles and chapters on cross-cultural vocational assessment, career development of women and racial/ethnic minorities, interest measurement, cross-cultural counseling, and race and ethnicity. She served as cochair (with Patricia Arredondo) of the writing team for the *Multicultural Guidelines on Education, Training, Practice, Research and Organizational Change,* which were approved by the American Psychological Association in August 2002 and published in the *American Psychologist* in May 2003.